To my daughter, Cathy

About the Author

James Brander is the Asia-Pacific Professor in the Faculty of Commerce at the University of British Columbia. He did his B.A. in economics at UBC, and completed a Master's degree and Ph.D. in economics at Stanford University. Prior to taking a position at UBC, he taught at Queen's University. He has published widely in academic journals, particularly in the areas of international trade policy and industrial organization, and also in the areas of finance and resource economics. He is the co-author of the most cited paper ever published in the *Journal of International Economics*, and is currently Managing Editor of the *Canadian Journal of Economics*. He has served as chair of the Policy Analysis Division in the Faculty of Commerce at UBC, and is currently Associate Dean of the Faculty. He is a research associate of the National Bureau of Economic Research (NBER), a prestigious U.S.-based research organization. He has also been active in consulting, and in government policy advising, particularly in the areas of international trade policy, and competition policy, and has been a frequent media commentator on these areas.

Contents

Chapter 8 The Theory of International Trade Policy 171

Chapter 9 International Trade Policy: Institutions 199

Chapter 13 Anti-competitive Practices: Economic Analysis 337

Chapter 14 The Theory of Price and Entry Regulation 357

Chapter 15 Major Areas of Private Sector Regulation 379

Preface and Acknowledgments

This book is intended for use as a textbook in courses dealing with public policy toward business. It is based on my lecture notes from a course entitled "Government and Business", taught in the Faculty of Commerce and Business Administration at the University of British Columbia. The first two editions of the book have been used in schools of business or administration for courses related to public policy. In addition, the book has been used for public policy courses in public adminstration programs, economics departments, and political science departments, and as a supplementary text for other courses in economics and other subjects. Many university level courses deal with public policy, and I believe that this book can be successfully used in most of them.

The book proceeds from conceptual principles to specific policy areas. Specific policies are viewed as applications of general policy principles and, after reading the book, students should be able to readily understand new policy issues that confront them.

The book offers an institutionally and theoretically up-to-date treatment of the major traditional areas of Canadian public policy toward business: competition policy, regulation, and public enterprise. This material has been updated and improved for the third edition. The book also deals with international trade policy, environmental and resource policy, and macroeconomic policy. All three of these areas have been expanded for the third edition. Specifically, environmental and resource issues have been split into two chapters and moved forward in the book, and the chapter on macroeconomic policy (Chapter 17) now contains more material on "open-economy" considerations and on long run economic growth.

Another significant change in the third edition is increased emphasis on the role of "fairness" in public policy. This material has been considerably expanded and moved forward, now appearing in Chapter 4. Compared with previous editions, there is now much more material on both axiomatic approaches to fairness (utilitarianism, etc.) and on situational ethics (i.e. particular examples of ethical dilemmas). Despite the expansions, the book continues to provide a streamlined overview of the major public policies that affect business and can be covered comfortably in a one-term course.

An important theme in the book is that policy can be viewed partly as the result of pursuit of "public interest" objectives by policy-makers, and partly as the result of competition for policy influence between various private interests. Both the "public interest" and "private interest" approach to policy are examined at a conceptual and institutional level, and many examples illustrating both interpretations of policy are provided.

Material in this book is drawn from several areas of study, including political science, philosophy, and psychology. The underlying discipline that contributes most to the central framework of the book is, however, economics. This reflects the fact that most policies affecting the business environment are focused on economic objectives. This book is not very technical, and presumes only that readers have a general familiarity with introductory economics. There are a few graphs and equations, but not many. The emphasis instead is on the basic insights and conceptual tools of economics, as they apply to business-related public policy.

I have accumulated many debts in the preparation of all three editions of this book. First, I would like to thank my wife and colleague Barbara Spencer, who made major contributions to the chapters on competition policy and made many other suggestions on all three editions. I would also like to offer special thanks to my father, Stuart James Brander, who read the manuscript for the first edition and provided many helpful comments. I have relied heavily on input from my colleagues at UBC, including the following people: Tony Boardman, Murray Frank, Keith Head, Len Hendriksson, Peter Nemetz, John Ries,

Tom Ross, Bill Stanbury, Mike Tretheway, Jim Vercammen and Bill Waters.

I have also benefitted from suggestions made by Ph.D. students at UBC including: Richard Arend, Clive Chapple, and Elizabeth Croft.

The book could never have been written nor revised without a major effort from research assistants. I would particularly like to acknowledge the assistance of: Jen Baggs, Rick Gleason, Fred Gower, Livia Mahler, Jo-Anne McLean, Diane Wilson and Monica Zhang.

Finally, I would like to acknowledge the contributions of people outside UBC, including reviewers and instructors from other universities. In this category I would like to recognize: G. Bruce Anderson, University of Manitoba, Paul Anglin, University of Windsor, Steve Globerman, Simon Fraser University, B. Pazderka, Queen's University, Asha and Venk Sadanand, University of Guelph, Zena A. Seldon, University College of the Cariboo, Allan Warrack, University of Alberta, and Bernard M. Wolf, York University.

I would also like to thank several anonymous reviewers and the staff at Wiley for their patience, efficiency and good judgement, particularly Karen Bryan, Michelle Harrington, John Horne, and Carolyn Wells.

1

Objectives and Overview

1.1 Introduction

This book is concerned primarily with government policies directed toward business. Such policies are an important focus of political debate, and are a staple item on the evening news. In addition, dealing with government policies toward business is a very important activity in the private sector, and implementing such policies is a major function of the public sector. This book is directed principally toward students in business, economics, and public policy, many of whom will deal with public policy issues professionally within either the public sector or the private sector. It should also be useful for other readers with a general interest in the analysis of public policy.

Most citizens of modern developed countries expect government policy to play an important role in their lives. We expect governments to provide law enforcement, education, and a variety of other goods and services, and we expect, or at least accept, that governments will finance these activities by imposing taxes, along with other means. Most of us also recognize that government policy has some influence on unemployment, inflation, interest rates, and general business conditions. Many people, however, are surprised when they discover the extent to which the business decisions of private sector firms are affected by government intervention. We might wonder what all this government intervention is intended to achieve, and why governments choose the policies that they do. We might also wonder whether the chosen policies are effective methods of pursuing the intended objectives. This book is concerned with these and related issues. More precisely, it offers a systematic method for analyzing government policy affecting business.

This analysis subdivides naturally into two questions:

1. What should the role of government be?
2. What factors explain the actual conduct of government?

normative

positive

The first question is sometimes described as "normative" or "prescriptive," because in answering it we are trying to suggest or "prescribe" what governments should do. The starting point in the analysis of this question is that government policy toward business should seek to promote the public interest. Therefore, consideration of question 1 is also called the "public interest approach" to policy analysis.

The second question is "positive" or "descriptive" in that it tries to explain or describe why things are as they are. It is possible that actual policies toward business will be just as normative analysis suggests they should be. Frequently, however, actual policies coincide very poorly with normative analysis, and we are forced to conclude that the general public interest was not the major determinant of policy.

In answering question 2, we normally assume that actual policy is the outcome of a "market" for political influence in which politicians are pursuing political or personal advantages, public sector managers are trying to advance their careers, and special interest groups, including business lobbies, are pursuing their private objectives as well. Analysis of question 2 is therefore often referred to as the "private interest approach" to policy analysis.

1.2 The Normative Approach to Policy Analysis

We have established that normative analysis starts with the assertion that government policy should seek to promote the public interest. Unfortunately, it is difficult to say exactly what the public interest is. Conceptions of the public interest are reflections of basic values and vary over time and across ethnic, social, religious, and even occupational groups. Nevertheless, there is a well-established set of goals that are widely accepted as legitimate objects of government attention. These goals are discussed briefly below, and will form the central themes of this book.

1. *Economic efficiency*: In rough terms, pursuit of economic efficiency corresponds to trying to make the per capita benefits from the consumption of goods and services as high as possible. In a world where simple economic scarcity and poverty remain the greatest problems, this objective is very important. In Chapter 2, the concept of economic efficiency is described more carefully.

2. *Macroeconomic stabilization and growth*: One of the most serious problems of market-based economies is that they are prone to cyclical swings in business activity and employment. After the experience of the Great Depression of the 1930s, most citizens of western (and many other) countries have come to regard stabilization of these cyclical fluctuations, and provision of reliable employment opportunities, as important objectives of government policy. More broadly, the objectives of macroeconomic policy are to smooth the business cycle, to keep unemployment rates low and stable, to keep inflation rates low and stable, and to assist in promoting economic growth.

3. *Fairness (equity)*: Pursuit of economic efficiency seeks to make the overall size of the "economic pie" as large as possible. Fairness or equity is concerned mainly with the distribution of that pie among different claimants. In Canada, for example, we have a system of taxation and social welfare that taxes the relatively well off and gives money to the poor. In addition to redistribution, public policy is also targeted toward other conceptions of fairness. For example, there are laws that seek to prevent discrimination by employers on the basis of sex, race, or (within certain limits) age, on the grounds that such discrimination is unfair in some fundamental way. Other ideas of fairness lead to public policy that seeks to protect the interests of children and others judged unable to adequately defend their own interests.

4. *Other social objectives*: Governments sometimes pursue objectives that are not directly related to economic efficiency, macroeconomic stabilization, or fairness. For example, Canadian governments have tried to promote "Canadian unity" and, simultaneously, to promote "multiculturalism." Some policies, such as limitations on gambling and alcohol consumption, have their roots in a desire to promote certain values. Such policies may be categorized simply as "other social objectives."

Any normative rationale for policy must be based on one of these four categories of objectives. For example, one important type of government policy toward business is environmental regulation, which, among other things, seeks to limit the damage done to the environment by various industrial activities. This policy is based primarily on the idea that unregulated business activity may cause inefficiently high levels of environmental damage. In other words, the normative rationale for environmental policy is based mainly on economic efficiency. In addition, some environmental legislation has it roots in the idea that fairness requires that certain aspects of the environment be protected for the benefit of future generations.

1.3 The Positive Approach to Policy Analysis

The positive approach to policy analysis focuses on the objectives, behaviour, and interaction of individuals and groups who influence policy decisions. Instead of focusing on what policy should be, as normative analysis does, positive analysis examines the reasons why policy takes the form it does. One important influence on policy decisions is voting. Another arises from special interest groups, including business lobbies, who spend time and energy trying to influence government policies. Public sector managers (or bureaucrats) themselves are an important influence, as are elected politicians. Chapter 5 of this book examines these various groups and their effect on the policy-making process.

1.4 The Major Policy Areas

Government policy toward business appears in many guises. There are, however, certain policy areas that are particularly important. The largest part of the book will be devoted to a systematic discussion of these major policy areas:

- international trade policy,
- environmental policy,
- competition policy,
- price and entry regulation,
- public enterprise and Crown corporations,
- macroeconomic stabilization policy and the public debt.

As this list suggests, government policy influences business activity in a wide variety of ways. Some policy areas, such as price regulation and Crown ownership, are directed toward specific firms and industries. Other policy areas are more like framework or background policies, since they are not targeted toward any specific firms, but affect the business environment broadly. Policies in this category would be macroeconomic stabilization policy and international trade policy. Perhaps the best way of seeing the influence of government on the private sector is by way of example. The following cases illustrate the important effect of government policies and decisions on business.

1.5 The Kemano Project: An Example of Public Policy Toward Business

In August 1997, the government of British Columbia and Alcan Aluminum signed an out-of-court settlement regarding the Kemano Completion hydroelectric project. As a result of the settlement, Alcan confirmed its intention to build a new aluminum smelter in Kitimat, B.C. to begin operations between January 2003 and January 2010. Alcan also dropped its court action against the province, and received compensatory benefits in the form of attractive contracts with the provincial Crown corporation B.C. Hydro.

The court action arose because, in early 1995, the government of British Columbia blocked the $1.3 billion power dam development known as the Kemano Completion Project. The Kemano project was to add a second phase to Alcan Aluminum's hydroelectric power-generating station in northwestern British Columbia. In 1987, Alcan had received permission from the provincial and federal governments of the day to undertake the project. Even in 1987 there were substantial objections to the project, primarily on environmental grounds. Specifically, the project would divert over half the water from the Nechako River, an important tributary of the Fraser River that in turn runs through the most heavily populated area of the province. Opponents argued, among other things, that the project was likely to damage the rich salmon runs in the Fraser River. However, after studying the project in considerable detail, both the B.C. provincial government and the Canadian federal government were, in 1987, strongly supportive of the project.

By 1995, new governments were in power in both British Columbia and Ottawa. B.C. premier Mike Harcourt argued that a new study undertaken by his government indicated that important, negative Fisheries Department evidence had been suppressed by the federal government in earlier studies, and he cancelled the project.

By the time the project was terminated in 1995, Alcan had spent approximately $500 million of the total $1.3 billion budgeted for the project. Alcan wanted full compensation for the money spent. However, the provincial government argued that the federal government had primary responsibility for any compensation to Alcan, while the federal government indicated reluctance to provide compensation.

The Kemano project illustrates two important aspects of government activity. First, governments must approve major projects undertaken by the private sector if those projects have significant environmental consequences or if the projects involve use of public (i.e., government-owned) land or resources. Since much of the economic activity in Canada falls into one or both of these categories, this implies a large impact of government policy on business planning. Second, government policy was also put into effect through B.C. Hydro, a Crown corporation entirely owned by the Province of British Columbia. B.C. Hydro's policies on buying surplus power from private producers such as Alcan reflect government policies on such activities. In an earlier period, or with a different government, B.C. Hydro might have been forced to support northern development by agreeing to purchase power from the Kemano project at prices more favourable to Alcan.

1.6 Mergers, Privatization, and Deregulation

In February 2000, the Government of Canada announced its final step in accommodating the merger of Canada's two major airlines, Air Canada and Canadian Airlines International. This completed a long period of public policy evolution in the airline industry. In the late 1940s and the 1950s, commercial air transport in Canada was controlled by a federally owned Crown corporation known as Trans-Canada Airlines (renamed Air Canada in 1964). The corporation's policy in this period was a direct reflection of federal government policy. In 1959, a private sector company, CP Air, was granted its first continental route. From the early 1960s until the mid 1980s, the airline industry in Canada was essentially a closely regulated "duopoly," with two major firms, Crown corporation Air Canada and CP Air.

Some small independent charter airlines, feeder airlines, and regional airlines also existed at various times. One charter airline,

Wardair, sought to become a full service national carrier in the 1980s, and one very successful regional carrier, Pacific Western Airlines, acquired CP Air in 1987, becoming Canadian Airlines. Canadian Airlines then took over Wardair in 1989. Also, most feeder airlines were acquired outright or became closely affiliated with one of the two major carriers, so the Canadian domestic air market was essentially a duopoly until the emergence of WestJet Airlines in 1996.

Until 1984, a government regulatory agency, the Canadian Transport Commission (CTC), regulated air fares and air routes. Thus the government, through the CTC, determined what prices the airlines could charge and what routes they could fly. Through CTC control over air routes, and in accordance with various bilateral agreements between Canada and other countries, foreign airlines were prevented from flying on domestic routes within Canada, and international routes were strictly regulated. Foreign carriers required Canadian permission to fly to or from a Canadian destination.

In 1984, Canada began a significant deregulation of its domestic airline industry, allowing free competition over air fares (leading to a substantial reduction in fares) and allowing domestic airlines more flexibility in determining the routes they would like to fly. This was followed by the privatization of Air Canada, with the Government of Canada selling Air Canada to private sector investors in two stages in 1988 and 1989. In 1993, Canadian competition policy authorities and Canadian regulators allowed U.S.-based American Airlines to purchase a substantial minority share in Canadian Airlines and to establish a strategic alliance with Canadian.

In 1995, the Canadian and American governments reached an open skies agreement, whereby Canadian and U.S. airlines would be able to freely serve routes between the two countries, without requiring special permission. Prior to 1995, the ability of the Canadian and American carriers to fly between the U.S. and Canada had been strictly limited. Ultimately, economic pressures induced Canadian Airlines to accept a takeover from Air Canada in 1999. After a complex series of government approvals the takeover went into full effect in the year 2000.

Like the Kemano project example, this example also illustrates the role of government policy and its influence on business activity. At various times the government owned the dominant firm in the airline industry, regulated prices in and entry to the industry, and had a major impact on the industry through its international agreements. Restructuring in the industry required the approval and participation of the Bureau of Competition Policy (as described more fully in Chapter 12) and transport regulators. In addition, the government continues its role in safety regulation of the industry and has an active, although evolving, role in the closely related airport business, as well as in the development and production of aircraft.

1.7 Globalization, Internationalization, and Canada's Role in the World Economy

Canadian public policy and Canadian business decisions are increasingly affected by events occurring outside Canada's borders. This situation is not unique to Canada. Most (and perhaps all) national governments have found that their ability to control domestic events has weakened progressively over the past two decades. In part, this is due to the increasing importance of processes that are global (or worldwide) in scope. Consider, for example, "global warming," which refers to the idea that the entire world, or globe, appears to be getting warmer. Global warming will probably have major economic effects on many countries over the next few decades, yet no one country can exercise much control over it because it is caused by the cumulative effects of activities occurring all over the world.

The phenomenon of "global production" refers to production structures in which a single final product draws on production activities carried out in a wide variety of countries. Thus, for example, a car "produced" in Canada may have significant components from a dozen or more other countries. Firms are particularly interested in finding the best possible place to carry out each productive activity, and will readily change locations as local wages, taxes, or other important factors change. This in turn reduces the control than any one national government can exercise over these firms, and also reduces the power of local labour unions, precisely because firms will readily move production from one country to another in the face of any profit-reducing changes in government policy or the labour relations environment.

Similarly, the emergence of global financial markets has reduced the ability of any one government to control domestic financial events, since financial market participants in any one country can readily transact in financial markets outside that country's borders, or at least outside its control. A street corner money-changer in Moscow who, among other things, makes U.S. dollar loans (and keeps a gun handy to aid in collection) is part of a global financial market, as is a large bank making computerized program trades involving perhaps 10 or 12 currencies simultaneously. Many financial transactions do not really occur in any particular country at all, but occur instead in the disem-bodied world of computerized financial networks. In general, the Inter-net has created a more unified global economy than has ever been known in the past.

The increasing significance of global processes and activities is often referred to as globalization. In essence, globalization refers to processes that transcend national boundaries. We can also consider activities that are merely international (i.e., that involve two or more countries), as opposed to global. For example, international trade between Canada and the United States cannot be called a global phe-nomenon, although it is international. Similarly, the increased eco-nomic integration of Western Europe is an important international event, but is not global in nature. However, the increasing importance of international interactions, even when they are not global in scope, also weakens and modifies the domestic authority and influence of national governments.

Ongoing globalization and internationalization have been caused in part by technological change, particularly advances in telecommu-nications (like the Internet) and transportation. Another major causal factor is worldwide population growth. As the world becomes more and more crowded, different groups of people come into more frequent contact with one another. The third major causal factor, however, is discretionary policy choice. For example, Canadian policy authorities in the 1980s, the 1990s and in the first decade of the 21st century have made a series of decisions, including joining the North American Free Trade Agreement, increasing immigration levels, reducing restrictions on foreign investment, and liberalizing financial regulation, that have increased the impact of global events on Canada. These policies could, in principle, be reversed if a more nationalist policy stance were to re-emerge.

One should not exaggerate the importance of globalization, since domestic events and domestic policy control remain the main influ-ences on the domestic economy. However, the twin phenomena of globalization and internationalization are important parts of the background to much of the discussion in this book. Chapters 8 and 9 are explicitly devoted to international trade policy and related institutions and issues. Chapters 10 and 11, on environment and resource policy, deal with many issues that are either international or global, and Chapter 17 includes some discussion of the international influences on macroeconomic policy. Even the traditional areas of government control over business, as exercised through competition policy, regulation, and Crown (i.e., government) ownership, are increasingly affected by international and global events.

1.8 Concluding Remarks and Outline of the Book

Two examples of government policy toward business were described in Sections 1.5 and 1.6. Facts were reported without judgements being made about the cases. Two natural questions do arise, however. First, were the government decisions reasonable: i.e., was there a sound normative rationale for intervention? Second, if the decisions were not good ones from the public interest point of view, why were they made? The first question is normative; the second is positive. In this book we explore general principles that will help us answer such questions, both for these and other cases of government involvement in business.

Part I of this book is devoted to the conceptual background of policy analysis. Chapter 2 reviews some basic economic concepts and shows how they can be applied in specific cases. Chapter 3 discusses the philosophical foundations for the role of government and the role of private enterprise in democratic societies, and provides a more detailed overview of the normative rationale for government policy than was provided in Chapter 1. Chapter 4 discusses the role of fairness as a normative rationale for government policy. Chapter 5 examines the positive, or descriptive, theory of government. Chapter 6 is devoted to the basic economic characteristics of firms and markets, focusing on imperfect competition as a reason for government intervention, and Chapter 7 outlines some of the more important features of Canada's business environment and general economic structure. Part II of the book takes up each of the major policy areas in turn, using the tools and ideas developed in Part I.

1.9 Bibliographic Notes

This book draws upon several subjects, each with its own well-developed literature, including public finance, industrial organization, public administration, business-government relations, and public policy analysis. Public finance is concerned with the economic principles of government expenditure and taxation. There are many useful text books in this area.

The subject of industrial organization focuses on the economic analysis of firms and markets and the associated public policy. Useful texts include Carlton and Perloff (1994), Green (1990), Tirole (1988), and the Handbook of Industrial Organization (1989) (edited by Richard Schmalensee and Robert Willig). Public administration analyzes the process of management in the public sector, drawing largely on political science and organizational behaviour for its conceptual core. Standard references in this area include Doern and Phidd (1992), Blakeney and Borins (1992), and Atkinson (1993). Business-government relations emphasizes the process of interaction between government and business. References include Baetz (1993), Crookell (1991), Stanbury (1993), and Taylor (1991).

Public policy analysis as a field is largely the application of public finance, industrial organization, and public administration to the substantive areas of policy: competition policy, environmental policy, etc. Useful public policy texts and readings include Viscusi, Vernon, and Harrington (1992), and Weimer and Vining (1992).

The journal *Canadian Public Policy* publishes accessible papers on public policy analysis and is a valuable source for student papers. The *Canadian Journal of Economics*, the *Canadian Journal of Public Administration*, and the *Canadian Journal of Political Science* all publish public policy material in their respective fields.

On-line Sources

Nowadays, the best source for current public policy information is the Internet. A good starting point for information related to the Canadian government is *http://canada.gc.ca.*

2
Four Useful Economic Concepts

Both the normative and positive analysis of public policy depend on four simple economic concepts: opportunity cost, marginalism, incentive effects, and economic efficiency. These concepts are discussed in turn below.

2.1 Opportunity Cost

Perhaps the most useful of all economic concepts is opportunity cost. The opportunity cost of any activity is defined as the value of the best foregone alternative. Consider, for example, a student who chooses to spend an evening studying, rather than going out with friends. The opportunity cost of studying is the value or enjoyment that the student would have obtained by going out. The application of opportunity cost to policy decisions means that any project or policy should be undertaken only if its value exceeds its opportunity cost. In other words, a project should be carried out only if its value exceeds the value of alternative projects.

The idea of opportunity cost seems so clear that one wonders why economists and other policy analysts emphasize it so much. After all, anyone who has had to decide whether to spend an afternoon working or playing tennis has confronted the concept of opportunity cost very directly. Surprisingly, however, this idea is frequently forgotten or misunderstood at the public policy level.

Vancouver's 1986 World's Fair, Expo 86, was widely hailed as a success. Furthermore, according to Expo's Chief Executive Officer, the roughly $300 million dollar deficit "would not cost one nickel of taxpayer money," because it would be covered by proceeds from the provincial government lottery, not from tax revenues.[1] An economist, however, applying the concept of opportunity cost, sees things differently.

To the economist, the $300 million of lottery revenues earmarked for Expo was $300 million that could have been used to reduce the tax burden, or spent on other projects such as reforestation, health care, education, and so on. The economist might agree that the $300 million spent on Expo was a worthwhile expenditure, but only if he or she could be convinced that Expo represented a better investment than alternative possible uses of the money. In any case, the $300 million certainly was a cost to taxpayers, because they had to forego the benefits of lower taxes or alternative projects.

Economists have been described as those who know the cost of everything and the value of nothing. The opportunity cost idea reminds us that concern about costs is really a concern about alternative values. The economist who criticizes Expo 86 is not (necessarily) a mean-spirited individual who wants to keep people from having fun. He or she is concerned that residents of British Columbia might have been better off if they had had the opportunity to spend more of their incomes on private expenditures, instead of paying taxes, or if the money had been used to replenish the declining forest stock, or for some other useful purpose. Added costs on any project leave us with fewer resources for alternative projects. This is the basic opportunity cost insight.

The fact that there is a general failure to recognize opportunity costs is revealed by the following very standard result from polls. In Gallup polls released on May 28 and May 31, 1990, (*Gallup Report.* Toronto: Gallup Canada, Inc., May 1990.) fully 85% of respondents indicated that Canadian governments are "not doing enough to ensure a clean environment," yet only 54% favoured paying an additional $100 annual income tax to "protect the environment," and only 14% favoured a $500 annual surcharge on income tax. More generally, when asked about their views on government policy, most people favour increased spending on education and hospitals, increased support for the poor and disadvantaged, and increased spending on a variety of other programs. They also favour lower taxes and lower deficits. Rather clearly, these objectives are not all consistent with each other.

A vote for higher expenditures on education must be seen as a vote for higher taxes, for higher debt (and higher future taxes), or for less expenditure on other programs. Opportunity cost tells us we cannot have our cake and eat it too.

Consideration of opportunity costs often brings economists into conflict with other professionals seeking to comment on public policy. Hospital administrators, doctors, and nurses regularly complain that current levels of support for health care are inadequate. They and many others argue that all citizens should have access to the best possible medical care. To an economist, the pursuit of the best possible medical care or the best possible anything is foolish because of opportunity costs. Health care could be improved by building major well-equipped hospitals every few blocks, but even the entire budget of all governments in Canada would not be sufficient for such a task. Is it reasonable to pursue the best possible medical care at the expense of all other government programs? Expenditures should be made on medical care only to the extent that the benefits exceed the opportunity costs. Given limited budgets, governments should optimize their expenditures, which requires funding any particular activity only to the extent that benefits exceed opportunity costs.

When airline regulators seek to make airline travel as safe as possible, or when environmentalists suggest that pollution should be minimized, they are failing to take account of opportunity costs. Even the educator who advocates that students have a right to free higher education is making a statement that troubles an economist. Would students have a right to free higher education if unrestricted demand were so high that expenditures on universities threatened to leave few resources for hospitals, roads, and other programs? In order to support the argument for tuition-free education, one would have to argue that the value to society is higher than the opportunity cost.

Opportunity costs should always be kept in mind, but sometimes the measurements required are very difficult. Just what is the value to society of having tuition-free higher education? And how can this be compared with the value of an alternative project such as providing grants to an ailing industry? These are difficult judgements, but unfortunately they do have to be made. If the assessment of opportunity costs is ignored, very wasteful decisions result.

If forced to demonstrate the benefits of tuition-free education, proponents of the policy would have to identify those benefits specifically. Such a policy would make students better off than they would otherwise be, but university students have much higher lifetime incomes than those who do not attend university, so this transfer of income can hardly be counted as a benefit on fairness grounds. There would be some people who would not go to university with tuition fees at current levels, but who would go to university if tuition were free. Some of these people would come from poor families. This, presumably, is the intended benefit. How large is this effect likely to be, and how large would it have to be to justify the cost? Would it be more efficient simply to provide aid to poor students? Trying to carry out the measurements required for opportunity cost analysis is surprisingly effective in exposing wasteful or inefficient policy proposals.

2.2 Marginalism

A second important tool of economic policy analysis is marginalism. Perhaps the best introduction to the marginalist approach is to see how it can be used to unravel one of the problems that perplexed early philosophers: the paradox of value. These philosophers could not understand why water, which was obviously very valuable, and in fact necessary for life, was so inexpensive, while diamonds, which contributed comparatively little to world welfare, were so expensive. If all the diamonds in the world were to disappear tomorrow, some people would be upset, but things would go on more or less as before. If water were eliminated, life would cease. Why are these prices inversely related to value?

The answer is that price is determined not by total value, but by marginal value. The marginal value of water is the value of a little more water. The price that a consumer is willing to pay for a litre of water depends on the marginal value of the next litre. If water is abundant and consumers already have as much as they want, their marginal willingness to pay for an extra litre is very low. Thus the price of water is low. Diamonds, on the other hand, are comparatively scarce. The marginal value of an extra diamond is high, and this is why the price is high. Prices reflect marginal value, not total value.

The implication of marginalist reasoning for public policy is that we must always compare the marginal benefit of policy programs with their marginal (opportunity) cost. Consider the following statement: "Education is more important than highways; therefore more money

should be spent on schools and less should be spent on roads." Statements of this sort are frequently made, perhaps with health care or the
environment substituting for education.

People who make such statements are failing to apply marginalist
reasoning; they are falling victim to the paradox of value. Most of us
would probably agree that in some absolute sense education is more
important than highways. This is a statement about total value. Logically, however, the claim that more money should be spent on schools
has nothing to do with total value. Such a claim depends on marginal
value, not total value.

Suppose that we already had well-equipped schools in every
neighbourhood, and that classrooms had lots of extra space, but that
people were driving on dirt roads in most of the community. Would it
still make sense to spend more on schools rather than highways? Obviously not. It makes sense to spend more on schools instead of highways only if the marginal value of school expenditures exceeds the
marginal value of road expenditures.

Definition: The **marginalist principle** states that any policy or
activity should be carried out as long as the marginal benefit
exceeds the marginal opportunity cost.

In other words, any activity should be carried out as long as the
marginal benefit exceeds the marginal value of alternative activities.
The optimum, or best possible, outcome arises when every activity is
carried out just to the point where marginal benefit becomes equal to
marginal cost.

The marginalist principle is a basic principle of decision-making.
It applies to public policy and to business decisions. For business firms
trying to earn as much profit as possible, the marginalist principle is
captured in the idea that firms should produce more output up to the
point where marginal revenue equals marginal cost. If marginal revenue exceeds marginal cost, output should be increased, because revenues will rise by more than costs and profit will increase. If marginal revenue is less than marginal cost, the firm will increase profit by
reducing output. The same idea applies to public policy, except that
public policy should be concerned with social benefits and costs, not
just financial profits and losses.

2.3 Economic Incentives

We all realize the power of economic incentives. Consider the following quote from a story in the Globe and Mail:[2]

> The cost of constructing a gravel road on a [native] reserve in northern Manitoba, independently estimated at a much lower figure, jumped to $1.38 million after the company in charge of the project was given pre-signed blank cheques. . . . The Department of Indian Affairs eventually paid out about 90% of the cost. . . . By issuing pre-signed blank cheques, the Indian band lost control of the project. . . . A Winnipeg engineering firm conducted an independent appraisal of the project and concluded that it should have cost between $275,000 and $330,000.

This description contains some obvious incentive problems. Giving pre-signed cheques to a firm engaged on a cost-plus project creates obvious incentives for the firm to pad expenses. The article went on to assign blame to the native band and to government officials for bad management. But what were the incentives facing the native band? It wasn't their money that paid for the road. Furthermore, what were the incentives facing government managers?

The idea of incentive effects seems very obvious, yet it is surprising how policy makers and individuals generally fail to anticipate incentive effects in context. A good example of insensitivity to incentive effects is provided by a Vancouver tennis club. The club recently eliminated monthly dues for juniors (tennis-playing children of adult members) on the grounds that this fee did not raise much revenue and that eliminating the fee would be helpful to families.

Many eligible children who had not previously been junior members promptly signed up. The club's capacity for juniors was quickly reached and a long waiting list formed. To the surprise and consternation of the club's directors, it soon became clear that anyone wanting to get a new junior into the club would face a long waiting list. The problem arose because, as soon as it became costless for juniors to join, every family had an incentive to enrol its children as members, whether or not the children had any interest in tennis. As a result, many of those who might have been very interested in tennis were prevented from joining by a long waiting list. After a trial period, the club restored dues for juniors.

Another good example of unanticipated incentive effects is the case of federal civil service buyouts. During the late 1980s, the Government of Canada, as part of an unsuccessful attempt to gets its deficit and debts under control, undertook a reduction in the size of the civil service. As part of this process, the government significantly increased the use of buyouts: civil servants would agree to quit or take early retirement in return for a cash payment. Seemingly, this would increase the incentive to leave and make downsizing the civil service easier. However, as described in the 1995 Report of the Auditor General of Canada, the program created perverse incentives. In particular, after it became clear that buyouts could be obtained, "normal" quits (i.e., quits without compensation) dropped sharply. Why quit without compensation when by hanging on to a job and negotiating for a cash settlement, a substantial reward can be obtained?

A second perverse effect of buyouts found by the Auditor General is that they disproportionately induce the best workers to quit. A poor worker in a well-paid job is probably earning considerably more than he or she could get in another job. Such people have little incentive to quit. Even with a buyout, quitting is probably unattractive for such a worker. On the other hand, a very good worker probably can get another good job. Such a person is close to the margin of leaving even without a buyout. Adding in a buyout then makes quitting very attractive. Thus a commonly observed effect of buyout programs is that they tend to induce a brain drain.

The Auditor General suggested targeting buyouts at workers the government particularly wants to get rid of. This too is a dangerous policy, because it gives people incentives to become poor workers in order to attract a buyout.

Economists expect people to follow their economic interests; noneconomists often expect people to leave their behaviour unchanged despite changing economic incentives. This was true of the tennis club. It is also true of people who are surprised when unemployment rises as unemployment benefits rise, or when landlords operating under rent controls choose not to maintain their rental units.

A particularly costly example concerns the ill-fated Scientific Research Tax Credit, which was introduced in Canada in 1984 and terminated in 1985. If this tax credit had been applied retroactively to a typical year, such as 1982 or 1983, the tax credit would have cost the government about $200 million. This seemed to various politicians like a small price to pay in order to be seen to be doing something to encourage research and development in Canada. Once the tax credit was in place, of course, business firms started classifying everything they could as research and development. When the program was terminated in May 1985 after being in effect for 17 months, it had cost the government about $3 billion in lost revenues.[3]

The basic idea of incentive effects is very simple: in considering the effects of any public policy we should expect people to follow their economic incentives. Anticipation of incentive effects will usually improve policy decisions, and an understanding of incentives will help the analyst understand why a particular policy worked out the way it did. In other words, recognition of incentive effects is fundamental to both normative and positive analysis.

2.4 Economic Efficiency

It is hard to find a discussion of business decisions or of public policy in which the term "efficiency" is not used freely. Unfortunately, there are several different, although related, concepts of efficiency, and confusion can result when different notions of efficiency are used in the same discussion. The following two concepts of efficiency are frequently used in economic policy analysis:

1. *Management efficiency (or production efficiency)*: Each economic activity is managed so efficiently that cost is minimized for the output levels chosen.

2. *Pareto efficiency (or allocational efficiency)*: Resources are allocated in such a way that it is impossible to make anyone better off without making someone else worse off.

The concept of management efficiency is easy to understand. Management inefficiency would mean that resources were being wasted: the firm or other organization would be using more inputs (and more money) than necessary. Another way of defining management efficiency is that it focuses on the question "Are we doing things the best way?" If not, we are being wasteful.

Pareto efficiency is a broader concept of efficiency than is management efficiency. It requires management efficiency as a necessary condition, but requires additional conditions as well. Ultimately, however, the concept of Pareto efficiency refers fundamentally to the absence of waste. If a situation is Pareto inefficient, it means that it would be possible to improve the welfare of at least one person without harming anyone else. It would be wasteful not to do so. Pareto inefficiency means that potential human welfare is being wasted.

The concept of Pareto inefficiency is closely related to deadweight loss. Consider the diagram in Figure 2.1.

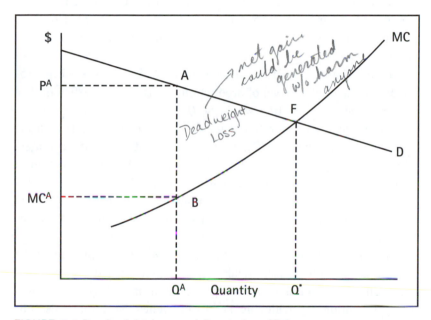

FIGURE 2.1 Deadweight Loss and Pareto Innefficiency

Figure 2.1 shows a demand curve, D, for some product. The normal interpretation of a demand curve is that it shows the quantity demanded for any price. The demand curve also shows, for any given quantity of consumption, the willingness of consumers to pay for a little more of the commodity. For example, at point A consumers are consuming quantity Q^A and would be willing to pay price P^A for a little more of the good. A consumer's willingness to pay for the next unit of a good can be taken as a measure of the consumer's marginal benefit from consuming that good.[4]

The curve labelled MC is the marginal cost of production. The marginal cost curve shows, for any given level of output, the marginal cost of producing another unit of output. The MC curve represents the minimum amount that owners of factors of production would be willing to receive to produce a little more output. At output level Q^A, the marginal benefit (as given by the demand curve) exceeds the marginal cost (as shown by the MC curve). This represents a situation of Pareto inefficiency.

The reasoning is as follows. If an extra unit of the product were produced, consumers would be willing to pay P^A and would suffer no loss in welfare. Owners of the factors of production would be willing to receive MC^A for the extra production with no loss in welfare. This would leave a surplus of P^A-MC^A, which could be refunded to consumers, or given to owners of factors of production, or given to a third party, or a mixture of all three. In any case, the welfare of some people could be improved without anyone being worse off. Therefore, production at the original level of production, Q^A, is Pareto inefficient. The efficient level of production would be Q^*.

The triangle ABF is referred to as a deadweight loss. This deadweight loss represents a net gain or surplus that could be generated, without harming anyone, by moving from the inefficient allocation of resources represented by output level Q^A, to the Pareto efficient allocation, Q^*. Pareto efficiency is sometimes referred to as allocational efficiency because it requires a particular allocation of scarce resources.

In Figure 2.1, the basic question is whether we are producing the appropriate amount of a particular good. If not, then the situation is Pareto inefficient. Producing the right amount of each good is a necessary condition for achieving Pareto efficiency. Note that this subsumes (or includes) the question of what activities to carry out (i.e., the question "Are we doing the right things?"). If we are not doing the right things, then we are carrying out some activities at a zero level despite the fact that surplus is available from them. Achieving Pareto efficiency would require that such activities be carried out at positive levels.

The concept of Pareto efficiency is a central benchmark, or point of comparison, used by economists in evaluating policy. It is, however, important to be aware of the limitations of this concept. As a practical matter, we never achieve full Pareto efficiency. All economic systems contain many distortions. In considering specific policies, we are always comparing one Pareto-inefficient situation to another. Thus, simply observing that a situation is Pareto inefficient is not really a sufficient reason for introducing or proposing a policy change. Only if the magnitude of the distortion were sufficiently large would there be a strong case for action.

One related policy criterion that can sometimes be applied is the concept of a Pareto improvement. We say that a Pareto improvement takes place if some people can be made better off and no one is made worse off. If we are in an Pareto-inefficient state, then it is possible in principle to make a Pareto improvement. Thus, we can use the concept of a Pareto improvement even if full Pareto efficiency is not achieved. If we move from situation A to situation B, and no one is made worse off while some people are made better off, then we satisfy the Pareto-improvement criterion whether or not situation B is Pareto efficient.

However, even Pareto improvements are rare. It is sometimes feasible to compensate the initial losers from some policy action so that in the end everyone gains. In general, however, it is very difficult to ensure that all affected parties are fully compensated. An easier criterion to satisfy is the criterion of potential Pareto improvements, as defined below.

> *Definition*: A **potential Pareto improvement** has taken place if the gainers have gained enough to be able to fully compensate the losers and still be better off.

Stated somewhat less precisely, a policy change creates a potential Pareto improvement provided that the gainers gain more than the losers lose, even if the losers are not actually compensated. If a potential Pareto improvement takes place, we say that there has been an improvement in efficiency. There are some technical difficulties associated with this concept, but it does allow us to make a connection between average levels of economic welfare and economic efficiency. Strictly speaking, however, in order to accept the idea that potential Pareto improvements are good, we must implicitly make the assumption that any resulting changes in the distribution of income are acceptable.

The difficulties associated with trying to apply either the Pareto-improvement criterion or the potential Pareto criterion arise in the case of intergenerational issues such as economic growth or resource depletion. Very often, the people who forego consumption and pay taxes to pay for some investment that will generate economic growth are no longer alive by the time the full benefits of the investment are realized. Conversely, when we consider the consumption of depletable resources, more current consumption may leave future generations worse off than they would otherwise be. In considering both of these intergenerational comparisons, the Pareto criterion is not helpful because it cannot be satisfied. Inevitably, one generation is made worse off to provide higher benefits for another. Just focusing on the potential Pareto criterion does not seem sufficient in itself to deal with the intergenerational tradeoff. Therefore, we end up considering distributional effects simultaneously with efficiency considerations.

In this book we will use the term "efficiency" as follows:

1. if a situation is said to be efficient, we mean that it is Pareto efficient.

2. if a situation is said to be inefficient, that means that it is Pareto inefficient.

3. if we say that one situation is more efficient than another, or that there has been an improvement in efficiency, it means that the potential Pareto criterion is satisfied.

4. if management efficiency is being discussed, then that term or its equivalent, production efficiency, will be used. Recall that management efficiency is a necessary condition for (Pareto) efficiency.

5. both allocational efficiency and economic efficiency are used as synonyms for Pareto efficiency.

Some analysts distinguish between static efficiency, which refers only to one-period analysis, and dynamic efficiency, which tries to deal with circumstances that evolve over time. The general concept of Pareto efficiency includes both static and dynamic efficiency.

It should be clear that efficiency is closely related to the marginalist principle. In fact, provided social valuations of different projects coincide with individual valuations, a situation that satisfies the marginalist principle from society's point of view will be Pareto efficient.[5]

As indicated in Chapter 1, efficiency is usually taken to be an objective of government policy because increases in efficiency are associated with increases in per capita living standards. One of the basic dilemmas of policy is that improvements in efficiency are often damaging, or at least apparently damaging, to fairness or equity objectives. Conversely, policies intended to promote fairness or equity are often very inefficient. For this reason, some people are hostile to the economist's apparent preoccupation with economic efficiency. At the very least, however, understanding economic efficiency is helpful in allowing us, for any given equity objectives, to seek the most efficient (or least inefficient) approach.

2.5 Bibliographic Notes

The basic economic concepts described here are presented in most economics textbooks. A standard introductory text is Stiglitz and Boadway (1994). Classic work on Pareto efficiency and its relationship to social welfare includes Arrow (1951), Bator (1957, 1958), and Little (1957).

Notes

1. Alan Daniels, "Expo legacy includes pride, hope, for future," *Vancouver Sun,* October 4, 1986, p. A10.

2. Geoffrey York, "Cost of road on reserve rose after blank cheques issued," *The Globe and Mail,* October 15, 1986, p. 1.

3. *The Globe and Mail,* December 29, 1986, p. 1.

4. The idea that marginal benefit is reasonably measured by willingness to pay as shown by the demand curve has generated some dispute. A discussion of the issues can be found in any good public finance textbook. See, for example, Boadway and Wildasin (1984). At least, however, willingness to pay is an approximation to marginal benefit.

5. It is possible, however, that social valuations might conflict with individual ones. For example, an individual might have a high willingness to pay for heroin, but society as a whole might take the view that this marginal benefit, as perceived by the individual, shoulld not get much weight in public policy.

3

The Normative Analysis of Government

Any normative view of government policy must be based on some fundamental philosophy. The basic philosophical issue concerns whether proposed or actual public policy interventions can be viewed as legitimate according to some acceptable and consistent set of values. In this book we cannot provide a detailed treatment of the philosophical basis of government. The first part of this chapter does, however, review the philosophical perspective underlying the normative analysis of policy articulated in this text. The rest of the chapter provides a categorization of the major normative rationales for government intervention in business.

3.1 Philosophical Foundations of Government Policy Toward Business

The first philosophical point to make is that different sets of values will, of course, give rise to different views of the legitimate role of policy. At some level, the choice of fundamental values is arbitrary, and anyone with even a limited knowledge of history can readily bring to mind several different sets of values underlying the role of the state.

In feudal Europe, the government consisted of the local feudal lord and ultimately a king or prince. Such governments regarded themselves as having an absolute right to intervene in the economic and personal affairs of the common people. In some areas this absolute right was thought to be a divine right, coming directly from the will of God. In others, the source of feudal rights was based more on a simple hierarchical or authoritarian view of human nature, which held that the natural obligation of every person was to have authority over his or her inferiors and to do the will of his or her superiors.

Modern Western philosophy can be seen in part as a reaction to feudal forms of organization and draws heavily from classical Greek views on the role of government. The basic element in this philosophy is the primacy or sovereignty of the individual. Individual rights, freedoms, and well-being are viewed as being the ultimate source of legitimacy for government action. Legitimate governments are those that would arise from social contracts to which all (or almost all) individuals would voluntarily agree.

Many philosophers and political economists see a natural link between ideas of individual sovereignty and private enterprise. Specifically, the philosophy of private enterprise rests on two conceptions of individual sovereignty: economic freedom and consumer sovereignty. Economic freedom is the idea that individuals should be free to enter voluntary agreements with other individuals concerning the production, distribution, and consumption of economic goods and services.

Consumer sovereignty means that each individual has a right to his or her own preferences and tastes, insofar as those tastes do not impinge directly on the rights of others. Furthermore, these preferences and tastes are, for any given technology, the ultimate determinants of what goods and services are produced. The job of the government is not to question or change those tastes, but to create an environment in which individuals can pursue their own objectives as effectively and efficiently as possible.

These ideas sound appealing when stated in the abstract, but most of us would not accept them as absolute principles. For example, economic freedom would imply that if one person were willing to grow poppies and produce heroin, and another were willing to buy the heroin at a mutually agreeable price, then they should be allowed to do so. Yet many societies pass laws against heroin production and consumption, and most of us agree with these laws. Most of the so-called victimless crimes are simple economic transactions that the state has decided to restrict: gambling, prostitution, consumption of various drugs, and so on.

Even consumer sovereignty is not sacred. It is not consistent with consumer sovereignty to have governments spending large sums of money on advertising campaigns intended to persuade people not to smoke, yet few of us oppose such policies. Governments also violate consumer sovereignty by choosing to subsidize opera and ballet, while they tax bowling alleys and professional wrestling, yet most people accept such policies as reasonable. In addition, most of us accept the idea that the principles of sovereignty should exclude certain groups, particularly the very young and those suffering from severe mental handicaps or disturbances.

In short, the individualist philosophy cannot be taken as absolute. It does, however, form the starting point for the normative analysis of government in Western market-based economies. There are exceptions and compromises, but the point is that such departures from the basic principles are seen as exceptions and compromises and must be carefully justified. This basic philosophical view leads naturally to political systems based on democratic principles and to economic systems based on private voluntary exchange (i.e., on private markets). Thus, the role of government in business affairs is seen, according to this view of the world, as a limited one that must be based on a strong case-by-case justification for intervention.

This philosophy based on individual rights is not universally held, even in Western countries, and is quite foreign in many parts of the world. Modern alternative views focus on the rights of a country (nationalism), or a class (Marxism), or a particular ethnic group, or a religious group to impose its will on individuals. Oddly enough, as individual rights are being embraced in many parts of the world (such as Eastern Europe) where they had been vigorously suppressed in the recent past, they are under attack in some of the Western countries where they have traditionally been most cherished.

For example, Kimball (1990, p.198) reports that a University of Pennsylvania student was admonished by university officials for embracing the notion of individual rights. The official argued what has become a fairly common position of the cultural left in North America: focusing on individual rights is racist because it argues against using race-based (or sex-based) preferential discrimination to correct perceived injustice.

In Canada, the 1991 Manitoba Aboriginal Justice Enquiry suggested the development of a separate native system of justice.[1] Through-

out the 1990s a variety of community-based aboriginal justice programs were introduced in Canada, and in 1999, the first large-scale
aboriginal justice system in Canada was started in Alberta. This
approach is inconsistent with individualist philosophies. It says, in
essence, that people should face different standards of justice depending on their race.

The enquiry argued that natives did suffer what, in effect, was
a different standard of justice within the conventional system. There
is, however, an important difference between differences that arise
from unintended or even illegal problems in the administration
of criminal justice, and race-based differences that are required by
law as matters of principle. In this book, we take the traditional individualist philosophy as the basis of normative analysis, in keeping
with the dominant themes in modern Western thought, recognizing,
however, that it is not absolute.

3.2 Private Enterprise and Individual Sovereignty

Market-based economic systems, with limited roles for government,
are consistent with the principle of individual sovereignty. This is not,
however, the real reason why Canada, the United States, and many
other countries have market-based economies. In fact, the converse is
probably true: philosophies that are based on the primacy of the individual are popular because the associated forms of economic organization have performed well. Market-based systems perform much better than tribal systems, much better than the hierarchical economic
systems of the past, and much better than centrally planned socialism
did in Eastern Europe and elsewhere. With few exceptions, the many
countries that have experimented with socialist central planning are
trying to move toward market-based systems.

There is, however, a considerable range among the market-based
economies concerning the appropriate role of government. Of the
major economies, the United States probably comes closest to the
purist approach of trying to promote competition while allowing private enterprise to make business decisions. Other countries, such as
France and Japan and now South Korea, have developed what has
been described as a corporatist approach, in which the government
becomes closely involved with large firms in planning major investment initiatives.

Similarly, in the world of former and current centrally planned countries (now often referred to as economies in transition or transitional economies), there is considerable variety. Some countries, such as Poland and the former East Germany (incorporated as part of the unified Federal Republic of Germany in 1990), have tried to adopt a Western European economic structure on a cold-turkey basis. Others, such as Russia, tried a third path of gradual reform in the late 1980s and 1990s, while a few, notably Cuba and North Korea, remain resolutely anti-market communist countries. It appears unlikely, however, that the policy stance of Cuba and North Korea will survive much longer. While it is still early to judge the economic performance of the former communist bloc countries, it seems that those countries that have taken a cold-turkey approach to reform are performing best, despite significant adjustment costs.

China is a particularly interesting case, partly because of its size (with a population over 40 times that of Canada), and partly because of its volatile policy history. During China's Cultural Revolution (1966 to 1976)[2] private markets were ruthlessly suppressed. We do not have reliable information about economic growth during this period, but it seems that per capita living standards actually fell from their already very low levels. In the reform period that has followed the Cultural Revolution, a major economic liberalization has been permitted, particularly in the agricultural sector, for small business generally in some parts of the country and, increasingly, for large-scale industry, especially in the "special economic zones" that have been granted more economic freedoms than the rest of China. The result has been a very rapid increase in per capita living standards, with real income per capita more than tripling between 1976 and 1999. Many senior government leaders want to call themselves communists or socialists, but are eager to reap the benefits of market reforms.

One reason that China has been able to perform well in recent years is that it has been able to control its population growth. It is questionable whether control of population growth could have been achieved so rapidly without the high levels of government control that seem to go hand in hand with authoritarian central planning.

3.3 Adam Smith and the Competitive Paradigm

Questions about the role of the state or the role of government have a long history in philosophical debate. Plato's *Republic*, written over two thousand years ago, is still read today by many students of political science. Our modern understanding of business and government really began, however, with the publication in 1776 of Adam Smith's *Wealth of Nations*. Smith was a philosopher at the University of Edinburgh in Scotland, but is now regarded as the first modern economist. He is responsible for one of the major themes in economic thought: competitive private markets harness private incentives, so they serve the public interest. The following quotations from Smith (1776) illustrate his point of view.

> An individual generally neither intends to promote the public interest nor knows by how much he is promoting it. . . . .By directing industry in such a manner as its product may be of greatest value, he intends only his own personal gain, and he is in this aim . . . led as if by an "invisible hand" to promote an end which was no part of his intention. (p.477)

> By pursuing his own self-interest, the entrepreneur frequently promotes that of society more effectually than when he means to promote it. (p.477)

> It is not from the benevolence of the butcher, the brewer, or the baker that we expect our dinner, but from their regard to their own self-interest. (p.18)

Whereas most people looked out into the world and saw chaos, Smith looked into the world and saw a remarkable degree of coordination and order. Consider the breakfast that Smith, in 18th-century Scotland, might have eaten. He might have had toast made from wheat grown in Eastern Europe; he would have spread marmalade, made from oranges grown in Spain, on his toast; and he would have drunk tea, brought from India, sweetened with sugar from the West Indies. He might have eaten with silverware made from South American silver, and his tablecloth might have been made from American cotton and his napkins from Chinese silk.

Coordinating even a simple breakfast was a remarkable accomplishment, beyond the capabilities of any single individual and probably beyond the abilities of most national governments of the time. What was the coordinating force, or invisible hand, that provided Smith with his breakfast? The invisible hand was private competitive markets. Somehow, many different individuals, mostly unknown to one another, pursuing their own self-interest through private competitive markets, achieved remarkable results. (Note, however, that some of the firms that may have been involved with providing Smith's breakfast had substantial monopoly power, such as the East India Company.)

When we reflect on how things get done, it is natural to assume that someone must give orders to make sure that the right products are produced in the right amounts and available at the right places. This is the method followed by the army: generals give orders to colonels, who give orders to majors, and so on. This is the command method; it is the obvious way of getting things done. It did not, however, produce Smith's breakfast. That was produced by a decentralized system of independent individuals acting in their own self-interest through market transactions.

Smith argued that market transactions, undertaken through the motive of self-interest, promote social welfare to a greater extent than do rival systems of organizing production, such as command systems. His main insight is very simple: if an exchange between two parties is voluntary, it will not take place unless they both believe they can benefit from it. This is the principle of voluntary exchange.

An implication of this argument is that little rationale exists for government intervention in private markets. Smith did recognize some exceptions. He acknowledged that the government might have a legitimate role in preventing concentrations of monopoly power, and he also believed that the government would have to provide some goods, such as national defence and roads, that would not be adequately provided by the private sector. He also recognized that for markets to function smoothly, governments must allow private property and must provide mechanisms for the enforcement of private contracts and the protection of private property and personal safety.

Smith's discussion of monopoly power raises an important distinction: private enterprise can be expected to work out well, but only if markets are reasonably competitive. Modern economists and other social scientists have inherited and emphasized the notion that competition is fundamentally important. Smith's basic legacy, therefore, is the idea that private competitive markets should form the basis of business organization.

In this book we will examine circumstances in which private markets do not perform well. These circumstances can be used to justify very substantial government influence on business affairs, but the point is that these policies will be viewed as particular cases that must be carefully justified. In other words, the basic question we will always ask with respect to any policy is "Why can't the private sector do it?"

3.4 The Meaning of Competition

As just indicated, a crucial part of Smith's argument is that markets must be competitive. This raises the issue of what is meant by "competition." The normal use of the term, by businessmen and politicians, and for that matter by Smith himself, refers to the rivalry among sellers (or buyers) in a market. Competition means a conscious striving against other firms for sales, possibly on the basis of price, but also on the basis of advertising, research and development, product quality, and other business variables as well.

Economists, however, have found it useful to work with an extreme notion of competition, perfect competition, which is defined by the following characteristics:

1. no buyer or seller has control over prices, which therefore are taken as given or exogenous by individual firms;

2. there is free entry and exit in the long run;

3. buyers and sellers have access to all information relevant to their production and consumption decisions.

Characteristic 1 indicates that competitive firms take prices as given, but does not say how or why such a situation would arise. We have in mind a market with many sellers, each selling a homogenous product. In such a case, no one firm could raise its price without losing its market to another firm. Thus, each firm would perceive its price as being determined by the market. Economists have been able to demonstrate that under perfect competition, and provided certain other conditions are met, private markets achieve Pareto efficiency. This is known as the first theorem of welfare economics. Furthermore, if redistributional goals are considered, then Pareto efficiency can be maintained by redistributing basic incomes and by allowing markets to operate freely without intervention. This is the second theorem of welfare economics. These two theorems are the modern abstract version of Smith's basic insight.

In addition to the theorems of abstract economics and to Smith's assertions, there are some political arguments for competition. The strongest of these is that high levels of competition promote the dispersion and decentralization of political and economic power. More forcefully stated, economic competition encourages, and may be central to, the development and maintenance of democratic political institutions.

Note that the suggested relationship is between competition and democracy, not between private enterprise and democracy. There have been (and still are) many examples of countries that were dominated by private enterprise and were simultaneously very undemocratic. In fact, economic monopoly power and political monopoly power seem to go hand in hand. Political dictators frequently use their political power to concentrate monopoly power in the hands of their friends and relatives, or even in their own hands, and conversely, concentration of economic power allows a small number of individuals to use economic power for political ends.

3.5 Normative Reasons for Government Intervention

So far we have emphasized the case made by Adam Smith and his intellectual descendants for private competitive markets as the basic organizational structure for business activity. Aspects of this argument are essentially ideological, but corresponding to the ideology is a well worked-out logical structure. This structure tells us the conditions under which private markets can be expected to perform well. It also tells us, however, when private markets will fail to work effectively.

As already indicated, the inefficiency arising from monopoly power is one important reason for active government policy. There are three major types of policy response to monopoly power. One type of response is to encourage or enhance competition so that a workable level of competition is achieved. This is, in large part, what competition policy attempts to do. A second type of response is to regulate industry directly, limiting the prices that can be charged and imposing other performance requirements. A third approach is direct government ownership, referred to in Canada as Crown corporations.

Monopoly power is not the only concern that arises about market economies. In general, as initially set out in Chapter 1, concerns about market performance fall naturally into four categories:

1. efficiency and market failure,

2. macroeconomic stabilization,

3. fairness and equity,

4. other.

3.6 Efficiency and Market Failure

Most of the specific policy areas that are discussed in this book draw on efficiency-based reasons for government intervention. We now recognize, based on the development of economic theory and on actual experience, that Adam Smith overstated the value of unregulated private markets. Private markets sometimes fail to achieve allocative or even management efficiency, and these departures from efficiency can be so severe that even very imperfect governments can be expected to offer improvements. In other words, there are some situations in which government intervention can raise per capita living standards, rather than simply redistributing wealth.

> *Definition*: A **market failure** is a situation in which private markets fail to achieve allocative (or Pareto) efficiency.

There are four major sources of market failure:

1. imperfect competition,

2. public goods,

3. externalities,

4. informational problems.

Each of these market failures is the rationale behind a major area of government policy, and each will be discussed carefully when the relevant policy areas are examined. In this section, the objective is to provide a brief explanation of each source of market failure.

3.6.1 Imperfect Competition

We have claimed above that perfect competition is efficient. Many industries, however, are not perfectly competitive. Individual firms have considerable control over market price and there may be barriers to entry. As described in Chapter 6, in such circumstances, profit-maximizing firms will charge prices that are too high and produce output levels that are too low from the allocational point of view. While the government cannot improve upon every minor departure from perfect competition, it does have a role in promoting competition and in regulating, or at least closely monitoring, areas where imperfect competition is inevitable.

For example, Hydro Quebec is a Crown corporation owned and controlled by the government of Quebec. Hydro Quebec is in the public sector to protect the province from the problems associated with private monopolies although continuing technological change makes market-based approaches a reasonable alternative. As of 2000, Ontario has sought to encourage open competition in electric power generation and transmission.

3.6.2 Public Goods

In virtually every country national defence is provided by the government. So are lighthouses and public parks. These are examples of public goods. A public good has the following characteristics:

1. a public good is nonrival in consumption: even though one person consumes the good, others may also;

2. a public good is nonexclusive: it is impossible (or at least very costly) to exclude anyone from consuming the good.

Consider a lighthouse. The fact that one ship's captain is warned by the flashing light to stay away from dangerous rocks does not prevent other ships from receiving the same warning. Thus, lighthouse services are nonrival in consumption. Also, it is virtually impossible to keep anyone from consuming the services of the lighthouse. Any passing ship will see the light. The services of a lighthouse are therefore nonexclusive.

Ordinary private goods, on the other hand, are rival and exclusive. If I consume an orange, it is gone and no one else can consume it. Furthermore, even if I do not eat the orange immediately, I can easily prevent others from consuming it. Public goods cause market failure because private markets will not provide public goods. The basic argument relies on incentive effects. If a good is nonexclusive, no consumer has an incentive to pay for the good once it is produced. After all, he or she will be able to consume it anyway, so why pay? In other words, each consumer has an incentive to be a free rider. Because no firm can expect to receive much payment for providing a public good, firms have very little incentive to provide such goods. The market will not provide public goods up to the point where the marginal social benefits are equal to the marginal social costs. It may not provide public goods at all. Government intervention is therefore called for.

3.6.3 Externalities

Roughly speaking, externalities are third-party effects. They arise when some person or group is affected by the economic activity of others, without markets to price the effect. For example, if a pulp mill discharges pollution that kills fish in nearby bodies of water, then fishermen are subject to a negative externality caused by the pulp mill. If a smoker sits beside a nonsmoker and proceeds to light a cigarette, then the smoker is imposing a negative externality on the nonsmoker (unless the nonsmoker enjoys the smoke, in which case the externality is positive). In the absence of government regulation, activities that generate negative externalities will be done too much and activities with positive externalities will be underprovided.

3.6.4 Informational Market Failure

The perfectly competitive model of business presumes that all parties to a transaction have access to the relevant information. In practice people are frequently underinformed. A consumer buying a personal computer has no way of assessing the dangers from radiation emitted by the monitor. If radiation screening is expensive, and consumers cannot tell safe radiation levels from unsafe ones, then firms will have an incentive to provide insufficient radiation screening. In such cases it often better simply to have the government impose standards for the product.

Imperfect information causes a variety of market failures. The basic source of market failure in situations of differential or asymmetric information is that the less informed party will not know the true marginal benefit to be derived from the transaction as clearly as the more informed party. In some of these situations, although not all, there is reason to believe that government intervention is appropriate.

It is worth noting that markets will respond to informational market failure. In situations where the buyer finds it hard to evaluate different products, sellers will seek certification for their claims, and external sources of certification will find a market for their services. In North America, the Consumers' Union, which publishes *Consumer Reports*, is basically in the business of determining and conveying to consumers information about the quality of different products. In addition, firms will have incentives to invest in their reputations for quality, so that consumers will trust the firm's products even if they (the consumers) cannot immediately distinguish quality differences among products. Both of these market responses can improve, but do not eliminate, informational market failure.

3.7 Macroeconomic Stabilization and Economic Growth

The following three basic facts about market-based economies play a major role in public policy discussions:

1. business activity is cyclical,

2. a significant but variable fraction of the labour force is always unemployed,

3. the price level is usually rising.

Point 1 refers to the idea that the pace of business activity tends to rise and fall, with corresponding increases and decreases in employment and in the growth of real incomes. This rise and fall of activity is referred to as the business cycle. Since the publication of John Maynard Keynes' *General Theory of Employment, Interest and Money* in 1936, it has been generally accepted that the government has a role to play in moderating the business cycle. Ideally, the economy would always operate close to its capacity, with little unemployed labour or capital. In an attempt to achieve this goal, the government uses its control over the money supply, interest rates, exchange rates, taxes, and government spending.

The unemployment rate rises and falls as the economy goes through recessions and expansions. Even at the best of times, however, there is substantial unemployment. In Canada, the lowest unemployment rate achieved in the period 1977 to 1999 was 6.6%, and this period contained three complete business cycles. There is always a lot of pressure for governments to help in the process of job-creation, particularly during recessions, and public discussions of any policy issue focus on the employment consequences of the policy.

It is important to distinguish, however, between policies that simply reallocate employment among regions or industries and polices that increase aggregate employment. If the Government of Canada undertakes a project in the home riding of an influential cabinet minister so as to expand employment in that area, it is not creating employment overall, but merely shifting potential employment from an alternative region where the project might have taken place. From a national point of view, the employment consequences of where to carry out a project cancel out, leaving other normative issues as the dominant considerations. Normative analysis of most policy areas, therefore, does not focus on employment issues. The presumption of the economic policy analyst is that unemployment problems are best tackled through broad-based macroeconomic policy.

From 1986 through 1999, inflation (the rate of price increase) has been low and stable, averaging approximately 3% per year and not exceeding 6% in any one year. Yet in the decade of the 1970s, inflation fluctuated sharply and rose well into double digits, reaching a local peak at 10.9% in 1974, and a still higher peak of 12.5% in 1981. Concern about inflation was probably the dominant economic policy issue of the 1970s. There is considerable evidence that high and variable levels of inflation are damaging to business activity, and national governments are therefore seen to have an obligation to keep the price level relatively stable. Unfortunately, governments have a natural incentive to create inflation by printing money to finance their budget deficits. Many countries have very high inflation rates for precisely this reason.

Keeping inflation under control in Canada is primarily the responsibility of the Bank of Canada (whose Governor is appointed by the Government of Canada). Since the early 1980s, the Bank of Canada (often referred to simply as the Bank) has been vigorously suppressing inflationary pressures. Whenever the economy starts to show signs of inflationary pressure, the Bank undertakes some action to relieve the pressure. Normally, however, such actions slow down the economy and tend to induce recessions. Ideally, the Bank would like to achieve a soft landing, in which the economy slows just enough to prevent inflationary pressures, but not enough to induce recession.

The cumulative path of economic recession and expansion determines the growth path of the economy, and, in the long run, the overall growth path is much more important than the particular cyclical pattern underlying it. Furthermore, through the compounding effect of exponential growth, rates of growth that seem modest when quoted on a year-to-year basis can completely transform a country if continued over a couple of decades. For example, a per capita real income growth rate of 6% per year will cause per capita real incomes to triple over the space of 20 years. Any policy that has a significant effect on growth rates is ultimately very important. Both macroeconomic policies and the other policy areas covered in this book can have a significant impact on growth rates.

This book does not emphasize macroeconomic stabilization, but Chapter 17 is devoted to a discussion of the main concerns surrounding stabilization policy. When considering other policy areas we will sometimes consider employment issues. Apart from this, however, specific policy areas focus mainly on market failure (or market inefficiency).

3.8 Other Rationales for Policy Intervention

Other rationales for intervention is a catch-all category that includes normative or public interest objectives that do not fit into the standard rationales for policy. In popular debate, of course, one hears any number of reasons for policy intervention. On close inspection, most of these other reasons either fit into one of the three categories we have just discussed or they are spurious rationalizations for special interests.

There are, however, some legitimate points to make here. Historically, the most important extra considerations are military. For example, many countries have taken the view that having a domestic steel industry is very important for national defense, and have therefore used government policies (such as subsidies and tariff protection) to ensure that the domestic steel industry survives. In Canada, probably the most important noneconomic influence on policy has been the desire to influence Canadian culture. Thus, Canadian policies include a variety of subsidies and local content regulations intended to foster the development of Canadian literature, music, arts, and other areas of cultural activity. Canadian cultural policy has also sought diversity of cultural activity as part of its program of multiculturalism.

Cultural policies are sometimes justified on efficiency grounds. For example, subsidies to the feature film industry are viewed by some as an investment in a potentially profitable domestic industry. However, if interventionist cultural policies really had to pay their way on economic grounds, we probably would not have many such policies.

Another important source of policy intervention is paternalism. Various censorship laws, regulations concerning drugs and alcohol, restrictions on the rights of children, and other areas of government intervention in the consumption decisions of individuals are due fundamentally to paternalism: the idea that some individuals need to be protected from themselves; that the state knows what is good for them better than they themselves do.

It may be hard to distinguish among possible rationales for a particular policy. For example, at various times in the recent past, political parties and even sitting governments in Canada have proposed a national child-care program along the lines of medicare. The basic objective would be to provide low-cost (i.e., publicly subsidized) day-care spaces. Some of the discussion underlying this proposal sounds like an efficiency rationale, and some seems to invoke a fairness rationale based on the idea of helping poor mothers, particularly single ones. However, it is hard to make the case that national day-care would be more efficient than existing private day-care. Even the fairness rationale is hard to establish against the counter-argument that there are simpler and more effective ways of helping poor mothers (single or married). Perhaps the real rationale falls into the other category and arises from a value judgement relating to the role of women. Specifically, the strongest proponents of national subsidized child-care seemed to be those who seek to increase the presence and success of women in the labour force as a matter of ideology or principle. At present, a large portion of child-care is carried out by mothers. A universal, national subsidized child-care program would reduce the privately perceived cost of day-care (even if total public and private child-care costs rose) and make it more attractive for mothers of young children to enter the labour force.

Almost all government programs consume resources. In particular, policies that seek to promote particular values typically impose significant net costs (relative to their overall size) on the government and on the economy as a whole. Canada's program of official bilingualism would be in this category, as would be funding for the CBC and, probably, national day-care. Such social expenditures require that the economy generate a sufficiently high level of income to support them. It is very difficult for social expenditures to increase without underlying economic growth to support them. Failure to fully appreciate this fact has caused many governments to perform poorly.

3.9 Jurisdiction for Government Intervention

It has been argued by many analysts that, at the practical level, jurisdiction for the four basic rationales for intervention should be divided up among different parts of the government. Specifically, it has been argued that most government agencies and departments should focus on economic efficiency, leaving stabilization and employment concerns to the Bank of Canada and the Department of Finance, and leaving concerns about equity mainly to the broad-based tax and transfer system.

This proposed separation of jurisdiction is reflected in actual practice, but only partially. Typically, every policy that surfaces in public debate is scrutinized for its effects on employment and its fairness as perceived by various interest groups. In any case, whether or not there is actual separation of function according to these four categories, this separation is conceptually useful.

In Canada, there is also ongoing conflict over jurisdictions of the different levels of government, particularly between federal and provincial governments. Canada is a federal state, which is a state with more than one substantive level of government. The study of how authority should be allocated among different levels of government is known as fiscal federalism. Because Canada was created in 1867 out of pre-existing political units, and because of Canada's large physical size, it is natural that the provincial level of government in Canada is very powerful. For example, provinces have authority over health policy and education policy, and share in jurisdiction over most areas of economic policy.

We do not have space in this book to examine the theory and practice of fiscal federalism very closely, but there are some general principles that should be stated. First, the general prescription for policies related to equity and redistribution is that they should be carried out by the highest level of government (i.e., by the federal government). The reason is because of incentive effects.

For example, in 1972, the federal government abandoned inheritance taxes, inviting the provinces to impose their own taxes. (Prior to 1972, the federal government set and collected a national inheritance tax but turned 75% of the proceeds over to the provinces. Three provinces had their own additional inheritance taxes.) Nine of the 10 provinces instituted inheritance taxes to replace the federal tax, but by 1983 all but one of these provinces (Quebec) had eliminated the taxes. This nearly complete removal of provincial inheritance taxes was caused by incentive effects.

The incentive for any one province was to reduce its inheritance tax to a level slightly below that of other provinces, so as to attract wealthy inheritors to the local economy. Provinces ended up in a tax-cutting war, leading to very low inheritance taxes. Since inheritance taxes are an important policy in reducing the importance of inherited privilege, this seems an inappropriate allocation of authority.

The same problem arises with welfare payments. Each province would have an incentive to pay less than its neighbours, to avoid importing people who would be a net drain on the economy and export such people to other provinces. The result would be a level of welfare payments below the level that would be settled on at the aggregate or national level.

Policies related to national public goods and to overall economic stabilization are also most efficiently handled at the national level. However, policies related to local public goods, local externality problems, and many other (but not all) problems arising from the failure of markets to achieve efficiency are best handled at the provincial level.

3.10 Cost-Benefit Analysis

In this chapter we have discussed the rationale for government policy intervention, but we have not discussed the techniques of policy analysis. For example, we have argued that public goods create a rationale for policy intervention, but we have not discussed how the government is to decide whether or not to provide a particular public good, or how much of the good to provide. The most important technique of policy analysis is cost-benefit analysis. A detailed discussion of cost-benefit analysis is beyond the scope of this book. The basic idea, however, can be easily stated. As the name suggests, cost-benefit analysis consists simply of trying to add up the costs of a project, add up the benefits of the project, and compare them.

Cost-benefit analysis first became widely used in the 1930s as a method for evaluating flood control projects in the United States, and became standard practice there for a wide range of projects by the early 1960s. In Canada, cost-benefit analysis had also become widely used by the early 1960s, and was formally incorporated into federal government policy analysis as part of the 1966 Planning Programming Budgeting (PPB) System.

Cost-benefit analysis can be applied to projects, programs, regulations, and other government actions. Before any regulation is adopted, it is useful to consider it from a cost-benefit point of view. For example, several Canadian provinces recently experimented with large increases in cigarette taxes, but found that enforcement costs were too high to make these taxes worthwhile. The basic problem was that cigarettes could be easily smuggled into a given province from other provinces and from the United States and sold illegally. This had the effect of dramatically reducing the tax revenue earned and undermining the objective of reducing cigarette consumption. Police forces then faced the problem of deciding whether to take personnel away from violent crime investigation, traffic control, and other areas so as to redeploy them to deal with cigarette smuggling. Ultimately, these high cigarette taxes would not pass a cost-benefit test.

One important area of application of cost-benefit analysis is the evaluation of power projects. Suppose that a government-owned power company (such as Manitoba Hydro) is considering building a new hydroelectric dam. The main output of the project would be electric power. In order to convert this output to a benefit the electric power must be evaluated. The normal method of valuation is to determine the maximum willingness to pay of potential customers. Recall from Chapter 2 (Figure 2.1) that marginal willingness to pay is given by the demand curve. Total willingness to pay for some quantity, Q, is the area under the demand curve up to point Q. This willingness to pay is taken as the measure of benefits.

The benefits will continue for many years, so the project generates a benefit stream through time. This introduces two complications. First, the future is hard to predict. Manitoba Hydro might have a good idea of what the demand for electric power will be next year, but there is considerable uncertainty associated with predicting demand for 10 or 20 years into the future. The normal approach is to construct an expected benefit. For each year, different possible demand levels would be considered and associated probabilities would be estimated. Based on this information an expected benefit can be calculated for each year.

The other problem associated with time is that benefits in the future are not as valuable as benefits today. Future benefits must be discounted in some way. Normally, a discount rate is applied. Thus, for example, future benefits might be discounted at the rate of 6% per year, 8% per year, or some other appropriate rate.

Similarly, the project also generates a stream of costs. The proper measure of costs should include the opportunity costs of the factors of production used to construct the dam. Typically, the opportunity cost is taken to be equal to the market value of these resources (such as the wage rate for labour, the market price of cement, etc.). Most of the costs of the dam will be up-front costs, but there will also be operating and maintenance costs that continue through time. To the extent that these costs are uncertain, expected values would be used. For each period, we can then subtract the cost from the benefit to obtain a net benefit, and add up all these net benefits as given by the formula

$$NPV = (B_0 - C_0) + (B_1 - C_1)/(1 + r) + (B_2 - C_2)/(1 + r)^2 + \ldots \quad (3.1)$$

where *NPV* stands for net present value, B_i stands for expected benefits in period i, C_i stands for expected costs in period i, and r is the discount rate. If the *NPV* is positive, then we say the project passes the cost-benefit test.

The individual terms in Equation 3.1 may extend for a long time, possibly into an indefinite future. Given typical discount rates, however, terms in the very distant future will have very little impact on the NPV and, as a practical matter, the NPV is normally taken over only a 25- or 30-year period. Some people have criticized this outcome on the grounds that it apparently undervalues the distant future. The future will receive more weight if the discount rate is lower. Choosing a discount rate therefore contains ethical judgements related to comparing future generations with the presents. For this reason (and others), different interested parties will often disagree over the appropriate discount rate.

Often the evaluation of benefits includes items other than the primary effect of the project. For example, a power project may have the extra (or ancillary) benefit of also providing flood control. If so, then these benefits should be counted as well. Similarly, the costs may include additional costs beyond the direct costs of building and running the dam. Perhaps the dam requires construction of a reservoir that will flood recreational land, or perhaps streams that are used for recreational purposes will be destroyed. These are legitimate opportunity costs of the dam and should be counted in the NPV calculation. Much of the difficulty in carrying out cost-benefit analysis arises from deciding where to draw the line concerning possible ancillary costs and benefits of the project.

3.11 Bibliographic Notes

The basic philosophy of individual rights is descended from 17th-century philosopher John Locke. Influential modern proponents of philosophies based on individualism are Hayek (1960) and Nozick (1974). An interesting application of the social contract approach to the theory of the state is provided by Rawls (1971), who argues that individuals placed behind a veil of ignorance concerning their own place in society would naturally choose certain principles for public policy. Smith (1776) is the classic reference on the benefits of private enterprise. Accessible accounts of the modern economist's interpretation of competition can be found in most microeconomic theory textbooks. The role of economic competition in maintaining political democracy is forcefully described in Friedman (1962). The normative approach to policy analysis is presented in the public finance textbooks listed at the end of Chapter 1. A valuable and up-to-date resource on cost-benefit analysis is Boardman et al. (1996).

Notes

1. David Roberts and Geoffrey York, "Judges urge separate native justice system," *The Globe and Mail,* August 30, 1991, p. A1.

2. The official dates of the Great Proletarian Cultural Revolution are 1966 to 1968. However, the economic and social policies associated with the Cultural Revolution dominated China until the death of Mao Tse Tung in 1976. The process of liberalization had begun before the death of Mao, but 1976 is probably the best year to take as the break point of Chinese economic policy.

On-line Sources

These are three of the highest profile policy institutes in Canada, and each offers perspectives on many of the issues discussed in this book. Ordered from left to right they are:

The Canadian Centre For Policy Alternatives, *http://www.policyalternatives.ca/*
The C.D. Howe Institute, *http://www.cdhowe.org/*
The Fraser Institute, *http://www.fraserinstitute.ca/*

4

Fairness and
Public Policy

4.1. What Is Fairness?

Perceptions of fairness dominate discussion of public policy. They also play an important role in our private lives. Most of us have a strong intuitive notion of what fairness consists of, and believe that our notions of fairness are based on important and clearly held values and ethical judgements. However, different people often hold sharply divergent ideas about fairness. It will be hard to implement public policy about fairness if we cannot agree on what fairness is. The first objective, therefore, is to see if we can establish some general principles of fairness.

Before proceeding, a brief comment about terminology is order. In philosophical discourse, and in ordinary language, the terms "fairness," "equity," "justice," "ethics," and "morality" are all used in slightly different ways, but with substantial overlap, so that distinctions among these terms are not very clear. For example, consider the following situation. You work for a successful small company. Your company is planning to hire some students as summer employees and asks you to interview four applicants and select one from the group for a summer job. It turns out that one of the applicants is the younger sister of your best friend from university. You know this younger sister slightly, and like her. Unfortunately, she is not the strongest candidate for the job. Nevertheless you want to hire her. We can ask whether such an act would be fair, equitable, just, ethical, and moral. It is not clear whether your answers to any of these questions could reasonably differ, although presumably they might.

Usually we think that morality and ethics are larger categories than fairness, in that morality and ethics deal with questions of what is good, which includes consideration of fairness, but is not restricted to such considerations. Thus, for example, some religious groups believe that it is immoral to drink alcohol or to gamble, but not because of anything to do with fairness. Similarly, we might conclude that lying is unethical, regardless of whether a given lie is actually unfair to anyone. It is harder to distinguish notions of equity and justice from fairness, since these terms are often used as synonyms. That is the practice adopted in this book. No distinction is made between fairness, equity, and justice, and fair acts are also presumed to be both moral and ethical.

4.1.1 An Example: The Case of Baby Jane Doe

The following case, eloquently described by Rachels (1993, pp.1-8), illustrates some possible principles of fairness. This case is not about business, but goes right to perhaps the most difficult area of debate: life and death. This case occurred in New York State and involved a child known as Baby Jane Doe. Baby Jane suffered from severe medical problems at birth, including spina bifida (an incomplete and protruding spine), hydrocephaly (fluid on the brain) and microcephaly (a small head, suggesting incomplete development of the brain). The question was whether an operation to partially correct spina bifida should be performed. This surgery would extend the child's expected life and, if she lived long enough, improve her ability to move, sit up, etc.

Opinions from two paediatric neurologists were obtained. Dr. A recommended against surgery, arguing that the child was unlikely to achieve any meaningful interaction with her environment, nor ever achieve any interpersonal relationships. Furthermore, he argued that the procedures and operations themselves would be painful and inflict needless suffering on the child, and, by extending her expected life span, would only extend the period of suffering that she and her parents would have to endure. Dr. B disagreed, arguing that there was a fundamental obligation to try to extend the life of the child, and that there was some chance, admittedly small, that the child could gain some positive experience from life.

The parents decided against surgery. There were, however, two legal challenges to this decision. First, lawyers representing a conservative right-to-life group petitioned the courts to order that surgery be performed, but this petition was denied. Second, the U.S. Department of Justice launched a suit on the basis that the child was a handicapped person who was being discriminated against on the basis of her handicap. This suit was also dismissed by the courts. The judge in the discrimination case found that the parents' decision "was a reasonable one based on due consideration of the options available and on a genuine concern for the best interests of the child" (Rachels, p.3).

This case caused substantial public debate arousing strong feelings on both sides. Strong feelings alone, however, do not help us very much. We want to know what was fair. Was it fair to deny the child surgery? In order to think carefully about fairness, we need to get beyond intuitive responses to the case and consider the underlying principles of fairness that might provide general guidance. In fact there are three central principles underlying the debate in the case:

1. the benefits principle,
2. the sanctity of life principle,
3. the freedom from discrimination principle.

4.1.2 The Benefits Principle

According to the benefits principle, the ultimate test of the fairness of a policy depends on the distribution of net benefits to the affected parties. Dr. A's recommendation against surgery was based on an assessment of the net benefits. He argued that both the parents and the child would be made worse off by the proposed surgery. The courts accepted the benefits argument. In making statements about the case, judges focused on whether the surgery would impose net benefits or net suffering on the child. In accepting the benefits principle, judges were accepting a principle that is widely held by philosophers and policy analysts. In this book we accept the benefits principle as a principle of fairness.

The conclusion that the benefits principle is an acceptable principle of fairness may strike the reader as so obvious as not to warrant much comment. What could assessments of fairness depend on except the benefits received or costs incurred by the affected parties? The answer has already been given. Both the sanctity of life principle and the discrimination principle are separate principles that may conflict with the benefits principle.

4.1.3 Sanctity of Life

The opposition mounted by the right-to-life group focused on the sanctity of (human) life principle. The essence of their argument went as follows: All human life is precious. Therefore, every individual is entitled to receive whatever treatment is necessary to preserve and extend that person's life. This implies that Baby Jane should receive surgery. Stripped to its essentials, under this principle, whether Baby Jane would suffer more (or less) as a result of surgery is not relevant. Surgery would almost certainly lengthen her life, and this implies that surgery should be undertaken. We all agree that human life is very valuable, and that major efforts to extend life will normally by justified. The question here, however, is whether the sanctity of life is an absolute principle, or whether other considerations are also relevant.

The courts rejected the idea that sanctity of life is an absolute principle, as do most analysts of public policy. The main reason for this rejection is that the sanctity of life argument leads to seemingly absurd implications. For example, it is well established that traffic fatalities can be reduced by reducing speed limits. If highway speeds were reduced from 100 km per hour to 20 km per hour, many lives would be saved. Thus, the sanctity of life principle would imply that highway speed limits should be reduced to 20 km per hour. However, virtually all drivers would oppose such low speed limits. As individuals, we are prepared to accept a slightly higher risk of death in return for being able to get from place to place quickly. We all take actions (like riding in cars or on bicycles) that increase the expected quality of our lives while reducing its expected duration. We all implicitly accept (through our own actions) that length of life is not the only thing that matters. Quality of life matters as well.

Even when dealing with a particular individual, most of us can think of situations where lengthening life does not seem right. The most obvious case is that of people who are terminally ill and in great pain. Most people who have seen a terminally ill person in great pain will favour administering pain-killing drugs, even if those drugs shorten expected life.

The point is that the sanctity of life principle does not hold up in all cases, and if it fails to hold up in some cases, then it is not really an absolute principle. It is not good enough to say that we should usually or sometimes seek to preserve human life at all costs, because we would then need some deeper principle (like the benefits principle) to tell us when sanctity of life applies. Thus, the deeper principle is the real principle, and focusing on sanctity of life as an absolute principle just introduces a layer of confusion into the analysis.

4.1.4 The Value of Life

Much policy analysis goes beyond the simple observation that sanctity of life is not absolute and actually seeks to place a monetary value on life. Life and death issues are very difficult for most of us to deal with. How often have we heard that some issue is "not just a matter of dollars and cents, but human lives are at stake." The implication seems to be that policies affecting human life transcend those that relate to mere business and economic issues.

For example, there is strong pressure from many quarters to raise the legal drinking age in various Canadian provinces, on the grounds that lives would be saved. It does in fact seem to be true that lives would be saved by raising the legal drinking age from 18 or 19 to 21. Even more lives would be saved by raising the drinking age to 25, or 30. Aside from all the problems associated with noncompliance and with substitution of other drugs for alcohol, the basic issue is that many young people get considerable pleasure from drinking. Somehow this pleasure must be compared with the associated loss of life.

The possibility of death is a risk that is influenced by individual decisions, and individuals deal with this risk in much the same way they deal with other business or consumer decisions. When a business executive chooses to drive through a snowstorm to attend an important meeting, he or she is implicitly trading off the value of attending the meeting against the increased risk of death or injury caused by driving in dangerous conditions.

Such reasoning also must enter public policy decisions. How much money is society prepared to devote to expensive life-saving equipment? Hospitals with fixed budgets confront that choice constantly, and are frequently in the position of having to deny life-saving treatments to some patients, because equipment is being used by other patients. At the public policy level, a decision to spend money on a subsidy to a Crown corporation is simultaneously a decision to allow some hospital patients to die sooner than they otherwise would if more life-saving equipment were available. The opportunity cost of every policy can be measured in lives lost. Choosing to spend some public money on highways rather than hospitals does reduce life expectancy for some people, or, put more crudely, it costs lives. It also raises the quality of life for many because it becomes possible for them to travel more easily.

Policy decisions implicitly place a value on human life. Most of us subscribe to the view that this value should be very high. One important distinction between modern Western society and other societies of the past and present is the high value placed on individual life. However, an appeal to suspend normal techniques of policy analysis in situations where human life is at stake does not make any sense, and is not really even possible. A very interesting attempt to determine a value of life for policy decisions in Canada is contained in Meng and Smith (1990), who obtain an estimate of $5.2 million as the policy value of saving a single life.

4.1.5 Nondiscrimination

The third principle advanced in the Baby Jane case was the nondiscrimination principle. The U.S. Department of Justice made the following argument:

> It is unfair (and illegal) to discriminate on the basis of disability. If Baby Jane had not been disabled, then she certainly would not be denied life-extending medical treatment. The failure to provide her with surgery would discriminate against her on the basis of her disability. Therefore, she should receive surgery.

The courts rejected this principle.

The basic conclusion reached by the courts is that discrimination is not necessarily unfair. In the Baby Jane case, the judge concluded that Baby Jane was indeed being denied surgery because of her disability, and this is discrimination. However, he also concluded that this discrimination was justified precisely because her disability made her unlikely to derive net benefits from the surgery.

A slightly different example will help make the point more obvious. Blindness is a major disability. We can readily agree that people should not be arbitrarily discriminated against simply because they are blind. It would seem unfair, for example, to deny university admission to someone simply because that person was blind. On the other hand, a blind person who applied for a job as an air traffic controller would be automatically rejected. In order to minimize the risk of air crashes, air traffic controllers require not just good vision, but very good spatial perception, along with other skills. Much of the selection for air traffic controllers consists of discriminating between people who have the required skills and those who do not. This obviously discriminates against blind people.

Thus, discrimination is not in itself a bad thing. Almost any reasonable selection process requires some sort of discrimination. For example, admission to the Faculty of Commerce at the University of British Columbia discriminates among students on the basis of grades received in previous courses. Nondiscrimination provisions in laws and policy statements have been interpreted by the courts as prohibiting unjustified or arbitrary discrimination, not all discrimination. But what makes a particular example of discrimination unjustified? Usually, the benefits principle is applied. Discriminating against blind people (or even against people with poor spatial perception) for the purposes of employment as air traffic controllers is fair and justified because the net benefits to affected parties are high. Discriminating against such people for admission to university would not provide any apparent net benefits and is therefore not justified.

4.1.6 Lessons To Be Learned from the Baby Jane Case

Our discussion of the Baby Jane case suggests that the benefits principle is valuable as a general principle of fairness. On the other hand, while the value of human life and concern about discrimination are certainly important to the case, the sanctity of life principle and the nondiscrimination principle are not admissible as general principles of fairness. They will often have considerable appeal, but careful consideration suggests that they are subsidiary to the benefits principle. More specifically, consideration of costs and benefits may sometimes lead to decisions that do not maximize expected life (as with high speed limits) and may discriminate (as with air traffic controllers). Not everyone would accept these arguments, but they are widely accepted and underlie the economic approach to policy analysis presented in this book.

What about Baby Jane herself? She did not have the surgery, but she surprised both Dr. A and Dr. B. Most infants with comparable disabilities die in the first year of life, but Baby Jane did not. In fact she made remarkable progress. By age 6 she was talking, attending a school for the disabled, and was able to get around in a wheelchair. She still suffered a significant degree of retardation and was profoundly disabled, but she could interact meaningfully with other people and was able get some enjoyment from life. She would have been even better off if she had received surgery to deal with spina bifida when she was an infant. Thus, the decision to deny surgery turned out to be unfortunate.

This makes another important point. The benefits principle used to decide against surgery was, according to the arguments presented here, the correct principle. However, even if we apply the appropriate principle, making the right decision requires, in addition, having correct facts about the case. Specifically, to apply the benefits principle, it is necessary to estimate the benefits, and this is difficult. In this case, Dr. A underestimated the benefits of surgery in the sense that he thought that Baby Jane's brain damage would prevent her from developing sufficiently to benefit from surgery. This turned out to be wrong.

It is, as already noted, sometimes difficult to get correct facts. If crucial facts depend on what will happen in the future, there is often unavoidable uncertainty. This uncertainty implies that good decisions do not always lead to good outcomes and, conversely, bad decisions do not necessarily lead to bad outcomes. If I decide to bet this week's grocery money on a horse race, that is almost certainly a bad decision, but if the horse happens to win, then I will have a good outcome. As for Baby Jane, it is difficult to know if the decision to deny surgery was a good one or a bad one, given only what was known at the time the decision was made. In general, it is important to realize that good decisions do not always lead to good outcomes, even if correct principles are being applied.

4.2 Moral Relativism and Conflicting Values

An important undercurrent of the Baby Jane case is that trying to determine what is fair depends heavily on underlying value judgements. Part of the disagreement in this case arises from different values with respect to human life and human suffering. People differ with respect to their strength of feeling about the value of extending life per se, as opposed to other considerations such as quality of life and possible suffering. Participants in the Baby Jane debate who placed a very high value on saving or extending human life favoured surgical intervention, whereas those who placed a very high value on preventing suffering may have opposed surgical intervention.

How are we to deal with competing value judgements? One response to this question is the doctrine of moral relativism. This doctrine holds that there is no way to determine that some values are superior to others. Thus, value systems may differ across cultures but none is better than any other. According to this view, asserting that one's own values are morally superior to other values is mere arrogance. The doctrine of moral relativism became particularly influential in the 1960s and 1970s and continues to have considerable impact. Moral relativism is an appealing counterpoint to apparent errors of the past. For example, various novels, movies, and anthropology textbooks have emphasized the excesses of the 19th-century Christian missionary movement in seeking to impose Christian beliefs and Victorian morality on various non-Western cultures. From the perspective of moral relativism, we might criticize such activities as unjustified interference.

Moral relativism seems particularly important in assessing individuals. William Shakespeare (1564-1616) is widely regarded as the most important English language dramatist, but he is not without critics. During the 19th century, Shakespeare was commonly criticized for being immoral because of the sexual content of his plays. One frequently criticized passage was a portion of Othello containing a brief description of a sexual act between Othello, who was black, and Desdemona, who was white. A leading editor and critic of the 19th century, Thomas Bowdler, undertook to edit Shakespeare's works so as to remove sexually offensive material. To us, Bowdler and others like him seem unreasonable. Shakespeare simply lived in a time and place (16th-century England) characterized by relatively liberal views about sex and sexuality, at least by comparison with the more restrictive standards of 19th-century England.

According to the standards of the late 20th century, Shakespeare's treatment of sex seems inoffensive, but he has been called anti-Semitic for his portrayal of the character Shylock in The Merchant of Venice.

Shylock, a Jew, has many characteristics that are taken as representing negative stereotypes of Jews. Should we judge Shakespeare to be a bigot or racist? By the standards of his time (or almost any other) Shakespeare was a person of remarkable tolerance and sensitivity. At a time when most literature in most countries was resolutely xenophobic (i.e., negative toward outsiders), Shakespeare treated individuals from a variety of ethnic backgrounds with sophistication and insight. His work contains sympathetic images of homosexuality, and some of his female characters would not be out of step with modern feminists. His work does not precisely match the political sensitivities of the present, but to view him as a bigot or racist seems to get the picture very wrong.

Other historical figures are open to more troubling criticism. What about George Washington and Thomas Jefferson (the first and third presidents of the United States)? Washington and Jefferson are regarded as the two most important contributors to the entrenchment of democratic principles in the American constitution and, by inference, are very important contributors to the development of democratic traditions around the world. Yet both were very substantial slave owners. By the standards of the late 18th-century United States, Washington and Jefferson were regarded as enlightened slave owners, who believed that slaves should be treated with dignity and protected by the rule of law. By modern standards, however, we would be hard pressed to imagine that anyone who tolerated the institution of slavery could be described as enlightened. How are we to judge Washington and Jefferson? The doctrine of cultural relativism helps us over this dilemma. We do not judge them relative to our standards, but relative to the standards of their own culture.

One may have misgivings, however, about the inherent acceptance of slavery implied by the application of moral relativism to Washington and Jefferson. This is a problem with moral relativism. It seems to prevent us from criticizing what appear to be obviously unacceptable practices. Quite a number of past cultures and some modern cultures regard slavery as perfectly acceptable. Cultures have been encountered in which infanticide (killing of unwanted infants) is common. As a less extreme example, the custom of purdah, although increasingly rare, still exists among some fundamentalist Muslims in India, Africa, and the Middle East. Under this custom, women are supposed to enter purdah (which means "behind the veil") after getting married. A woman in purdah is not allowed to be seen, except in extreme emergency, by any adult males except her husband and close family. Most modern Canadians would be hard pressed to accept that slavery, infanticide, or even purdah represent a set of values that can be viewed as just as good as ours.

A second problem of moral relativism is that it eliminates the concept of moral progress. Over the past century in Canada, there has been a dramatic change in women's rights and privileges. A century ago, women could not vote or hold public office and had very limited rights in a variety of areas relating to business and control of property. These restrictions on women have been eliminated and most Canadians would say that the current system is more fair, and superior from an ethical or moral point of view. If we accept moral relativism, however, such statements make no sense. Moral relativism tells us that we have no basis for judging values of 100 years ago to be inferior to our own. They are simply different, and that is all that can be said. Thus, the biggest problem with moral relativism is that it provides no basis for choosing between conflicting views, for it implies that all values are equally admissible.

One area where moral relativism has been applied is in evaluating bribery. During the 1960s and 1970s, several North American corporations that were expanding into international markets ran into trouble over bribery. For example, as described in Velasquesz (1992, pp.207-208), Lockheed Corporation (a U.S.-based aircraft producer) provided a Japanese lobbyist with the year 2000 equivalent of $40 million to pay bribes in Japan from 1972 to 1975. These bribes helped Lockheed obtain major contracts to supply aircraft in Japan. Lockheed Chief Executive Officer (CEO) Carl Kotchian subsequently stated: "I knew from the beginning that this money was going to the office of the Prime Minister [Kukeo Tanaka]." Kotchian also argued: "I should have declined such a request [for bribe money]. However, in that case I would most certainly have sacrificed commercial success." During an investigation by the U.S. Congress, Kotchian made the case that bribery on this scale was a common business practice in Japan, and that it is defensible for U.S. firms to adopt local ethical standards even when those standards differ from U.S. standards. Thus, he was arguing that ethical standards are relative. What is wrong in the United States might be right somewhere else.

In contrast, someone who took an absolutist (as opposed to relative) view of ethical standards would say that bribery and the associated dishonesty are universally unethical. Even if bribery is more common in Japan than in the United States, and even if it is easier for Japanese government officials to get away with taking bribes than it is for their American counterparts, it is still unethical to participate in such bribes. Thus, Kotchian's actions in bribing the Prime Minister of Japan are no different in principle than if he had sought to bribe the President of the United States.

Subsequent investigation showed that many other companies were also paying bribes to government officials in Japan (and in other countries). However, it turned out that Lockheed was paying larger bribes than most other companies and was reputedly viewed as an unusually easy source of bribes. Thus, Lockheed was escalating the alleged bribery custom, not just following it. Second, when the Lockheed scandal became known in Japan there was widespread public resentment and several Japanese government officials were arrested. Thus, bribery on this scale could be not be called accepted practice in Japan. Ultimately, U.S. authorities did not fully accept Kotchian's ethical relativism defence, but they did not take a fully absolutist position either. Mr. Kotchian escaped personal prosecution, but he was forced to resign and Lockheed was fined for fraud. Largely as a result of this case and the subsequent congressional investigation, the U.S. Congress passed a law in 1978 containing a universal prohibition on bribery.

Pragmatically, most policy analysts take an eclectic view of moral relativism in which some moral values are taken as relative and some are taken as absolute. Furthermore, even in cases where we think absolute standards apply, we recognize that individuals are influenced by their environment. Thus, for example, a young child who grows up in a criminal environment where stealing and fighting are common might be inclined to view stealing and violence as acceptable behaviours. We can understand this and make some allowance for it without accepting such a value system as morally equivalent to mainstream Canadian values.

4.3 Value Conflicts or Misunderstanding?

As just indicated, some disagreements over policies reflect differences in fundamental values. Debates over issues such as capital punishment and abortion clearly derive principally from basic value differences. However, conflicts over values, while fundamental, may be less significant sources of policy difficulties than is commonly recognized. Schelling (1981) tries to illustrate that what seem to be value conflicts are often misunderstandings. He writes that he frequently asks his students whether gasoline rationing is a good response to gasoline shortages, such as those that affected the United States in 1973-74. Schelling finds that his students generally approve of rationing. Each person gets ration coupons providing the right to a fair share of the available gasoline and no more. Schelling then says that he opposes gasoline rationing, and would prefer to let the market ration gasoline through higher prices.

At this point his students infer that his basic values differ from theirs; that he is less sensitive to the needs of the poor, more committed to the market system as a process, and less concerned about the consequences of unbridled capitalism than they are. Schelling then proceeds to argue that, if his students like rationing, they should agree that people should be allowed to sell their gasoline ration coupons. At first this proposal has little appeal, for it means "that the rich will be able to burn more than their share of gas, the poor being coerced by their very poverty into releasing coupons for the money they so desperately need" (p.40).

Eventually, however, the point is recognized that the poor would like to be able to turn gasoline ration coupons into money. Whereas gas coupons can be used only to buy gas, money for which they might be sold can be used to buy milk or groceries. At worst, the coupons can still be used by a poor person to buy gas. In addition, more attractive possibilities also become available. Someone with the interests of the poor at heart can hardly oppose this proposal, which certainly makes the poor better off.

The next point is that, with a market for ration coupons operating, the coupons are really just like cash. If gas costs 70 cents per litre, and ration coupons sell for 30 cents per litre, then the net price of gas is $1 per litre, which is precisely the price that would clear the market in the absence of rationing. A gas station that sells 10 litres takes in $7 in cash and $3 worth of ration coupons that could have been sold for cash. When a poor person (or anyone else) receives ration coupons for 100 litres from the government, he or she is receiving the clumsy equivalent of $30 dollars.

But then why not pay $30 to the poor directly? One could avoid all the red tape and processing costs of the ration system, greatly reducing the cost of the program, and the government would not have to give this special ration coupon money to everyone, but could target it to the poor. The direct costs could even be recovered by a tax on gasoline. This would be better for the poor, the nonpoor, the gas stations, and the economy as a whole.

Schelling is usually able to persuade his students that their concern about gasoline fairness is misplaced. Their fundamental concern is about the fact that the poor are poor, not that they may consume less gasoline than the wealthy. The efficient response, if that is the problem, is to give the poor more money and to allow the market to do its job of allocating resources efficiently.

Schelling, a professor at Harvard, is, if anything, probably more sympathetic to the plight of the poor than most of his students. Certainly his disagreement with them over the value of rationing did not really arise from major differences in basic values. His disagreement simply illustrated the point that popular perceptions of fairness are biased toward favouring interference in specific markets, even when the underlying problem could be much more effectively addressed in some other way.

4.4. Major Philosophical Approaches to Fairness

The time has come for an important admission. Philosophers, theologians, and many other people have been thinking about principles of fairness for a very long time, but no consensus has been reached on an appropriate set of rules for fairness. While many principles of, and approaches to, fairness have been proposed, all have flaws. Most influential views of fairness incorporate some version of the benefits principle, but even this principle is not immune to all criticism. This section reviews some of the major systematic approaches to fairness. The approaches considered here are the utilitarian approach, the social contract approach, and what may be referred to as procedural fairness (sometimes called the rights approach). Note that each of these approaches implies a rejection of cultural relativism in that each suggests a set of absolute standards or criteria by which we may judge fairness.

4.4.1 Utilitarianism

Utilitarianism can be thought of as an example or refinement of the benefits principle. In our discussion of the Baby Jane case we noted that the benefits approach focuses on the benefits and costs (which are simply negative benefits) of surgery to the affected parties. We were, however, not very specific about exactly whose benefits count and about what weight or importance should be applied to each person's benefits.

It seems clear that the benefits or costs of surgery to Baby Jane are important and should be given high weight. But what about the parents? One of the concerns expressed by Dr. A was the idea that the parents might suffer as a result of surgery. He had in mind a situation in which surgery would be performed and the life of the infant would be extended, requiring great financial and personal sacrifice from the parents, who would be required to care for a hopelessly disabled child, possibly for the rest of their lives. He also thought that surgery would be damaging to the child's best interests, but concern for the parents strengthened, in his mind, the case against surgery.

Now let us consider a similar but slightly altered hypothetical situation. Suppose that the surgery would provide a small chance of improvement for the child, but would probably have no effect. However, suppose further that the surgery is very expensive to the parents and, over and above these costs, will require a very large subsidy from the health-care system, leading to fewer medical resources being available for other sick children.

What is fair in this case? In essence, this is a situation where benefits to the child must be weighed against costs to the parents and costs to other parties. Some people would argue that the case should be decided purely with reference to the child's benefits, implying that surgery should be undertaken, but this position is hard to maintain. As we imagine increasingly large costs to the parents and to the rest of society, and increasingly small benefits to the child, at some point this claim becomes ridiculous. Would we, for example, require the parents to reduce themselves to abject poverty to obtain one more day of life for the infant? (Or one more hour? or one more minute?) The conclusion is that the costs and benefits incurred by the parents, and by others, do matter. But how much? Are benefits to all parties to be evaluated equally, or do benefits to some people matter more than to others?

Utilitarianism gives a clear answer to these questions. The basic utilitarian position was developed by David Hume, Jeremy Bentham, and John Stuart Mill in the late 18th and early 19th centuries. The utilitarian position is that an action is good if it increases total utility or happiness. Put slightly differently, utilitarianism is based on the axiom that moral and fair decisions are those that maximize total utility. A common, although somewhat vague, statement of utilitarianism is that we should seek the greatest good for the greatest number.

The utilitarian position tells us that in deciding whether to perform surgery on Baby Jane, we must add up the expected effects on her utility (or happiness), on that of her parents, on that of other potential users of the resources consumed by her surgery, etc. When we add these things up, if the sum is positive, then surgery is the fair and moral thing to do. If not, then surgery is not appropriate. Note that even if surgery would be of substantial expected benefit to Baby Jane, but imposed costs on others that were judged to exceed Baby Jane's benefit, then utilitarianism would say that surgery should not be done.

John Stuart Mill, the most influential exponent of utilitarianism, saw it as supporting a very liberal social position. For example, note that utilitarianism does not distinguish between the utility of a king as opposed to a poor person. Mill regarded it as very unfair that thousands of ordinary young men would be drafted into an army and sent off to fight and die in wars whose principle objective was to secure greater glory for a king. Utilitarianism would of course rule out such activities. By treating everyone equally, utilitarianism is a very democratic principle. Second, utilitarianism underlies the modern liberal position that if an act increases the utility of the person performing the act and harms no one else, then the act is justified. Mill saw utilitarianism as an essentially kind doctrine that saw good in the things that gave people happiness, rather than focusing on religious and other moral codes that emphasized personal sacrifice as the source of virtue.

Mill and other utilitarians also felt that utilitarianism provided a strong rationale for redistributing income from rich to poor. The basic argument is that, in general, an extra dollar of income is more valuable to a poor person than to a rich one. More concretely, a morsel of food provides more extra utility for a hungry person than for someone with more than enough to eat. Thus, taking a dollar (or a morsel of food) from a wealthy person and giving it to a poor person would tend to raise total utility because the poor person's perceived increase in utility would exceed the wealthy person's perceived loss. Such redistribution is therefore justified on utilitarian grounds.

More broadly, proponents of utilitarianism feel that all reasonable moral positions eventually boil down to adding up the benefits and costs of actions. When we try to defend other principles, such as the sanctity of life, or nondiscrimination, or a particular set of religious rules, we usually end up arguing that these things are good because they increase total benefits. In doing this we tacitly accept the utilitarian position.

Despite the appeal of utilitarianism, however, it has some serious flaws. The first one is that it assumes that utility or happiness is comparable across individuals. Some critics assert that comparison of happiness across individuals is simply impossible. Does it seem possible to assert, for example, that one person will get 50 units of utility from a new car whereas someone else would get only 40? If such comparisons cannot be made, then utilitarianism cannot be applied.

Other critics assert that even if interpersonal comparisons of utility can be made, it is wrong to do so. In particular, utilitarianism would seem to unfairly favour people who have greater capacity for happiness or, more crudely, those who are the most efficient "pleasure machines." We all know people who seem very happy and seem to derive great enjoyment from life. We also know people who are often depressed and may take little pleasure in things that most of us would enjoy. Should we compound this existing asymmetry by giving even more to the happier people because they are more able to take more pleasure in things?

Another flaw in utilitarianism is that it seems to offer very weak protection for individual rights. Suppose that by sacrificing one person, everyone else benefits substantially. Is it fair to sacrifice that one person? This dilemma is a very common theme in legend and literature, and comes up often enough in practice. Consider the following situation. Two ethnic groups, the blues and the greens, live in a town. A young green girl is brutally murdered and an unidentified blue male is seen leaving the scene. The green people are very upset and relations between the blues and greens, already tense, are now about to explode into violence. The two police investigators working on the case have no leads on tracking down the murderer, and are getting desperate as tensions in the town mount. Before the murder, they had been planning to arrest a blue "career criminal," released from prison about a year ago, who is known to be responsible for a string of recent robberies and assaults. Instead of arresting him for these robberies and assaults, however, they charge him with the murder of the green girl and, by fabricating some evidence, are able to obtain a conviction in the murder case. Tensions in the town die down and further violence is avoided.

A utilitarian analysis suggests that the police may be justified in their actions. If the arrest and conviction of the blue career criminal prevented violence that would have caused, let us say, the deaths of several innocent people, then the police action appears to have generated net benefits, since the only person really harmed by these events was the blue criminal. Furthermore, although he was not guilty of murder, he was guilty of other crimes that would have been sufficient to put him in jail.

Despite this analysis, most readers of this book will conclude that it was unfair to arrest and convict the blue criminal for a murder he did not commit. We feel that the blue's basic rights were violated, that due process was not followed. One suspects that even the police themselves, while arguing that what they did was justified in some aggregate sense, would still agree that it was unfair to the blue criminal. In fact, several cases of this type have come to light in recent years, and while there is some understanding of the police position, there is little overall doubt that such actions are unfair. Thus, utilitarian analysis seems to point us in the wrong direction. The problem is that there is little room in utilitarianism for any concern about rights or due process.

We can construct more extreme examples that demonstrate the same point. Suppose that some people (and there are such people) derive great pleasure from inflicting pain on others. Suppose that a large group of such people "beat up" or assault an innocent victim. Since there is only one victim but many "assailants", it is possible that if we add up the utility gains of the latter, these gains could exceed the utility cost to the victim. Thus, utilitarianism could favour this action. But even thinking this way seems ridiculous. Of course, we say to ourselves, assaulting an innocent person is completely unfair no matter how much pleasure some (sadistic) people might get from it. We regard the pleasures obtained by sadists from harming others as not a legitimate type of utility, and we believe that the victim has a right to freedom from arbitrary assault.

These examples suggest that simple utilitarianism is not acceptable as a general principle of morality or fairness. People have offered more sophisticated versions of utilitarianism that seek to address these and other concerns, including the possibility of excluding certain types of utility as not legitimate. It is still an open question as to whether it is possible to construct a reasonable theory of fairness based on utilitarian ideas. However, there is no simple utilitarian principle that seems to capture certain important intuitions about fairness.

4.4.2. Social Covenants and Contracts

Another conception of fairness and ethics is based on the social covenant or social contract approach. The basic idea here is that a fair system is one that we would all voluntarily agree to join. Thus, the system is viewed as a social contract that we have all agreed to accept. The social contract approach was first developed by Locke, Rousseau, and Kant, but the most influential modern proponent is Rawls (1971). It is the Rawlsian version that will be discussed here.

Rawls envisions what he calls an original position. All relevant individuals are present in the original position. However, no person knows who he or she is. Some social structure will emerge following the initial position, and each of us will assume our identities at that time. Initially, however, we do not know anything about our identities. In the initial position an individual does not know what sex he or she will be, and does not know whether he or she will be intelligent or unintelligent, rich or poor, tall or short, beautiful or ugly, or whatever. Thus, in the original position people are behind a veil of ignorance.

Rawls makes two central claims about the veil of ignorance. First, he argues that agreements reached from behind the veil of ignorance should be taken as fair. In other words, he proposes that rational discussion in the original position is a fundamentally fair process. Second, Rawls also argues that rational people in the original position would adopt a "maxi-min" principle. Specifically, society should be ordered so as to maximize the well-being of the worst-off person.

Many critics, especially economists, do not find Rawls' claim that the maxi-min principle would arise from the social contract to be convincing. Suppose, for simplicity, there are 1,000 individuals, all behind a veil of ignorance. Suppose they are choosing between the following situations. In Situation 1, each person will get 50, which we take to be a short and hard life. In Situation 2, 999 people will get 100, which corresponds to a long and pleasant life, and 1 will get only 49, which, of course, is just slightly worse than 50. You do not know which of these 1,000 people you will be. Would you prefer Situation 1 or Situation 2? If the maxi-min principle is correct, you should choose Situation 1. Most people, however, prefer Situation 2. They are willing to take some small risk of being marginally worse off to obtain the very likely prospect of being much better off than in Situation 1. You would have to be extremely risk averse to prefer Situation 1.

Even if the maxi-min principle does not necessarily derive from a social contract, it might be taken as fundamental in itself. Rawls points out that the maxi-min principle does not imply the equal division of well-being (or of income). Suppose we agreed that there was no reason in principle why one person should receive more than another, and accordingly agreed that everyone should receive the same income, irrespective of what he or she did. Total income would simply be shared among the all individuals equally. The obvious problem is that few people would work very hard under such a system. In a large population, an individual's income would be almost totally unaffected by his or her own work effort, and the resulting incentive to work would be weak. Work effort would not drop to zero, but it would be diverted into personally enjoyable rather than economically productive activities. Total output might well drop to something approaching zero. Certainly, average income and welfare would drop precipitously. In short, the efficiency costs of the equal sharing principle would be enormous. Everyone, including the worst off person, would be made worse off under such a system. In order to provide incentive effects that make everyone better off, some degree of inequality may be necessary.

The maxi-min principle is, like utilitarianism, another example of the benefits principle. It is, however, quite a different example. Utilitarianism sought to maximize the sum of benefits to all individuals. The maxi-min principle seeks to maximize only the benefits of the worst-off person. Thus, both utilitarianism and Rawlsian maxi-min focus on the distribution of benefits, but they propose different weights on different individuals.

The maxi-min principle seems to put excessive weight on the very worst-off person, while ignoring everyone else. If we think about the real world, the situation of the worst-off person is hard to define. Would the worst-off person be an infant who has a very difficult and painful delivery and then quickly dies? If so, then we should devote all efforts to preventing infant mortality. No pleasures would be allowed: no food beyond the minimum necessary for efficient work effort, no nice clothes, no pleasures of any sort so long one child died in delivery. But even this effort would probably not be enough to prevent all infant mortality. Enormous sacrifices could be required for relatively little benefit.

Alternatively, if all potential people participate in the original position, then perhaps the worst-off (potential) people are those who never are born. Presumably, there will always be more potential people than can be accommodated, so the worst-off person gets nothing no matter what we do. In this case the maxi-min principle provides no guidance whatsoever. Thus, the maxi-min principle seems hard to operationalize, and it seems to point us in questionable directions even if it is operationalized.

Even if we reject the maxi-min principle, the social covenant idea is still very interesting. The appeal of the social contract seems to be that if a group of people, with all their special interests stripped away, could voluntarily agree on social rules, then those rules would necessarily be fair. Thus, the social contract is based on the idea that fairness derives from a particular procedure that is viewed as fair. The feature of this procedure that seems to make it fair is that people must voluntarily agree. In effect, each person has the right to opt out and cannot be forced to participate. Unfortunately, while the social contract idea has appeal, it is not at all clear what a group of disembodied souls operating behind a veil of ignorance really would agree to. Thus, it too is very hard to operationalize.

4.4.3 Procedural Fairness or Rights?

The appeal of the social contract approach is not based on an evaluation of benefits, but on the idea that fairness is whatever derives from fair procedures. It therefore focuses on procedural fairness. This should be distinguished from distributive fairness, which focuses on the ends or results of some process. Basic utilitarianism is therefore a matter of distributive fairness. Rawls' maxi-min principle is also a statement about distributive fairness.

There is a conflict among philosophers over whether procedural fairness or distributive fairness is more fundamental. We have seen that Rawls tried to finesse this conflict by using a notion of procedural fairness (the social contract) to derive a fundamental principle of distributive fairness, but this attempt is not very persuasive. We have also seen that many of the strongest objections to utilitarianism are based on the concern that it ignores basic rights. Since rights are simply a commitment to particular procedures, this critique of utilitarianism amounts to the idea that it is more important to focus on procedures than on outcomes. One more example might clarify the point. Consider how we would feel if a large and healthy but poor young man snatched the purse of a frail but well-off elderly woman. There might be some differences of opinion over this transfer of wealth, but most of us would regard it as unfair on procedural grounds, despite its progressive redistributive effect. Even if the poor young man would benefit more than the elderly woman from the money (implying that the theft would raise total utility), it seems to most of us that theft, especially when carried out under the threat of violence, is usually an unfair procedure and violates important basic rights of the elderly woman. Put simply, the primacy of procedural fairness is captured in the aphorism "the ends do not justify the means," while the primacy of distributive fairness is reflected in the response that "if the ends don't justify the means, what does?"

Nozick (1974) and Hayek (1960) are strong proponents of the primacy of procedural fairness or rights. They both argue that society's obligation is to provide fair procedures, and focus on the idea that procedures should be noncoercive: that society's institutions should allow voluntary choices and should avoid paternalism and coercion. Note, however, that procedural fairness described in this way does not guarantee egalitarian outcomes. Procedures that require equality of opportunity will allow some people to do better than others because of differences in fundamental (and inalienable) abilities, because of differences in luck, and possibly for other reasons as well.

The biggest problem with the rights approach is that it is difficult to agree on what basic rights and procedures should be adopted. As indicated, perhaps the most widely accepted candidate for being a fundamental right is the right of noncoercion. Defining noncoercion precisely is not easy, but it is taken to mean than no individual can be forced to take positive action that he or she does not want to take. Thus, for example, if my neighbour's house burns down, I have no obligation to provide my neighbour with a bed for the night. As long as I do not actively harm my neighbour, what I do is my own business. I might choose to help my neighbour, and almost certainly would, but that is up to me. It cannot fairly be forced on me by the government.

Note that this principle might be viewed as drastically cutting down on the scope of acceptable redistributive activity carried out by governments. A wealthy person could not be forced to pay taxes that were simply redistributed to the poor. A wealthy person might voluntarily choose to pay taxes in return for government-provided goods and services, such as roads, police protection, etc., but might not choose to support welfare, unemployment insurance, and other redistributive programs. In fact, Nozick's statement of the rights approach is regarded as the intellectual foundation of the libertarian position, which argues for minimal government.

One could of course propose other rights (or procedures) that implied highly redistributive and interventionist government programs. There have, for example, been proposals in both Canada and the United States for constitutionally guaranteed rights for a certain level of medical care or for guaranteed employment. Rights of this type would create claims on other people and would therefore conflict with rights of noncoercion.

For almost any set of rights that is proposed, it is possible to think of examples that make those rights seem less than absolute. One of the most cherished (and hard-won) rights in modern democratic societies is the right of free speech. But even this right should not be absolute. As has been frequently observed, it should not, for example, provide a right to yell "Fire!" in a crowded theatre.

One important widely accepted right is the right to the control and integrity of one's person (i.e., one's own body). Thus, for example, kidnappers do not have the right to kidnap and assault an innocent victim. We feel that the victim has the right of control over his or her body. Similarly, police do not have the right to torture accomplices to a crime, even if those accomplices are withholding important information. So far, so good.

But what about the following hypothetical example. Suppose that a woman, call her Anne, has a unique factor in her blood that can attack and destroy HIV, the virus that causes AIDS. A serum based on her blood can cure people with HIV infection. Unfortunately, while this factor can be artificially augmented, fresh donations of blood from

Anne are required to produce serum. Scientists are hopeful of producing a purely artificial version of the serum but have not yet succeeded.

Doctors have told Anne about the situation and have asked her for regular blood donations. Anne does not like giving blood and has a very negative view of the behaviours associated with transmission of HIV. She therefore refuses, even though a single blood donation would save many lives. Would the government have the right to force her to give blood? Would Anne be justified in holding out for high payment for her blood? The answers to these questions are not obvious. Under current Canadian law Anne could not be forced to give blood and could not demand payment for it.

Now suppose further that Anne goes into the hospital for some routine minor surgery. Doctors seize the opportunity to take enough of her blood to provide the basis for research focused on artificially reproducing the unique factor that kills HIV. Are doctors justified in doing this? They have certainly violated her right to control over her own body. Readers may be uncertain of what is appropriate in this case (which is loosely based on a real example, although not involving HIV). By changing the example slightly, however, we can make a much stronger case for breaching Anne's right to control of her own body. Suppose the disease is not HIV infection, but a new highly lethal airborne virus that threatens to kill half the population. Suppose further that only a small amount of blood is required, causing little inconvenience to Anne. We could construct an example in which it would seem fair to violate Anne's right on essentially utilitarian grounds.

Thus, the rights approach also has flaws. First, it is far from obvious exactly what fundamental rights of fairness are appropriate. Second, it is hard to think of any rights that stand up as absolute principles in the face of careful scrutiny. As a practical matter, most democratic constitutions use some mixture of rights-based and benefit-based approaches. Thus, for example, the Canadian constitution incorporates a series of individual rights but allows them to be overridden in cases of overwhelming public interest.

For our purposes, we recognize that there is no simple approach to fairness that will serve as a foundation for analyzing public policy. However, it is helpful to be aware of major philosophical approaches to fairness when thinking through particular issues and examples. Thus, confronted with a particular problem, we can ask ourselves whether a proposed course of action would satisfy utilitarian requirements, whether it is something that would emerge in a social contract setting, and whether it is consistent with certain basic rights. All of these perspectives are helpful and relevant.

In most circumstances, whether in designing a constitution, formulating a corporate ethics policy, or determining a set of standards for student conduct at a university, we can readily agree on some basic rights and ethical standards. However, implementing these rights can be difficult and typically depends on the leadership of a few individuals. Consider the student conduct example. In many courses students are given assignments worth some fraction of the course mark. Sometimes the professor may allow or even encourage joint work by students, but often the assignments are to be done on a purely individual basis. If the assignments are to be done individually, we can all readily agree that each student would have a right to be free from demands to share answers with other students. Furthermore, we can also agree that sharing answers is not fair or ethical, since it harms those students who do abide by the rules. Nevertheless, coercion to share answers in such a setting commonly arises. In such situations, the leadership role of one or two students can make a large difference. If an influential student makes a clear statement that sharing answers is not appropriate, then often the entire group of students will settle into a noncheating or ethical equilibrium, whereas otherwise a cheating or unethical equilibrium might prevail.

4.5 Individual and Group–Based Fairness

So far we have focused on the individual as the unit of analysis, asking what things are fair from an individual point of view. It is, however, important to be aware that there is a distinction to be drawn between individually based concepts of fairness and what might be referred to as group fairness. Human beings seem to have a natural tendency to identify strongly with group membership and to define themselves in part by group identity: as members of one sex, of a particular racial or ethnic group, of a religious group, of a social class, of a union or management, on the basis of physical disabilities, etc. It then seems natural to examine both procedures and outcomes on a group basis. In recent decades, notions of group fairness seem to have gained importance relative to notions of individual fairness. Thus, there has been, for example, increasing emphasis on whether various racial or ethnic groups are appropriately represented in universities and in certain occupational categories.

The problem is that group fairness can readily conflict with individual equality of opportunity. For example, as described in D'Souza (1991, p.3), during the 1980s the University of California at Berkeley instituted race-based quotas for admission. The basic policy statement from the university administration was that the student body should "reflect the population of the state of California." Students were classified by race as Asian, black, Hispanic, native, or white, and different admission standards were applied so as to achieve the appropriate mix of students. The net effect was that individual members of groups with high admission scores were rejected in favour of individuals with lower admission scores from other groups. This conflicts with individually based notions of equality of opportunity. Well-meaning people have argued forcefully both for and against the policy. Partly as a response to the Berkeley case, there has been a strong backlash against policies of preferential discrimination in California, and legislation making preferential discrimination on the basis of race or sex illegal in many situations has been enacted. The point, in any case, is that group fairness and individual fairness are difficult to reconcile.

Aside from race, the other major group distinction of current political concern is between men and women. There has been a strong attempt to increase female participation in traditionally male occupations such as policing and firefighting. In a recent case, a Kitchener man, Jake, and his wife, Kim, made a formal complaint to the Ontario Human Rights Commission.[1] The man took 18 months away from his job as a carpenter to take courses so as to meet basic academic requirements for a firefighter's position. He then took the Kitchener Fire Department's aptitude test, on which he scored 83%. As a result, his application was rejected because the cutoff for white males was 85%. However, the cutoff for women was 70%, well below the score Jake received. Jake argued that this policy constituted discrimination based purely on his sex and race. In an interesting twist, his wife Kim also argued that not only did this discrimination adversely affect Jake, but it also adversely affected her and their two children.

Until recently, women were not considered for jobs as firefighters. It seems relatively uncontroversial that this discrimination against women was unfair. Given this history, fire departments have a higher portion of men than they would have had under a fairer system. Is fairness served by trying to get an appropriate proportion of women by discriminating against men and in favour of women at entry level? As Jake pointed out, he was in no way responsible for past discrimination in fire department hiring. Furthermore, he had not benefited from discrimination in fire department hiring. In fact, men who had previously discriminated against women in hiring and who had presumably benefited from this discrimination were now senior fire department officials who were discriminating against him. This does seem to violate norms of fairness based on individual rights, but arguments can be constructed to justify it on utilitarian grounds, or on group fairness grounds.

Managers in both private and public sector settings are increasingly forced to confront group fairness issues. For example, Dauphinee and Ramkhalawansingh (1991, p.52) describe the Toronto City Council policy on equal opportunity as seeking "to eliminate discrimination on the basis of race, creed, colour, national origin, political or religious affiliation, sex, sexual orientation, age, marital status, family relationship and disability."

In order to obtain a contract from the City of Toronto, or do other business with the City, a firm must satisfy the City Council that it has a commitment to equal opportunity as just defined. Agencies that work for the city must also "report on representation and salaries of different groups" and "are required to develop an action plan to identify and remedy employment practices that inhibit the full participation of designated group members in the workplace."

The requirement to keep records of representation of different groups can be quite difficult. Looking at the list of characteristics described by the City, this would seem to mean keeping track of the number of employees in at least three racial categories (visible minority, native, and other), several creeds and colours, many national origins, several religious affiliations, two sexes, at least three sexual orientations, several age groups, etc. In practice, such programs usually just require information on three categories: race, sex, and disability, but employers must be prepared to respond to any allegations of bias on the basis of other categories. At a minimum, this is costly. It would also seem to conflict with basic notions of privacy. Suppose, for example, that someone does not wish to be categorized by his or her race.

A more significant problem with such policies is a likely contradiction between nondiscrimination or equal opportunity and full participation of members of designated groups. It not entirely clear exactly what full participation of members of designated groups means, but it is closely related to the objective of equal group outcomes or proportional representation. The underlying assumption of policies such as that adopted by the Toronto City Council seems to be that nondiscriminatory practices will lead to proportional representation in various employment categories.

Many people involved in group fairness debates simply assert as a matter of ideology that group differences in choices or performance must be due to discrimination in some form or other.[2] It is certainly true that overt race-based and sex-based discrimination has played an important role in relative occupational success in the past. For example, until the late 1960s, most medical schools in Canada, as a matter of policy, admitted very few women.[3] This existence of past discrimination does not imply, however, that nondiscrimination necessarily leads to equal performance or proportional representation of various groups. For example, it seems unlikely, based on what we know about occupational preferences and the distribution of physical strength across males and females, that a neutral system would give rise to equal numbers of male and female firefighters.

D'Souza (1991, p.224) has argued forcefully that group fairness policies can be very divisive, especially if they are aggressively pursued. He reports the feelings of several American students of various backgrounds who attend universities with vigorous affirmative action programs, including categorization by race. Students report that "Ethnic separatism [is] a constant theme." D'Souza argues that whether students start out with a sense of alienation from the mainstream or not, by the time they finish with such programs, feelings of alienation and fragmentation have usually developed or worsened.

Issues related to group fairness are difficult and confusing. Most of us have a hard time grappling with the basic principles involved. For example, most of us want to accept some fundamental notion of individual equality before the law, but are sympathetic when confronted by, for example, native demands for different treatment before the law. This fundamental contradiction is addressed in the Charter of Rights and Freedoms, where a series of equality before the law provisions are described, followed by the statement that none of these provisions are to undermine the special treatment of natives.

Most people have strong emotional reactions to particular group fairness issues, such as the native issue, but are unable to articulate consistent conceptual positions to support their emotional response. Many of us assume that we want to help people and that people with opposing views must have bad intentions. People who disagree with us on matters relating to group fairness issues can then be labelled as racists (or sexists, or whatever). It is, for example, easy to call someone a racist for arguing that natives should be treated as different from other citizens in some fundamental way, but equally easy to call someone a racist for arguing that they should not.

Race and sex are not the only categories over which group fairness is considered. In Canada, freedom of association, intended as an individual right, has been viewed by the courts as providing fundamental protection for labour unions, including the rights of labour unions to exclude from certain jobs those workers who do not wish to belong to the union. This would seem to conflict with basic individual freedoms concerning freedom of choice, and seems to stretch the notion of freedom of association, but this was part of a political battle over union-based group rights. In Canada there also has been a high degree of attention paid to regional groups and considerable discussion of regional fairness. This concept has been used to justify taxing the population at large so as to provide income support for regions with below average incomes. Unfortunately, the poor in well-off regions pay their share for such policies, and the greatest beneficiaries are often people who are already well off but who happen to live in poor regions. Regional redistribution is a very crude and inefficient way of trying to achieve distributive fairness.

Politicians and special interest groups can be very imaginative in thinking of ideas of fairness that can be used to justify their own objectives, and we find that the word "fairness" enters almost every policy debate. Notions of group fairness seem to be particularly susceptible to political use. Somewhat surprisingly, economists place relatively little emphasis on fairness in analyzing particular policy areas. This follows from a general presumption among economists that fairness objectives are best pursued at the broadest possible level, which is the national system of taxes and transfers (such as welfare, unemployment insurance, and old age pensions). More specific policy areas should, according to this view, focus on economic efficiency.

4.6 Tradeoffs Between Efficiency and Fairness

The first point that economists usually make about public policies toward fairness is that there is a tradeoff between fairness and efficiency, principally because of incentive effects. One of the basic conclusions of most influential views of fairness, such as utilitarianism or the Rawlsian maxi-min principle, is that we would like to redistribute from the relatively well-off so as to help the relatively disadvantaged. In countries like Canada, we do this through a progressive tax and transfer system. Low-income people receive income from the government in various ways, including welfare, and from subsidized or free services such as medical care. Tax rates are modest at moderate income levels and rise to high levels as income rises. Maximum tax rates in 1999 (inclusive of federal and provincial income tax) were in excess of 50% in some provinces.

But why stop at 50% or 55%? Why not have tax rates of 70% or 80% on high income earners? Surely that would be even fairer. The problem is that if tax rates at high levels of income are very high, the incentive for high-income people to work will be low. Socialist governments in Britain in the 1970s raised marginal tax rates on high-income earners to levels above 80%. Strangely, these high taxes collected very little revenue. Highly productive people either reduced their work effort and income and/or increased the time and effort devoted to tax avoidance activities. High-income people were obviously made worse off by this policy of confiscatory taxation, but so were low-income people, because there was less money to redistribute to the poor and highly valued services were withdrawn from the economy. This policy was inefficient in the Pareto sense: it made all parties worse off.

To give an example of tax avoidance, consider the following anecdote. A lawyer recently defended (unsuccessfully) a person, whom we shall call Mr. X, accused of commercial fraud. Mr. X set up a firm to sell franchises that would in turn sell tax advice to the public. A franchisee would pay $5,000 up front, and give an I.O.U. to Mr. X for $15,000, in return for a franchise to sell this particular tax advice. Mr. X would provide a receipt for $20,000 to the franchisee.

The franchisee would never sell any tax advice, nor would he or she ever pay the $15,000. There would, however, be a claim for a $20,000 loss on his or her taxes, thereby reducing them by about $10,000 (assuming a marginal tax rate of 50%), and saving $5,000 net of the $5,000 fee paid to Mr. X. Mr. X would pocket the $5,000. Over the course of a few years, Mr. X took in $5 million. He ran into trouble when Revenue Canada started disallowing the $20,000 deductions claimed by franchisees, who then started complaining.

The striking point about this case is not that Mr. X dreamed up a fraudulent scheme and ended up in jail. Rather, it is that he was able to attract hundreds of clients, consisting largely of doctors, lawyers, accountants, and business people, whose clear intent was to defraud the tax system. None of them went to jail, or were even assigned penalties by Revenue Canada. This particular scheme went undetected for the first year, and is only slightly different from many tax avoidance schemes that are legal. Indeed, if Mr. X had produced any tangible output, such as brochures that franchisees were to sell, he probably would have avoided prosecution. Tax avoidance costs are an inefficiency cost of high income tax rates.

Many policies intended to promote fairness have efficiency costs. Free medicare is an example. If medical attention is free, trips to the doctor will be made more frequently than necessary, and will sometimes be used by people who are simply lonely as a way of getting some attention. In general, there will be no incentives for efficiency.

Another anecdote will illustrate this point. When I returned to British Columbia after several years in Ontario, I was, for a period of three months, not covered by the B.C. medical plan. (Medical bills were to be sent to Ontario to be reimbursed.) I was taking monthly allergy shots at the time, and shortly after arriving I was due for a shot. I did the easiest thing: I went to the emergency ward of a hospital. My bill (in 1999 dollars) was about $83, and I could see why. I had been processed by three people: a receptionist, a nurse, and a doctor. I had filled in forms that would have to be processed by others, and I had sat in an impressive hospital waiting room with all kinds of expensive equipment standing by.

If anything, $83 was less than the cost of my visit. It was, however, more than I was willing to pay, so I investigated alternatives before getting my next shot. I found a small clinic. Two mornings a week, a nurse gave allergy shots to all people who showed up. I came in, got my shot, waited a few minutes, paid my bill, and left. This time my bill (in 1999 dollars) was $8.33, in accordance with the resources consumed.

The clinic was far more efficient than the hospital, but incentives to use clinics are generally very weak. If I had not been in the unusual situation of having to process my own medical costs, I never would have discovered the difference in costs. Because most people face no incentives that would bring resource costs to bear on individual behaviour, the medicare system is more expensive than it needs to be. It might, of course, still be important to have free medicare. We might decide that the fairness objectives of universal free medical care are so significant that we are willing to pay high resource costs.

Rent controls are another example. Most people who favour rent controls do so because of some sense of distributive fairness; they want to help poor tenants. Once again the efficiency costs are large, because of incentive effects. Landlords will stop maintaining controlled apartments, and will not build new ones. One of the most well-established empirical regularities of economic policy analysis is that areas subject to strict rent controls end up with housing shortages, imposing large costs on anyone looking for a place to live. Landlords then screen prospective tenants on the basis of their (the landlords') personal preferences, and the poorest tenants are frequently unable to find any accommodation at all.

Another important example is unemployment insurance. If unemployment insurance is very generous, unemployed workers will remain unemployed longer and will be much choosier about the jobs they will accept. This raises the natural rate of unemployment and increases the total efficiency losses associated with unemployment. There is no easy way out. As Thomas Schelling (1981, p.43) has remarked:

> Offering 90 percent of normal pay [as unemployment insurance] can make unemployment irresistible for some . . . Providing only 40 percent . . . makes life harder than we want it to be. There is nothing to do but compromise. But a compromise that makes unemployment a grave hardship for some makes it a pleasant respite for others, and we cannot even be comfortable with the compromise.

Similarly, if benefits to unwed mothers are very generous, unmarried teenage mothers will be more inclined to keep their babies, rather than give them up for adoption. This raises the overall public costs associated with raising such children, not to mention reducing their prospects for a happy life. Raising such benefits even reduces incentives to avoid unplanned pregnancies. However, reducing benefits to unwed mothers would make life much harsher for those unmarried women who have and keep their children, and, perhaps more disturbingly, would make life harder for their children as well.

All of these examples point out the fundamental problem with policies that give resources to the disadvantaged. By their very nature, these policies are providing rewards for being disadvantaged, and will tend to reduce private incentives to avoid such circumstances. This does not mean that we should not have such policies. It does mean that we have to recognize the associated efficiency costs.

When we argue that programs intended to promote fairness cause inefficiency, we do not mean simply that they consume resources. We expect medicare, employment insurance, welfare, and such things to consume resources. The inefficiency refers to the problem that the costs of delivering the desired results are higher than they need to be. Very often the incentive effects of social programs can be improved. The objective is to seek out least-cost methods of achieving fairness in public policy.

4.7 Improving Fairness and Efficiency

Despite the unavoidable conflict between fairness and efficiency, most economists would argue that it would be possible to improve on both the efficiency and fairness of current policies. Most such improvements rely on market-like incentives. One point to emphasize is that universal social programs are suspect. A universal program is one that applies to everyone, irrespective of income. For example, all Canadians receive free medical care and all are eligible for the Old Age Pension. In effect, the government taxes money and gives it back. Unfortunately, the resources consumed in the process are substantial. A more accurate analogy is that the government taxes $1 and gives back 75 cents. The difference is a pure deadweight loss or waste. Taxing the well-off to give to the poor is one thing. Inefficiencies are created, but they may well be justified on grounds of fairness. Taxing the well-off even more and then refunding part back to them, consuming the rest in the process, however, seems less appealing.

Suppose, for example, that we want to improve the efficiency of medical care without reducing fairness. In Canada, health care is a very large and important industry, accounting for over 10% of national output. The industry consists of private providers of health care (doctors, nurses, many hospitals, laboratories, etc.), but most payments in the system are provided by governments, not by individuals. The exact administrative details vary from province to province (since health care is a provincial responsibility) but certain aspects of the overall health-care system are governed by the Canada Health Act, which is federal legislation. In particular, provinces are required to provide universal access to the major parts of the health-care system (acute-care hospitals and most doctors' services) at no cost to the user.

A possible modification in the system would be to adopt modest users' fees, not enough to make medical care inaccessible to people with low incomes, but sufficient to provide some incentives in the direction of efficiency. In addition, substantial amounts of revenue would be collected, easing the problems associated with rapidly growing government debts. People who could really not afford even modest user fees could be given vouchers. (Vouchers are like tickets or licences. Each voucher is worth a specified sum of money. The government gives vouchers to individuals who qualify, these individuals use the vouchers to buy the service in question, and then the seller can have the vouchers redeemed by the government for their nominal value.)

Another possibility would be to introduce a system of catastrophe insurance to cover the costs of catastrophic illness. Depending on how such a system was implemented, it might be similar to the existing health premiums that exist in most provinces. However, such a system could also incorporate some incentive elements by linking the amount of the premium to certain high-risk behaviours (such as driving, smoking, or dangerous occupations).

Those who suggest the use of modest user fees, possibily supplemented by catastrophe insurance, do not advocate complete or even substantial elimination of the current medicare system. There are benefits from some elements of universal health care. For example, we all have an interest in providing immunization for relevant diseases. This benefits the immunized people, and it benefits the rest of us by reducing our exposure to infectious disease. Similarly, as carefully described by Kesselman (1980), universality has some adminstrative and other advantages.

Vouchers can be used for other things in addition to medical user fees. They could be used as an alternative to rent controls. If we believe that some people deserve assistance in paying for housing, we could provide them with vouchers for perhaps $200 per month (or whatever) and have them compete on the open market for housing. This would increase the demand for housing, and would bring forth a corresponding increase in supply, which would be much more efficient than public sector housing.

Many economists have suggested a more radical proposal to substitute for current welfare and employment insurance programs: a guaranteed annual income. A guaranteed annual income would provide a certain minimum payment per person (appropriately adjusted for age and family size) and would allow people to keep some fraction (such as 50%) of personal earnings above the minimum. People with very low earnings would get substantial payments from the government; people with higher earnings would receive smaller payments from the government, but would still be better off as a result of earning more income themselves. At some still higher level of earnings, government payments would fall to zero, and at higher levels, positive income tax would be paid by the individual to the government.

This system is sometimes called a negative income tax, because it supplements incomes below the threshold level. The greatest advantage of the negative income tax is that it provides some incentive to work and earn income. Current welfare provides no such incentive. Current welfare schemes provide for a certain minimum income, then for every dollar of income that is earned, the welfare payment is reduced by one dollar, making the effective tax rate on earnings 100%! Welfare recipients are, in effect, discouraged from earning income. In addition, it is possible (although not certain) that the administrative costs of welfare programs could be reduced by such a plan, which could be administered as part of the tax system.

Depending on the specific details of the negative income tax (tax rate used, base income rate, etc.), it is possible that the negative income tax could increase the total expenditure burden by providing net payments to the working poor who do not currently receive welfare or other direct assistance. Thus, it might be difficult to contemplate moving to a negative income tax at a time when government budgets are under great pressure.

Over the past decade, quite a few changes have been made that serve to improve the incentive properties and fairness of the tax/transfer system. Thus, it is now harder than it used to be to find examples of obvious efficiency. Unfortunately, however, improvements in the structure of the tax/transfer system are modest in importance compared to the continuing large excess of expenditures over revenues, and lead to an increasing accumulation of public debt. This debt in turn has implications for intergenerational fairness, since it is a burden for future generations to contend with.

4.8 The Role of Business Ethics

We often hear complaints about the ethical standards of the business community. Recent scandals in the investment and securities industry are the latest focal point of such concerns. In recent years, business ethics have also been criticized in connection with environmental pollution, manipulative advertising, and a variety of other issues. Even highly successful businessmen will often bemoan the state of ethics in business, arguing that ethical standards are not what they used to be.

Most of us favour ethical behaviour, at least in the abstract. Some observers, however, such as Milton Friedman (1972, p.32), have taken a refreshingly clear stance against social responsibility in business. Friedman argues that "the social responsibility of business is to increase its profits." If society does not like pollution, we should tax it, and let profit-maximizing business firms respond (as they will) by reducing pollution. Not only would it be naive to expect voluntary reductions in pollution, it would also be counterproductive. Firms that adopted less polluting but more expensive methods of production would earn lower profits and tend to decline in relative importance compared to those who did not. The "good guys" would be punished and the "bad guys" would win.

Similarly, according to Friedman, we should not expect or want business executives to decide which cultural activities to support (with money that would otherwise go to shareholders or to the government in taxes). Business should supply goods and services that people are willing to pay for, not presume to paternalistically decide on social policy.

There is, however, more to the issue of business ethics than Friedman suggests. In particular, ethics and social values play an important role in influencing economic efficiency. Suppose, for example, that business people generally subscribe to a policy of honesty. Agreements could be made over the phone, contracts would not have to be written down, lawyers would not have to be consulted, and transactions could be concluded quickly. Much business is in fact conducted in this way.

If, on the other hand, dishonesty were the norm, then verbal agreements would never be sufficient and written contracts would be required for everything. Furthermore, if contracts were violated, then redress through the court system would be required, which would be very expensive for all parties, including society at large, which pays for the courts. Many Pareto-improving transactions would be foregone altogether, simply because the two parties could not trust each other to fulfil the terms of the transaction. It is frequently alleged that such problems are an important part of why certain less developed countries remain less developed.

The trust problem is also an important explanation for why, in certain countries, business is dominated by a particular ethnic group or even by a few families. Within the group people can trust each other, and it is much more efficient to do business with people you can trust than with people you cannot trust.

Business honesty generates positive externalities. Honesty may be a good policy for the person in question, because of reputation effects, but in addition, his or her honesty creates benefits for others as well, including business associates and third parties. Because honesty is associated with positive externalities, there is reason to believe that private incentives will provide too little of it. The standard policy solution of subsidizing honesty seems impractical.

However, social values and personal ethics can be an important substitute for policy. If business people are honest because they have a personal commitment to honesty, or because their friends will ostracize them if they prove to be dishonest, then honesty will be promoted without the need for active public policy. Business will run much more efficiently as a result. Many sociologists have linked the 18th- and 19th-century economic development of the West to the rise of the Protestant religions and their emphasis on the values of honesty, thrift, and hard work.

Honesty is only one example of an ethic that is important to general business efficiency. Thrift and hard work are also important. So are loyalty and altruism. A business enterprise in which employees are willing to help each other, even when no direct credit is forthcoming, will generally operate more effectively than one in which employees engage in backstabbing.

In addition to promoting business efficiency, business ethics also have a direct effect on the psychological well-being of the population at large. Most people simply feel better when they are in an environment where they believe they can trust others, and where they believe they are contributing to something worthwhile. They are also more likely to emulate such behaviour if they observe it in others. (This is a standard observation from psychology. For example, a motorist is much more likely to stop to help someone with a flat tire if he or she has recently seen someone else stop to help a motorist in distress.)

The state of business ethics does play an important role in economic efficiency and, more generally, in overall social well-being. To a large extent, the evolution of business ethics simply reflects changing social and religious values, and there is little that public policy can do to change business values directly. Policy does, however, have some impact. If, for example, the tax system is so full of loopholes that it encourages business decisions to made principally for reasons of tax avoidance, not only does this have direct efficiency costs, but it also undermines the business ethic that business is supposed to produce value for money, not defraud taxpayers. Similarly, if governments are seen to reward successful lobbying by bailing out failing businesses, this has the indirect cost that all citizens become a little more cynical. They will tend to modify their behaviour accordingly, reducing their willingness to pay taxes and to contribute to the general public welfare.

If we accept the proposition that business ethics is important, and if we can agree on what a general statement of business ethics might consist of, there is still the problem of implementation of ethical standards. As mentioned earlier, leadership within an organization is very important in implementation. At the level of public policy, there are several actions that might make implementation of ethical standards easier. One such action is legislative protection for whistle-blowers. A whistle-blower is someone who reports or publicizes serious ethical or legal problems. In recent years there have been many cases of individual employees reporting, for example, illegal dumping of toxic wastes, or falsification of research findings, or other serious ethical failures. Frequently, however, these whistle-blowers have themselves suffered, perhaps being fired or demoted, and frequently finding it difficult to find a new job. Legislative protection can reduce these costs.

Another possible action is to increase the legal responsibility borne by boards of directors. In particular, the law could view boards of directors as having an explicit social obligation as well as a corporate obligation. Thus, for example, a director who failed to undertake due diligence concerning toxic waste dumping might be held financially or criminally liable. Similarly, outside auditors who fail to appropriately investigate situations of obvious fraud, or outside lawyers who contribute to their clients' attempts to carry out illegal activities, might reasonably be held partially responsible.

4.9 Attitudes Toward Fairness in the Marketplace

One of the difficulties in establishing policies that are both efficient and fair is that we seem to have trouble thinking consistently about fairness. This point has been demonstrated clearly by Kahneman, Knetsch, and Thaler (1986), from which the following examples are taken.

A large (random) sample of individuals were presented with several examples of business behaviour and were asked if the behaviour was unfair or acceptable. Some of these situations are reported below:

1A. A company is making a small profit. It is located in a community experiencing a recession with substantial unemployment but no inflation. There are many workers anxious to work at the company. The company decides to reduce wages and salaries 7% this year.

    Acceptable 38%   Unfair 62%

1B. A company is making a small profit. It is located in a community experiencing a recession with substantial unemployment and inflation of 12%. The company decides to increase wages and salaries only 5% this year.

    Acceptable 78%   Unfair 22%

2A. A shortage has developed for a popular model of automobile, and customers must now wait two months for delivery. A dealer has been selling these cars at list price. Now the dealer prices this model at $200 above list price.

    Acceptable 29%   Unfair 71%

2B. A shortage has developed for a popular model of automobile, and customers must now wait two months for delivery. A dealer has been selling these cars at a discount of $200 below list price. Now the dealer sells this model only at list price.

    Acceptable 58%   Unfair 42%

3A. A small company employs several people. The workers' incomes have been about average for the community. In recent months, business for the company has not increased as it had before. The owners reduce the workers' wages by 10% for next year.

    Acceptable 39%   Unfair 61%

3B. A small company employs several people. The workers have been receiving a 10% annual bonus each year and their total incomes have been about average for the community. In recent months, business for the company has not increased as it had before. The owners eliminate the workers' bonus for the next year.

　　　Acceptable 80%　　　　　　Unfair 20%

Each pair of questions presents two similar situations. Situations 1A and 1B are objectively identical as far as real income is concerned. In each case workers are presented with a 7% cut in real income. Despite the objective equivalence of the situations, intuitions about fairness differ very significantly. Imposing a 7% real wage cut in the presence of 12% inflation is judged to be fair, while offering a 7% real wage cut in the absence of inflation is judged to be unfair.

Situations 2A and 2B make a similar point. In each case the car dealer raises price by $200. The list price is, of course, completely arbitrary, and has no direct bearing on the welfare of consumers in any case. Yet raising the price $200 above list generates many more assessments of unfairness. Similarly with Situations 3A and 3B, perceptions of fairness concerning a wage cut change dramatically, depending on the semantic issue of whether or not some part of regular income is referred to as a bonus.

In general, perceptions of unfairness are very sensitive to how the situation is framed or described. Slight changes in description can produce very dramatic changes in the intuitive response of most people. People are more strongly influenced by the connotations of the description than by the economic realities of the situation.

This has three very disturbing implications. First, it means that perceptions of fairness are easily manipulated, a fact which many self-serving politicians and business people frequently take advantage of. Second, it means that individual perceptions of fairness tend to be inconsistent, which makes it very hard to determine what we mean by fairness. Third, even if people seem confident in their perceptions of fairness, we must wonder what these perceptions are based on if they are so easily manipulated.

4.10 Concluding Remarks

This chapter makes the point that concerns over fairness have a long history of analysis and still generate much disagreement and debate. In part this is because some of the issues that arise, such as the Baby Jane case, are difficult ones that trouble us as individuals, even before considering differences in viewpoints across individuals. A person's attitudes toward fairness are strongly influenced by the culture and environment in which that person develops and lives, and we observe that different cultures of the past and present have major differences in their conceptions of fairness and morality. One possible implication of these differences is the doctrine of cultural relativism, which holds that we have no basis for asserting the superiority of one value system over another. While acknowledging the importance of keeping cultural relativism in mind, especially when judging individual behaviour, we considered three major attempts to provide absolute standards of fairness. These major approaches are the utilitarian approach, the social covenant approach (especially as applied by Rawls (1971)), and the rights or procedural approach. This chapter also noted the distinction between group-based and individual-based conceptions of fairness. The chapter then made the important point that there are tradeoffs between fairness and efficiency, but suggested how it might be possible to improve both fairness and efficiency at the same time. The role of business ethics was discussed, as were some problems associated with assessing fairness in the marketplace.

Despite the difficulties in determining an absolute set of criteria for fairness, it is important that fairness considerations be handled rigorously in public policy analysis. One useful step that acts as a complement to the cost-benefit analysis described in Chapter 3 is to identify the likely distributional effects of proposed policies: who gains and who loses, along with an assessment of how much they gain or lose. We can then ask whether this pattern of distributional changes meets some reasonable standard of fairness.

4.11 Bibliographic Notes

Useful introductory overviews of morality and fairness and related topics include Brown (1986) and Rachels (1993). An influential philosophical position on fairness is that of Rawls (1971). Useful discussions of the tradeoff between efficiency and equity can be found in Rhoads (1985) and Schelling (1981). Implications of attitudes toward fairness for market behaviour are discussed by Khaneman, Knetch, and Thaler (1986). A useful collection of readings on business ethics is Poff and Waluchow (1991), which includes Friedman's (1970) paper.

Notes

1. *MacLeans Magazine,* September 14, 1992, p. 23.

2. The other point of view, that group differences in performance arise in part from intrinsic differences rather than discrimination, is contained in Hernstein and Murray (1994).

3. In 1959–60 women made up 9% of first-year medical students in Canada. This percentage rose modestly to 11% in 1964–65, and was a full 47% in 1987–88. See *Canadian Medical Educational Statistics, 1990,* vol. 12, Ottawa: Association of Canadian Medical Colleges. The argument for being restrictive in allowing female enrolment was that women would be likely to waste their expensive medical educations by getting married and giving up their careers.

On-line Sources

For more information about corruption, a useful place to start is:
http://www.gwdg.de/ uwvw/icr.htm

5

The Positive Theory of Government

5.1 Introduction

The normative analysis of government is concerned with what governments should do. It is prescriptive in nature. The positive analysis of government, on the other hand, tries to explain why governments choose the policies they do. In other words, positive analysis seeks to understand why current policies have come about and tries to predict future directions in policy. The positive theory of government is sometimes referred to as public choice theory.

It might be the case that actual policy coincides very well with normative prescriptions. If so, positive analysis need go no further. We frequently see examples, however, of policy decisions that seem hard to explain on the basis of any clear normative principles. Why, for example, have rent controls often been in force in many Canadian cities, despite the fact that almost all economic policy analysts agree that rent controls are a bad policy?[1] Why is it often alleged that government contracts seem to be awarded on the basis of reasons that have little to do with basic normative criteria? Why, for that matter, is there so much concern over conflict of interest in policy-making?

The answer to these questions and others like them is that we expect politicians and civil servants to be motivated by the same fundamental force that motivates private sector economic behaviour: self-interest. Politicians wish to be re-elected. Civil servants wish to do well in their careers. Sometimes these incentives lead to policies that are not in the general public interest. Furthermore, various special interest groups devote substantial amounts of effort to trying to influence public policy in their favour, typically at the expense of the public at large.

This chapter presents a brief analysis of the forces that control government policy. This analysis is based on incentive effects. Incentives facing policy-makers are created by two major external forces: voting patterns and lobbying by special interest groups. Both of these forces affect the self-interest of policy-makers. In addition, policy-makers have personal, direct self-interests that affect the conduct of policy. In this chapter, these three major determinants of the incentives confronting policy-makers are examined in turn.

Section 5.2 is devoted to a discussion of voting, Section 5.3 deals with special interests and the related process of transfer-seeking, and Section 5.4 addresses direct self-interest.

5.2 Voting

It is obvious that voting influences public policy. Furthermore, virtually all citizens of modern democracies would argue very forcefully that voting should influence public policy, and that voting is the operational foundation of democracy. Most of us probably think that voting and democracy are synonymous.

Even if we agree that voting should be the basis of policy, there are still many procedural issues that must be decided. The most obvious operational issue that arises is the question of who should vote. Should convicted criminals be able to vote, should teenagers, the illiterate, the mentally retarded, the clinically insane? How should immigrants be treated in the voting process?

After settling on who should be allowed to vote, the next issue is how voting should be translated into policy. There are two basic approaches: direct democracy and representative democracy. Direct democracy involves direct voting by the citizenry on policy issues. In Canada, direct democracy is not uncommon at the local level. For example, municipalities commonly hold referenda on major civic construction projects, such as bridges and roads. The referendum will contain a proposal and financial plan, and voters are able to vote for or against. At the provincial and national levels, on the other hand, direct democracy is very rare. One exception was the 1980 referendum brought forward by the government of Quebec concerning sovereignty association with Canada. The people of Quebec were asked whether they wanted the government of Quebec to negotiate with the Government of Canada to remove itself from provincial status and establish instead a more independent association with Canada. The outcome of the vote was 60% against the proposal, 40% in favour.[2] A second referendum on essentially the same question was held October 30, 1995. In this case just under 51% voted no and just under 49% voted in favour. There was also a national referendum on a proposed new constitution for Canada (called the Charlottetown Accord) in 1992. This referendum failed by a vote of approximately 54% to 45%. (The missing 1% is due to spoiled ballots and rounding).

National and provincial referenda are, however, very rare. Almost all policy decisions at these levels of government (and most local policy decisions as well) are made by representatives, rather than by the public directly. Canada's political system is almost exclusively one of representative rather than direct democracy. There are good reasons for this. In the first place it would be impractical, if not impossible, to have citizens vote directly on most policies. Second, representatives can make use of expert opinion and presumably make better decisions as a result, especially on technical matters. It would make very little sense, for example, to have a national referendum over the design of military aircraft. The reason is that most citizens would be incapable of making an informed judgement without taking enormous amounts of time and effort. Instead, we elect representatives whom we trust to make good decisions on our behalf in accordance with general objectives that we elect them to pursue.

Representative democracy puts severe restrictions on the way in which voters can influence policy. Individuals make a host of market decisions every day, and governments make hundreds, perhaps thousands of important decisions per year, yet voters can only choose or recall their representatives at infrequent intervals of several years. Some important policy-makers, such as Supreme Court of Canada Justices, are not elected directly, but are appointed by an elected government and serve until retirement, which may be a very long time. Because they are called upon to interpret a vague constitution that seeks to entrench various rights, some of which conflict with each other, Supreme Court Justices are among the most important policy-makers in the country.[3]

There are limited options available to a voter in making choices. A voter may prefer the position of one candidate on one issue, of a competing candidate on a second issue, and may find his or her view on some other issue totally unrepresented. Yet the voter must choose one of the candidates (or abstain altogether), who will then represent him or her on every issue.

It is not impossible to introduce elements of direct democracy into modern politics. In some states in the United States, citizens have the right to bring forward direct referenda (called initiatives) in state elections. In a typical state election, voters will vote for candidates to represent them and, in addition, will vote directly on several initiatives. It is through this method that voters of Massachusetts were able to restrict property taxes to 2.5% of assessed value, against the recommendations and wishes of most politicians. In recent years, some political forces in Canada have been advocating more extensive use of direct democracy.

Voting for political representatives is a very important part of the political process. A second important part of policy formulation is voting within government. Modern government is really government by committee, and understanding the way in which committee voting works is very important to an understanding of the policy-making process. Different committee voting systems have different properties. The following subsection considers properties of representative voting in more detail, and subsequent sections present a theory of party platforms, and discuss surprising and interesting properties of committee voting.

5.2.1 Representative Voting

In Canada, as in all modern democracies, the public elects representatives who then have responsibility for the actual formulation of policy. The system is one of representative democracy. It is interesting to consider how the outcome of direct democracy might differ from the outcome of representative government. Capital punishment is not legal in Canada, despite the fact that a majority of Canadians support capital punishment.[4] In the United States, a majority of the population favours national gun control, yet gun control has made very little progress in the U.S. Congress. These are two cases where national referenda would clearly lead to a different policy outcome than does representative government.

Why does policy under representative government differ from that under direct democracy? There are at least three major reasons. First, as already mentioned, there is the matter of expert judgement. Representative governments have the capacity to obtain expert judgements and may therefore be in a position to make more informed judgements about some policy matters. Second, representative governments are more subject to interest-group lobbying than are private individuals.

Third, the representatives are different from the population at large. In general, politicians have higher incomes, are better educated, and come from more advantaged backgrounds than the average citizen. In addition, politicians tend to share certain personality traits and values, just as other occupational groups do. As a result, politicians have, as a group, a slightly different set of values and principles than the general population has. This is probably why Canadian politicians as a group have tended to oppose capital punishment while public opinion has tended to be in favour.

It should be emphasized that differences between policy and public opinion are not very large, and certainly cross-country differences in policy are closely related to cross-country differences in public opinion. The correspondence between policy and public opinion is, however, far from complete.

There are several ways in which representatives may be elected and governments formed. Virtually all modern democracies have a party system at the national level. Various individuals who stand for office align themselves with a particular political party and present a common platform or set of policies to the electorate. Not all party members might agree with the platform, but they find that the advantages of party alignment outweigh the costs.

In Canada, as in most countries, representatives are elected on a regional basis. Each member of parliament (MP) must be elected from a particular riding or area. One result of this process is that regional competition for policy advantages contributes substantially to political debate in Canada. Each MP has a strong incentive to pursue the interests of his or her riding (or constituency within the riding) at the expense of the general public interest. For example, any MP who could persuade the government to grant defence contracts in his or her riding would face improved local re-election prospects, even if the local bidders presented higher cost, lower quality bids than bidders in other parts of Canada.

In part, of course, the system of regional representation has arisen because regional issues are important in Canada. In addition, however, the regional representation system reinforces the importance of regionalism.

5.2.2 Hotelling's Theory of Political Parties

It is hard to predict the behaviour of political parties. Party platforms are based on a combination of pragmatic attempts to get re-elected and ideological commitments to particular policy agendas. One very simple theory of party platforms, first suggested by Hotelling (1929), is presented below. The basic assumptions of the theory are as follows:

1. there are two parties,
2. each party wishes to maximize the number of votes it receives,
3. voters are uniformly (evenly) distributed over a single left-right dimension.

These assumptions are simplifications of reality, but they allow us considerable insight into political platform formulation.

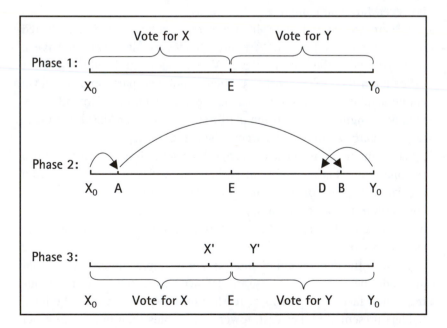

FIGURE 5.1 Hotelling's Theory of Political Parties

As indicated by assumption 3, voters are spread evenly over a single left-right dimension. We can represent this policy dimension by a line, as illustrated by Figure 5.1. Call the parties Party X and Party Y. Where will the parties locate their platforms on the line?

Suppose the parties begin at the extreme polar positions: Party X at the extreme left, Party Y at the extreme right. In this situation, if each voter votes for the party closest to his or her preferred position, each party will get exactly half the votes. If, however, Party X were to move slightly to the right, to point A on the diagram, it would gain votes. The voters to the left of point A will continue to vote for Party X, and the voters between point A and the extreme right will be evenly split between the two parties. Thus Party X will gain a majority of the votes.

In fact, the further to the right Party X moves, the more votes it gets. It can maximize its votes by moving as far to the right as it can, while still being to the left of Party Y. This is represented in the diagram by point B. Point B maximizes votes for Party X, given Party Y's position at the extreme right. If, however, Party X were to move to B, Party Y could then maximize its votes by leapfrogging over Party X and moving to point D. Party X would then move, and so on. The equilibrium or resting point of this process occurs with both parties beside each other at the middle of the spectrum, as represented by point E.

The prediction of this theory is that the two parties will cluster around the middle of the political spectrum. In practice, parties do not usually arrive at the midpoint of the spectrum by leapfrogging one another; they are more likely to approach the center by gradually moving from an extreme position. This gradualist dynamic path would be implied by slight modification of Hotelling's theory. If instead of maximizing votes, political parties were satisfied by moving just sufficiently far from their initial positions so as to gain a majority, then we would see such behaviour. In any case, the end equilibrium of the process seems to be very descriptive of actual party policies in countries like Canada and the United States, where there is typically (although not always) comparatively little difference of substance between major parties in overall party platforms.

The assumption that voters are spread uniformly is unnecessary. Voters could be spread, for example, according to a normal (bell-shaped) distribution over the spectrum, or according to some asymmetric distribution. The general statement of Hotelling's theorem is that political parties will tend to cluster around the median (or middle) voter.

Hotelling's theory has two main implications. First, in a system dominated by two political parties, policy platforms will not differ very much between the two parties. Second, the overall policy platform will closely match the preferences of the median (or middle) voter. This is the median voter principle.

The presence of additional parties can complicate Hotelling's analysis, as can the recognition that policy issues are multidimensional rather than unidimensional. One interesting question that emerges is whether, in a multi-issue world, free entry of political parties produces policies that are in line with voter preferences. In addition, as already mentioned, party platforms reflect ideology as well as pragmatic vote-maximizing. Despite these qualifications, however, Hotelling's principle has considerable descriptive power.

The median voter property of the Hotelling model seems to be desirable from the normative point of view. What could be more democratic than to have the median policies adopted? One fundamental problem, however, is that voting does not take intensity of preference into account. Suppose that we have a population of 100 people and that we are considering a policy that 60 people prefer. Assume that the average monetary value of the policy to these 60 people is $10 each. Assume further that the other 40 people dislike the policy and would have their welfare reduced by (in monetary terms) $100 each if the policy were implemented. The policy would generate costs of $4,000 whereas the benefits would be only $600. The median voter, however, is one of the 60 who favour the policy, so, if the median voter were to determine the outcome, the policy outcome would be inefficient in the sense that the costs would far exceed the benefits.

5.2.3 Committee Voting and the Power of the Agenda Setter

Consider the following problem. A committee of three cabinet ministers must select one out of three alternative projects. The three cabinet ministers are the Minister of Fisheries, the Minister of Forests, and the Minister of Energy. The three projects include one reforestation project, one fishery enhancement project, and one energy project. Only one project can be funded. How is the funded project to be chosen?

The first voting system that comes to mind is majority voting. Suppose that each minister votes for his or her most preferred project. It would not surprise us if each minister voted for the project from his or her own ministry, so that each project had one vote and no project had a majority. What should be done next? One approach is pairwise majority voting: the committee members decide between one pair of projects using majority voting, then decide between the winner of that vote and the third project using majority voting.

In order to determine the outcome, we will need to know the preferences of all three committee members. Suppose the preferences are as shown in Table 5.1.

TABLE 5.1

Ministry	Reforestation	Fishery Enhancement	Energy
Forests	1	2	3
Fisheries	3	1	2
Energy	2	3	1

This table means that the Minister of Forests likes the forestry project best, the fishery project next, and the energy project least. The Minister of Fisheries likes the fish enhancement project best, etc.

The person who can set the agenda (the order of votes) can, in this situation, determine the project to be selected. For example, suppose the agenda setter favours the energy project. He or she should set up the first vote between reforestation and fishery enhancement. In this first vote, the reforestation project gets votes from the Minister of Forests and the Minister of Energy and wins by a vote of 2-1.

The reforestation project is then put up against the energy project. In this vote, the Minister of Energy and the Minister of Fisheries both vote for the energy project and it wins by a vote of 2-1. Thus the energy project is the overall winner.

Imagine now that the agenda setter had wanted the fisheries project to win. In this case, the first vote would have been between energy and reforestation, which, as we have just seen, is won by the energy project by a vote of 2-1. The energy project would then be put up against the fisheries project. This time, according to the preferences given in the above table, both the Minister of Fisheries and the Minister of Forests vote for the fishery project, so it becomes the overall winner. The reader can verify that it would also be possible for reforestation to emerge as the winning project, depending on the order in which pairwise votes were taken.

In this case, the agenda setter has great power. Note, however, that the agenda setter does not always have power. If the first choice of all three ministers were the energy project, then the order of pairwise votes would not matter: the energy project would always win. Thus, the power of the agenda setter depends on the preferences of the committee members. In a wide range of circumstances, however, an agenda setter can exercise considerable influence.

There is no best voting procedure. As we have seen, overall first-choice voting may produce no winner. Pairwise voting is subject to manipulation by the agenda setter. If each alternative is put up against each other alternative in round-robin fashion, this process may cycle endlessly, with no project emerging as the winner. This phenomenon is sometimes referred to as the paradox of voting.

Another voting scheme for committees is approval voting, in which each member of the committee votes for all the alternatives of which he or she approves, with the winning project being the one with the most approval votes. Still another voting method is point voting: each member of the committee is given a certain number of points to be allocated among the alternatives as he or she sees fit. Someone who is almost indifferent may divide up the points more or less evenly. Someone who cares passionately about a project may give all his points to that project. The project with the most points wins. This method allows intensity of feeling to be taken into account.

Each method of voting has advantages and disadvantages. Which voting method is best depends on a variety of factors, including the number of committee members, the number of alternatives, the importance of the policies, and other issues as well. We do not have space here to go into the properties of committee voting in detail. However, the reader should be aware that different voting systems will generally produce different policy outcomes.

5.2.4 Vote-Trading

As already indicated, individual members of a government will not, in general, fully support the platform of the governing party. Similarly, each member of a committee will normally have a different set of policy objectives. Furthermore, there are many issues over which policy must be formulated. One member of a government or a committee may be very sensitive to environmental protection, another may be very interested in fishery enhancement, a third might be very concerned about the pricing of natural gas, etc. How are actual policies decided upon? One explanation of the process, first described by Downs (1957), is referred to as vote-trading or logrolling.

Vote-trading means that different members of the policy-making group form coalitions to support one another's policy proposals. For example, a city council member who cares about creating more park space may agree to support another city council member's proposal for building a bridge, in return for a positive vote on park development. Downs has argued that this vote-trading (or influence-trading) process has certain desirable properties. However, the outcome of this process may easily differ from the policies prescribed by pure normative analysis.

5.2.5 The Normative Significance of Voting

One of the lessons that most people absorb from childhood is the idea that voting has considerable normative significance. Thus, people will often argue that a particular policy is good simply because it has won popular support, or that a political party has a certain legitimacy because it has been elected. Because we accept the process of voting as a good process, we accept the outcome as normatively appropriate (i.e., as a guide to what should be done) even if, as individuals, we would prefer a different alternative. Thus, for example, the 1988 Canadian general election was fought largely on the basis of whether Canada should enter into the Canada-U.S. Free Trade Agreement (FTA) (the forerunner of NAFTA, the North American Free Trade Agreement). Debate over the issue was vigorous, but when the party favouring the FTA (the Conservatives) won the election, there was general (though far from universal) agreement that the FTA should be implemented. The other political parties (the Liberals and the NDP) had sought to obstruct the FTA's progress prior to the election, but cooperated in its speedy implementation after the election.

This approach could be used to establish principles of fairness. We could say that fair policies are those that the political process has produced. Thus, for example, the political process has (at present) decided that it is fair to enforce contracts requiring people to retire at age 65, but not fair to fire people because they have AIDS. In essence this is a social contract approach to fairness, as described in Chapter 4. We agree, as part of a social contract, that voting is a fair procedure. Therefore the outcome is taken to be fair.

In practice we do not take a position as extreme as this, in part because we recognize that there is no best electoral system, and electoral outcomes depend on the details of the system. For example, either the Australian electoral system (in which second place votes count) or the German system (in which some seats are allocated on the basis of overall popular vote) would have led to a different electoral outcome in 1988 and defeat for the FTA. Furthermore, we are often in the position of saying that something is unfair, despite the fact that it has arisen through the political process. Therefore, we think that factors beyond electoral legitimacy are important in assessing fairness, although electoral legitimacy has some significance.

5.3 Special Interest Groups and Transfer-Seeking

We have argued that one major influence on policy and policy-makers is voting. The second major external influence on policy-makers is interest-group activity. While the influence of voting on policy is obvious and relatively uncontroversial, the influence of interest groups is both subtle and a cause for concern.

It is worth distinguishing between two types of special interest groups: those concerned primarily with their own economic self-interest, and those trying to promote particular moral or social values. We will refer to these as economic interest groups and social interest groups, respectively. Sometimes a single interest group will undertake both kinds of activities. For example, the Canadian Labour Congress, a coalition of Canadian labour unions, is a strong proponent of policies that will benefit its members directly, but it also supports a variety of social policies that have little to do with the direct economic welfare of its members. Similar statements could be made about the Canadian Federation of Independent Business (CFIB). For example, the CFIB lobbies for policies such as lower taxes on small business, but it also undertakes activities intended to promote a general philosophical position in favour of free enterprise.

Despite the dual focus of some interest groups, most can be classified fairly easily into one of the two categories. So-called pro-life (anti-abortion) and pro-choice (pro-abortion) groups, for example, are focused on a fundamental conflict of values that has relatively little to do with the economic self-interest of the people involved. Even with interest groups such as these, the individuals involved may be pursuing their own self-interest at some level, but such groups are sufficiently different from economic interest groups that it is important to make a distinction between the two.

Some obvious economic interest groups include individual unions, specific industry lobbies, professional associations, and regional lobbies. It should be noted, of course, that even the most purely self-interested groups will usually claim, at least in public, that they have the public interest at heart.

5.3.1 Transfer-Seeking

Transfer-seeking (often called rent-seeking) is the process of devoting resources to trying to obtain (or simply retain) economic benefits by having them redistributed from others rather than by creating new wealth. When the CEO of a major corporation spends his or her time and company's money trying to persuade the government to provide special grants to his firm, this is transfer-seeking. The CEO is trying to redistribute wealth from taxpayers to the firm, and is using up resources in the process. Litigation in court is an example of transfer-seeking. When Mr. A sues Ms. B, Mr. A is trying to redistribute wealth from Ms. B to himself. No new wealth is created, and all the resources used up in the process, as represented by lawyers' fees, court costs, and lost time (leading to lost income) of Mr. A and Ms. B, represent net losses to society at large.

An even more obvious form of transfer-seeking is theft. A thief is trying to redistribute wealth from his victims to himself, and all the resources consumed in the process represent net losses. If a thief breaks into a car, causing $200 worth of damage to the car in order to steal a stereo worth $300 (which will perhaps be sold for about $100), then the $200 in damage, the value of the thief's time, and the value of victim's time that will be used in getting the car repaired and in buying another stereo are all pure losses.

The more resources devoted to transfer-seeking, the more potential output we lose. If we spent all of our time transfer-seeking, nothing would be produced and we would all be very poor. Transfer-seeking is

essentially a parasitic activity. From the individual point of view, however, transfer-seeking can be very attractive. An individual faces the
choice of how best to allocate his or her resources in the pursuit of various objectives. If suing someone, or lobbying the government, will
lead to a higher private return than working in some wealth-creating
or productive activity, then there is a clear private incentive to undertake the transfer-seeking activity.

Transfer-seeking has three major consequences:

1. resources consumed in transfer-seeking are wasted from the
   social point of view,

2. there is a wealth transfer from society at large to the transfer-
   seeker,

3. the policy induced by transfer-seeking usually has pure waste
   associated with it.

One classic example of transfer-seeking is the firm that seeks to
obtain a monopoly franchise for some service. Such a franchise would
be worth a substantial amount in expected future profits. A company
that thought it could obtain such a franchise would be willing to use
up a lot of resources in the process of getting the franchise. Several
companies may compete for this right, and the resources consumed in
this process are costs as indicated by point 1 above. Second, once a
company has a franchise, it can charge a monopoly price. This illustrates point 2; the outcome of the transfer-seeking is a transfer from
one group (consumers) to another (the firm). Finally, there will be a
deadweight loss from the resulting monopoly power, as indicated by
point 3.

The first analytical treatment of transfer-seeking and monopoly is
due to Tullock (1967), who argued that transfer-seeking greatly
increases the cost of monopoly power. Figure 5.2 illustrates a monopoly situation.

The demand curve, D, shows the quantity demanded for any possible price. The average cost, AC, and marginal cost (the cost of producing another unit of output), MC, are assumed to be constant, in
which case they must be the same. The monopolist wishes to maximize
profit. Marginal revenue is shown by the curve MR. The marginalist
principle for profit-maximization by the monopolist implies that it
should choose price (and output) so that marginal cost is just equal to
marginal revenue.

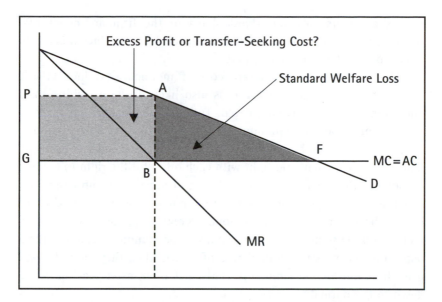

FIGURE 5.2 Transfer-Seeking as an Additional Cost of Monopoly Power

As described further in Chapter 6, there is an efficiency loss or welfare loss associated with the monopoly. This loss is represented by triangle *ABF*, and arises because a monopolist restricts output to a point at which willingness to pay (as shown by the demand curve) exceeds marginal cost. Thus, society is foregoing consumption that would generate a net surplus. This lost surplus is the standard efficiency loss (or deadweight loss) due to monopoly.

Consider the rectangle *PABG*. It is equal to the price cost margin times the quantity sold. Costs are assumed to include all direct costs plus a normal return on capital, risk-taking, and entrepreneurial ability, so the price cost margin represents a pure or above normal profit per unit. The rectangle *PABG* therefore represents the total above-normal profit earned by the monopoly.

Under pure competition, the price would equal average cost and consumers would pay lower prices, expanding the difference between their willingness to pay and the actual amount paid. (This difference is consumers' surplus). Under pure competition, the area *PABG* would be part of consumers' surplus. Under monopoly, the area *PABG* is extracted from consumers by the monopolist. This represents a pure transfer from consumers to shareholders of the firm. Consumers might not like this transfer, but it does not appear to be inefficient in itself. Consumers are worse off, but shareholders of the firm are better off. Apparently, only the triangle *ABF* is an efficiency loss, since it is a loss to consumers that no one else gets.

This is the standard welfare cost of monopoly. Tullock (1967) argued, however, that area *PABG* is also likely to be a welfare loss, once transfer-seeking is considered. Tullock pointed out that there is competition to become a monopolist, especially in cases where monopoly power is created by government policy. Potential monopolists will lobby the government and fight with each other for the right to exploit consumers. How many resources will be consumed in the process? Tullock argued that approximately all of the potential above normal profits will be consumed in the monopoly creation process. After all, if there is a large supply of people wishing to be monopolists, and if their opportunity cost is the normal rate of return, then they should compete the value of the monopoly rents, net of transfer-seeking costs, down to the normal return.

A closely related transfer-seeking situation is created by import quotas, which are described in Chapter 8. Import quota licences restrict the right to import goods to certain importers, and restrict the total amount imported. This creates quota rents, since the scarce supply of the desired product allows importers to charge considerably higher prices for sales than they have to pay for goods on the world market. The competition for these quota rents will, however, use up much of the potential returns in transfer-seeking costs.

In Canada, as in most developed countries, quotas and the associated quota rents are a relatively minor business phenomenon. In many other countries, however, the creation of quota rents is very important. Many economists argue that the pervasiveness of transfer-seeking activities is one of the greatest barriers to economic development in a significant number of countries.[5]

Transfer-seeking situations are common. In many cities, entry into the taxi business is restricted by local government, creating large rents and large transfer-seeking costs. As already mentioned, litigation is an example of transfer-seeking, as are theft and other economic crimes. In recent years considerable controversy has arisen over insider trading in financial markets. This is largely a transfer-seeking activity, since insiders transfer wealth from shareholders of firms to themselves. Business lobbying is mainly a transfer-seeking activity, as are strikes in the workplace. The ultimate transfer-seeking activity is war.

The costs of transfer-seeking are high. The direct economic costs are substantial, but there is a second cost as well. If the general perception is created that rewards in society are a return to special privilege created by lobbying or dishonesty, then the motivation to succeed through the creation of new wealth (i.e., through productive activities) is very much reduced. If auto industry pioneer Henry Ford or steam engine inventor James Watt had decided to lobby for government grants before proceeding with their commercial enterprises, we might all be walking to work.

Two final points should be made about transfer-seeking. First, services should not be confused with transfer-seeking. Services such as health care, education, financial services, etc. are productive even though no physical output is produced. It is true that most transfer-seeking activities appear in GNP accounting (see Chapter 8 for a discussion of GNP) under the services category, so the value of services is overstated in GNP accounts, but most services are productive in the sense that they add to the stock of things that make people better off. The one category of services that probably is largely transfer-seeking is legal services, since most legal activity involves attempts to redistribute income and wealth.

Magee (1991) argues that litigation imposes a significant burden on the U.S. economy. He states:

> The costs of litigation-specific economic predation include: the failure to accumulate capital because of the erosion of property rights, the time wasted fighting spurious claims, the economic loss of engineers, doctors, and executives who become redistributive litigators, and the discouragement of innovation because of excessive product liability.

Magee is not hopeful about legislative change, however, because a near majority of legislators and the entire judiciary are members of the interest group that uses litigation positively: the legal profession itself.

The second concluding point is that even if we could, we would not want to eliminate all transfer-seeking activity. While it is true that transfer-seeking is economically inefficient, the transfers of wealth created by transfer-seeking may, in some cases, be beneficial from a broader point of view. The court system is one example. If Ms. Sparks is careless in using her barbecue and sets her neighbour's house on fire, we regard it as appropriate that the neighbour be able to seek redress in court, even though the costs to the government and the parties involved may well exceed the magnitude of the settlement. While the court system is an extremely inefficient way of making transfers of income, it is probably necessary that the court system be available for use in settling disputes in order to maintain certain principles of justice.

A second possible example of beneficial transfer-seeking involves some charitable organizations. When the Canadian National Institute for the Blind lobbies governments to provide money for training guide dogs, it is transfer-seeking. When it asks for donations, it is transfer-seeking. Not many of us would speak out in opposition. The general point is that most people would approve of the wealth transfers created by some transfer-seeking activities on equity grounds, even if considerable economic inefficiency is created.

Despite the possibility that the transfers caused by transfer-seeking might be socially worthwhile in some cases, it should be emphasized that the equity effects of most transfer-seeking activity would be regarded by many as highly undesirable. Specifically, it is those who already have substantial influence who are in the best position to undertake successful transfer-seeking activity. This strengthens the basic presumption against transfer-seeking. It has even been argued by Olson (1982) that the basic success of a society is closely related to its ability to keep transfer-seeking institutions to a minimum so that as many resources as possible are devoted to productive pursuits.

5.3.2 The Transitional Gains Trap

One interesting phenomenon related to transfer-seeking is the transitional gains trap, described by Tullock (1976). The argument is that successful transfer-seeking by an interest group will lead to transitional gains only. The idea is best illustrated by example.

In many North American cities, taxi drivers are required to have special licences to operate. In New York City these licences are called "medallions." The number of such medallions is fixed at well below the number that would emerge in a competitive market. As a result, taxi cabs can charge higher fares, and drivers and taxi companies can earn above normal profits. However, getting a medallion is not cheap. Medallions must be purchased from someone else, and these medallions are valuable, for they confer the right to monopoly profits. Medallions have sold for prices well in excess of $100,000 in New York City. In fact, the market price of medallions should equal the present value of the stream of monopoly profits arising from ownership of the medallion.

From the driver's point of view, the cost of buying the medallion exactly offsets the monopoly rent he expects to earn. His overall return is back down to the normal level, the level equal to the opportunity cost of those people willing to be taxi drivers, which is quite low. If one objective of the medallion policy was to increase the income of taxi drivers, then we have the original problem back again. In addition there is deadweight loss arising from the monopoly power created by the policy.

The basic problem is that the value of the policy is capitalized in the cost of getting into the protected group. Net of the entry cost, returns to entrants are at the normal level: at the level of the entrant's opportunity cost. At least, this is what we expect if there is a competitive supply of people wishing to get into the protected group. It then becomes very hard to undo the policy, for removing the policy will reduce the net returns to the protected group below normal levels. Specifically, the expensive medallions that New York taxi drivers regard as valuable assets would suddenly lose their value.

The original beneficiaries of the policy do earn windfall rents. Their benefit does not disappear. From the policy point of view, however, the benefits are only temporary, for soon there is a new group that requires the protection just to earn a normal return.

In Canada, a good example of the transitional gains trap in action is the Dairy Quota system. In the 1960s a quota system was initiated in the dairy industry. The objective was to raise the incomes of dairy farmers. The policy was effective in that quotas reduced output so that higher prices could be maintained in the industry. In effect, the policy created monopoly power in a previously competitive industry. Dairy farmers are forced by law to be part of a producers' cartel administered by marketing boards.

Current dairy farmers must buy or inherit quotas from the people who received the quotas originally or bought them subsequently. The value of monopoly rents created by the quota system is capitalized in the price of quotas, so the net effect of the quota does not raise the overall income of a farmer who must buy quotas in order to be allowed to produce and sell output. Consumers pay high prices for milk, taxpayers subsidize the industry, and the current farmers earn only normal returns.

5.3.3 Economic Interest Groups

Economic interest groups have a major influence on public policy toward business. Unfortunately, it is hard to determine the extent of interest-group activity in Canada. Using various indicators, the total amount of professional lobbying activity increased dramatically during the 1980s and 1990s. In September 1989 the Lobbyists Registration Act went into effect. The Act requires lobbyists to register themselves and their clients, if applicable, in a public record called the Lobbyists Registry.

The Registry contains two categories: Tier I lobbyists are professional consultants representing clients; and Tier II lobbyists are trade associations, unions, etc. that lobby strictly on their own behalf. The leading lobbying areas are international trade, government procurement, and regional economic development.

The Registry applies only to federal government lobbying. In addition, there is an enormous amount of lobbying at provincial and local government levels and, furthermore, large corporations will typically have a significant staff unit, headed by a senior executive, devoted to business-government relations. In total, all this lobbying activity represents a very substantial amount of transfer-seeking.

Not all lobbying is transfer-seeking, however. Lobbyists actually do produce something of value: information. A successful lobbyist is one who can provide cabinet ministers, members of parliament, and senior public servants with useful information. This information is offered as a return to the policy-maker for spending time with the lobbyist. A lobbyist who offers very biased or inaccurate information, or who has nothing to offer, will not have much access to senior policy-makers. It might be the case that the amount of useful information produced by lobbyists is small compared to the total amount of resources consumed in lobbying, in which case we would assume that lobbying is mostly transfer-seeking. It is, however, possible to make a case that lobbying has a productive component.

A second argument that can be made for the value of lobbying by economic interest groups is that it helps to offset some basic public policy biases. In fact, business lobbies and consumer lobbies can often be found arguing for policies that are closer to the policies suggested by normative policy analysis than are the policies offered by politicians. For example, business lobbies have argued for trade liberalization, reducing the government budget deficit, removing rent controls, and generally restricting the role of government in the economy. In the absence of such lobbies, it is argued, governments would be even more tempted than they already are to try to gain short-term political advantage by political adventuring in policy areas where they do very little good.

This argument may be too generous to lobbyists. Certainly much, and probably most, lobbying is pure transfer-seeking that acts to the detriment of the public interest at large. The extent of lobbying and the analysis of many examples suggest that economic interest-group lobbying is very effective. Why?

Lobbying is effective because a small well-organized group with a lot at stake will have much more incentive to get involved in the political process than will a broad diffuse group. The CEO of a major corporation has a strong incentive to lobby the government for grants or special protection. If successful, he or she may save his or her own job and earn hundreds of thousands of dollars, possibly millions of dollars, in higher income. The losers in the deal are taxpayers. Most taxpayers will not even be aware that the deal is proceeding, and the liability for any one taxpayer is small, perhaps a few dollars. No one is going to pay the airfare to Ottawa to argue over a few dollars. This theme will reoccur in several places in this book. Interest groups are effective because the benefits of lobbying are concentrated and the costs are diffuse. Therefore, the beneficiaries have an incentive to get involved; individual losers do not.

5.3.4 The Ultramar Case

In late 1985, Ultramar Canada Inc. purchased the eastern refineries and service stations of Gulf Canada. At the time, the refineries in Quebec were operating at about 74% capacity. According to industry analysts, refineries need to operate at about 85% capacity to earn a reasonable return.[6] Ultramar planned to close the Montreal refinery it had purchased from Gulf, resulting in layoffs to about 430 workers. This closure would allow Ultramar's other refineries to operate at close to 100% capacity. Industry analysts regarded this as a natural development. It was viewed as part of the necessary adjustment required for the market to react to shortfalls in the demand for oil caused by the expansion of other energy sources in Quebec, notably natural gas and hydroelectric power. In economic terms, closing the refinery would increase efficiency in the industry. Investment Canada and the federal cabinet reviewed the sale and saw no reason to intervene.

The Conservative government of Canada immediately felt pressure from interested parties. The refinery workers' union took the issue to court, seeking an injunction to keep the refinery open. Local citizens groups, local religious groups, and politicians from the refinery area started lobbying the government. A Conservative cabinet minister from the Montreal area resigned from cabinet over the issue, claiming that the government had been blackmailed by the big oil companies. She and two other Montreal MPs publicly demanded that the prime minister overturn the decision to allow the sale. Rumours began to circulate in the press that Ontario ministers were in favour of the sale and closure so as to increase refining activity in their own ridings.[7]

In most of the press, coverage focused on the Quebec vs. Ontario issue, on lobbying from various groups, on the battle between Liberals and Conservatives for political support in Quebec, and on the employment losses from the closure. Politically, the government fared poorly over the issue. Very little attention was paid in the public debate to the basic normative analysis of the sale and refinery closure.

From the normative point of view, there was no reason for the government to block the sale. This case was, in fact, a perfect example of the market working. Demand for oil in Quebec was falling, largely as a result of increased output from the James Bay hydroelectric project and as a result of expansion of natural gas pipelines in Quebec, both of which involved expansions of employment in those industries. Oil is a comparatively dirty high-cost fuel that is inferior to natural gas and hydroelectric power for many purposes. The way the market works is by causing production to fall in areas of declining demand and by reallocating resources to superior products. This is the value of private markets and is the reason why market-based economies perform so much better than centrally planned ones.

Forcing the refinery to stay open to save 430 jobs in an obsolete refinery makes no more sense than paying 430 workers to dig holes in the ground and then fill them in again. It is true that being laid off is a hardship for the workers, but if that is the real issue, then the appropriate government response is to help them find new jobs, perhaps by retraining, perhaps by improving the business environment generally, and perhaps by direct job search assistance. Alternatively, the government or the firm could have compensated the laid-off workers with lump sum payments that would ease their transition to new employment.

In the end, the sale did go through and the refinery was closed, although it was a near thing. The government sweetened the deal by providing a large subsidy of $55 million to a Montreal petrochemical producer. (The sale price of the Gulf assets was about $120 million.) A Financial Post editorial of January 25, 1986, had the following summary comments:

> The weight of evidence shows that there is an excess of refining capacity in the Montreal region. . . . The loss of jobs at the former Gulf operation is a harsh result. But the government didn't close the refinery. It was a business decision. To say that the government is responsible for the job loss is tantamount to saying that the government should thwart any industrial rationalization no matter what the long term benefits may be. . . . Is it the job of government to keep injecting taxpayers' money into declining or outdated or inefficient industries and companies?. . . The view persists that political loyalty can be bought.

The point of this example is that even a policy decision that was fairly clear on normative grounds generated a large amount of interest-group activity. Indeed, it is unlikely that the sale and closure would have gone through had it not been for strong lobbying by the companies involved and by other interested parties in favour of the sale. Furthermore, even though the sale and closure itself was an efficiency improving move, when the $55 million subsidy to the petrochemical firm is taken into account, the overall costs may outweigh the benefits.

5.3.5 Social Interest Groups

Social interest groups also have a major influence on policy, and have proven to be quite effective in changing the political center of gravity. Most Americans are not opposed to abortion and support the idea that birth control is very important in improving the economic circumstances of less developed countries. Nevertheless, U.S. anti-abortion groups were successful in the 1980s in eliminating U.S. contributions to international birth control agencies that include abortion as a possibility, although some contributions were subsequently restored.

In Canada, organized lobbies on both sides have made abortion a very sensitive issue. Environmental lobbies have made politicians very concerned about environmental issues. Relatively small humanitarian, religious, and ethnically based interest groups have had a large impact on immigration policy. In the 1970s, Canadian nationalist groups, representing a small fraction of the population, induced governments of the day to spend large sums of money on very questionable subsidies and policy adventures in the energy sector.

Why are social interest groups more effective than their numbers alone might suggest? One reason is that members of social interest groups are often one-issue voters. They will vote for the candidate coming closest to their position on the issue they care about, irrespective of other issues. This affects a candidate for office in a clear way. Suppose there are 100 voters, 20 of whom feel strongly that activity A should be outlawed, and who will vote for any candidate taking their position. Suppose the other 80 voters see nothing wrong with activity A, but are concerned about a variety of issues, so that a candidate who opposes activity A has only a 10% chance of losing any particular voter in this group.

Under a system of direct democracy, an up or down vote over activity A would result in a landslide in favour of making the activity legal. A candidate in an election for a representative government would, however, have an incentive to oppose activity A. By doing so, he or she will gain 20 votes for certain and lose an expected vote total of 10% of 80, or 8 votes, producing a net gain of 12 votes.

There are other reasons for the effectiveness of social interest groups. They make life difficult for policy-makers; they are prepared to spend their own time taking up the time and energy of busy politicians. They put elected officials in an adversarial position in newspapers and on TV, which is very damaging to political fortunes, and they make campaign contributions. As a result there are strong incentives for policy-makers to be very sensitive to the demands of social interest groups.

It is not clear whether the power of interest groups is good or bad. Many people resent interest-group lobbying, feeling that it leaves ordinary citizens under-represented in the political process. But any citizen may join (or create) a social interest group. Interest groups are one way in which intensity of preference is taken into account in the political process. If 10% of the population feels passionately about something, while the other 90% feels only a slight preference for the opposite policy, is it obvious which policy direction is appropriate?

There have, of course, been some disastrous policy outcomes from the interest-group process. Perhaps the most striking example was the Prohibition period in the United States. In 1919 (and until 1933), alcohol consumption was made illegal in the United States, largely as a result of the efforts of organized lobbies, particularly the Anti-Saloon League and the Women's Christian Temperance Union. A clear majority of Americans at the time occasionally drank alcohol,[8] and a substantial minority continued to drink alcohol despite Prohibition.

The resulting flagrant violation of the law by many citizens, including police, judges, and politicians, caused a general decline in respect for the law. The costs of trying to enforce Prohibition were enormous. In addition there was a substantial loss of tax revenue because the alcohol industry was forced underground, and, perhaps most importantly, the profits from illegal alcohol distribution allowed organized crime to establish itself as a major force in the United States. The point here is not to argue that alcohol is good or bad. The point is simply that a small focused minority can have considerable influence.

The power of social interest groups suggests that an organized minority can be very effective in exploiting or at least controlling a disorganized majority. This is ironic, because political scientists have traditionally concerned themselves much more with the possible exploitation of a minority by a majority. In nondemocratic political systems there have been some appalling examples of minority exploitation. The case of Jews in Nazi Germany is one example that comes to mind readily, and the persecution of Ukrainians in the Soviet Union in 1930s and the apparent attempted genocide of Armenians in Turkey in the early 20th century may have been equally terrible. It is hard to find anything comparable under democratic governments. It may be that the power of interest groups in representative democracies tips the balance in favour of organized minorities, provided they have the right to vote. Some political scientists have coined the term "minoritarianism" to describe the apparent bias in favour of organized minorities in the public policy process.

5.3.6 Lobbying: Who and How

Lobbying activity in Canada has increased significantly since the early 1980s, and has become a complicated process that many large firms and industry associations engage in. Many firms will say that they do not particularly like the process but cannot afford to be absent from the corridors of influence and power, especially given the political changes that have occured since the early 1980s. Prior to then, most decisions were made within the relevant government departments. Lobbyists could lobby the minister of the relevant department directly, or they could interact with officials (i.e., civil servants) in the department, secure in the knowledge that their input would be passed up the line to the minister. During the middle and late 1980s, the new Conservative government increased the policy influence of ministerial staff, as distinct from the civil service. Thus, each minister would interact with the departmental officials and with his or her own (political) staff. This meant that lobbyists then needed to lobby both the departmental bureaucracy and the minister's staff. Furthermore, the Conservatives also created parliamentary committees so as to increase the influence of ordinary members of parliament. However, this also meant that lobbyists needed to interact with a third group. Finally, power has been increasingly decentralized to provincial governments, which implies that lobbyists need to devote more effort to provincial-level lobbying.

Each of these changes introduced by governments in the 1980s was part of a general policy to decentralize political power, bringing it closer to the grass roots and reducing the monopoly power on policy that was previously exercised by the senior civil service in combination with cabinet. This sounds reasonable. However, as power was decentralized, the scope for lobbying greatly increased. In effect, these changes brought the Canadian system closer to the American model, where power is more decentralized (because the Senate, the House of Representatives, and the Adminstration share power) and levels of lobbying are much higher than in Canada.

To be an effective lobbyist, Fleischmann (1993) recommends the following steps:

1. understand where the interested parties stand,
2. formulate a proposal that will satisfy most of your members' concerns and leave room for concessions the government will require,
3. seek out other interest groups that share your position,
4. coordinate individual efforts so governments will hear the same view from different sources,
5. avoid confrontation on the issue,
6. be reasonable and keep your sense of humour.

To illustrate point 3, Fleischmann offers the example of lobbying over supply management policies. For many years in various agricultural sectors, Canada has had supply management that raises prices above what they would otherwise be. Farmers' associations, such as the Dairy Farmers of Canada, had been very successful in lobbying efforts to create and maintain the supply management system, despite the opposition of a lobbying organization called the Grocery Products Manufacturers of Canada (GPMC). In recent years, the GPMC formed an alliance with unions in the food processing sector, with restaurant associations, and with others to increase their lobbying strength. As a result, it has been more successful in its lobbying efforts. (However, as described in Chapter 9, international pressures have been very important in leading to plans to weaken Canada's supply management system.)

5.3.7 Interest Groups and Financing of Political Parties [9]

One potentially important way for interest groups to obtain influence is through campaign contributions. A significant fraction of campaign expenses are provided from public (i.e., taxpayer) sources. Tax credits and direct subsidies by the federal government to political parties, combined with publicly funded contributions to individual candidates, have accounted for about 40% of total expenses in recent elections. The other 60% comes from private sources, raising the question of whether interest groups are heavily involved in campaign financing.

Typical individual contributions are fairly small, and relatively few people actually make donations. Most (annual) contributions by individuals are on the order of $100 to $200, and only just over 1% of the population makes contributions to political parties. Corporate contributions are much larger, but not as large as might be expected, and almost never exceed $100,000. This level of corporate contributions in the 1990s was, in real terms, dramatically less than during the 1960s and early 1970s.

This comparatively low contribution level is consistent with the claim, made by all parties, that large political contributions will not buy policy favours. It is believed by some observers, however, that large contributions do at least help the donor gain access to cabinet ministers and other senior policy-makers. Access does not guarantee influence, but it is the first step.

The campaign financing process is subject to some regulation under the Canada Elections Act. While there are no limits on the contributions made by particular donors, political parties and individual candidates are subject to limits on campaign spending. These limits are very low compared with campaign spending the United States. A typical Canadian member of parliament spends only about 5% of what a member of the U.S. House of Representatives spends to get elected, and spends less than 1% of what a typical member of the U.S. Senate spends per election.

In Canada, each contribution of $100 or more to a political party or candidate must be disclosed. In addition, parties are limited in the amount of electronic media advertising they can buy during election campaigns. The limits for each party are based largely on its success in the previous election. Overall, although there are some concerns about campaign financing, it seems that campaign contributions do not act as a major conduit of interest-group influence in Canada. In particular, total contributions of interest groups other than corporations and labour unions have always been very modest, in sharp contrast to the U.S. experience.

5.4 Direct Self-Interest

So far we have considered the two major external sources of pressure on policy-makers: voting and interest-group lobbying. These external pressures are important because they affect the self-interest of policy-makers. Politicians will be sensitive to voting pressures, and they will be sensitive to interest-group lobbying. In addition, however, policy-makers are subject to direct self-interest. Decisions that they make affect their own welfare directly, leading to conflicts of interest, and at the very least, policy-makers can be expected to take advantage of the perquisites of their positions. We will focus separately on the bureaucracy and on elected officials.

5.4.1 The Theory of Bureaucracy

Strictly speaking, a bureaucracy is a nonelective government body characterized by a hierarchical system of specialization that formulates and implements government policy. It has also become common for any complex hierarchical system of organization, especially if associated with fixed rules and red tape, to be referred to as a bureaucracy, even in the private sector. In this book, however, the term "bureaucracy" is used in the strict sense, and refers only to government. It is used synonymously with the terms "civil service" and "public service."

The history of literature owes much to bureaucracy. The earliest Egyptian literature was dominated by rules of conduct for young officials in the imperial bureaucracy. The Chinese imperial bureaucracy of eunuchs has been immortalized in the writings of many Chinese scholars, including Confucius, and both Plato and Machiavelli wrote their best known works on the subject of bureaucracy. Much of this literature has been very critical of bureaucracy, although usually employing a subtle and ironic style.

In some countries, such as Japan and France, employment in the senior bureaucracy is accorded the highest status, and is regarded as appropriate for only the most able and intelligent. In Victorian England, the senior bureaucracy in the Foreign Office and the Colonial Office were drawn from the highest ranks of society, the domestic civil service was next in status, with employment in the universities, in the professions (law and medicine), and in business ranking much lower.

In North America, however, as in most of the modern world, the bureaucracy is viewed with suspicion, and government managers are often viewed as inferior to their business counterparts. In Canada, senior bureaucrats are sometimes referred to as mandarins, evoking images of the powerful but rigid and wasteful bureaucracy of imperial China.

Our question is "What do bureaucrats do?" One answer is provided by Niskanen (1971), who presents what might be described as a Leviathan theory of bureaucracy. The elements of Niskanen's theory are as follows:

1. The bureaucracy carries out valuable programs that society at large and the elected government are willing to pay for.

2. The bureaucracy will maximize its own welfare, which is directly correlated with slack: the difference between the budget it receives for a program and the minimum cost of carrying out the program. This slack is consumed by the bureaucracy in various ways: thick carpets, large staffs, generous expense accounts, etc.

3. The bureaucracy knows the true cost of its programs much better than elected officials. As a result the government will pay the budget asked for by the bureau as long as the benefit of the program exceeds the budget cost.

The main implication of this theory is presented in Figure 5.3.

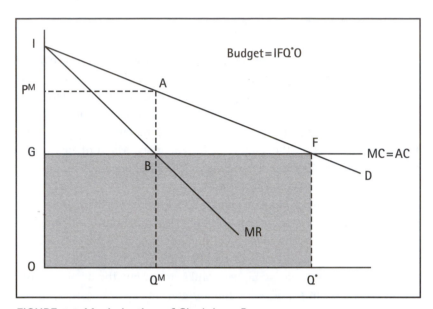

FIGURE 5.3 Maximization of Slack by a Bureaucracy

In Figure 5.3 there is a demand for the service provided by the bureau, denoted D. The average and marginal cost of production are equal and denoted by the line $MC = AC$. The normatively efficient outcome would be to offer amount Q^* of the program at a cost equal to AC times Q^*, as represented by the shaded area under the average cost curve. If the good could be provided by a monopolist on a price per unit basis, the monopolist would supply output Q^M and charge price P^M, leaving consumers with surplus IAP^M.

Under Niskanen's theory of bureaucracy, the bureau is able to set both the quantity of service and the total budget. The political authority is assumed to accept the total budget offer as long as the total budget does not exceed the total (gross) benefit of the service. If the bureau wishes to maximize slack, it will offer amount Q^* for a budget almost equal to the entire area under the demand curve up to Q^*. In other words, it will ask for a budget equal to the minimum cost, plus almost all the surplus associated with the program. As long as there is some residual surplus left, the government will accept the bureau's offer, and taxpayers will wind up with almost no surplus from the program. The outcome is worse for taxpayer-citizens than from private monopoly.

This theory is an extreme and inaccurate version of bureaucratic behaviour. Even Niskanen would not say that it is accurate. One point is that Niskanen's theory assumes that the bureaucracy merely implements policy (i.e., produces desired services), but does not formulate policy. However, a growing literature (e.g., Blais (1986)) is stressing the role of bureaucrats as architects of policy. Niskanen's theory does, however, illustrate two important insights. First, bureaucrats have an incentive to create slack in government programs because they are not subject to any market discipline. Second, a bureaucracy has even more potential monopoly power than a private monopoly. These insights contain a lot of truth and explain much of what we see. The real world is not as extreme as Niskanen's model, but the model does contribute to an overall understanding of bureaucracy.

These ideas were well expressed by Sir Humphrey Appelby,[10] fictional permanent secretary in the U.K. Department of Administrative Affairs:

> The Civil Service does not make profits or losses. Ergo we measure success by the size of our staff and our budget. By definition a big department is more successful than a small one. . . . This simple proposition is the basis of our whole system. Nobody had asked the NW controller to save 32 million pounds. . . . Suppose everybody started saving money irresponsibly all over the place?

In defense of bureaucrats, it should be pointed out that the Foreign and Colonial bureaucracies of Victorian England and the modern Japanese bureaucracy are widely regarded as very good managers. Part of what is needed for bureaucratic success is a sense of professionalism and esprit de corps. Part of what is needed is a set of analytical tools that can aid in making good decisions, and, more importantly, an incentive structure that encourages good performance. In most bureaucracies, salary is related to the importance of the task as measured by the number of people under one's supervision and the size of the budget being managed. This creates an incentive to maximize slack. It would make more sense to give bonuses for carrying out tasks at lower cost, as in the private sector.

5.4.2 Conflict of Interest and Self-Interested Politicians

Perhaps the most obvious explanation of why actual policies might differ from normative prescriptions is simply that a policy-maker wishes to enrich him or herself through the use of government policy. A government official may accept bribes or kickbacks in return for awarding contracts to certain firms rather than others. He or she might make policy decisions intended to improve the profitability of firms owned by friends, family, and even him or herself.

In Canada there have recently been some much publicized cases of conflict of interest in political office. The increased emphasis probably reflects increased media scrutiny and increased access to information more than increases in dishonesty in government. When discussing conflict of interest in Canada, one point should be remembered. Despite the fact that corruption and abuse of political power are common in Canadian history, including very recent history, corruption is the exception rather than the rule.

5.4.3 Examples of Conflict of Interest

On May 12, 1986, the Minister of the Department of Regional Industrial Expansion (DRIE), Sinclair Stevens, resigned amid charges of conflict of interest. The prime minister appointed a commission of enquiry, headed by Chief Justice William Parker of the Ontario Supreme Court, to investigate the charges. During the enquiry the following facts emerged.[11] Mr. Stevens complied with federal conflict of interest guidelines by placing his assets in a blind trust, administered by National Trust, when he joins Cabinet. His principal asset was his controlling interest in Gill Construction Ltd., which in turn had an effective controlling interest in a holding company called York Centre Corp. The purpose of a blind trust is to prevent a cabinet minister having control over his assets while in a position to make policy affecting the value of those assets. In principle, a minister does not even know the composition of his or her asset portfolio while it is being administered in a blind trust.

Mr. Stevens' problems arose because his wife and his personal secretary continued to be closely involved with the affairs of York Centre Corp. during his tenure as Minister of DRIE. In particular, Mrs. Stevens negotiated a $2.6 million loan for York Centre from a consultant to Magna International, an auto-parts manufacturer negotiating for and receiving millions in subsidies from DRIE. In addition, Mrs. Stevens negotiated, on behalf of York Centre, with a number of other firms that Mr. Stevens had dealings with as Minister of DRIE. For example, Mr. Stevens made a trip to Seoul, Korea, in 1985 to discuss DRIE-related matters with the Hanil

Bank, including the possible operations of the Bank in Canada. Accompanying him on the trip were his wife, and the CEO of York Centre Corp., who also met with the Hanil Bank representatives.

Mr. Stevens retained the services of an investment house, Gordon Capital Corp., on behalf of the government, at a time when he allegedly knew that York Centre was seeking financial assistance from Gordon Capital. He also appointed J. Trevor Eyton to an attractive board position controlled by DRIE, and authorized payment for services to two Toronto brokerage firms when he knew that all of these parties were being approached by York Centre for assistance.

Mr. Stevens clearly failed to avoid the appearance of possible misconduct, which is the normal standard for being allowed to stay in the Cabinet. Whether he was in legal violation of conflict of interest guidelines turns on the question of whether Mr. and Mrs. Stevens discussed the affairs of York Centre. The lawyers for Mrs. Stevens have argued that "it is logical to assume that Sinclair Stevens did not discuss the [York Centre] companies with his wife." The alternative view is that Mr. Stevens was, in effect, managing the affairs of York through his wife, and using his position as minister of DRIE to extract favours from the business community. Conflict of interest guidelines do not explicitly prohibit the spouse of a cabinet minister from involvement in the management of the minister's portfolio, but many people have argued that husband and wife should be presumed to be in each other's confidence over personal financial affairs.

One has some sympathy for Mr. Stevens. First of all, the blind trust notwithstanding, he could not help but know that his principal financial holdings were tied to York Centre. No portfolio manager is going to sell off a minister's principal asset, especially if it is in a company in which the minister previously took a major management interest. Furthermore, Mr. Stevens happened to be Minister of DRIE at a time when his company, York Centre Corp., was in serious financial difficulty. A large portion of his personal wealth was tied up in York Centre and he could not be expected to ignore its situation. Furthermore, the Canadian business community is not that large, and it is inevitable that many of the firms to which York Centre would turn for assistance would also be involved with DRIE. Many people believe that Mr. Stevens was a decent person caught in a difficult situation, but the extensive management activities of his wife appear to violate at least the spirit of the conflict of interest guidelines.

Consider, in addition, the position of a business executive dealing with Mr. Steven's wife. If that firm was in a position to be affected by

DRIE policy, or was actually negotiating with DRIE, what was the executive to assume when the wife of the minister came soliciting a loan on behalf of a firm in which the minister was known to have a substantial holding? Even if no threats or promises were made, or even intended, the executive's position was clearly compromised, for he or she must reasonably have anticipated that direct self-interest might be a factor in the minister's decisions.

The Commission of Inquiry released its report on December 3, 1987. The report concluded that Mr. Stevens was in conflict of interest 14 times while in the Cabinet. The report commented that Mr. Stevens had shown a "complete disregard" for the standard of conduct expected of public office holders.

In 1994, the prime minister of Italy, Silvio Berlusconi, come under suspicion of tax fraud and corruption. He was subsequently forced to resign his position as prime minister (although he continued to hold his seat in parliament) and was indicted on fraud and corruption charges in 1995. Furthermore, throughout the controversy over his status, he used his position as an influential member of parliament to try to block new anti-monopoly regulations that might have a negative impact on his business interests, notably his ownership of several television channels. His television channels, which dominate Italian TV, have taken a strongly partisan position on a variety of political issues, including elections involving Mr. Berlusconi. Mr. Berlusconi is the latest in a long series of Italian political leaders who have been accused of corruption and fraud, including several with close connections to the Italian Mafia. Mr. Berlusconi has subsequently sold some of his TV holdings.

In all countries, including Canada, there is a long history of corruption in public office. In many political jurisdictions in the world, including many U.S. cities and states, bribes are an expected part of an elected official's income. It is remarkable, for example, that former U.S. President Lyndon Johnson was able to accumulate an immense personal fortune, despite spending his entire life in relatively modestly paid political positions and having no known outside income. It should be pointed out, however, that the increasing frequency of public conflict of interest cases in Canadian politics that occurred in the 1980s and early 1990s almost certainly reflects increases in the scrutiny of senior public officials and in the standards we expect them to observe, rather than an increase in self-interested behaviour. This increase in expectations and in scrutiny has created incentives to reduce blatant seeking of personal financial gain from political office. Such activity is not likely to disappear in the near future, but we might reasonably expect a significant reduction.

5.5 Bibliographic Notes

The paradox of voting was first analyzed by de Condorcet (1785). The most important modern contribution to the theory of voting and social choice is Arrow (1951, 1963), who demonstrated that no social choice rule, including any kind of voting, could satisfy a modest set of desirable requirements. Hotelling (1929) is the source on the Hotelling theory of political parties, and Downs (1957) is the classic work on vote-trading. Other important contributions to the theory of voting in a representative democracy are Black (1958), Buchanan and Tullock (1962), and Buchanan (1967).

The basic theory of transfer-seeking is set out in Tullock (1967), and the transitional gains trap is analyzed in Tullock (1976). Valuable discussions of interest-group effects on public policy include Schultze (1977) and Pross (1992). Discussions of interest groups in Canada include, Simpson (1988), Stanbury (1993), and Fleischmann (1993). The theory of bureaucracy is associated with Niskanen (1971). Related work includes Spencer (1980). A discussion of deputy ministers in Canada is contained in Osbaldeston (1989).

Notes

1. In Frey et al. (1984, p. 988) it is reported that 96% of a randomly chosen sample of U.S. economists agreed with the statement "A ceiling on rents reduces the quantity and quality of housing available." Only 3% disagreed.

2. The Quebec Referendum was held on May 20, 1980. The question, as reported in Fitzmaurice, John. *Quebec and Canada: Past, Present and Future*. London: Hurst and Co. (1985, p. 301), read:

    > The government of Quebec has made public its proposal to negotiate a new agreement with the rest of Canada, based on the equality of nations; this agreement would enable Quebec to acquire the exclusive power to make its laws, levy taxes, and establish relations abroad, in other words, sovereignty—and at the same time maintain with Canada an economic association including a common currency; no change in political status resulting from these negotiations will be effected without approval from the people through another referendum.

    On these terms, do you give the government of Quebec the mandate to negotiate the proposed agreement between Quebec and Canada?"
    The voter turnout was 84%.

3. The importance of the Supreme Court as a policy-maker was made very clear on January 28, 1988, when it decided that Canada's abortion law

was in violation of the Charter of Rights. This decision made abortion on demand at least temporarily legal in Canada. This is clearly a policy decision by the Court, for the Charter of Rights certainly does not address the issue of abortion directly, and is capable of quite different interpretations. Similarly, in 1985, the Supreme Court decided that the Charter right of due process applies to anyone physically present in Canada, not just to Canadian citizens and landed immigrants. This was interpreted to mean that the Canadian government could no longer summarily deport illegal immigrants and other visitors. The result has been a large influx of unauthorized immigrants who, as discussed in Chapter 9 in the section on immigration, have rights to legal representation and welfare benefits once they enter Canada. It is unlikely that such a policy would have been passed by either referendum or legislative methods.

4. The September 1990 *Gallup Report* shows that 60% of a randomly chosen sample of adult Canadians favoured capital punishment, 33% opposed capital punishment, and 7% were undecided. This represents a drop from a 1982 Gallup finding that 70% favoured capital punishment, with only 19% opposed, and 11% unsure. In 1987 a free vote on reinstatement of capital punishment was held in the House of Commons. Reinstatement was defeated by a 148–127 margin.

5. A very well-documented account of these and related problems as they apply to Peru is found in de Soto (1989).

6. David Hatter, "Why Quebec keeps losing," *Financial Post,* January 18, 1986, p. 3.

7. Richard Cleroux, "Gulf sale controversy threatens to explode into full-blown crisis," *The Globe and Mail,* January 13, 1986, p. A5.

8. The April 20, 1987, *Gallup Report* estimates that 78% of Canadian adults (age 18 and over) consume alcoholic bereages.

9. This section is closely based on notes generously provided by my colleague, W.T. Stanbury of the University of British Columbia. For a much fuller account of campaign financing, see Stanbury (1991).

10. Lynn and Jay (1984), p. 59.

11. *The Globe and Mail,* February 17, 1987, pp. A1, A2, and A10.

On-line Sources

For information about the Canadian government, see

http://canada.gc.ca/programs/pgrind_e.html

6
Firms
and Markets

6.1 Introduction

In Chapter 3 we established the basic idea that competitive free enterprise is an effective form of economic organization. If, however, markets are not very competitive, we cannot be nearly so confident about the benefits of private enterprise. As argued in Chapter 3, imperfect competition is an important rationale for government intervention. Most markets will not be perfectly competitive, so the real questions become "Is there a workable or reasonable level of competition?" "What happens in markets where there are only a few firms?" "How do public policies of various types affect markets?" An essential step in answering such questions is to understand the basic characteristics of firms and markets. The objective of this chapter is to provide an overview of the theory of the firm and the theory of markets. The study of firms and markets is often referred to as industrial organization.

6.2 The Firm

Markets are composed of firms, and these firms determine the performance of each market. Firms produce most of what is consumed and are the basic unit of organization in modern market-based economies. Firms vary tremendously in size and scope. Many firms employ only one or a few workers and carry out highly specialized tasks. On the other hand, very large firms, such as Toyota and Microsoft, employ thousands of people and have budgets larger than that of most national governments. Most firms are specific to one location in their operations, but some firms operate in hundreds of locations. Corporate fortunes can change quickly. In the early 1980s, the entire combined operations of Microsoft (computer software) and Intel (computer processors) were tiny compared to carmaker General Motors, yet both Microsoft and Intel overtook General Motors in market value (but not sales) in 1995.

In Canada, most large firms are corporations, which means that they are legally incorporated and have limited liability in the sense that the shareholders of the firm cannot be held personally liable for the firm's debts beyond their own investment in the firm. In certain industries, however, such as legal services, the corporate form is not allowed, and firms are organized as partnerships, with each partner having personal liability for the firm's debts. In addition, many firms, especially small ones, choose not to incorporate. Table 6.1 offers a list of Canada's largest corporations.

These numbers could be compared with those of major corporations in other countries.[1] The largest U.S. corporation (by sales) in 1999 was General Motors, with sales equivalent to about C$230 billion (i.e., about seven times the sales of its Canadian subsidiary), followed by Ford at just over C$200 billion, and Wal-Mart at just about C$200 billion.

Despite the great diversity of the business world, there is one great unifying principle: private sector business firms of all types are in business to earn profits. (Government-owned firms are likely to have objectives other than the pursuit of profits.) The basic activity of any firm is to acquire inputs, to use them in some productive process, and to market the output. The inputs are purchased at market prices or provided by the owners of the firm directly. The revenue of the firm is the output quantities multiplied by the prices at which the outputs are sold. Costs can be divided into two categories: contractual costs, which are the costs of purchased (or rented) inputs, and noncontractual costs, which are the opportunity costs of the factors provided by the owners of the firm (including their own labour). The firm's economic profit is revenue minus total costs. Thus, an economic profit of zero includes a return to the owners of the firm equal to their opportunity cost. (This opportunity cost is sometimes referred to as normal profit.)

TABLE 6.1 Canada's Largest Corporations in 1998 (in 1998 dollars) by sales

By Sales	Company	Operating Revenues or Sales ($millions)
1	General Motors Canada	33,600.0
2	BCE Inc.	33,191.0
3	Ford Motor of Canada	27,911.6
4	Northern Telecom (Nortel)	22,099.8
5	Royal Bank of Canada	17,586.0
6	Seagram Co. Ltd.	17,339.1
7	CIBC	16,871.0
8	Chrysler Canada	16,688.0
9	Bank of Montreal	14,515.0
10	Trans Canada Pipelines	14,242.8

Source: *Canadian Business,* Performance 2000, 1998.

Accounting statements do not report economic profits directly. One problem is that it is difficult to measure normal profits and include them as a cost. Another problem is that even contractual costs and revenues can be hard to measure. For example, if the firm buys a computer that will last for several years, how should the cost of the computer be assigned? Ideally, costs should be assigned in accordance with economic depreciation. For example, if a new computer that comes to market renders the purchased computer obsolete, reducing its market value to zero, then the old computer should be written down to zero immediately, but accounting conventions operate differently. There are, of course, conventions for dealing with almost any situation that might arise, but these conventions do not (and cannot) coincide exactly with economic fundamentals.

Accounting statements do report a variety of calculations related to economic profits, the most useful of which is the rate of return. The rate of return takes total revenue minus total contractual costs, subtracts taxes paid (which can be thought of as part of costs), and divides by the equity capital of the firm. (Equity capital is the financial capital provided by the shareholders of the firm.) Table 6.2 shows two examples of rate of return calculations.

TABLE 6.2 Rates of Return
Royal Bank of Canada Annual Report 1999
Consolidated Statement of Assets and Liabilities ($ millions)

Assets

Cash resources	23,042
Securities	50,559
Loans	163,227
Other	33,822
	270,650

Liabilities and Shareholder's Equity

Deposits	187,897
Other	65,542
Subordinated debt	4,596
Shareholders' equity	12,615
	270,650

Net income (Revenue − Cost) = 1,757
Rate of return = Earnings/Equity = 1,757/12,615 = 13.93%
Source: *Royal Bank Annual Report 1999.*

Nortel Networks 1999
Consolidated Balance Sheet (U.S.$ millions)

Assets	20,725
Liabilities and Shareholders' Equity	
Current liabilities	7,019
Other liabilities	2,244
Shareholders' equity	11,462
Total liabilities and shareholders' equity	20,725

Consolidated Statement of Income (U.S.$ millions)

Revenue	19,365
Costs and expenses	18,300
Net income	1,065

Rate of return = Net income/Equity = 1,065/11,462 = 9.2%

Source: *Nortel Networks Financial Statements, September 1999.*

The rate of return is a very useful measure of profitability, provided measured costs and measured revenues coincide reasonably well with actual economic costs and revenues. A firm acting in the interests of its current shareholders should, other things being equal, try to maximize the rate of return. (Shareholders might also be interested in the risk characteristics or variability of the rate of return.) Rates of return equal to the competitive rate of return on financial capital represent normal profits, and rates of return above the competitive market rate represent above normal profits.

High earnings and rates of return allow the firm to pay out higher dividends to shareholders or retain the earnings in the firm. Over the long run, a firm that pays no dividends but reinvests earnings in new projects should have faster growth in the value of shares than a comparable company that pays out its earnings in dividends. From the shareholder's point of view, it is better to have the money paid out in dividends if the shareholder can make better use of the money than the firm can.

An important aspect of the modern corporate world is that the owners of the firm (the shareholders) do not control the firm. Firms are controlled by top management and, to some extent, by boards of directors, who are supposed to represent the shareholders. However, the interests of boards of directors, top management, and shareholders may diverge substantially, raising an important possible source of market inefficiency. Government regulation is increasingly concerned with controlling and correcting such market failures.

Because of the problems created by this separation of ownership and control, many people have questioned whether modern corporations really do maximize profits. It has been argued by Jensen and Meckling (1976) among others, that the modern corporation is nothing more (and nothing less) than a complex mesh of contracts between self-interested individuals. The managers are, in effect, the agents of the shareholders and bondholders, so the analysis of principal and agency relationships subsumes the theory of the firm as a special case. Managers would be expected to maximize their own welfare, which will coincide only partially with maximizing the profits of the firm.

The agency approach to the theory of the firm contains many valuable insights but, for a variety of reasons, the traditional idea that firms strive to maximize profits has proved to be very robust. One reason is the survivor principle: firms that fail to maximize profits will tend to disappear. In this book we treat the idea that firms maximize profits as the main unifying element in the theory of the firm.

We should, however, keep in mind that firms are much more than profit-maximizing automatons. They are complex organizations that are similar in many ways to other organizations. Furthermore, to say that firms are in business to make a profit does not really answer the question of why firms exist or why they take the form they do. We do not address such questions here, but the reader should be aware that a significant literature on the firm as an organization does exist, as noted in the bibliography to this chapter where some sources are given.

6.3 Market Structure

The next useful step in industrial organization is classification of markets into five distinct market structures: monopoly, dominant firm, oligopoly, monopolistic competition, and perfect competition. This ordering ranks market structures from the least to the most competitive. In examining the different market structures, we will use a different ordering. The natural starting point for analysis is the theory of perfect competition. Monopoly is the next easiest market structure to understand, the dominant firm structure is a small modification of pure monopoly, and monopolistic competition is considered next, leaving the most difficult and the most interesting market structure, oligopoly, until last.

6.3.1 Perfect Competition

Perfect competition was defined in Chapter 3. That definition is repeated here. Perfect competition requires the following three conditions:

1. no buyer or seller has control over prices, which are therefore taken as given or exogenous by individual firms;

2. there is free entry and exit in the long run;

3. buyers and sellers have access to all relevant information necessary to their production and consumption decisions.

Recall also that in order for condition 1 to hold it is necessary that there be lots of buyers and sellers. It is also important that firms produce homogenous products. If there were meaningful product differentiation, then firms would experience some control over product price. In

Chapter 3 it was stated that perfect competition is efficient. Figure 6.1 illustrates this assertion using the cost curves of a competitive firm.

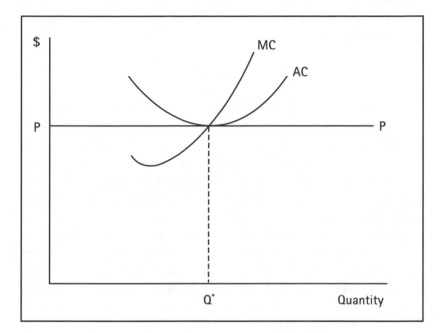

FIGURE 6.1 The Firm's Long-Run Equilibrium Under Perfect Competition

In Figure 6.1 the price is taken as constant, as illustrated by line *PP*. For a purely competitive firm, marginal revenue is equal to price: because price is constant, selling one more unit produces extra revenue equal to the price; there is no price decline to be concerned about. Marginal cost is shown by curve *MC* and average cost by curve *AC*. As is customary in economic analysis, these cost curves are assumed to include normal profits.

The marginalist principle for the profit-maximizing firm requires that the firm set marginal cost equal to marginal revenue, which in this case is the price. The firm will therefore produce where the marginal cost curve crosses the price line. In addition, free entry implies that no above-normal profits be earned in the long run (at least for marginal firms). If above-normal profits were being earned, more firms would enter the industry and price would fall until profits fell to their normal level. This implies that in the long run price must equal average cost. Furthermore, it is a property of marginal and average quantities that marginal cost must cut average cost at the minimum point of the average cost curve. Figure 6.1 illustrates all this. In long-run equilibrium the following condition holds:

$$P = MC = AC = Min\ AC$$

where *P* stands for price, and *Min AC* stands for minimum average cost.

The basic efficiency comes about because market price is, as described in Chapter 2, a measure of society's marginal benefit from consuming a little more of the good. Thus marginal cost and marginal benefit are equated, satisfying the marginalist principle from the social point of view and implying that no potential Pareto improvements are possible.[2]

In the real world there are not many industries that we would describe as perfectly competitive. The standard examples are drawn mainly from agriculture. There are thousands of wheat farmers, and no one farmer has any control over price. Price is determined by market conditions, and any single farmer can sell all he wants at that price. Entry into the industry is relatively free, so there is little reason to expect above-normal profits. One point about agricultural markets, however, is that they have become so heavily subsidized by governments and dominated by marketing boards that one can hardly point to them as examples of Adam Smith's competitive ideal.

There are many industries that are highly competitive, such as restaurants and retail trade, but in most of these industries individual sellers have some control over price, so they are better described by some other market structure, such as monopolistic competition.

6.3.2 Monopoly

The polar opposite of perfect competition is monopoly. Monopoly means that there is a single seller in the market. Unlike a perfectly competitive firm, a monopolist confronts a downward sloping demand curve. In fact, the monopolist faces the industry demand curve. Because demand is downward sloping to the firm, the firm recognizes that if it wants to sell more output, it must (other things equal) charge a lower price. This means that the marginal revenue curve lies below the demand curve (i.e., marginal revenue is less than price). Marginal revenue consists of the extra price obtained by raising sales by one unit of output, minus the value of the price reduction for all other units sold.

Furthermore, because the monopolist is not confronted by entry of new firms, it is quite possible for the monopolist to earn above-normal profits in the long run. These above-normal profits are sometimes referred to as monopoly rents. The price and output configuration that maximizes profit is obtained by choosing the output level so that marginal revenue is equal to marginal cost. The monopoly solution is illustrated in Figure 6.2

As shown in Figure 6.2, there is an inefficiency or deadweight loss associated with monopoly. The socially efficient level of output is Q^C, which is the output level at which the marginal cost of production just equals the price or marginal benefit to consumers. This is the output level that would emerge under perfect competition. The competitive price would be P^C. The monopolist charges a higher price, P^M, and produces a lower quantity, Q^M, creating an efficiency loss represented by triangle *ABF*. This diagram is very similar to Figure 2.1, and the rea-

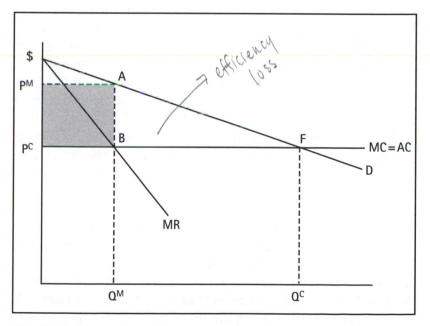

FIGURE 6.2 Monopoly Profit Maximization

son underlying the idea that area *ABF* represents an inefficiency is the same.

The above-normal profit of the monopolist is shown by the shaded rectangle. This rectangle is the markup of prices over average cost (inclusive of normal returns to the shareholders) times the output. This above-normal profit is a transfer from consumers to the owners of the firm. This transfer is not inefficient in itself, although it may be viewed as undesirable from an equity standpoint.

A monopoly may have other effects. A monopolist may fail to achieve management efficiency: it may fail to minimize costs for the output chosen, as if the entire cost curve were shifted up. The failure to minimize costs is sometimes referred to as X-inefficiency.

Monopolies may arise for several reasons. The most important one is increasing returns to scale. Increasing returns to scale (IRS) means that there are advantages to producing large quantities of output. Strictly speaking, IRS is normally defined to occur if a proportionate increase in inputs leads to a more than proportionate increase in output. Thus, for example, there are increasing returns to scale if a doubling of inputs causes output to more than double. At the level of the firm, if input prices remain fixed, then increasing returns to scale are reflected in an average cost curve that is downward sloping: average cost falls as output rises. Constant returns to scale (CRS) arise when a proportionate increase in inputs causes output to increase by the same proportion. In this case, if input prices are fixed, the average cost curve would be flat. Decreasing returns to scale occur if output increases by a smaller proportion than inputs and would tend to make average cost slope upwards if input prices were fixed. Some writers use the term "economies of scale" to refer to downard sloping average cost and "diseconomies of scale" to refer to upward sloping average cost. Thus increasing returns to scale are the main cause of economies of scale.

Most production processes have increasing returns to scale over some range of output. Therefore, a typical firm will have a U-shaped average cost curve that is declining over some range of output, then fairly constant for some range of output, then upward sloping. However, the long-run average cost curve may also be nearly L-shaped for some technologies. Both U-shaped and L-shaped cost curves are illustrated in Figure 6.3.

The lowest output at which the firm reaches an average cost very

close to the minimum average cost possible is called the minimum efficient scale (MES). Monopoly arises when the MES is very large relative
to market demand. If the MES lies outside the demand curve, then

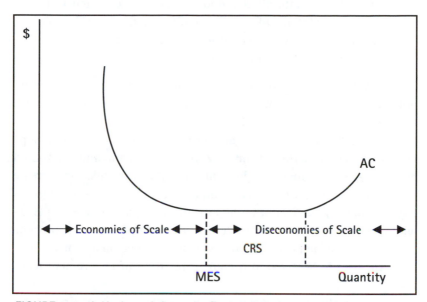

FIGURE 6.3a A U-shaped Average Cost curve

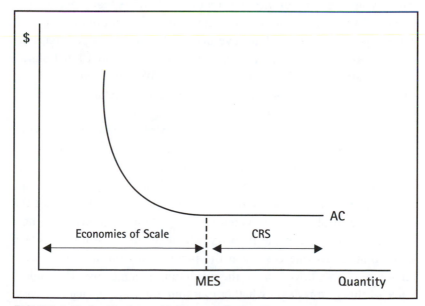

FIGURE 6.3b An "L-shaped" Average Cost curve

monopoly is certainly the natural outcome. If, however, the MES is very small relative to market demand, then the market is likely to be highly competitive.

> *Definition*: A **natural monopoly** arises when increasing returns to scale are sufficiently significant that any feasible level of demand can be met at lower average cost by a single firm than by two (or more) firms.

In addition to natural monopolies, monopolies can be created by other means. One important type of monopoly is legal monopoly: monopoly created by law. Most countries have patent protection, which gives the developer of a new product the right to be a monopolist for a certain period of time (17 years in Canada and the United States for most products). In addition, governments may create monopoly franchises. This was common in earlier times. The Hudson's Bay Company was given a monopoly franchise by the King of England to be the monopoly fur trader in British North America. In some (mostly low income) countries today, it is not uncommon for monopoly franchises to be given to friends or relatives of government leaders.

A monopoly may be created by the amalgamation of firms in an industry in combination with the creation of barriers that prevent entry by new firms. Such situations were relatively common in the late 19th and early 20th centuries, but have been reduced by competition policy in Canada and its equivalent, anti-trust policy, in the United States. Pure private monopoly is now rare in the Western democracies. In cases of natural monopoly, firms are either closely regulated or owned outright by the government.

One recent development in the analysis of monopoly is the contestability hypothesis developed by Baumol, Panzar, and Willig (1982, 1988). This hypothesis stresses the importance of potential entry. The basic idea is that even if there is only one firm or a few firms in the industry, the industry may still behave in some way approaching the competitive ideal if it fears potential entry. More specifically, if new firms are able to enter the industry whenever industry prices exceed the minimum average cost, then the incumbent firm or firms will be unable to charge prices above the minimum average cost. The importance of this idea rests on whether exit and entry are sufficiently easy. Many observers feel that the contestability hypothesis is not likely to be a reliable guide to industry behaviour in very many (if any) cases. As indicated above, if entry is restricted in some way, then we expect monopoly price markups to emerge.

6.3.3 Dominant Firms

Although pure private monopoly is rare, a closely related market structure is fairly common. This is the dominant firm structure. In such markets there is a single firm that controls a large share of the market (usually 50% or more), and a competitive fringe consisting of several or even a large number of small firms. The large firm has market power, and acts much as an ordinary monopolist, except that its behaviour is constrained by the presence of small rivals. The small firms act more or less as perfect competitors, taking market conditions as set by the dominant firm. If the dominant firm sets a price that is very high, then the small firms, taking that price as given, will produce and sell a lot of output.

The dominant firm acts as a monopolist on what is called the residual demand curve: the industry demand curve net of what is supplied by the competitive fringe. The dominant firms occasionally undertake predatory actions (such as reducing price with the intent of driving some of the smaller firms out of business) if firms in the competitive fringe become too aggressive. Such actions are, however, in violation of competition policy in Canada and anti-trust policy in the United States and are therefore not very effective as a disciplining device on competitors.

Some of the major examples of dominant firm industries are computer operating systems (Microsoft), photographic supplies (Eastman Kodak), detergents and toiletries (Proctor and Gamble), jet aircraft (Boeing), and canned soups (Campbell). Apart from the Canadian subsidiaries of U.S.-based dominant firms (such as Campbell Soups Canada), there are not many true dominant firms in Canada, because most large Canadian firms are in oligopolistic industries. One fairly close approximation to the dominant firm structure would be the role of Northern Telecom (Nortel) in telephone equipment.

6.3.4 Monopolistic Competition

Just as the dominant firm structure is close to monopoly, monopolistic competition is close to perfect competition. This is the market structure associated with industries such as restaurants, corner grocery stores, clothing, movie theatres, hotels, etc. As in perfect competition, entry and exit costs are relatively low. Also, minimum efficient scale is reached at output levels that are low relative to total market demand. Each firm has only a small share of the total market and any consumer has a wide range of choices available. Typically, there is considerable product differentiation, with each firm offering its own, sometimes unique, product qualities. As a result, each firm faces a demand curve that is slightly downward sloping: its sales will rise if it lowers its price and will fall if it raises its price. Firms' demand curves are, however, very elastic or price sensitive; large increases in price will drive most consumers away because there are many close substitutes in the market. Still, the key difference between perfect competition and monopolistic competition is that under the latter individual firms perceive that they have some control over the price they receive, whereas under perfect competition firms simply take price as given.

Firms feel the general competitive pressure of the market, which keeps prices within certain bounds. Thus, movie theatres cannot depart very far from the going price for movie seats, and restaurants that fail to offer quality commensurate with price soon go out of business. In the long run, because of free entry, profits are driven to their normal level, with price equal to average cost. The long-run equilibrium of monopolistic competition is illustrated in Figure 6.4.

In Figure 6.4 you can see that the equilibrium under monopolistic competition implies that firms will be producing on the downward sloping portions of their average costs curves. This can be compared with perfect competition, under which firms produce at the minimum points of their average cost curves.

This market structure is important and growing, because it is the natural market structure for many service industries that are growing in importance. Monopolistic competition is very rarely a target for competition policy or heavy regulation because of its highly competitive nature.

6.3.5 Oligopoly

The most interesting market structure for public policy considerations is oligopoly. Oligopoly literally means few sellers. In practice, however, oligopoly refers to all market structures that do not fit into one of

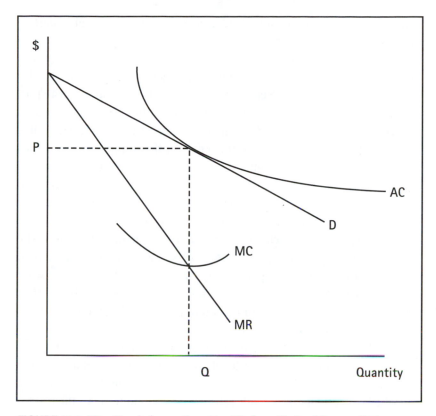

FIGURE 6.4 The Firm's Long-Run Equilibrium Under Monopolistic
            Competition

the other four categories. Oligopolistic industries may have as few as
two firms in the industry or as many as 20 or more. The main characteristics of oligopoly are as follows:

1. each firm (or each major firm) faces a downward sloping demand
   curve,

2. firms are in a strategic position relative to one another.

The second characteristic is important, because it means that firms
recognize that the fortunes of any one firm depend very much on what
its rivals do. For example, the performance of General Motors depends
very much on pricing and product decisions made by Ford, and, perhaps more importantly, by Toyota. In other words, firms are highly
interdependent. This can be contrasted with monopolistic competition,

where firms compete in some general sense but no one rival is particularly important.

It is, of course, hard to draw a strict line between oligopoly and monopolistic competition, and some industries may be on the border between the two. The more competitive oligopoly structures merge into the less competitive monopolistic competition situations. Nevertheless, it is conceptually useful to distinguish between the two market structures. Oligopoly can also be contrasted with the dominant firm structure, where firms on the competitive fringe take market conditions as given, rather than viewing themselves as important strategic players in the market. In the computer software applications industry, Microsoft is close to being dominant, but there are two or three other large firms, including IBM and Novell, along with many small firms. In 2000, Microsoft was found by a U.S. judge to have a monopoly position in relevant parts of the "operating system" market, but the software industry as whole is on the borderline between the dominant firm structure and oligopoly. The same could be said of Intel and the computer processor industry.

In oligopoly, entry barriers may or may not be important, and there may or may not be high levels of product differentiation. Most major manufacturing and resource industries could probably be described as oligopolistic: oil refining, automobile manufacturing, steel, most mining, semiconductors, and consumer electronics industries. In Canada, banking has traditionally been a major oligopoly, although recent regulatory change has increased competition in the financial service industries.

Firms in an oligopoly face conflicting incentives. On the one hand, they face an incentive to collude. Successful collusion can replicate monopoly outcomes, with correspondingly high profits for the firms involved. As a result, there are many examples of formal collusive arrangements (called cartels) in jurisdictions where they are allowed, and informal collusive arrangements in jurisdictions where cartels are illegal (such as Canada).

There is, however, a conflicting incentive that is also very strong: the incentive to cheat on the collusive agreement. If a group of producers has restricted output to the monopoly level and a high price is available, the incentive for any one producer to sell more output at a slightly lower price is very strong. Consequently, collusive arrangements are notoriously unstable. The most prominent recent example of the rise and fall of a cartel is the OPEC oil cartel. Table 6.3 shows the pattern of oil prices over the recent past. The unstable price behaviour corresponds to the instability of collusion.

TABLE 6.3 Recent Oil Prices: Brent Crude Oil (Official Contract) (current) U.S.$ per barrel

1970	1.80	1980	30.22	1990	23.72
1971	2.19	1981	32.50	1991	19.31
1972	2.47	1982	32.86	1992	19.31
1973	3.27	1983	29.73	1993	17.00
1974	11.58	1984	28.74	1994	15.54
1975	11.53	1985	27.62	1995	14.62
1976	12.38	1986	14.44	1996	17.57
1977	12.39	1987	18.49	1997	14.47
1978	12.70	1988	14.94	1998	9.52
1979	17.26	1989	18.23	1999	15.68
				2000	22.15 (1st quarter)

Sources: *Energy Prices and Taxes, 1994*, International Energy Agency Statistics; *The Economist.* "Economic Indicators," July 1-7, 1995, p. 96; British Petroleum website.

Even in the absence of collusion, oligopoly firms are necessarily forced to think about their own positions vis-à-vis those of their rivals, and may adopt either very aggressive strategies or relatively acquiescent ones. Senior managers spend a lot of time considering the behaviour of their rivals (the so-called competitive environment).

The basic problem in maintaining collusion arises from the fact that if one firm were to choose its share of the monopoly output, the other firm's best response would be to produce more than its share of the monopoly output. This suggests that a stable situation might arise when both firms are selecting an output that is a best response to the other firm's output. This is the central idea in a formal model of oligopoly originally proposed by Cournot (1838).

6.3.6 The Cournot Model of Oligopoly

The simplest version of the Cournot model is with only two firms—the case of duopoly. The basic setting is that of two firms producing a homogeneous product. The two firms make simultaneous decisions concerning how much output to produce in a given period. Cournot used the example of two firms producing bottled water from mineral springs. Readers who have consumed Perrier or Evian bottled water will recognize that this industry is no less fashionable today than it was 160 years ago.

Firms act independently or noncooperatively, but they recognize their interdependence. For Firm 1, its profit-maximizing output depends on the amount that Firm 2 produces. For example, suppose industry demand is given by a linear function of the form $P = 100 - Q$, where P is industry price and Q is industry output. If we let $q1$ be the output of Firm 1 and $q2$ be the output of Firm 2, then $Q = q1 + q2$. Suppose that Firm 2 produces 50 units of output. It follows that the demand facing Firm 1 is given by $P = 100 - 50 - q1 = 50 - q1$. Firm 1 will then take this demand curve and figure out its profit-maximizing output, setting marginal cost equal to marginal revenue. It therefore determines its best response to Firm 2's output of 50. Firm 1 is assumed to determine its best response to every possible output of Firm 2. Thus, we can think of Firm 1's desired output as a function of Firm 2's output. This function is called a best-response function.[3] Firm 2 also determines its best-response function. Two best-response functions (one for each firm) are illustrated in Figure 6.5.

Cournot proposed that the equilibrium or expected outcome would occur where the best-response functions cross. This is the Cournot equilibrium. At this point, each firm is choosing the best output it can given the output chosen by the rival. At any other point, at least one firm is dissatisfied with its output choice and would like to change it.

The Cournot model has several plausible features that can stated here. First, the combined output level will exceed the monopoly level, and total profits (summed across the two firms) will be less than the monopoly level. As more firms are added, total output rises, price falls, and total profits fall. Thus, the industry gets more competitive as more firms enter. As the number of firms gets very large, the industry approaches the perfectly competitive outcome.

The Cournot equilibrium is a special case of a Nash equilibrium, which is defined as follows.

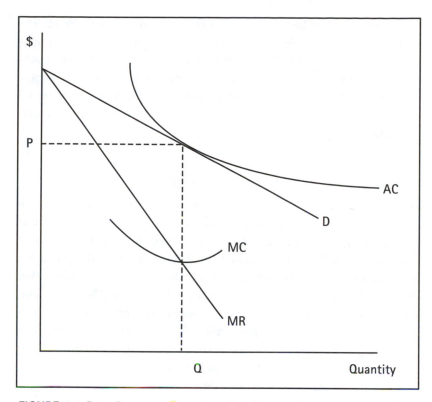

FIGURE 6.5 Best-Response Functions for Cournot Duopoly

Definition: A Nash equilibrium in a strategic game arises when each player selects a strategy that maximizes that player's payoff, given the strategies chosen by the other players.

From this definition we can see that a Cournot equilibrium is a Nash equilibrium for a game in which each player simultaneously chooses its output as its strategy choice. More realistic oligopoly games, in which firms choose research and development levels, investment levels, advertising levels, prices, or other variables, can be studied using the Nash equilibrium. In a sense, all of these models build on the Cournot model.

One very simple modification of the Cournot model arises if, instead of assuming that firms move simultaneously, one firm moves first. This leader firm is then in a position to anticipate the follower's reaction. In particular, the leader realizes that for any output it chooses, the follower will choose its best response. This means that the outcome will be somewhere on the follower's best-response function. The leader then simply chooses the point on the follower's best-response function that is best for the leader and selects the corresponding output. This model is called the Stackelberg model. More detailed analysis of the Cournot model and related models of oligopoly can be found in most intermediate microeconomics textbooks, and in industrial organization textbooks.

6.3.7 Oligopoly and the Prisoner's Dilemma

Strategic situations form the subject matter of game theory. Formal game theoretic modelling is beyond the scope of this book. There is one very simple game theoretic structure, however, that captures the basic oligopoly incentive problem very well. This structure is the prisoner's dilemma. Consider a two-firm industry (a duopoly) in which firms may charge either a high (collusive) price or a lower price. Note that this setting is different from the Cournot model in two respects. First, firms are choosing price rather than quantity. Second, their choice is discrete in that they have only two prices to choose from. In the Cournot models firms can choose any one of a large number of possible quantities. Despite these differences, however, the incentive structure of this game is similar to the Cournot model.

The strategy of charging a high price is referred to as cooperation; charging a lower price is referred to as defection. If both firms cooperate or charge high prices, both firms do well, essentially sharing in the monopoly profits. If one firm charges a high price and the other defects, the defector takes most of the sales in the market and does very well, but the other firm does very poorly. If both firms defect, both make modest profits. This payoff structure is illustrated in the following box or matrix.

		FIRM 2	
		Cooperate	Defect
FIRM 1	Cooperate	40 40	0 70
	Defect	70 0	20 20

The first element in each cell is Firm 1's profit (or payoff); the second element is Firm 2's profit. Combined profits are highest under the strategy of mutual cooperation. If, however, Firm 1 believes that Firm 2 intends to charge the collusive price, then Firm 1 has an incentive to defect, for by defecting it can raise its profit from 40 to 70. Furthermore, even if Firm 1 believed that Firm 2 was likely to defect, then the best strategy would be to defect also, for by defecting Firm 1 gets 20, while if it remains true to the agreement, it will get nothing. Similar reasoning applies to Firm 2. Thus, for each firm, no matter what the other does, its best strategy is to defect. (A strategy that is best no matter what the rival does is referred to as a dominant strategy.) It is likely, therefore, that mutual defection will be the outcome, even though the firms could earn twice as much by colluding. Note that mutual defection is a Nash equilibrium: given the strategy chosen by the rival, each firm is doing the best it can.

The original version of the prisoner's dilemma dealt with two suspects in a crime, rather than two firms. In the original version each prisoner was induced to confess (defect) in the hope of getting a lighter sentence, even though both suspects would do best if neither confessed.

If firms (or prisoners) had to make single, once-and-for-all choices, it is hard to believe they would do anything other than defect. If, however, the interaction between the firms is repeated, there is a much better chance of maintaining cooperation. In a repeated game, there is an incentive to cooperate if the firms believe that cooperation in this period will bring forth cooperation from the rival in the next period, while defection today will induce defection by the rival next period. Thus, cooperation may be maintained in a repeated game, although if one firm believes it may not be around next period, or if the one period gains from defection are very high, then defection will result.

It is a fortunate thing for consumers that oligopoly situations have a prisoner's dilemma aspect to them, for this is what maintains reasonably vigorous levels of competition even when only a few firms are involved. We cannot say in general how much competition is enough, but, as indicated above, even industries with only a few firms can be highly competitive. There are many alternative theories of how oligopolies behave.

6.4 Modes of Rivalry

There are many things that firms do to compete with each other. Most
of these strategies are of relevance principally in oligopoly situations,
but they may arise in other market structures as well. The first, and
most obvious, area of competition is over price and quality. Perfectly
competitive firms, oddly enough, do not compete over price. They simply bring their output to market for sale at what they take to be the
going price. In all other market structures firms recognize that they can
affect total sales by changing price. Even under monopoly, although
the monopolist does not face direct competition from firms producing
similar outputs, the monopolist is in competition for the consumer's
dollar with firms producing other products. If the price of tickets to
sporting events gets high enough, consumers will turn to other forms
of entertainment.

In addition to price and product competition, firms compete with
advertising and other marketing practices, through research and development, and they may undertake predatory actions to deter or prevent
entry. For example, firms may carry excess capacity to deter other
firms from entering an industry, or they may engage in the occasional price war to convince potential entrants that entering the industry
would be a poor idea. In Chapter 12, where competition policy is taken
up, we will examine public policy response to these and other strategic actions that firms might undertake.

6.5 The Structure-Conduct-Performance Approach to Policy

The main concern of (normative) public policy toward business is the
performance of an industry. Performance means the extent to which
the industry achieves allocational (or Pareto) efficiency, both at a point
in time and over time. Unfortunately, it is very difficult to measure performance directly.

Because measuring performance directly is difficult, public policy
and academic research in industrial organization has made use of the
structure-conduct-performance (SCP) approach. This approach is based
on the idea that market structure is the fundamental determinant of the
conduct (or behaviour) of firms, and that conduct is in turn the fundamental determinant of performance. For example, the theory of market

structure suggests that an oligopoly consisting of two or three firms is likely to engage in certain forms of conduct, such as collusion, that in turn lead to (socially) inefficient performance. Therefore, public policy might focus simply on the market structure and either regulate or break up small group oligopolies accordingly, rather than trying to measure the actual performance of the industry.

The key requirement for the application of the SCP approach is a measure of structure. Typically, a measure of seller concentration is used. One could, for example, look at the four-firm concentration ratio, which is simply the market share of the largest four firms in an industry. Both the four-firm concentration ratio and the eight-firm concentration ratio have been commonly used. A slightly more sophisticated measure of concentration is the Herfindahl index, which is the sum of squared market shares for all firms in an industry. Thus, if there are three firms with shares of 0.5, 0.3, and 0.2, the index would be $(0.5)^2 + (0.3)^2 + (0.2)^2 = 0.38$. The index must lie between 0 and 1. Under monopoly the Herfindahl index is 1, while if there are many small firms, the index would approach zero.

Another central focus of concern in SCP analysis is barriers to entry, particularly if those barriers are deliberate strategic devices. For example, it has been argued that brand proliferation in the breakfast cereal market has been used as an explicit barrier to entry, which might explain why a handful of companies dominate a market that would seem ideal for substantial competition. Carrying excess capacity is another strategic barrier to entry, because the excess capacity signals to potential entrants that incumbent firms can easily increase production in the event of entry, making life difficult for an entrant. In essence, if an industry has a low concentration ratio and has apparent strategic barriers to entry, it is a natural candidate for policy investigation.

6.6 Bibliographic Notes

There is an enormous literature on the theory of firms and markets. Much of the relevant material can be found in intermediate microeconomics textbooks such as Pindyck and Rubinfeld (1999). Adam Smith (1776) is the original source on the nature of the firm. More recent classics on the nature of the firm include Coase (1937), Alchian and Demsetz (1972), and Chandler (1977). Jensen and Meckling (1976) is

the standard reference on the agency theory of the firm, and an excellent set of real examples of agency problems are analyzed in Milgrom
and Roberts (1992). Non–profit–maximizing theories of the firm are
presented by Cyert and March (1963), Nelson and Winter (1982), and
Simon (1979). Two valuable sources on the firm as an organization are
Brown (1992) and Milgrom and Roberts (1992). The classic work on
oligopoly is Cournot (1838). Standard textbooks in industrial organization are Carlton and Perloff (1999) and Tirole (1988). High-level
reviews of most topics relating to the theory of firms and markets can
be found in Schmalensee and Willig (1989). Influential books on business strategy include Porter (1980) and Ghemawat (1991) and
Mintzberg and Quinn (1991). Axelrod (1984) provides a very interesting description of prisoner's dilemma experiments. The SCP approach
to analyzing markets was pioneered by Bain, Joseph S. *Barriers to New
Competition*. Cambridge, Mass. Harvard University Press, 1956.

Notes

1. *Business Week*, July 10, 1995.

2. In fact, Richard G. Lipsey and Kelvin Lancaster (1957) have shown that
   full efficiency is ensured only if all markets are perfectly competitive. If
   some markets are inefficient, then tampering with other, possibly competitive, markets may also be called for. This is known as the theory of the
   second best. As a practical matter, however, the basic policy rule is that
   the closer to perfect competition, the better.

3. More formally, if we let demand be $P = a - Q$, then revenue for firm 1 is
   $R1 = (a - (q1 + q2))q1 = aq1 - q1^2 = q1Q2$. The associated marginal revenue (given by derivative $dR1/dq1$) is $MR = a - 2q1 - q2$. If we assume
   marginal cost (MC) is a constant equal to c, then the profit-maximizing
   choice of output by firm 1 is given by $MR = MC$ or $a - 2q1 - q2 = c$.
   Rearranging this so as to isolate q1 yields the best response function for
   firm 1: $q1 = (a-c)/2 - q2/2$. Firm 2's best-response function can be
   derived in the same way and is therefore $q2 = (a-c)/2 - q1/2$. Solving
   these two linear equations in two unknowns simultaneously yields the
   Cournot equilibrium, which in this case would be $q1 = q2 = (a-c)/3$.

7

The Canadian Business Environment

Public policies toward business operate in a complex environment. Good decision-making in government or in business requires an understanding of this environment. This chapter provides a brief selective survey of Canadian economic structure and other aspects of the business environment. Section 7.1 considers population and demography, and Section 7.2 focuses on recent macroeconomic trends. Section 7.3 is devoted to industrial structure, and Section 7.4 examines the role of government. Finally, Section 7.5 briefly discusses Canada's place in the world economy.

7.1 Population and Demography

The population of Canada was 24.9 million at the 1981 Census,[1] rose to 28.1 million as of July 1, 1991, and was approximately 30 million in mid-1999. By international standards, Canada is a country with a modest-sized population. China, the world's most populous country, has a (1995, p.1) population of approximately 1.2 billion, and the United States has a population roughly 10 times that of Canada. Japan's population is over four times as large as Canada's, and France, Italy, Germany, the United Kingdom, and Mexico are each more than twice as populous.

Most of Canada's population is concentrated in Ontario and Quebec, which account for 37% and 25% respectively. British Columbia accounts for 12% of Canada's population and Alberta for 9%, while

Manitoba and Saskatchewan together account for 7%. The Atlantic
Provinces as a group have about 9% of the population, and the Yukon
and Northwest Territories together comprise less than half a percent of
the total. One of the striking features of Canada's population is that it
is concentrated in a narrow strip adjacent to the U.S. border. Canada
is, from the demographic point of view, a long thin country.

One very important demographic factor for public policy analysis
and for strategic planning in business is the age structure of the population. Table 7.1 shows the age structure as of 1999, and Figure 7.1
shows the pattern of births over the period 1947 to 1999. These data
illustrate an important phenomenon known as the baby boom. Over
the period 1947 to 1961, the number of births grew very rapidly in
Canada, but then a fairly dramatic reversal took place: births (and the
birth rate) fell sharply throughout the 1960s. The birth rate levelled out
in the early 1970s to about 15 per thousand of the population, and then
fell gradually to its level of about 12 in 1999. Demographers had been
expecting a significant rise in births in the 1980s as an echo effect of
the baby boom (i.e., as baby-boom women had their own children).
Baby-boom women have, however, had fewer children and have
delayed having them longer than expected.

Since the end of the baby boom, population has continued to
increase but current fertility rates would, in the absence of large immigration flows, lead to a situation of zero population growth at a pop-

TABLE 7.1 Canada's Age Structure, 1999 (thousands)

Age	Total	% of Population
0–14	5917.4	19.4
15–19	2061.9	6.8
20–29	4172.9	13.7
30–39	5042.1	16.6
40–49	4818.4	15.8
50–59	3454.3	11.3
60–69	2374.9	7.8
70–79	1777.7	5.8
80–89	744.8	2.4
90+	126.9	0.4
	30,491.3	100.0

Source: Statistics Canada CANSIM Matrix 6367.

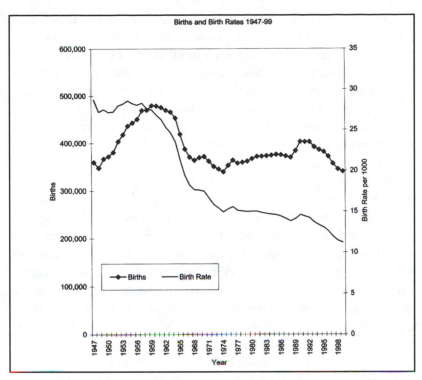

FIGURE 7.1 Births and Birth Rate 1947–1999

ulation of under 35 million in the early part of the 21st century.[2] The large immigration flows of the late 1980s and 1990s would, however, if continued, lead to an indefinitely growing population.

The baby-boom generation has had a major impact on business and on public policy. During the 1950s and early 1960s, child-related businesses did very well: manufacturers of diapers, baby food, and related items experienced a period of rapid growth. As this generation grew into childhood, great public policy emphasis was placed on education: education faculties at universities were created and expanded, new schools sprang up in all parts of Canada, and business activity focused on family- and child-oriented products.

The movement of this generation into adolescence coincided with the so-called Youth Movement of the late 1960s and early 1970s. This was a period of significant social unrest in many Western democracies, especially the United States and France, and extending to Canada. While this period of unrest was fuelled by protest against the Vietnam War, the sheer relative size of the baby-boom generation was an important contributing factor.

As young and middle-aged adults, members of the baby-boom generation have turned out to be much like their parents in most important respects, subject to some evolution of social attitudes.

The movement of the baby boom into adulthood and middle age has, therefore, had a predictable effect on the social environment, on public policy, and on business. The flood of baby boomers into the labour market, along with the increasing labour-force participation of women, taxed the capacity of the economy to absorb new workers during the 1970s and early 1980s.

When the baby boom moves into retirement, serious public policy issues will have to be addressed. Two major problems will materialize. First, the ratio of nonproductive to productive people will rise significantly, greatly straining the capacity of the productive base to support a high standard of living for themselves and the elderly. When Canada's retirement age was lowered to 65 in the 1960s, the ratio of productive workers to retired workers was about 6:1. It has since fallen to about 4:1, and, if retirement patterns remained unchanged, would fall to about 3:1 early in the 21st century.[3] Second, demands on the health-care system will grow substantially, placing a great burden on taxpayers.

These pressures are already being felt to some extent, but the pressures will get much greater before they decline. The public policy answers are fairly obvious. Average retirement age will have to rise so as to maintain a sufficiently high ratio of productive to nonproductive people, and the medical-care system will increase its relative consumption of society's resources or else fall in quality.

Another demographic phenomenon that requires emphasis is the increasing labour-force participation of women. Table 7.2 reports women's labour-force participation for the period 1965 to 1999.

As this table shows, very significant increases in female labour-force participation occurred during the decades of the 1960s, the 1970s, and 1980s. In the 1990s, however, female labour-force participation appears to have levelled off in the high fifties. The increase in labour-force participation of women that has occurred since the 1960s has had a number of important effects. The character of the workplace has changed, and women's demands on public policy have changed as well. Increasing labour-force participation has also increased the economic independence of women. As a result, the divorce rate has risen because both women and men face less economic incentive to remain married to a spouse they would prefer to leave. In the case of women, this incentive

TABLE 7.2 Labour–Force Participation Rate of Women 1965–1999

Percentage of Females Age 25+ in the Labour Force)

1965	31%
1970	35
1975	40
1980	46
1985	52
1990	57
1994	57
1999	59

Source: CANSIM Matrix 3472.

arises from their ability to support themselves; in the case of men it arises because the divorced husband's financial obligation is lowered if his wife can support herself.

It is important to see this evolution in female labour-force participation in perspective. Women have always made major economic contributions. In the past, however, most of these contributions were in the form of household production: cooking, child-rearing, gardening, farming, washing clothes, making clothes, etc. Throughout most of history, women's duties in and around the household have been a full-time job. What has happened in recent times is that technological innovation in the household appliance industry, in the clothing industry, and in the food processing industries have greatly reduced the labour required to achieve a given level of household production. Washing machines, dryers, dishwashing machines, vacuum cleaners, radio and television (to amuse children), and the availability of ready-made clothes and ready-made food have reduced the demand for labour in the household. As a result, women have shifted their economic activity outside the household and into the formal labour market. Indirect effects arising from increasing urbanization (itself caused mainly by technological innovation in agriculture) have also played an important role in moving women into the formal labour market.

As is typical with social attitudes, attitudes toward working women have tended to follow economic incentives. A 1987 Gallup poll[4] reported that 47% of Canadians answered "yes" to the question "Do you think married women should take a job outside the home if they have young children?" In 1960, the fraction of Canadians answering "yes" to this question was only 5%, and even in 1970 was only 13%. (The proportions answering "no" were 93% in 1960, 80% in 1970, and 48% in 1987. The other respondents were undecided.) Respondents were also asked if married women should take a job outside the home if they did not have children. In 1960, a full 30% answered "no" to this question, but by 1987 the percentage answering "no" was down to 7%. Gallup has not asked these questions since 1987, because they have ceased to be controversial.

One significant trend is an increasing preponderance of elderly women, because women are outliving men by a significant amount. In 1931, life expectancy for Canadian men stood at 60 years and women were only slightly ahead at 62 years. By 1995, the life expectancy of women had risen to about 81 years, while the life expectancy of men had risen to about 75 years. Thus Canadian women live, on average, almost 10% longer than Canadian men.

The educational attainment of Canadians continues to evolve significantly. Table 7.3 shows the recent history of educational attainment in Canada.

Virtually 100% of children between the ages of 6 and 11 attend elementary school and close to 100% of those age 12 to 17 are in secondary school. About one-third of the population between the ages of 18 and 24 attends some form of post-secondary education in any given year (including universities and community colleges).[5] Slightly more women than men now attend university in Canada, but men continue to significantly outnumber women in graduate programs.

7.2 Macroeconomic Trends

The environment of business is determined largely by macroeconomic conditions (the state of the business cycle). As discussed in Chapter 3, moderating the business cycle and controlling the macroeconomic environment is an important function of government policy. The macroeconomic environment refers mainly to three variables: inflation, unemployment, and per capita real Gross National Product (GNP) or the closely related Gross Domestic Product (GDP).[6] (Interest rates and exchange rates are also important influences on these three variables and therefore also receive a lot of attention in macroeconomic analysis.)

The objectives of policy are to keep the unemployment rate low, to keep the inflation rate low, and to promote growth in real incomes,

TABLE 7.3 Highest Educational Attainment
(Percentage of Population Age 15 and Over)

	Elementary	Secondary		Post-Secondary		
		Some	Completed	Some	Diploma/Cert.	Degree
1961	47.0%	29.8%	10.7%	5.4%	3.1%	4.0%
1977	25.2	36.2	10.9	9.7	8.5	9.4
1990	16.4	35.3	13.2	11.3	11.0	12.8
1996	*	36.8	23.1	2.3	24.5	13.3

* Note: This number includes both elementary and some secondary.

Sources: *Education in Canada*, Statistics Canada Catalogue No. 81-229 and 1996 Census *Nation* tables.

usually measured by per capita GNP. Table 7.4 reports the recent history of these three variables.

In mid-1995, the U.S. unemployment rate was 5.6%, reflecting the persistent difference of about 4% that has opened up between Canada and the United States in the past 20 years. As for other countries, Japan and Switzerland typically have low unemployment rates, and their rates were 3.1% and 4.0% respectively in mid-1995. Other high-income countries in Western Europe tend to have similar unemployment rates to Canada, whereas the high-income Asian countries normally have lower unemployment rates.

Perhaps the most striking and most important piece of information in Table 7.4 is the extent to which real per capita GNP, which approximately measures average living standards, grew between 1950 and the late 1980s. Real living standards, as measured by GNP per capita, nearly tripled between 1950 and 1989. Furthermore, living standards have risen in almost every year prior to the 1990s. Only in sharp recession years has real per capita GNP failed to grow. This means that living standards today are much higher than they were 45 years ago, and significantly higher than they were even 20 years ago. By historical standards this is remarkably good performance. There is no period in modern world history that has close to this record for continued improvement in living standards. This strong sustained economic performance is often forgotten in the general day-to-day concern over economic fluctuations.

Real GNP is not a perfect indicator of living standards. GNP is the total value of goods and services produced by factors of production owned by domestic residents, measured by market prices. It includes much activity of questionable value (including various types of trans-

TABLE 7.4 Unemployment and Inflation Rates in Canada, 1950–1999

Year	Unemployment	Inflation	Real per Capita GDP (1999 dollars)
1950	3.6%	2.9%	$ 10.8
1955	4.4	0.0	12.2
1960	7.0	1.2	13.2
1965	4.0	2.4	15.6
1970	5.7	3.3	18.0
1975	6.9	10.8	21.3
1980	7.5	10.2	24.4
1985	10.5	4.0	26.7
1990	8.1	4.5	28.8
1991	10.3	5.6	27.9
1992	11.3	1.5	28.8
1993	11.2	1.8	28.1
1994	10.4	0.2	28.9
1995	9.5	2.2	29.1
1996	9.7	1.6	29.2
1997	9.2	1.6	29.9
1998	8.3	1.0	30.4
1999	7.5	1.9	30.7

Sources: *Economic Indicators.* Economic Reference Tables, August 1995; Statistics Canada, World Bank Matrix 6549, 9957.

fer-seeking), it does not properly include subtractions for environmental damage, it cannot cope very well with product innovation, and, perhaps most importantly, it does not account for the value of household production or the value of leisure. Nevertheless, it is the best widely available measure we have of aggregate economic performance.

Even accepting per capita GNP at face value, there are some causes for concern. First, the growth rate was much lower in the 1970s and 1980s than in the 1960s, and in the 1990s hardly grew at all. The early 1990s was a period of recession in Canada, and recessions are not unusual. However, it is unusual for per capita real income to take as long to return to its pre-recession levels as it has in the 1990s. The parents of most university-age children are, on average, much better off than their own parents were, who in turn were much better off than their parents. It is far from clear, however, that current Canadian university students will be better off than their parents. Also, even moderate unemployment rates, reflect a lot of individual frustration, and there have been bouts of unacceptably high inflation. Even if the business cycle has been moderated by macroeconomic policy, it is still sufficiently strong to create costly uncertainties in business planning and in individual lives.

One important feature of Canada's business environment is the extent to which it varies from region to region. Some parts of the economy are traditionally depressed, such as most of Atlantic Canada and parts of Quebec, and some, such as British Columbia and Alberta, have been more volatile than the country as a whole. Table 7.5 gives some indication of this regional variation by reporting the recent history of regional unemployment rates.

There is also significant variation in regional incomes, with Alberta, British Columbia, and Ontario having per capita incomes above the

Table 7.5 History of Provincial Unemployment Rates, 1950–1999

	Canada	Atlantic	Quebec	Ontario	Prairies	B.C.
1950	3.6%	7.8%	4.4%	2.4%	2.3%	4.4%
1955	4.4	6.6	5.9	3.8	2.5	5.2
1960	7.0	10.7	9.1	5.4	4.2	8.5
1965	4.0	7.4	5.4	2.5	2.5	4.2
1970	5.7	6.0	7.0	4.4	5.0	7.7
1975	6.9	9.8	8.1	6.3	4.0	8.5
1980	7.5	11.1	9.8	6.8	4.3	6.8
1985	10.5	16.0	11.8	8.0	9.2	14.2
1990	8.1	12.8	10.1	6.3	7.1	8.3
1991	10.3	13.9	11.9	9.6	8.1	9.9
1992	11.3	14.9	12.8	10.8	9.3	10.4
1993	11.2	15.5	13.1	10.6	9.2	9.7
1994	10.6	15.2	12.2	10.0	8.6	9.5
1995	9.5	14.2	11.3	8.7	7.4	9.0
1996	9.7	14.6	11.8	9.0	7.1	8.9
1997	9.2	14.8	11.4	8.5	6.2	8.7
1998	8.3	13.7	10.4	7.2	5.7	8.9
1999	7.5	12.7	9.9	6.8	5.5	8.7

Sources: *Bank of Canada Review*, various issues; Statistics Canada Matrix 3472.

TABLE 7.6 Employment Share (Percentage) by Sector and Industry

	1947	1960	1970	1975	1980	1985	1990	1995	1998
PRIMARY									
Agriculture	25.9	11.3	6.5	5.2	4.5	4.2	3.3	3.1	3.1
Other primary	2.9	3.0	2.8	2.6	2.8	2.6	2.2	2.1	1.9
Total	28.8	14.3	9.3	7.8	7.3	6.8	5.5	5.2	5.0
SECONDARY									
Manufacturing	24.7	24.9	22.7	22.1	19.7	17.5	15.9	15.3	15.7
Construction	5.7	7.2	6.0	6.5	5.8	5.2	5.8	5.4	5.4
Transport, communication, other utilities	7.7	7.5	8.4	8.7	8.4	9.0	8.7	7.4	7.4
Total	38.1	39.6	37.1	37.3	33.9	31.7	30.4	28.1	28.5
TERTIARY (Service)									
Trade	13.4	16.2	16.7	17.2	17.2	17.7	18.0	17.5	16.9
Finance, insurance, real estate	2.6	3.8	4.6	4.9	5.7	5.6	6.0	5.9	5.5
Community, business and personal service, public administration	16.4	25.0	31.9	32.8	36.1	39.5	40.3	43.9	44.1
Total	32.4	45.0	53.2	54.9	59.0	62.8	64.3	67.3	66.5

Sources: Statistics Canada Catalogue No. 71-001; Statistics Canada Matrix 3472.

other provinces. Before-tax incomes in these provinces are about 35% higher than in the poorest provinces (Newfoundland and Prince Edward Island). However, once government taxes and transfers are taken into account, average provincial incomes are considerably more equal, and if differences in housing prices are considered, it turns out that real income is remarkable similar across the provinces.

7.3 Industrial Structure

7.3.1 Sectoral Shares of Business Activity

In this section we examine the structure of Canada's economy. The objective is to gain some understanding of the relative importance of different parts of the economy. It is natural to subdivide total business activity into three broad categories: the primary sector, the secondary sector, and the tertiary or service sector. The primary sector is related to direct use of the major physical natural resources: fishing, farming, energy, mining, and forestry. The secondary sector consists mainly of manufacturing and fabrication of physical goods, and the service sector includes the activities of the financial industry, the civil service, the personal and business service industries, and retail and wholesale sales or trade.

Historically, Canada has been viewed as a producer of primary products. Even today, one sometimes hears that Canadians are principally hewers of wood and drawers of water. As indicated by the following tables, however, this view of Canada is very misleading. Table 7.6 shows the employment share of the major sectors of the economy.

Table 7.6 shows clearly the trend away from employment in the primary and secondary industries toward employment in the tertiary or service parts of the economy. In the early post-World War II period, the three major sectors were roughly equal; in 1998, the service sector accounted for over two-thirds of total employment. The service sector is a little less important in total output than it is in employment, reflecting the relatively high capital to labour ratio in the primary and secondary sectors. Table 7.7 shows the share of national output, as measured by Gross Domestic Product (GDP), accounted for by the major sectors.

The GDP shares indicate a strong shift into services, although not quite in proportion to the shift indicated by the employment data. Some people have expressed concern over the decline of the primary and secondary sectors and the expansion of the service sector. This phenomenon is sometimes referred to as the de-industrialization of North America. (The United States and Canada have had a similar experience.) Concern about de-industrialization is related to the physiocratic idea that physical or material things are the source of value. Somehow we are worse off, according to this reasoning, if more time is spent producing services and less time is spent producing physical goods.

Like many misleading ideas, this one contains a half-truth. Many socially unproductive activities of the transfer-seeking type are included in the service component of GNP. Moving a higher fraction of activity into transfer-seeking is welfare-reducing for the society as a whole. For example, the service part of GNP includes the incomes earned by lawyers who may have spent the entire year arguing divorce cases against each other: arguing over the distribution of wealth rather than

TABLE 7.7 GDP (Percentage) at Factor Cost by Sector and Industry

	1926	1950	1960	1970	1980	1985	1990	1995	1998
PRIMARY									
Agriculture, fishing, trapping	19.0	10.6	5.2	3.5	2.6	2.4	2.4	2.1	1.8
Forestry	1.4	2.3	1.3	0.8	0.6	0.6	0.5	0.8	0.7
Mines, quarries, oil wells	3.2	3.9	4.0	4.0	4.6	4.3	3.9	4.4	3.9
Total	23.6	16.8	10.5	8.3	7.8	7.3	6.8	7.3	6.4
SECONDARY									
Manufacturing	21.6	29.2	26.4	23.3	19.7	19.6	17.9	18.5	17.8
Construction	4.2	6.0	6.0	6.3	6.4	6.1	6.6	5.2	5.4
Transport, communication	12.9	9.2	9.6	8.9	7.2	7.4	8.1	8.6	7.9
Utilities	0.0	2.2	2.8	2.9	3.2	3.4	3.1	3.2	3.4
Total	38.7	46.6	44.8	41.4	36.5	36.5	35.7	35.3	34.5
TERTIARY									
Trade	11.0	12.2	12.8	12.4	10.7	11.2	11.5	12.6	12.1
Finance, insurance, real estate	10.2	9.2	11.6	11.3	14.8	15.0	15.7	16.4	16.5
Community, business and personal service, public administration	16.6	15.3	20.4	26.5	30.7	29.9	30.4	28.7	30.6
Total	37.8	36.7	44.8	50.2	56.2	56.1	57.6	57.7	59.2

Sources: Urquhart, M.C. and K. Buckley. 1983. *Historical Statistics of Canada*, 2nd ed. Toronto: Macmillan Co.; *Canadian Economic Observer*, Statistics Canada Catalogue No. 11-210; Statistics Canada Matrix 4677.

producing anything of net value. (Each lawyer's services are of value to his or her client, of course, but the net value is zero in the sense that the lawyers cancel each other out.)

Police services and prison services are included in the service sector. Police services are very valuable, but if an increase in police services reflects an increase in crime and a corresponding increased need for police, we can hardly argue that society is better off. In 1950 there were 1.2 police per thousand persons, but by 1998 this fraction had increased to 1.8 per thousand. However, this number was down from its peak reached in the early 1990s. A deduction should be made from GNP to account for criminal and noncriminal transfer-seeking activities and for the resources that go into controlling such activities. (The appropriate deduction would be much larger for the United States than for Canada.)

The point that should be emphasized, however, is that services can be just as valuable as material goods. If a consumer is willing to pay $25 for a haircut, then the service of cutting the consumer's hair is just as valuable as a $25 compact disc that the consumer might also be willing to buy. There is nothing wrong with services, and there is nothing wrong with having the service sector of the economy increase in size, provided those services represent net value creation, not transfer-seeking.

In fact, the increasing share of services in the economy reflects increasing wealth. Overall, consumption of services is income elastic: as their income rises, consumers tend to spend a higher fraction of it on services and a lower fraction on the consumption of physical materials. For example, food consumption varies little by income class in Canada. The relatively wealthy consume about the same amount of food per capita as the relatively poor. Instead of using higher incomes to buy larger physical quantities of food, people spend extra money on services, such as the services of restaurants (which contribute to the growth of the trade sector). Note also the steady growth in the financial (and related) sector, possibly reflecting increased attention to investment-related activities by individuals.

The increasing relative importance of services as an employer also reflects labour-saving technological innovation in the primary and secondary sectors. Services, by their very nature, are labour intensive and have comparatively little scope for substitution of physical capital for labour. Labour has been released from the primary and secondary sectors and absorbed by the service sector. We have just as much physical production as before, and in addition we have more services to consume. This process is a major reason why per capita living standards in Canada have risen to their very high current levels.

One final point to make is that there is considerable variation in industrial structure by region. In general, the Western provinces are more closely linked to primary resource-based industries, while a relatively larger share of economic activity in Ontario and Quebec is devoted to secondary manufacturing. All regions have large service economies.

7.3.2 Market Structure

In Chapters 3 and 6 we emphasized the importance of market structure to economic performance. Market structure refers basically to the degree and type of competitiveness in a particular industry. It is hard to measure competitiveness directly, but one commonly used indicator of market structure is the concentration ratio, which shows the share of the industry accounted for by the largest firms in the industry. For example, a four-firm sales concentration ratio would show the share of sales accounted for by the largest four firms in the industry.

It is, of course, not clear what we mean by an "industry." Is tennis shoes an industry, or is it part of the athletic shoes industry, or simply part of the footwear industry? In general, the higher the level of aggregation (i.e., the broader the definition of industry), the lower we expect the concentration ratios to be. There are several categorizations of industries, corresponding to various levels of aggregation. These categories are described by the Standard Industrial Classification (SIC) used by Statistics Canada. The industrial breakdown used in Tables 7.6 and 7.7 corresponds to the one-digit level of aggregation. A finer subdivision of industries is given by the two-digit level of aggregation, a finer level still by the three-digit level, and so on, down to the seven-digit level, where each industry is identified by a seven-digit number. Table 7.8 corresponds to the three-digit level of aggregation. Thus, for example, the mining industry (a one-digit classification), when broken down to the three-digit level, is characterized by concentration ratios above 75%.

7.4 The Role of Government

The objective in this section is to provide an overview of the role of government in the economy. Governments affect the economy in many ways, including through the various policy areas described in subsequent chapters of this book. This section is devoted mainly to data describing the size of government and the evolution of the public debt. These issues are also taken up in Chapter 17. Table 7.9 shows how the ratio of government expenditures to income has grown over the past 60 years.

The striking feature of Table 7.10 is the extent to which deficits grew between the mid 1970s and mid 1990s. During the late 1990s, the federal government was able to eliminate the federal deficit and move to a surplus position, but with a large accumulated debt. As will be described in Chapter 17, stabilization policy suggests that government should run

TABLE 7.8 Sales Concentration Ratios in Nine Industrial Sectors

Sector	Typical Industry Concentration (CR4) Ratio
Agriculture	Very low
Forestry	20%
Mining	2/3 of industries have CR4 > 75%
Manufacturing	1/2 have CR4 > 50%
Transportation, communications, utilities	Very high
Wholesale trade	Low to moderate
Retail trade	Low to high
Community, business and personal services	Low in most cities
Finance, insurance, real estate	Moderate to high in finance and insurance; moderate in real estate

Source: Green (1990), p.75–90.

TABLE 7.9 Total Expenditure of all Government Levels as a Percentage of GNP (millions of current dollars)

Year	Expenditure	GNP	% of GNP
1935	$ 1,093	$ 4,301	25.4%
1940	1,689	6,714	25.2
1945	5,029	11,863	42.4
1950	4,080	18,700	21.8
1955	7,498	28,865	26.0
1960	11,380	38,832	29.3
1965	16,531	56,531	29.2
1970	31,088	87,765	35.4
1975	68,454	169,002	40.5
1980	124,925	302,064	41.4
1985	223,567	463,656	48.2
1990	317,162	645,608	49.1
1995	389,489	769,096	50.6
1996	396,038	788,372	50.2
1997	381,291	832,256	45.8
1998	377,075	860,316	43.8
1999	396,234	891,780	44.4

Sources: Economic Reference Tables (August, 1995) Department of Finance, Ottawa. P. 19,101; Statistics Canada Matrix 6572, 3315 and 3776, 7093.

TABLE 7.10 Deficits, Debt Service, and GNP (all levels of government, millions of current dollars)

Year	Revenues	Expenditures	Balance	% of GNP	Interest on Debt (% of GNP)	Interest on Debt (% of Rev.)
1935	922	1,093	(171)	-4.0	6.5	30.4
1940	1,622	1,689	(67)	-1.0	4.1	16.8
1945	3,338	5,029	(1,691)	-14.3	4.3	15.3
1950	4,634	4,080	554	3.0	2.9	11.7
1955	7,458	7,498	(40)	-0.1	2.3	8.9
1960	10,710	11,380	(670)	-1.7	2.8	10.2
1965	16,688	16,531	157	0.3	3.0	10.0
1970	31,800	31,088	712	0.8	3.7	10.2
1975	64,170	68,454	(4,284)	-2.5	3.9	10.2
1980	116,308	124,925	(8,617)	-2.9	5.6	14.4
1985	191,031	233,567	(31,325)	-6.8	8.7	21.0
1990	290,033	371,162	(27,129)	-4.2	9.9	22.0
1995	321,073	373,760	(52,687)	-6.5	7.6	19.2
1998	351,317	371,250	(19,933)	-2.2	7.1	18.0

Source: Statistics Canada Matrix 3317.

deficits in recessions, but Canada went through four complete business cycles from 1975 to the mid 1990s, without running a surplus.

In the 1990s, several provinces took major steps in dealing with their fiscal structures, and most were in a balanced budget position by the end of the 1990s, or were running surpluses. The one major exception to this was British Columbia, which experienced substantial deficits throughout the late 1990s. As of 1998, Ontario was also running a modest deficit so the combined federal and provincial fiscal position was still in deficit, as shown in Table 7.10.

During the 1970s, generous social programs in education, social services, and health care were entrenched, and during the late 1970s interest payments on the debt began to grow sharply. None of these areas of expenditure can be easily reduced. The ratio of deficits to GNP (and debt to GNP) have been higher in the past (at the end of World War II), but the ratio of debt service (interest payments on the debt) to GNP was high throughout the 1990s. There is some disagreement over exactly what the burden of high government debt is, as will be discussed in Chapter 17, but one obvious point is that all major areas of government expenditure aside from interest on the debt have been under pressure, resulting in lower levels of real services.

Concerns about government debt forced the possible restructuring of social programs onto the policy agenda, although many of the reforms might be valuable in their own right, quite apart from their fiscal impact.

Another important structural change in government policy over the past decade has been the privatization of Crown corporations such as Air Canada, Alberta Government Telephone, and many others, as discussed further in Chapter 16.

7.5 Canada in the World Economy

The main objective of this chapter is to describe the Canadian business environment. So far we have focused on purely domestic issues. It is important, however, to give some indication of Canada's place in the world economy.

7.5.1 International Trade Flows

Chapters 8 and 9 are devoted to international trade policy, but it is worth noting here the importance of international trade to Canada. Throughout the 1990s, Canada exported about one-quarter of its GDP. Table 7.11 reports the relative importance of Canada's trading partners.

The clear implication of Table 7.11 is that Canada's major trading partner is the United States. It consumes about 20% of Canadian GNP, more than any single province except Ontario. The U.S. economy is clearly a very important part of Canada's business environment. Japan and the rest of Eastern Asia are small but growing trading partners and have displaced Europe as the second most important trading area for Canada. The "NIC" category consists mainly of the East Asian countries (other than Japan).

7.5.2 World Living Standards and Population Growth

On the whole, the picture painted in this chapter is a relatively rosy one. Canadians are very well off overall, and there are no acutely threatening features in the domestic business environment. Canada is, however, along with a handful of other Western market-based democracies, very different from the rest of the world in two important respects. First, Canada is much richer than most of the world. Second, Canada could,

TABLE 7.11 Merchandise Trade by Principal Trading Areas, 1998

Country	Exports	Imports
United States	84.7%	68.2%
Japan	2.7	4.7
European Union	5.2	9.0
NIC	2.0	7.9
Mexico	0.46	2.6
Other Countries	4.94	7.6

Source: *Department of Foreign Affairs & International Trade 1998 Annual Trade Report.*

depending on immigration policy, achieve population stability.

Table 7.12 shows some cross-country comparisons of living standards. Making cross-country comparisons is difficult; simply taking local GNP figures and multiplying by market exchange rates can be very misleading, because the prices of nontraded goods (such as housing and medical services) vary substantially across countries. Ideally, one would like to compare the real purchasing power of average incomes across countries. A data set known as the Penn World Tables constitute a very substantial effort to determine the relative purchasing power of average incomes in different countries. Some of the results are reported below.

It should be noted that movements in exchange rates can sometimes cause problems in making real income comparisons across countries. However, the data reported here are based on real purchasing power and therefore are less susceptible to this criticism. That is, the numbers presented here show how much in the way of real goods and services that an average resident in each country can purchase. In any case, this table gives an accurate big picture concerning real income comparisons. As one expects, there are wealthy countries and poor countries. It is, however, hard for people living in areas like Canada, the United States, Western Europe, and the emergent parts of East Asia to comprehend what per capita annual incomes of less than $2,000 or $3,000 really mean, let alone the desperate circumstances of countries like Madagascar. An unfortunate fact is that the bulk of the world's population is in the poorest countries, although the rapid growth of real income in China, the world's most populous country, is moderating that effect.

Perhaps of more concern is that it is the poorest countries that have the most rapidly growing populations, since there is reason to believe that these high population growth rates, particularly in Africa,

TABLE 7.12 Comparisons of Living Standards, 1998
(Adjusted Per Capita Purchasing Power in 1998 C$)

Country	Population Increase 1970–1998	Per Capita Real Income Increase 1970–1998	1998 Real Income Per Capita
U.S.A.	31%	59%	32,952
Canada	43	77	28,673
Hong Kong	69	286	27,763
Australia	49	57	27,011
Switzerland	13	24	25,653
Germany	6	67	24,987
Japan	21	112	24,777
France	16	64	24,058
United Kingdom	6	74	23,649
Italy	7	79	21,609
Israel	100	86	17,775
Chile	56	86	10,694
Mexico	89	66	10,565
Poland	19	80	8,456
Brazil	72	81	7,042
China	51	266	4,069
India	79	109	2,678
Ivory Coast	163	−24	1,962
Nigeria	127	24	1,523
Madagascar	113	−49	927

Source: World Bank macro data tables (1999) converted to 1998 Canadian dollars.

are an important cause of poor economic performance. Economic growth is discussed further in Chapter 17.

The path followed by the rest of the world is very important for Canada's business environment. Economic development in the rest of world means markets for Canadian products, opportunities for Canadian-based multinational firms, and sources of supply for imports. More importantly, however, the increasing gap between rich and poor in the world economy, along with the problems created by excessively rapid population growth in low income countries, could easily promote war, revolution, and ecological decline. These concerns loom as major considerations for public policy at the international level, and as possible influences on domestic policy.

7.6 Bibliographic Notes

Much of the material in this chapter is taken from primary data sources produced by Statistics Canada. Other useful sources of primary data include the Department of Finance *Economic Review* and the *Bank of Canada Review*.

Notes

1. Economic Reference Tables (August, 1995) Department of Finance, p. 1

2. Royal Commission on the Economic Union and Development Prospects for Canada (1985), Ministry of Supply and Services: Ottawa: vol. 2 (of 3), pp. 52-59.

3. Economic Council of Canada (1991), p. 11.

4. *The Gallup Report*, Monday, March 23, 1987, The Gallup Poll of Canada.

5. Statistics Canada Catalogue No. 81-220.

6. Gross Domestic Product (GDP) and Gross National Product (GNP) differ slightly from each other. GDP measures the total amount of economic product produced in Canada. It is therefore the best measure of total activity and is the appropriate variable for describing economic activity. A small (but growing) part of GDP is due to foreign-owned factors of production, so not all GDP corresponds to earnings of domestic factors. When earnings to foreign factors are subtracted from GDP, and foreign earnings of domestic factors are added, the residual is GNP. GNP is therefore the appropriate measure of the earnings of domestic citizens and is used in making standard of living comparisons.

On-line Sources

For recent statistical information about British Columbia, see:

http://www.bcstats.gov.bc.ca/data/bcfacts.htm

For recent statistical information about Canada, see:

http://www.statcan.ca/start.html

For Canadian information about business, Industry Canada is a good place to start: *http://strategic.ic.gc.ca/engdoc/main.html*

8

The Theory of
International Trade Policy

8.1 Introduction

International trade is a very important part of Canadian business activity. Between 1985 and 1999 exports and imports each averaged about 25% of GDP.[1] In addition, many firms producing for the domestic market are in competition with imports, and many other firms are dependent on imports as inputs for their own production. In total, at least 40% of private sector activity in Canada is closely connected to international trade. It follows that international trade policy, which is policy focused on effecting trade flows, is correspondiryly important. Furthermore, Canada is one of the few countries in the world in which international trade policy has frequently dominated political debate.

Thus, Canada is a trading nation, and recent trade policy developments, including NAFTA and the formation of the World Trade Organization, are likely to increase the relative importance of trade. However, the extent of trade varies from province to province and region to region within Canada, with some regions being heavily involved with trade, while other are more self-sufficient. Also, trade patterns vary regionally. Western Canadian trade with Asia is largely resource based (including agricultural products), whereas southern Ontario's trade with the United States is mostly in manufactured products.

Canada's trade flows with the United States are substantial. In addition, there are substantial trade barriers within Canada (as described in Palda (1994)) that might be expected to impede inter-provincial trade and expand trade between Canadian provinces and American states. Despite these facts, McCallum (1995) has shown that Canadian provinces trade much more with each other than they do with the United States, after adjusting for size and distance. Thus, we should keep in mind that there is still a very substantial movement of goods and services across provincial boundaries within Canada.

This chapter focuses on the theory, vocabulary, and main concepts of international trade policy. This discussion falls naturally into the following categories. Section 8.2 deals with the basic economics of international trade, including the traditional theory of comparative advantage. It also emphasizes the relationship between industrial organization and international trade. Section 8.3 surveys the major instruments of trade policy, and Section 8.4 reviews the normative reasons for trade policy. Section 8.5 undertakes a positive analysis of international trade policy, and Section 8.6 contains concluding remarks. Chapter 9 describes the history, institutions, and major issues in trade policy.

8.2 The Basic Economics of International Trade

8.2.1 Comparative Advantage

Consider the following problem. You are a senior manager in a multinational corporation, Hi-tech Inc. You produce a specialized high-technology product. Each finished product contains components that must be produced and assembled. Thus, a given worker might work in either component production or in assembly. Your firm has production facilities in two countries: Canada and Caledonia. Canadian workers are somewhat more productive than Caledonian workers. One Canadian worker can produce enough components for four products per month, or can assemble four finished products per month, given the components. In Caledonia, one worker can produce enough components to produce two finished products per month or can actually assemble one final product per month. These basic data are illustrated in the following table.

Output per Worker per Month

	Components	Assembly
Canada	4	4
Caledonia	2	1

At the moment, you have 120 workers under contract in Canada and 240 under contract in Caledonia. No workers can be laid off in the short run. Assuming that the costs of transporting components are minor, how should production be allocated between Canada and Caledonia so as to maximize output per month?

One possibility would be to have the production facility in each country produce complete products, doing both production and assembly. In this case, the Canadian plant would allocate 60 workers to components and 60 to assembly, producing 240 finished products per month. In Caledonia, 80 workers would be allocated to components and 160 to assembly, yielding an output of 160 finished products per month. The firm's total output over both countries would be 400 products per month.

A second possibility would be to have Caledonia specialize in component production. If all workers in Caledonia produced components, they could produce enough for 480 final products. If these components were then transported to Canada they could be assembled by the 120 Canadian workers, yielding a total output of 480 products per month. This second allocation of labour, involving specialization and trade, is in fact the allocation that maximizes output. The gain over autonomy or "autarky" is 80 products. These 80 extra products represent the gains from trade.

The pattern of specialization is important. If Caledonia were to specialize in assembly, then 60 Canadian workers would produce 240 sets of components per month for export to and assembly in Caledonia, enough to keep the workers in Caledonia fully occupied. The other 60 Canadian workers would be divided into 30 workers producing components for assembly in Canada and 30 assembling finished products. Thus, 120 finished products would come from the Canadian plant and 240 from the Caledonian plant, yielding a total of only 360 finished products, which is actually less than the production under autarky. This production information is summarized below:

	Total Production
Autarky (no trade)	400
Caledonia specializes in components	480
Caledonia specializes in assembly	360

Why are there gains from having Caledonia specialize in component production? It cannot be that Caledonian workers are better at producing components than Canadian workers, for Canadian workers are in fact twice as efficient in component production as Caledonian workers are. The answer is related to opportunity cost. In Canada, moving one worker from assembly to component production means that components for four extra products can be produced, but four fewer units are assembled. The opportunity cost of extra components is one less product assembled per set of components. In Caledonia, on the other hand, the opportunity cost of an additional set of components is only one-half in lost assembly. The reason it pays the firm to have Caledonia specialize in components is that the opportunity cost of component production is lower in Caledonia than in Canada. In other words, Caledonia has a comparative advantage in component production.

> Definition: A country is said to have a **comparative** advantage in the production of X if the opportunity cost of producing more X is lower in that country than in other countries.

A dentist who is very good at cleaning patients' teeth would still be better off hiring a dental hygienist to do cleaning and focus his or her time on more sophisticated dental work. The opportunity cost of cleaning teeth is just too high from a dentist's point of view. Cleaning teeth is not a dentist's area of comparative advantage, even if the dentist is very good at it. The dentist has a comparative advantage in sophisticated dental work and will earn more income by specializing in such work. Similarly, it pays for a country to specialize in its areas of comparative advantage.

The idea of comparative advantage was first described by an English stockbroker and economist named David Ricardo. Ricardo's famous example involved England and Portugal. Ricardo first assumed that England was absolutely more efficient in producing cloth than Portugal, and that Portugal was absolutely more efficient in producing wine. Under these circumstances, there are obvious advantages to having England specialize in the production of cloth and export it to Portugal, while Portugal specializes in wine and exports it to England.

Ricardo then imagined that England was not only more efficient in cloth production, but also in wine production. Suppose, for example, that each English worker could produce four units of wine per time period or, alternatively, four units of cloth, and that each worker in

Portugal could produce two units of wine or one unit of cloth. Suppose, before trade, that each country is producing both products. Now consider the following thought experiment. Move one worker in England from wine production to cloth production. This reduces wine production by four units and increases world cloth production by four units. Simultaneously, transfer three workers in Portugal from cloth to wine. This increases wine production by six units, more than compensating for the reduction in English production of wine, while cloth production falls by only three units, less than the gain in England. In aggregate, the gain is one unit of cloth and two units of wine.

This thought experiment demonstrates the gains from trade. Portuguese workers need not fear being undercut by more efficient English workers, and English workers need not fear cheap Portuguese labour. Both groups can be made better off through specialization (according to comparative advantage) and trade.

It is true, of course, that real wages in each country will depend on absolute productivity levels, and that English workers will be better off than Portuguese workers because they are more productive. If productivity levels in Portugal increase, then workers in Portugal will earn higher real wages. Regardless of absolute productivity levels, however, both sides can gain from trade.

The Ricardian model of comparative advantage is a very simplified view of the world. It ignores the costs associated with moving workers from one industry to another, which may be substantial. It also assumes away complications created by imperfect competition and increasing returns to scale. Nevertheless it illustrates powerfully the most important idea in trade policy: there are gains from trade.

An implication of the theory of comparative advantage is that countries trade with each other because they are different. If the nature of production and demand were the same in each country, there would be no comparative advantage because the opportunity cost of each good would be the same in each country. There are several reasons why production possibilities are different in different countries. Most importantly, different countries have different basic resources or factor endowments. Also, climate, education levels, consumer tastes, and technology all contribute to differences in comparative advantage across countries. Thus, the theory of comparative advantage explains why Canada might export forest products to Japan and import coffee from Brazil.

8.2.2 Comparative Advantage, Competitive Advantage, and the Exchange Rate

In policy debates one often hears the terms "competitive advantage" and "competitiveness."[2] From the point of view of an individual firm, having a competitive advantage means being able to produce a product of given quality at a lower cost than its international rivals. It is less clear what a national competitive advantage might be, and it certainly does not follow that policies that would make firms more internationally competitive are necessarily in the national interest.

The most obvious way for a firm to improve its competitive advantage is to lower its costs directly by paying lower wages and lower taxes. While the firm itself would certainly benefit from such cost reductions, it would not necessarily be good for the country as a whole. We could always be more competitive by lowering real wages, but the cost would be a lowered standard of living. Similarly, firms would be more competitive if they did not have to pay taxes, but that would mean giving up the socially provided services that those taxes pay for. Arguments that Canadian policy should do something to offset the competitive advantage of relatively low-wage or low-tax countries such as the Philippines or Mexico are highly questionable.

An alternative way for a firm to become more competitive is to improve its productivity. This might come about from having more productive workers, a more stable and predictable political environment, better infrastructure (roads, communications systems, etc.), or other sources. A competitive advantage that derives from increased productivity is in the national interest. In fact, high productivity is precisely what allows Canadian workers and citizens to have high wages and high standards of living.

Perhaps the most important short-run influence on competitive advantage is exchange rate movements. The exchange rate is the rate at which one currency can be exchanged for another. In this book we refer to the exchange rate as the foreign currency price of a unit of domestic currency. For example, if one Canadian dollar can be exchanged for 73 cents of U.S. currency, then the exchange rate is U.S.$0.73. When an exchange rate appreciates, it means that the foreign currency price of the domestic currency is rising. For example, if the Canadian dollar were to rise from U.S.$0.73 to U.S.$0.80, we would say that the Canadian dollar had appreciated. Conversely, if the value of the Canadian dollar fell to U.S.$0.70, we would say that the dollar had depreciated, or the exchange rate had fallen.

An appreciation of the exchange rate increases the purchasing power of the domestic currency on world markets. It is therefore good for consumers, especially if they are planning foreign vacations. However, an increase in the exchange rate also tends to reduce the competitive advantage of Canadian producers. The Canadian firm requires a certain price, in Canadian dollars, to cover its Canadian dollar costs. If the value of the Canadian dollar rises, that price translates into a higher foreign currency price than before. This makes it easier for foreign producers to undercut the Canadian producer.

Consider the following example. Suppose a producer of Canadian plywood can produce one standard-sized sheet of plywood for C$5. If the U.S. exchange rate were 70 cents, then a price of U.S.$3.50 would cover these costs. Suppose now that the Canadian dollar rose in value to 80 cents. In order to cover costs of C$5, the firm would now have to earn U.S.$4 in the U.S. market, making it more vulnerable to U.S. competition.

Short-run movements in the exchange rate are influenced by many factors, including a variety of government policies. In the long run, exchange rate movements reflect comparative advantage. Consider the example of England and Portugal described above, and suppose that initially England could produce both wine and cloth more efficiently (in labour time) than Portugal. Suppose further that at the initial exchange rate England was able to sell both wine and cloth more cheaply than Portugal. In other words, a Portuguese importer could take escudos (the Portuguese currency), exchange them for British pounds, buy British wine (or cloth) and save money over what it would have cost to buy the wine or cloth in Portugal.

Such a situation could not persist. This process of buying British pounds with Portuguese escudos would bid up the price of English pounds (as measured in escudos). The appreciation of the pound-escudo exchange rate would continue until importing English wine into Portugal was no longer profitable, and wine would begin to be exported from Portugal to Britain instead. In the long run, the exchange rate will adjust so that domestic producers of the good in which a country has a comparative advantage have a competitive advantage over foreign rivals in world markets.

If Portuguese productivity were to improve drastically, so that Portuguese firms could undersell British firms in both wine and cloth, the exchange rate would eventually have to adjust, with the higher levels of Portuguese productivity being reflected in an appreciation of the Portuguese currency. This appreciation would mean that Portuguese workers could then buy more goods on world markets: they would experience an increase in their real wages.

One problem with exchange rates, which we will not go into in any detail here, is that short-run fluctuations can temporarily create a competitive disadvantage in some industry where a country has a long-run comparative advantage. There is often pressure on governments to do something to protect the industry in question. The cause of a temporary loss of competitive advantage is usually related to domestic monetary stabilization policy, and that is where the solution should be sought.

On balance, it is reasonable to be concerned about competitiveness at the national level, as long as we keep in mind that competitiveness is not an end in itself but is desirable as a way of increasing living standards. If we become more competitive as a result of productivity improvements, then living standards will rise, but there is no point in trying to become competitive by lowering living standards.

8.2.3 Increasing Returns to Scale

Ricardo's reasoning assumes constant returns to scale. If labour is the only factor of production, this means that output per worker stays the same no matter how much output is produced. More generally, with many factors of production we say there are constant returns to scale if a proportionate increase in all inputs yields the same proportionate increase in output. Real production processes, however, are often characterized by increasing returns to scale, which means there are advantages to producing large quantities of output. At the level of the individual firm, increasing returns to scale are reflected in an average cost curve that is downward sloping: average cost falls as output rises, at least up to some limit.

Not all production processes have increasing returns to scale, but many do, especially those with large overhead or fixed costs. For example, it is frequently argued that automobile production has increasing returns because of the high costs of getting the assembly line set up for a particular model. Once the assembly line is set up and calibrated, it is relatively easy to produce additional cars. Thus, good performance in automobile production requires long production runs. The production of electric power is another industry with substantial economies of scale.

The presence of increasing returns to scale is an additional cause of international trade. Furthermore, the presence of increasing returns to scale expands the gains from trade. Consider a small country, such as Chile. Left to itself, such a country could not economically produce certain goods, such as jet aircraft and mainframe supercomputers, both of which have very substantial increasing returns to scale. The market size of Chile is small enough so that only a small demand for either of these products exists. Therefore, if such goods were produced they would be produced at very high average cost. Now introduce a second country, Argentina, which we will assume is similar to Chile. If one firm were to produce jet aircraft for both markets, it would achieve a lower average cost than in the autarky case. Thus, incentives would be created for a firm in one country to produce jet aircraft and export some of its production to the other country. The same point applies to mainframe supercomputers.

In the real world, both Chile and Argentina take part in a much larger trading community and neither produces jet aircraft or mainframe supercomputers, but both countries benefit by being able to import such products from low-cost producers in other countries. The point is that increasing returns to scale implies that there are advantages to specialization and trade, even if countries are very similar. Increasing returns to scale is therefore an important cause of trade. A dramatic illustration of the importance of increasing returns to scale is provided by the Canada-U.S. Auto Pact of 1965.

The Auto Pact is an agreement or treaty between Canada and the United States creating free trade in automobiles, at the wholesale level, between the two countries. Before 1965, when the Auto Pact came into effect, Canadian automobile production was protected by tariffs: special taxes were levied on imports of automobiles. The result was that the major automobile producers, General Motors, Ford, and Chrysler, produced full model lines in Canada. Given the comparatively small Canadian market size and the correspondingly short production runs, Canadian automobiles were produced at a high average cost. After the Auto Pact, Canadian auto plants specialized in a few models that were produced for the entire North American market. Other models were imported from plants in the United States. The net effect was a significant decline in the real price of cars for Canadian consumers, increased profits for the firms, and higher real wages for workers. Furthermore, automobiles have become Canada's leading export and leading import.[3] In 1999, automotive products accounted for fully 27% of Canadian exports by value and 24% of Canadian imports. (The Auto Pact will be discussed in more detail in Chapter 9.)

The economics of automobile production are very similar in Canada and the United States. It would thus be hard to tell which country had a comparative advantage relative to the other. We normally think that comparative advantage is determined in part by relative factor endowments. Thus, for example, we might expect that countries with large relative supplies of unskilled labour would have a comparative advantage in producing goods that can effectively use a lot of low-skilled labour, and countries with substantial natural resources would have a comparative advantage in resource-based products. However, Canada and the United States have relatively similar factor proportions, so factor-based explanations cannot really explain the advantage of large scale trade in autos between the two countries. This trade between Canada and the United States in automobiles is not based on comparative advantage; it is based on economies of scale.

Figure 8.1 illustrates how increasing returns to scale (or economies of scale) generate gains from trade. Figure 8.1 contains a downward sloping average cost curve. Before trade, the firm is producing low levels of output and suffering a high average cost. After trade, output expands and average cost falls. These declines in average cost may accrue to firms in higher profits, to consumers in lower prices, or to workers in higher wages and salaries.

The result that firms move down their average cost curves after trade liberalization is sometimes referred to as rationalization of the industry. At the practical level, it is important to know where the scale economies arise and how significant they are. Most Canadian economists have emphasized product-specific plant-level scale economies. This suggests that gains do not come so much from having large diversified firms as from longer product runs on the factory floor.

The Auto Pact was viewed as very successful. It proved to be the forerunner of the wide-ranging Canada-U.S. Free Trade Agreement (FTA) of 1988, which in turn was the foundation for NAFTA (including Canada, the United States, and Mexico), which went into effect in 1994.

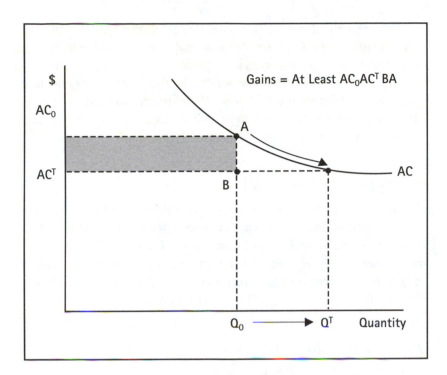

FIGURE 8.1 Economies of Scale and Gains from Trade

8.2.4 Market Structure

One other implicit assumption made in Ricardo's reasoning, in addition to constant returns to scale, is that markets are perfectly competitive. If markets are perfectly competitive, then prices equal marginal cost (as was described in more detail in Chapter 6). Therefore, prices will be high if costs are high, and such goods will be imported if they are produced more cheaply abroad (as they will be if foreign countries have a comparative advantage in this good).

If, however, foreign production is controlled by a monopolist, then it is no longer true that price will equal marginal cost. The price will also include a monopoly mark-up. Thus, the foreign price might even be higher than the domestic price despite the comparative advantage in production enjoyed by the foreign country. The domestic country might, under such circumstances, end up exporting this good. Foreign consumers will then benefit from lower prices arising from higher levels of competition in their markets.

This example illustrates two points. First, market structure (degree of competition) itself influences trade patterns. Second, the consequence of trade is to increase competition, because firms in different countries are induced to compete with each other. Some firms may lose profits in this process, but the more efficient firms will gain and consumers will benefit. The net benefits will exceed the losses to the less efficient firms, leading to additional gains from trade.

8.3 Types of Trade Policy

Having discussed the basic economics of international trade, we are now prepared to discuss trade policy more directly. The next step is to go over the main instruments of trade policy. The most common objective of trade policy is to restrict imports. Such policies are referred to as "protection" because they protect the domestic industry from foreign competition, and they will be discussed next.

8.3.1 Import Restricting Policies

A list of protective policies follows:

1. tariffs,
2. quotas (or quantitative restrictions),
3. government procurement polices,
4. administrative barriers to trade (red tape),
5. other regulations.

Before discussing these policies in detail, it should be noted that most countries also practice export promotion: a policy of encouraging exports. The main tool is subsidization. As will be discussed in Chapter 9, most countries have agreed (under the General Agreement on Tariffs and Trade (GATT), now embodied in the World Trade Organization (WTO)) not to use explicit export subsidies. Nevertheless, many policies are followed that have the effect of export subsidies, including simple production and/or investment subsidies to export-oriented firms and subsidized financing of exports. It is also possible that countries could discourage exports or encourage imports, and they occasionally do. This involves using the same policies that are used for protection or export promotion in reverse.

8.3.2 Tariffs

Definition: A **tariff** is a special tax levied on an imported good or (more rarely) on an exported good.

Tariffs may be expressed in "ad valorem" terms, which means as a percentage of the price, or, alternatively, they may be expressed as specific tariffs, which are fixed sums that are independent of the price, such as $1 per unit. Historically, tariffs are by far the most important type of trade policy. The earliest tariffs no doubt precede the beginning of recorded history, and even today tariffs exercise an important influence on trade flows and government budgets. Tariffs are popular with governments because they raise revenue for the government, and they are also popular with import-competing domestic industries. An important example of tariffs in Canada is in the area of textiles and clothing, where ad valorem tariffs of about 20% are applied to most products originating from outside Canada, the United States, or Mexico.

8.3.3 Quotas

Quotas, or quantitative restrictions (QRs) are fixed limits on imports. Quotas are usually implemented using licences. Thus, for example, a licence may be obtained from the government allowing an exporter to export up to some specific number of units of the good. Quota licences may be sold off to exporters (or to importers), creating revenue for the government, but, more commonly, at least in Canada, quotas are simply given away and therefore generate no government revenue. Import-competing domestic industries tend to prefer quota protection to tariff protection. Quite a few products are subject to both quotas and tariffs.

One interesting special kind of quota is the so-called voluntary export restraint or VER. This is a quota that is voluntarily agreed to by the producers and monitored and controlled by them. In its effect on the consumer, a VER is no different from an ordinary quota. Unlike ordinary quotas, however, VERs cannot raise revenue for the government, nor can they be given to domestic importers. Furthermore, VERs can be a tool to facilitate collusion among exporters. As described by Harris (1985), VERs allow exporters to restrain competition among themselves by, in effect, acting as a cartel agreement limiting the output of each firm. Ries (1993) presents evidence that the 1981 VER on

Japanese automobiles exported to the United States and Canada resulted in significant increases in profitability for Japanese exporters.

8.3.4 Government Procurement

When it comes to government procurement of Goods and Services, most
countries give preference to domestic producers. This means that a
domestic government will give preference to a local supplier, even if a
lower price could be obtained elsewhere. The United States claims that
Canada's federally and provincially owned Crown corporations follow
strong "buy Canada" policies, especially in telecommunications and
transportation. The United States claimed (prior to implementation, in
1989, of the FTA) that the Canadian federal government followed an
informal 10% rule, meaning that a domestic supplier would always be
preferred as long as its price was within 10% of the best foreign price.[4]
Such a policy creates an incentive for domestic suppliers to quote higher prices than they otherwise would. The extent to which preferential
purchasing causes price to rise depends on the level of local competition.

8.3.5 Administrative Barriers to Trade

The term "administrative barriers" refers to the cost of filling in forms,
lining up at customs offices, waiting to get permission to export, and
all the other administrative procedures that make it harder (and more
costly) to export rather than to produce and sell locally. While it is difficult to measure the effects of administrative barriers to trade, many
small business people argue that such barriers are a serious impediment
to trade, especially for Canadian producers hoping to sell in Asia. As
discussed in the next chapter, administrative barriers between Canada
and the United States were substantially reduced by the FTA and its
successor, NAFTA.

8.3.6 Regulatory Barriers

Regulation is discussed in Chapters 14 and 15. Quite frequently, regulations seem to be focused on a nontrade objective, such as making
sure the food supply is safe, or making sure that monopoly power is
not abused, but in fact they often serve to keep foreign products out of
the domestic market. In Canada, this process is most serious in the area

of marketing boards, which are accused of acting simply like producer cartels (see Chapter 15), and which certainly use their power to exclude foreign products.

8.3.7 Interprovincial Trade Barriers

Our discussion of trade policy refers generally to national trade policies pursued by sovereign governments, especially the Canadian government. In Canada, however, provincial governments also carry out policies that affect interprovincial trade and international trade. Strictly speaking, the federal government in Canada has exclusive jurisdiction over international trade policy, so provinces are unable to impose tariffs or quotas. Provinces do, however, use preferential purchasing, administrative barriers, and regulatory barriers in an effort to assist local producers and discriminate against producers from other provinces and countries. Interprovincial barriers to trade are considered by many to be a fairly significant source of economic inefficiency in Canada.

8.4 Normative Reasons for Trade Policy

8.4.1 Overview of Reasons for Intervention

In our discussion of the economics of international trade, the main point of emphasis is that there are gains from trade. The apparent policy implication is that the best policy is a policy of free trade. In other words, countries should not use tariffs, quotas, preferential procurement policies, export subsidies, or other interventions in the business activity associated with international trade. This is, in fact, the prescription made by Ricardo, and this prescription is widely accepted by modern economists.

There are, however, a few complications. First of all, even if we agree that free trade is the best policy for the world as a whole, it does not follow that every country faces a unilateral incentive to avoid trade barriers. In fact, much of the international conflict over trade policy reflects an attempt by one country to gain from interventionist trade policy at the expense of other countries. From the nationalist public interest point of view, it might be normatively defensible to pursue a policy whose principle effect is to transfer benefits from other countries, leading to trade policies of the beggar-thy-neighbour variety.

Second, the prescription that free trade is the best policy does not hold perfectly. Especially in the presence of economies of scale and imperfect competition, there are potential benefits to be obtained from intervention. A list of normative rationales for trade policy follows:

1. raising revenue

2. noneconomic objectives (e.g., military or cultural objectives)

3. monopoly tariff (to exploit monopoly power in world markets)

4. the infant industry argument for protection

5. profit-shifting

6. domestic market failure

7. domestic redistribution

8. retaliation against foreign trade barriers

9. increasing employment ?

10. improving the trade balance ?

Of these 10 reasons for trade policy intervention, the most important politically are the last two, and particularly item 9, increasing employment. It is a rare discussion of trade policy that does not dwell on employment effects. I have, however, put question marks after both the employment and trade balance rationales for trade policy intervention. The reason for the question marks is that most existing evidence and most theoretical analysis suggest that interventionist trade polices do not increase aggregate national employment or improve the trade balance. In other words, most economists would argue that the employment and trade balance rationales for policy intervention are spurious. Each of the rationales for intervention is discussed below.

8.4.2 Raising Revenue

Historically, the most important reason for tariffs, and for trade policy intervention in general, is simply to raise revenue for the government. There is general agreement that governments have some legitimate functions. It follows that these functions must be paid for in some way. Virtually any source of finance has efficiency costs associated with it. For example, personal income taxes reduce work incentives, corporate income taxes reduce corporate activity, money creation creates an inflation tax, borrowing by the government reduces private invest- ment, and so on. Application of the marginalist principle suggests that the appropriate way to raise revenue is to impose taxes in such a way that the marginal efficiency loss is the same on all taxes, including tar- iffs. This will imply positive tariffs.

In practice, most tariffs are above the efficient level from this pub- lic finance point of view. In the past, however, tariffs were a relative- ly efficient form of taxation because collection costs were much lower than for other taxes. It was relatively easy to identify goods coming from overseas, because such goods would come through the dock areas of port cities. The customs official could stand near the dock and col- lect duties as goods came ashore. Collecting income taxes or business taxes was much more difficult, because citizens and businesses would have incentives to lie about their incomes and there was little govern- ments could do about it. Income taxes did not become important sources of revenue until the 20th century.

Nowadays, tariffs contribute only a small fraction (about 3%) of federal government revenue. Tariff revenues contribute nothing to provincial government revenues. Amalgamating provincial and feder- al budgets shows that tariff revenue is less than 2% of total govern- ment revenue in Canada. Over the post-World War II period, trade lib- eralization under GATT has dramatically reduced the importance of tariff revenues for Canada and most other developed countries. The FTA and NAFTA have further reduced tariff revenues in Canada. In many low-income countries, however, tariffs and sales of quota rights remain an important revenue source.

8.4.3 Noneconomic Objectives

National governments can use trade policy to pursue military, cultur- al, or other objectives not directly related to the economic criteria of efficiency, stabilization, or equity. For example, many countries use tariffs and quotas to protect a domestic steel industry for military reasons, and in Canada trade policies are used to promote Canadian culture.

8.4.4 The Monopoly Tariff

The monopoly, or so-called optimum, tariff refers to the idea that
countries might be able to exploit monopoly power in world markets.
Consider, for example, Brazil's position in the world coffee market.
Brazil is a large enough producer to affect the world price of coffee; if
Brazil has a very good crop, world prices fall. Each individual producer, however, is much too small to have any influence on world prices.
Therefore, individual producers are perfect competitors, and, in the
absence of government intervention, would not earn any monopoly
profits from the world coffee market. If, however, the government
imposed an export tariff on coffee, it would raise the world price
toward the monopoly level, and the government would earn monopoly
profits from the tariff revenue.

Similarly, if a country were a large enough buyer of a particular
product, it could use an import tariff to take advantage of its market
power. Obvious opportunities to use a monopoly import tariff are not
very numerous, but opportunities for export tariffs are fairly common.

Nevertheless, monopoly tariff arguments are rarely heard in political discussion, even in private, and they are never heard in public
political debate. The reason is that export tariffs are not very well
received by producers, since they (the producers) do not benefit directly and in fact may lose. Producers would prefer a policy of quantity
restrictions, without export taxes, so that they earn the monopoly
rents. Since producer groups are effective special interest groups, supply restraint is more common than export tariffs.

8.4.5 The Infant Industry Argument for Protection

While the revenue-raising motive for tariffs is probably as old as the
institutions of government and international trade themselves, the
infant industry argument is also rather venerable. In Canada, for
example, it was used in the early days following Confederation to justify the national policy of high tariffs against U.S.-manufactured
goods. The argument for infant industry protection runs as follows: in
general, free trade is the best policy. A country might not, however, be
able to achieve its natural comparative advantage, especially if other
countries are already well established in the relevant industries. For
example, Canada might potentially be a successful producer and

exporter of high-technology computer hardware, but, forced to compete with U.S. giants such as IBM, Hewlett-Packard, and Apple, the Canadian industry might never have a chance to get going. A potential entrant must be prepared to suffer large losses while it trains its labour force, acquires a consumer base, and so on.

The infant industry argument suggests, therefore, that such industries be given protection in their early years, or infancy, to allow them a competitive advantage in the domestic market until they can compete internationally. It is argued that Japan has followed a successful infant industry policy in areas such as consumer electronics and semiconductors.

This argument is related to the concept of learning by doing, which refers to the idea that, for some types of production, experience is important in improving productivity. This certainly sounds persuasive. We all know that it takes time for a firm to become efficient and profitable. If we know it, however, bankers, investors, and entrepreneurs know it too, and if computer hardware is a potentially profitable industry for Canadian firms, investors should be willing to accept short-term losses in return for long-term gains. Private financial markets exist precisely for the purpose of providing financial support for firms with good investment opportunities. If it can be argued that private financial markets are not doing their job, that there is some market failure in financial markets, then infant industry protection might be appropriate. The point to be emphasized is that there must be some market failure for the infant industry argument to make sense. The infant industry argument is really a special case of the domestic market failure rationale for intervention.

The other possible market failure justification (aside from imperfect financial markets) for the infant industry argument is based on positive externalities. Suppose that the domestic country has a potential comparative advantage in some industry. Suppose further that there is no labour with the appropriate skills and that if one firm did train workers, they would soon quit to start their own firms. Thus, any firm would confer on other firms benefits that it could not capture itself. In such a situation the industry might never get going, although if it did get going to the extent that a large skilled workforce was available, then many firms could survive. It might be reasonable to get the industry started using an infant industry tariff.

One practical problem with the infant industry argument for protection is that there are currently some very old infants around, and some industries that are in their second childhood. Even a very good set of policy analysts in government will not pick winners 100% of the time, and it must be expected that some attempts at infant industry protection will not be successful. The problem is that it becomes politically very difficult to abandon an industry that needs protection to survive. The cost of supporting industries that pass from infancy to old age without any intervening period of maturity must be set against the benefits of any successes.[6]

8.4.6 Profit-Shifting

The profit-shifting argument for interventionist trade policy focuses on the presence of imperfect competition in international markets. The basic idea is that government policy can be used to increase the domestic share of the above-normal profits that may be available in imperfectly competitive industries. An argument along these lines was made by the NDP government of British Columbia in the early 1970s in connection with the automobile insurance industry.

The government argued that foreign-owned automobile insurance companies were making large profits that should be retained in British Columbia. The provincial government decided to exclude private firms from the market and set up a Crown Corporation to provide auto insurance. Subsequent events suggested that the auto insurance business was (and is) very competitive, with little in the way of above-normal returns. The principle of trying to capture excess profits is, however, not unreasonable.

The simplest case of profit extraction involves imposing tariffs on imports from a foreign firm with monopoly power. Such a tariff will divert some of the monopoly profits into the domestic treasury. It will also act in part as a tax on consumers, but on balance the country can gain from the appropriately chosen tariff. A more interesting case arises when there is a domestic firm in the market as well, or if there is a potential domestic entrant. The outcome of a tariff depends on the way in which firms interact, but the tariff can be expected to damage the competitive position of the foreign firm, shifting profits from the foreign firm to the domestic one.

In a slightly different form of profit-shifting, profits in world markets are the target. In this case, subsidization of a domestic firm may enhance its competitive position and increase its profits, at the expense of rivals, sufficiently for there to be a net gain to the domestic economy. A simple example (based on descriptions in Brander (1986) and Krugman (1987)) should make the point clear.

Suppose that two countries are capable of producing a particular good. For concreteness, let us call the good 150-seat passenger aircraft and let us call the countries America and France. Also, assume that there is one firm in each country that can produce the good. We will call the firms Boeing and Airbus respectively. Suppose that the internal market for this product is small in both countries, and that most consumption of the product is in other countries (as it might well be for a particular type of aircraft). We can then take the profit earned as the appropriate measure of national benefit from this product for each of the two countries.

We assume that each firm must choose either to produce the product or not. We also assume that the market is profitable for one firm if it is the only entrant, but that the market will be unprofitable if both firms enter and must share the market. The profits or payoffs are shown in the following table. The first number in each cell is the payoff to Boeing (and America), while the second number is the payoff to Airbus (and France).

| | | Airbus | | |
		Enter		Not Enter
Boeing	Enter	-5 -5		100 0
	Not Enter	0 100		0 0

Given this payoff matrix, the outcome is indeterminate. If either firm enters, the other would prefer not to. If, for example, Boeing entered while Airbus did not, then Boeing would earn a return of 100 and Airbus would earn nothing. If Airbus did enter, its return would be -5, so it would prefer not to enter. Similarly, if Airbus enters and Boeing does not, then Boeing would prefer not to enter. What can government policy do? Suppose that the European government offers a subsidy of 10 to Airbus if it enters. The payoff structure becomes as follows.

| | | Airbus | | |
		Enter		Not Enter
Boeing	Enter	-5 5		100 0
	Not Enter	0 110		0 0

In this case, the outcome is clear: Airbus will enter and Boeing will not. The basic reason for this outcome is that the subsidy makes entering a dominant strategy for Airbus. Entering is the best strategy for Airbus no matter what Boeing does. If Boeing enters as well Airbus still earns 5, which is better than the zero it gets if it does not enter. If Boeing does not enter then Airbus gains 110 by entering. Thus Airbus should certainly enter. Knowing that Airbus will enter for certain, Boeing should not enter, for it will lose 5 for certain. Thus, Airbus will earn 110 and Boeing will earn nothing. This policy has insured a net gain of 100 to France (which equals 110 minus the subsidy of 10). Profits have been shifted to Airbus, hence the term "profit-shifting."

8.4.7 Other Market Imperfections and Retaliation

Both the infant industry argument for protection and the profit-shifting argument for policy intervention are based on the presence of market failure. Other possible market failures might also create a rationale for interventionist trade policy. With any market failure, however, the question becomes whether trade policy is the best way of dealing with the problem. For example, if imperfect financial markets are the reason for advocating infant industry protection, many people would argue that it makes more sense to try to improve the workings of financial markets directly.

There is little to say about retaliation. International trade laws allow the use of protection as retaliation in some circumstances. It is much easier for a national government to resist domestic pressures for protection if it can legitimately raise the spectre of foreign retaliation. Thus, the threat of retaliation can be a force that works against protection. In order for retaliation to be taken seriously as a threat, however, it must sometimes actually be used.

8.4.8 Domestic Redistribution

One major aspect of trade policy is that it can be used to redistribute income and wealth within a country. For example, tariff protection for an industry located in region X will tend to raise the income of that region at the expense of other regions. More directly, tariff protection for a particular industry will tend to raise the incomes of people involved in that industry. It is possible that the government might use trade policy with a specific normative intent to redistribute income. Most analysts would claim, however, that trade policy is a very poor tool to use in pursuing redistributional objectives. In recent years it has been argued that increased trade liberalization in the world as a whole has put downward pressure on the incomes of low-skilled workers in high-income countries such as Canada and the United States. These workers are now coming into more direct competition with low-skilled workers around the world. The other half of the argument is that this same trade liberalization has put upward pressure on returns to high-skilled labour in high-income countries.

8.4.9 Employment

Politically, the most important rationale for trade policy intervention is employment promotion. Almost every discussion of trade policy focuses on the employment consequences of the policy under consideration. For example, during the debate in Canada and the United States leading up to ratification of NAFTA, former U.S. presidential candidate Ross Perot became famous for asserting that tariff reductions under NAFTA would give rise to a "giant sucking sound" as jobs and factories moved from the United States to Mexico.

Despite the attention paid to the employment effects of tariff and quota protection, the main conclusion of economic analysis is that protection in the form of tariffs and quotas (or in any other form) tends to decrease rather than increase total employment. In short, the employment argument for protection is spurious.

The conclusion that protection is not helpful in promoting employment is based partly on historical experience. During the Great Depression of the 1930s, many countries increased tariffs in an attempt to protect industries damaged by the decline in business activity. The net effect was apparently to reduce employment further and make the depression worse. Conversely, the trade liberalizations of the postwar period seem to have boosted employment and economic activity.

There are good reasons why protection is likely to be damaging to aggregate employment. First, however, it is important to observe that protection certainly does increase employment in the protected industry. If quotas and tariffs in the textile industry were removed it is probable that many of the workers would lose their jobs. On the other hand, higher tariffs and stricter quotas would expand employment in the industry. The problem is that protection in one industry, such as textiles, is damaging to employment in other industries.

There are at least five reasons why protection for one industry reduces employment in other industries:

1. Because of protection, prices will be higher for the output of the protected industry. This means that industries that use that output as an input for their production will face higher costs and have lower employment. Textiles, for example, are used as an input in the clothing and apparel industry and in various other industries.

2. Because of protection, employment will be higher in the protected industry. Some of this higher employment will simply be in the form of workers bid away from other industries, rather than in the form of workers taken from the pool of unemployed workers. If the industry in question has higher than normal wages, workers might even prefer to wait in an unemployment queue for these high-wage jobs, rather than work in lower-paying jobs elsewhere. (The textile industry is not a high-wage industry but many protected industries are.)

3. Other countries are likely to retaliate, reducing employment in export industries.

4. Even if protection is successful in reducing net imports, there will be adjustments in the exchange rate that tend to induce a corresponding decrease in exports. This is the least obvious but most important reason why protection does not increase aggregate employment.

5. Finally, protection will normally have net economic costs, thereby reducing average living standards. This effect will be small for protection in any one industry, but, to the extent that it occurs, there will be a depressing effect on aggregate economic activity.

For all of these reasons, employment that is created in one industry tends to be offset by employment lost in other industries. The case is not absolutely clear cut, however. It is possible that by protecting very labour intensive industries, while output declines in more capital intensive industries, aggregate employment might be slightly raised. The problem with this policy is that it would reduce average capital intensity in the economy, effectively reducing productivity and real wages.

The main conclusion of this section is that protection can be very effective in redistributing employment among regions or among industries, but it is not likely to increase aggregate employment.

This view of trade liberalization is widely accepted by economists, yet in the aftermath of the FTA (first implemented in 1989), there were many assertions that Canada lost jobs as a result of the agreement, although such assertions died down by mid-1990s. This issue is discussed more fully in Chapter 9.

8.4.10 The Trade Balance

It is sometimes argued that protection can be used to improve the balance of trade (exports minus imports). The first counter-argument is that it is not clear why having a positive balance of trade should be a policy objective. Second, protection will generally not improve the trade balance. Protection will decrease imports, but it will also tend to decrease exports. The balance of trade is determined mainly by considerations other than the cost of imports.

8.5 The Positive Theory of International Trade

Despite the long list of normative reasons for activist trade policy, the conclusion at the end of Section 8.4 is that the case for trade policy intervention is not very strong. Raising a little revenue with the tariff may be appropriate, but the other rationales would apply in at most a small number of cases, and the employment and trade balance rationales are viewed by most economic analysts as spurious. Why then is interventionist trade policy so common and so important? The answer probably lies in the positive analysis of policy.

A positive analysis requires understanding who the gainers and losers are from any policy. Consider the textile industry. The beneficiaries of protection are the workers who are able to keeps their jobs and the owners (shareholders) of firms in the industry. (The owners' interests are represented by the Canadian Textiles Institute.) Furthermore, regions in which this industry is concentrated also benefit from protection.

The losers are harder to identify. Consumers of clothing, which includes all residents of Canada, are certainly losers. They pay higher prices for clothing and other products made from textiles than they otherwise would, and the range of choice is more limited. The consumers most seriously affected by quotas are low-income consumers, because it is the low-quality low-price part of the market where the effects of quotas are most strongly felt. (This results from the fact that suppliers, restricted by a quota, tend to substitute high-price high-value items for low-price items. This is the so-called quality upgrading effect of a quota.) Other losers are people who would have jobs in other industries, particularly export industries, if protection in the clothing industry were reduced. It is hard to identify these people in advance; all we can say for sure is that there would be such people.

Note that there is a major asymmetry between the losers and the gainers from protection. The gainers know who they are, the issue is very important to them, and they are represented politically by well-organized lobbies. Furthermore, the gainers are geographically concentrated and are represented by elected politicians whose major policy objective is to maintain or increase protection in the industry. The losers, on the other hand, are geographically dispersed, so they have no political representation. They are not represented by any organized lobby, and the costs of protection, although very high when added up over all losers, are not all that high for any one consumer, which implies that no single consumer has an incentive to buy airline tickets to Ottawa to lobby for his or her views. Most importantly, the losers do not even know who they are. Certainly, potential beneficiaries from expanded employment in other industries cannot identify themselves; and most consumers are not aware that tariffs and quotas in textiles and clothing even exist, and that they are paying more than necessary for their clothing.

In the 1985 Interim Report of the Clothing and Textile Board, which was supposed to provide objective policy recommendations to Cabinet, there was not one single mention of consumer interests, or of the effects of protection in clothing and textiles on the rest of the economy. Virtually the entire report was devoted to the concerns of producer interests. In 1988 the Clothing and Textile Board was amalgamated into the newly formed Canadian International Trade Tribunal, which does take a more balanced view. In 1990 this tribunal recommended a substantial (28%) cut in tariffs on textile imports.

It is not surprising that the costs of protection exceed the benefits, but the extent of the excess cost is surprising. Costs per job saved in this industry were estimated to be over U.S.$160,000 per job in the

United States and over U.S.\$124,000 in Europe, as of 1980.[7] (To convert to year 2000 dollars, these figures can be approximately doubled.) Hazeldine (1981) obtained more modest but still very substantial costs of protection in Canadian textiles.

Trade policy in clothing and textiles is explained very well by the principles of transfer-seeking described in Chapter 5. More generally, trade policy seems to be very responsive to special interest groups. This point will be clearly demonstrated by some of the trade issues discussed in Chapter 9. In addition, trade policy also stems from a general misunderstanding about the so-called general equilibrium effects of trade policy described in connection with the employment rationale. Politicians and individual citizens see that protection can save jobs in any one industry, but there is very little recognition that it reduces jobs in others.

8.6 Bibliographic Notes

The original source on the theory of comparative advantage is Ricardo (1817). Important subsequent developments were suggested by Eli Heckscher and Bertil Ohlin. A sophisticated review of international trade theory is Jones and Kenen (1984) and Grossman and Rogoff (1995). A standard textbook on international trade theory is Krugman and Obsfeldt (1994). The importance of market structure considerations for Canadian trade policy was pointed out by Eastman and Stykolt (1967). Helpman and Krugman (1985, 1989) offer a treatment of increasing returns to scale and imperfectly competitive market structures in international trade, and their implications for international trade policy. A survey of work on market structure and trade policy is Brander (1995). The original analysis of profit-shifting is due largely to Brander and Spencer (1985).

Notes

1. In calculating this number, we have followed the recent Department of Finance practice of not counting earnings on Canadian-owned foreign investment as an export, or Canadian earnings of foreign-owned investments in Canada as an import. If these items were included, exports and imports would exceed 30% of GDP.

2. Michael Porter has contributed to the popularization of the debate over competitiveness with his 1990 book, *The Competitive Advantage of Nations*. Rugman and D'Cruz (1991) discuss Canada's prospects for improved competitiveness and offer a critique of Porter (1990).

3. There is always a practical difficulty in deciding what Canada's biggest export industry (or import industry) is because of aggregation questions. For example, is wheat an industry, or is Number 2 red winter wheat an industry, or is agricultural products the relevant industry? However, even at the broadest level of aggregation commonly used, automotive products are the largest category. Thus, for example, automotive exports exceed forest products and energy products in value.

4. "American Concerns," Office of the U.S. Trade Representative, in Cameron (1986).

5. Peter Morton, "Long way to go before our trade walls tumble," *Financial Post*, September 2, 1991, p. 3.

6. A very interesting attempt to estimate the effects of infant industry tariffs is Head (1994).

7. "Soaked by Protectionists," *The Economist*, September 13, 1986, p. 15.

On-line Sources

One of the most prominent commentators on international trade is Paul Krugman. His writings can be found at: *http://web.mit.edu/krugman/www/*

9
International Trade Policy: Institutions

9.1 Canadian Trade Patterns

As background to any discussion of Canadian trade policy, there are two important facts to keep in mind. Canada trades a great deal, and most of that trade is with the United States. Both of these points were made in Chapter 8. The following table shows, however, that the United States has not always dominated Canadian trade flows to the extent it does now.

TABLE 9.1 Major Canadian Trading Partners 1926–99
Share of Total Trade (Exports plus Imports)

	1926	1955	1970	1985	1990	1995	1999
U.S.A.	49	67	67	75	72	76	80
United Kingdom	28	13	7	3	3	2	2
Japan	0	1	5	5	5	5	3
Other	23	19	21	17	20	17	15

Sources: M.C. Urquhart, and K. Buckley. *Historical Statistics of Canada*, 2nd ed. 1983. Macmillan: Toronto; Statistics Canada, Catalogue No. 65-001; DFAIT pocketfacts economic indicators, (1999).

The relative importance of trade has increased substantially. In 1960, exports accounted for 15% of GDP. In the following years trade grew steadily, so that exports stood at 33% of GDP in 1993. The relative importance of international trade more than doubled over the period of 33 years, which represents a dramatic increase in the openness of Canada's economy. The composition of trade has also changed significantly. As late as the early 1960s, most of Canada's trade was, using the terminology of Chapter 8, comparative advantage trade. Canada exported largely forest products, wheat, minerals, and other products based on Canada's primary resources. Imports were concentrated in finished manufactured products.

As we enter the 21st century, primary product exports are still important, but Canada's trade is dominated by intra-industry trade: two-way trade flows in similar products, particularly automobiles. Table 9.2 shows the composition of Canada's trade flows in 1999.

Table 9.2 Canadian Trade Flows by Product Class, 1999

	Exports	Imports
Automotive products	27%	24%
Industrial goods and materials	15	19
Forest products	12	1
Machinery and equipment	22	34
Energy products	8	3
Consumer goods	3	12
Other goods	13	7
Total	100%	100%

Source: Statistics Canada, Catalogue No. 65-001P; Department of Finance.

The striking point about Table 9.2 is that the largest export category, automotive products (mostly automobiles), is also a very large import category. About one-quarter of Canada's trade involves exporting and importing automotive products, mostly two-way flows between the United States and Canada.

Although this chapter is primarily about trade, it should also be noted that investment flows are very important. Investment flows include direct investment, as when a foreign corporation builds a factory in Canada, and they also include portfolio investment, as when a foreign corporation or individual buys bonds issued by a Canadian company or a government. Both inward and outward investment flows are very significant for Canada. Investment flows are discussed more fully in Chapter 17.

With this background in mind, we now proceed to an examination of trade policy institutions. Section 9.2 provides a brief history of trade policy in Canada and elsewhere. Section 9.3 describes the World Trade Organization (WTO) and it precursor, the General Agreement of Tariffs and Trade (GATT). Section 9.4 discusses other international institutions that affect trade policy. Section 9.5 summarizes Canadian trade policy institutions. Section 9.6 is devoted to Canada-U.S. trade relations, and Section 9.7 discusses the North American Free Trade Agreement and its forerunner, the Canada-U.S. Free Trade Agreement. Section 9.8 discusses Canadian immigration policy, and Section 9.9 provides bibliographic notes.

9.2 A Brief History of Canadian and World Trade Policy to 1947

In recent years there has been much discussion of trade wars and the "new protectionism." In fact, however, the current world trading system is, by historical standards, relatively open or liberal. Trade policy has a long history. A reasonable place to start, however, is with the mercantilist philosophy associated with 17th- and 18th-century Europe.

9.2.1 Mercantilism

Mercantilism is the idea that a country is better off if it exports more than it imports. Mercantilism arose from the observation that if a country's exports exceeded its imports, then it would be accumulating whatever asset was used as the means of payment for exports, usually gold. People thought that just as an individual would become better off by accumulating gold, so too would a country. The policy implication of mercantilism was that imports should be restricted through the use of tariffs. This policy implication fitted in rather well with the incentives of monarchs, who found tariffs a very convenient way of raising revenues to support their opulent lifestyles. In fact, kings, queens, and princes had been using tariffs in this way long before they heard of mercantilism.

Although the doctrine of mercantilism has a certain appeal, and has surfaced regularly in modern policy debates, it was essentially misguided and tended to make countries worse off, not better off. In the first place, not all countries could simultaneously export more than they imported, since total imports must equal total exports for the world as a whole. The attempt by each individual country to run a trade balance surplus doomed some countries to policy failure. The main effect of mercantilism was simply to reduce trade. All countries, including those following successful mercantilist policies, bore the opportunity costs of foregone gains from trade.

Another problem caused by successful mercantilist policies of the 17th and 18th centuries arose from the fact that gold is not a productive asset. A successful mercantilist country would export productive materials and accept gold in exchange. The gold would then sit in vaults in the possession of private citizens or the state. The individuals who owned the gold would be well off, but the gold itself did not produce anything. Unless the gold was used to finance new investment through financial intermediation, the holding of gold inventories created a net deadweight cost to the society at large. The most successful mercantilist nation of the 16th, 17th, and 18th centuries was Spain, and, perhaps as a result, it experienced slower economic growth and slower improvements in living standards than other European nations.

9.2.2 The British and U.S. Experience

In Britain, Adam Smith's (1776) *Wealth of Nations* and the early 19th-century work of David Ricardo did much to dispel the prevailing wisdom of mercantilism, and had a major effect on policy. Protection, as measured by the average import duty (total tariff revenues divided by the total value of imports), peaked in Britain at over 50% in the 1820s and fell to just under 10% by 1870, where it stayed until 1929.[1] The Great Depression of the 1930s was associated with a rise in tariff protection among most trading nations. In Britain the average import duty had risen to about 45% by 1940.

The U.S. average import duty peaked at about 70% in 1813, reached a low of just over 10% in the mid 1920s, and rose sharply as a result of the Smoot-Hawley tariff of 1930. The Smoot-Hawley tariff rates averaged about 60% on those items that had tariffs, although the overall average import duty rose to only about 20%, partly because the tariff was so high on many goods that imports stopped altogether and therefore generated very little revenue.

The Smoot-Hawley tariff was a policy reaction to the Great Depression, which had begun in earnest in 1930, following the stock market crash of 1929. The objective of the Smoot-Hawley tariff was to protect American jobs. Imports fell, but so did exports, for reasons discussed in Chapter 8. Many other countries also adopted high tariffs in response to the Smoot-Hawley tariff, and international trade fell sharply. The Smoot-Hawley tariff is thought by most international economists to be one of the great policy mistakes of U.S. history. Although it was a very popular piece of legislation at the time, for it seemed to promote employment, it was a major reason for the depth and length of the Great Depression.

9.2.3 Canadian Trade Policy History

Canadian trade policy history begins at Confederation in 1867. The major trade policy issue of the time was whether Canada should enter into a free trade agreement with the United States. Prior to Confederation, the United States had a reciprocity agreement establishing free trade in primary products with the British North American colonies that became Canada, but the United States had withdrawn from the agreement in 1866. After Confederation, the Canadian government, under Conservative Prime Minister Sir John A. MacDonald, tried to negotiate a limited free trade agreement with the United States to cover primary products and a substantial group of manufactured articles. These negotiations failed because the United States was unwilling to extend any agreement to include Britain, which Canada insisted on.

In something of a policy reversal, MacDonald then developed the so-called National Policy, which passed into law in 1879, establishing high tariffs in the manufacturing sector. The intent of the policy was to promote development of Canada's manufacturing sector along the lines of the "infant industry" rationale described in Chapter 8. In addition, the policy was intended to strengthen East-West links in Canada as part of the extension of Canada to include the Western provinces and territories.

After 1879, both Liberal and Conservative governments continued trade policy negotiations with the United States. In 1911, the Liberal government of Sir Wilfred Laurier concluded a free trade agreement with the United States. Much of the support for this agreement came from Western Canada, where farmers and other primary producers were upset about having to pay high prices for Canadian-produced machinery rather than being able to buy lower-cost goods from the

United States. Also, the newsprint and forest products producers from the West wanted free access to the U.S. market.

The 1879 National Policy of high tariffs was successful in that it achieved its two main objectives. It did foster a domestic manufacturing industry, mostly in Quebec and Ontario, and it did increase East-West economic interaction. However, the manufacturing industry was largely of the branch plant type: a U.S. producer would establish a branch plant in Canada so as to "jump" the tariff wall and serve the Canadian market. These small-scale branch plants were not able to realize economies of scale and were not competitive in world markets. Canadian workers had correspondingly lower real wages than their U.S. counterparts, and potential gains from trade were lost. As is described in the following discussion of GATT and the WTO, high tariffs on industrial goods were gradually reduced during the post-World War II period as a result of multilateral trade negotiations sponsored by GATT.

As a result of acrimonious debate in Parliament, the Liberals were forced to call an election before the trade agreement could be passed into law. The election was fought mainly on the free trade issue, with the Conservatives running on the slogan "No truck or trade with the Yanks." The Liberal party lost the election, ending prospects for a U.S.-Canada free trade agreement for the immediate future.

During the Depression, Canada, like most developed countries, adopted higher tariffs. During the 1930s, the British Preferential Trading System established reciprocal tariff preferences between Canada and Britain. Prior to this Canada had allowed British goods into Canada at preferentially low rates, but these preferences had not been reciprocated. Canada's average import duty had peaked at about 30% in 1879, fell in the 1920s, and peaked again at just under 20% in 1932.

One other important development of the post-war period was the rise of the multinational corporation (MNC). MNCs now play a major role in international trade, finance and investment.

9.3 The WTO and the Multilateral Trading System

9.3.1 A Brief History of GATT: Precursor to the WTO

The present-day multilateral trading system, of which Canada is a part, is based primarily on the WTO, which has its origins in GATT. GATT was originally drafted and signed in 1947, and can be viewed primarily as a reaction to the costly trade wars of the 1930s, and partly as an aid to the reestablishment of commercial relations among the nations emerging from World War II. At the time, GATT was thought to be a temporary device to assist in trade liberalization, pending the formation of a permanent international agency for regulation of international trade, to be called the International Trade Organization (ITO). However, the charter of the ITO was never ratified by the governments of the major participating countries. Instead, an elaborate set of institutions associated with GATT gradually developed on an ad hoc basis, including GATT dispute resolution panels, the GATT secretariat, and various other components.

Thus, from 1947 until 1994, GATT was both an international agreement and an international institution. It had a physical presence in the form of a small permanent secretariat in Geneva. As an agreement or contract among the countries involved (which were referred to as the contracting parties), GATT provided (and still provides) a common set of rules for the conduct of international trade in goods. However, GATT had two other important functions. First, it provided an independent forum for the monitoring, discussion, and settlement of trade disputes, and, second, it served as a sponsor for multilateral negotiations on trade policy.

GATT's role in settling trade disputes between disputing pairs or groups of countries was not supported by any enforcement machinery, but the decisions of GATT panels had a certain moral authority, reflecting GATT's history of relatively impartial and well-reasoned verdicts. GATT was a convenient mechanism for taking trade disputes out of a domestic political environment, where self-interested business and labour representatives and opportunistic politicians are dominant and where foreign interests are unrepresented and frequently misunderstood.

The most important aspect of GATT, however, was its contribution to multilateral trade negotiations. These negotiations have been conducted in a series of "rounds," eight of which have been completed. The most recent, known as the Uruguay Round, began in 1986 and was formally completed in April 1994. All of the GATT negotiations have been built around two major themes or principles: nondiscrimination and trade liberalization. The nondiscrimination principle is that each country should have a unified (i.e., nondiscriminating) structure of tariffs with respect to all other GATT countries. The first two GATT rounds, held between 1949 and 1951, focused on trying to get each country to reduce tariffs on imports from participating countries down to the level of tariffs then in force for the most favoured nation. The net effect was to substantially lower tariffs.

Further rounds then focused on promotion of trade liberalization (reduction of trade barriers) generally. The most successful of these rounds was the sixth round, known as the Kennedy Round, held from 1964 to 1967. The Kennedy Round succeeded in obtaining across the board tariff cuts in manufacturing industries that left most Western industrial countries with average tariff duties of only about 7%. If one were to try to pick a particular ending date for Canada's National Policy of protection in manufacturing, the date at which the Kennedy Round negotiations were completed would be a good candidate.

The seventh round of negotiations, the Tokyo Round, stretched over the period 1973 to 1979. The Tokyo Round achieved a further reduction of tariffs, which was phased in over the period 1980 to 1986, reducing average tariff rates in manufacturing to about 5%. The main objective of the Tokyo Round, however, was to reduce or restrict non-tariff barriers to trade. Only modest success was achieved.

The Uruguay Round proved to be the most difficult. The most divisive issue related to trade in agriculture. Agriculture was explicitly omitted from earlier GATT agreements, largely because several countries, including members of the European Union (EU), subsidized agriculture heavily for political and social reasons, and resisted having these subsidies cut. In the early stages of GATT, the United States had also wanted to omit agriculture for domestic political reasons. Since GATT rules out export subsidies, bringing agriculture under normal GATT rules would have required major changes in the agricultural policy of the EU, the United States, Canada, and other countries. By the time of the Uruguay Round, Canada and the United States were prepared to make such changes and argued strongly for including agriculture under GATT rules, while the EU still resisted. The agenda for the Uruguay Round also included intellectual property rights and trade in services. Nontariff barriers were also under consideration again, since little progress had been made in the Tokyo Round. The Uruguay Round was supposed to be completed by the end of 1990, but it went through a series of postponements and extensions and stretched on for several more years. Substantive negotiations concluded with agreement in December 1993, and the new Uruguay Round Agreement was signed in April 1994 in Marrakesh, Morroco, marking the formal conclusion of the round.

In the end, the Uruguay Round achieved more than had been anticipated. Most significantly, the Uruguay Round Agreement created a major new international organization, the WTO. This organization is similar to what had been envisioned for the ITO in 1947, albeit almost 50 years late. Only 23 nations had signed the first GATT agreement in 1947, and only eight of those nations had implemented GATT when it first went into effect on January 1, 1948 (although the others soon followed). By the time the Uruguay Round drew to a close in 1994, GATT had 125 members (or contracting parties), all of whom signed the Uruguay Round Agreement.

Getting international agreement among the negotiators representing the member countries was difficult, but was not the end of the story. In most member countries, the agreement then had to be ratified by domestic legislatures and the agreement had to be proclaimed by the government before it could go into effect for that country. This was where the charter for the 1947 ITO had failed. This time, however, all aspects of the Uruguay Round Agreement were ratified by the United States, Canada, and most other major trading nations. Implementation of the Uruguay Round Agreement, including the WTO, went into effect as scheduled on January 1, 1995. By this date, 75 countries out of the 125 who signed the Uruguay Round Agreement had ratified it and were full-fledged members of the WTO. As of November 1999, full membership in the WTO was up to 135 countries.

9.3.2 Structure of the WTO and its Relationship to GATT

The WTO supersedes or takes over all institutional aspects of GATT. GATT is now just an agreement; it is no longer an institution. In essence, the GATT panels, GATT secretariat, GATT personnel, etc. have simply been renamed as corresponding WTO bodies.

In addition to creating the WTO, the Uruguay Round included substantial revisions to the GATT treaty, mostly involving further tariff reductions. (Technically, the most current version of GATT is referred to as GATT 1994, to indicate that it incorporates the changes arising from the Uruguay Round, and to distinguish it from the old, pre-1994 version.) The Uruguay Round also gave rise to a series of other agreements, including, among others, the General Agreement on Trade in Services (GATS), an Agreement on Trade-Related Aspects of Intellectual Property Rights (known as the TRIPS Agreement), an Agreement on

Trade-Related Investment Measures (called the TRIMS Agreement), an Agreement on Article VI of GATT (anti-dumping), an Agreement on Subsidies and Countervailing Measures, an Agreement on Agriculture, and an Agreement on Clothing and Textiles.

Thus, the WTO can be viewed as an umbrella organization embracing GATT and a number of other agreements covering a wide range of international issues. In keeping with this umbrella approach, the administrative structure of the WTO contains three governing councils. There is a WTO Council on Trade in Goods dealing with the GATT 1994 Agreement and other agreements relating to trade in goods. There is also a WTO Council on Trade in Services that has jurisdiction over the GATS Agreement, and there is a WTO Council for TRIPS dealing with the TRIPS Agreement. In addition to these three councils, there are various committees devoted to a variety of special issues, such as the Committee on Trade and Environment and the Committee on Trade and Development. Formation of the WTO was also accompanied by a minor upgrading of WTO enforcement power and legal standing (relative to the previous standing of GATT) in member countries.

As previously indicated, the initial 1947 group of GATT signatories consisted of 23 countries. This included Canada and its major trading partners. The 125 countries that signed the Uruguay Round Agreement account for the vast majority of world trade. Significant non-members include China and most members of OPEC (the Organization of Petroleum Exporting Countries). The case of China is particularly interesting because it was one of the original 23 signatories to GATT. However, following the communist takeover in 1949, China abandoned any attempt to meet GATT obligations and its membership was converted to inactive status. At present China is seeking to have its membership in GATT reactivated and to obtain membership in the WTO. This is, however, subject to difficult negotiations over a variety of issues, especially intellectual property rights. In essence, the United States and other countries have argued (with substantial evidence to support the case) that China allows patented and copyrighted material to be readily pirated. These countries insist that China must crack down on this practice before being allowed to resume active status in GATT and obtain membership in the WTO. Alleged human rights abuses in China have also become an issue.

In the past, low-income countries have sometimes been allowed to opt for partial access to GATT; that is, they could enjoy many of the benefits of GATT without having to meet all of GATT's obligations. It could be argued that China should be granted active GATT status and WTO membership on this basis. However, given China's very rapid economic growth and its increasingly important and even aggressive stance in world political affairs, many countries are reluctant to allow China any kind of preferential treatment of this type. On the contrary, they would like to use possible WTO membership as leverage to rein in China's policy agenda.

9.3.3 The Main Features of GATT

Each of the many agreements now incorporated in the WTO contains a long list of articles and subsidiary material. The key elements of the WTO are articulated in the GATT articles, and repeated in the articles of other agreements. Article I of the GATT sets out the nondiscrimination provision, requiring each member of the WTO to grant most favoured nation status to all other members, and prohibiting the development of new preferential trading arrangements. There are some exemptions from the nondiscrimination principle. If a group of nations eliminates tariffs among themselves on substantially all goods, establishing a free trade area or customs union, they are not required to extend the tariff removals to other GATT countries. Some special agreements, such as the Canada-U.S. Auto Pact and the Multi-Fibre Agreement in the textile industry, have received specific exemption, and there is a general exemption for developed countries that wish to provide tariff preferences on imports from low-income countries. It was on the basis of this exemption that Canada for many years imported automobiles from Korea duty free, while maintaining tariffs of 9% on automobile imports from other countries (except the United States). The nondiscrimination principle was the mechanism through which GATT achieved its early success in lowering trade barriers and facilitating world trade.

Article III of the GATT requires that goods from all countries be treated the same as domestically produced goods, once tariffs have been paid. This would seem to imply that nontariff barriers, such as quotas, and administrative barriers are not allowed under the WTO, and this was the intent of the article. In practice, however, nontariff barriers have increased and proved hard to remove during the 1980s. During the first part of the 1990s nontariff barriers have been fairly stable.

Another important feature of GATT is a set of three articles dealing with what is often called contingent protection. Article VI deals with the use of special tariffs (called anti-dumping duties) to offset the effects of dumping, which means selling exports at abnormally low prices. Article XVI deals with the use of special tariffs or duties to countervail the effect of foreign subsidies on exports, and Article XIX (referred to as the escape clause) allows the use of temporary protection to limit imports that are causing or threaten to cause serious injury to domestic producers. Thus, all three of these articles deals with the application of protection that is contingent on some particular event (dumping, subsidies, or serious injury), hence the term "contingent protection." Contingent protection has given rise to considerable conflict among GATT members, and has been used particularly aggressively by the United States. All three of these GATT articles were substantially elaborated in new WTO agreements, as discussed in Section 9.3.5.

9.3.4 The WTO Agreement on Agriculture

Prior to conclusion of the Uruguay Round, one of the weaknesses of GATT was an inability to extend its general principles to all industries. The two most important industries to which general GATT principles did not apply were agriculture and clothing and textiles. In the Uruguay Round, two new agreements were obtained, dealing specifically with these two industries. Formally, these are new WTO agreements, distinct from GATT, but the basic objective is to begin to apply GATT principles to these industries.

Agriculture, which is covered by the Agreement on Agriculture, has long been a major problem in international trade. The difficulty arises from the fact that many countries wish to protect and support domestic agriculture by using tariffs, quotas, and other policy tools to limit foreign access to domestic agricultural markets. In addition, many countries provide direct subsidies to domestic producers. Levels of protection and subsidy in agriculture have been far higher than would be permitted if agriculture had been subject to normal GATT rules. Table 9.2 shows the results of an OECD study that calculated the net subsidy-equivalent transfers to the agricultural sector (incorporating the effect of direct subsidies and protection) in a range of countries.

TABLE 9.3 Agricultural Support, 1992

Country	Total Subsidy Equivalent (1998 C$ billion)	Subsidy per Capita Equivalent (1998 C$)
Australia	2.5	144
Canada	7	530
European Union	250	730
Japan	120	965
New Zealand	0.1	24
Norway	7	1560
Unites States	150	710

Source: *Agriculture Policies, Markets, and Trade* (Paris: OECD, 1993).

As shown by Table 9.3, agricultural support is very substantial. In Canada, for example, agricultural support amounted to about $500 per person in 1992, or about $2,000 for a family of four. Recalling from Chapter 7 that about 3.3% of the Canadian labour force works in agriculture, and noting that the labour-force participation rate in Canada was about 65% in 1992, this implies a net subsidy-equivalent of about $23,000 per person employed in the agricultural sector. Per capita levels of support were even larger in the European Union, Japan, and the United States. Norway actually had the largest per capita subsidies, showing that it is not just the major agricultural nations that subsidize agriculture heavily.

Support for such subsidy programs comes from three main sources. First, the agricultural sector in most countries is a powerful lobby of the type described in Chapter 5. Second, and perhaps more important, there is a strong historically based cultural or social foundation for agricultural support. In Canada, for example, the idea of supporting the family farm has had considerable influence in public policy debate. Finally, having a large agricultural sector is viewed as a form of insurance, in that countries want to ensure a secure supply of food in case of war or natural disaster. This has been a particularly strong influence in Japan and parts of Europe, especially among those old enough to remember the food shortages of World War II.

In order to understand the effects of agricultural subsidies, it is helpful to consider the European Union (EU) first. The EU consists of most of the countries of Western Europe, the largest of which are

France, Germany, Italy, Spain, and the United Kingdom. The EU maintains a policy known as the Common Agricultural Policy (CAP). The CAP[3] is, in essence, a very large subsidy to European, particularly French, agriculture, which guarantees prices for agricultural commodities produced in the EU. Products are purchased by the CAP at these high prices and are then resold on world markets at prevailing market prices, or put in inventory. CAP prices typically run about 100% above world prices for butter and milk products, and close to 50% above world prices for wheat.[4] In addition to the direct cost of CAP, EU consumers also pay much higher prices than necessary for food.

The policy of high guaranteed prices is a subsidy to farmers and encourages high production levels. When resold on world markets, this production causes world prices to fall and reduces the incomes of farmers in other producing countries, such as Canada. In 1986, the United States began a policy of subsidy warfare with the EU (then known as the European Economic Community or EEC), and agricultural prices were forced down further, causing considerable hardship in other countries such as Canada, Australia, New Zealand, and Argentina, while creating a glut of agricultural products on world markets. Most of the period between the 1970s and early 1990s was a period of agricultural surplus, with large inventories being stockpiled in major agricultural nations.

Beginning in the mid-1980s, the United States, Canada, and several other major agricultural producers began a major negotiating effort in GATT to try to reduce agricultural support levels, notwithstanding the strong agricultural lobbies in their own countries. Serious disagreement between these countries and the EU (especially France) brought the Uruguay Round to a standstill on several occasions, but eventually a new agreement was reached. Thus, agriculture is no longer to be exempt from international trade rules.

The Agreement on Agriculture achieved two important objectives. First, all agricultural trade barriers are to be converted to tariff equivalents; then these tariffs are to be significantly reduced over time. Specifically, developed countries are to reduce these tariffs by 36% over six years, and developing countries are to reduce agricultural tariffs by 24% over 10 years. Tariffication of agricultural protection will require the dismantling of important components of Canada's system of agricultural marketing boards. As reported in Ritchie (1994), the initial 1995 tariff equivalents for Canada's major marketing board agricultural products are 192% for eggs, 280% for chicken, 283% for milk, and 351% for butter. These extraordinarily high tariffs indicate just how restrictive the marketing board system has been. Even after a 36% cut these tariffs will still be very high. The second objective achieved by the Agreement on Agriculture is a 20% reduction in direct subsidies to farmers. On the whole, these reforms are much weaker than Canada and the United States had wanted to achieve, but they represent a substantial change over the status quo. Canada's position as of the year 2000 calls for the complete elimination of direct subsidies in agriculture.

As time proceeds, some of the controversy over agriculture may become moot. As pointed out elsewhere in this book (especially Chapter 11), the world is going through a population explosion, and sooner or later food shortage rather than food surplus is likely to become important. Famines in parts of Africa have already become fairly common over the past decade and are likely to become more frequent given the extremely high population growth rates in Africa. Donations from surplus stocks of European and North American agricultural produce have been the main source of aid in responding to these famines, and stockpiles are now substantially lower than a decade ago. More significantly for international food prices, real income growth combined with modest, but still positive, population growth in East Asia, especially China, continues to increase the demand for food products.

9.3.5 Other New WTO Agreements

The other major industry that had been exempt from standard GATT principles was clothing and textiles. The domestic interest group background to protection in the clothing and textile industries has been touched on in Chapters 5 and 8. At the international level, trade policy in clothing and textiles was governed by an agreement, sanctioned under GATT beginning in 1974, commonly referred to as the Multi-Fibre Agreement (MFA).

The MFA was really nothing more than an agreement by the developed countries that dominate GATT to exempt clothing and textiles from GATT principles. The MFA allows countries such as Canada, the United States, and members of the EU to impose high tariffs (between 20% and 25%) and restrictive quotas on imports of clothing and textiles from less developed countries with a comparative advantage in these industries.

The problem arises because most developed countries have entrenched clothing and textile industries, but these industries cannot compete with clothing and textile production in countries like Taiwan, South Korea, the Philippines, Pakistan, and Sri Lanka. As a result, there was strong domestic lobbying to restrict imports of clothing and textiles.

The costs of protection are high in the importing countries; they are even higher in the exporting countries. Clothing and textiles happen to be very good industries for countries in the early stages of industrialization. The Industrial Revolution in Britain was built on these industries, and the industrialization of the Northeastern United States in the 19th century was also centered on clothing and textiles. More recently, Japan did very well in the clothing and textile industries in the early phases of its postwar development, and is now letting the industry wind down as real wages in Japan rise above the level that can be supported by the industry. More recently, Hong Kong has done well in this industry, but Hong Kong's wages are also rising above the level that can be supported.

This is an industry that requires skills, in the sense that a skilled worker can accomplish much more than an unskilled worker, but the skills are acquired fairly quickly and by on-the-job practice (learning by doing) rather than by formal education. The capital requirements are not trivial, but they are not prohibitive, and will allow a resourceful entrepreneur with a few employees to establish a profitable business in a few years. It is the ideal industry for a poor country with an eager and disciplined workforce. This path will be easier for such countries to follow if the MFA is abolished and clothing and textiles come under normal GATT regulations.

The Agreement on Textiles and Clothing concluded as part of the Uruguay Round in 1994 requires that MFA restrictions on trade in textiles and clothing be gradually phased out over a 10-year period. At the end of this period (i.e., in 2005), textiles and clothing will be covered by GATT 1994, and will be treated like other manufactured goods in that they must be free from quotas and subject to, at most, very low tariffs.

The Uruguay Round incorporated several other important new agreements. The TRIPS Agreement represents a success for the strong U.S. efforts to protect intellectual property rights. American producers had complained that a large number of countries, especially in East Asia, allow relatively free copying of books, compact disks, prescription drugs, computer programs, and other items embodying intellectual property, without adequate compensation to the originators of these materials. The new TRIPS Agreement requires that patents and copyrights in these areas be honoured in accordance with specific rules similar to those in force in North America and Europe.

The one area of trade intervention that was increasingly active over the 1990s was contingent protection, described briefly in Section 9.3.3. The problem is that many companies have adopted the practice of bringing forward anti-dumping and countervailing duty cases simply to harass foreign rivals. Such complaints may be made to domestic authorities or to the WTO (formerly GATT) itself. Complaints made to domestic authorities have tended to become highly politicized in a number of countries, especially the United States, leading to decisions that seemed to be based on pure transfer-seeking (as described in Chapter 5) rather than on the merits of the case. Three Uruguay Round agreements seek to reduce these problems by providing clear guidelines on when and how contingent protection can be applied.

One such WTO agreement is the Agreement on Subsidies and Countervailing Measures, which is an elaboration of the Article XVI of GATT. The basic idea of Article XVI and this agreement is that governments are not supposed to offer export subsidies to specific firms or industries. Furthermore, a wide range of other subsidies, even if not directly targeted at exports, are also countervailable. If such subsidies occur, if they are beyond a certain size, and if they actually confer benefits on subsidized firms, then exports from those firms are subject to the application of countervailing action. Such action is normally in the form of a special tariff, referred to as a countervailing duty, levied on the subsidized products. In order for a countervailing duty to be applied, there must be evidence that the subsidy has actually injured or is likely to injure competing producers in the export market. An example of a subsidy or countervailing duty case is discussed in Section 9.8.7 on the Canada-U.S. softwood lumber dispute.

A similar additional agreement is the anti-dumping agreement, officially named the Agreement on Implementation of Article VI of GATT 1994. Article VI allows national governments to retaliate against dumping by imposing special tariffs called anti-dumping duties. Dumping occurs if an exported product is sold in the export market for a price below its normal value. In practice, this is defined to occur if the product is sold in the export market for a price below its cost of production or for a price below its normal home market price. In order for an anti-dumping duty to be applied, the domestic firms that initiate the complaint must be judged to have suffered injury as a result of the dumping. Note that the anti-dumping duties are similar in principle to countervailing duties applied in subsidy cases. The principal difference is that anti-dumping applies to an action taken by foreign firms (i.e., dumping), whereas countervailing duties are to offset an action taken by foreign governments (i.e., subsidies).

These two agreements also put sunset clauses on anti-dumping and countervailing duties. Many countries were particularly concerned about the U.S. use of anti-dumping as long-term protection, in violation of the spirit of GATT. In particular, as of 1994, the United States had about 300 outstanding anti-dumping duties in place, about 10% of which had been in force for 20 or more years![5] European countries have also been active in applying anti-dumping duties and undertaking related actions. Such duties now expire automatically after five years, although they can be renewed after a new investigation.

A related issue is now covered by an Agreement on Safeguards, an elaborated version of Article XIX of GATT. This agreement allows a country to limit imports that cause or threaten to cause serious injury to domestic producers, even if those imports are not dumped or subsidized. In 1986, the United States used its version of the escape clause provision to impose a 35% tariff on exports of Canadian cedar shakes and shingles.

The Uruguay Round also produced agreements on investment and on trade in services. The basic idea is to bring similar principles of nondiscrimination and freedom of movement to investment and trade in services as have been established for trade in goods. These agreements establish certain general principles along these lines, but with a number of important exceptions, including financial services.

Having the agreements in place is important, but the value of such agreements depends very much on the level of institutional support. An important form of institutional support provided by the WTO is in the form of adjudicating tribunals. Countries can make a complaint about another country's trade practices and have the complaint adjudicated by the WTO. In addition, countries can still take unilateral actions again other countries, and these actions may be admissible under the WTO agreements, but policy actions have greater legitimacy if they arise from adjudications within the WTO.

9.3.6 Future of Multilateralism

Some observers have questioned whether multilateral agreements (GATT and the WTO) can achieve any more than they already have. One problem is the expansion in GATT's size from 23 to 132 members. Rather obviously, it is much harder to reach agreement in a group of 132 than in a group of 23. In addition to the pure numbers problem, distinct blocs have emerged among the population of WTO members. Thus, for example, there are a number of issues that divide high-income and low-income countries. Other issues divide North America and Europe, and so on.

The original 23 countries were a comparatively similar group, dominated by the wealthier Western democracies. The effects of trade liberalization are much easier to deal with politically if the liberalization occurs between relatively similar countries. Such reductions in trade barriers allow economies of scale to be realized, and they encourage competition and rationalization within industries. They do not, however, require major changes in the overall industrial structure of a country, and they do not put much downward pressure on the wages of large groups of workers.

On the other hand, trade liberalization between high-wage developed countries, such as Canada and the United States, and low-wage countries with high rates of population growth causes adjustment problems for both groups. This kind of trade puts downward pressure on the market wage of low-skilled workers in the developed countries, for the simple reason that those workers are effectively in competition with the very large supply of low-skilled, low-wage workers in the poorer countries. There are still gains from trade, of course, but they accrue to workers in the developed countries whose skills are scarce in the poorer countries and to owners of other scarce factors of production. Adjustment problems are also created for the low-income countries.

Because of these and other difficulties, the WTO may not be able to make progress on further multilateral liberalization. Partly out of frustration with multilateral negotiations, pairs or small groups of countries (e.g., Canada, the United States, and Mexico; the EU) have undertaken their own negotiations in an attempt to benefit from those trading gains that can be obtained without political and economic disruption. Many people predict that bilateral or small group trading agreements are likely to be the pattern of future trade policy changes, with the world dividing into trading blocs of relatively similar countries or contiguous regions.

As indicated earlier, the Uruguay Round lasted from 1986 to 1994—longer than any previous round and almost twice as long as initially planned. The difficulties in reaching agreement led many observers to predict the demise of the liberal multilateral trading system that has emerged in the latter half of the 20th century. In fact, however, the Uruguay Round Agreement was considerably more far-reaching than initially planned in 1986. Thus reports of the demise of multilateralism proved exaggerated or at least premature. The future is, however, very uncertain. As discussed further in Chapters 10 and 11, an important agenda item for further multilateral negotiation under the WTO is trade and the environment.

9.4 Other International Institutions

In addition to the WTO, there are three other international agencies that have an influence on trade patterns and policy. These are the World Bank, the International Monetary Fund (IMF), and the United Nations Conference on Trade and Development (UNCTAD).

9.4.1 The World Bank

The World Bank and the IMF both arose from the Bretton Woods Conference of 1944. The conference was dominated by the United States and Britain, although 44 allied nations were represented, including Canada. The purpose of the conference was to set up a regulatory system for the conduct of international business in the world that would emerge from the ashes of World War II. The World Bank was set up in 1945, and its basic function was (and is) to provide financial assistance for the development of economically productive projects. The financial capital of the World Bank is obtained partly through contributions by member nations, and partly from borrowing money on international markets. The World Bank is supposed to earn enough revenue to cover its costs and should not require an ongoing subsidy from member countries.

The membership of the World Bank has expanded from 44 to 181 nations (as of 2000). The focus of the World Bank's activities has changed from postwar reconstruction loans to trying to aid in the development process of less developed countries. The World Bank is best viewed as an international development agency.

The World Bank has its headquarters in Washington DC and consists of five related organizations. The original and largest is the International Bank for Reconstruction and Development (IBRD), which borrows and lends money on commercial terms. During the late 1990s it provided about U.S.$18 billion per year in development funding. The International Finance Corporation (IFC) is a second organization, set up in 1956 to promote direct private investment in developing countries, that will take equity positions in some projects. Unlike the IBRD, which makes loans to governments, the IFC provides financing directly to the private sector. The IFC is small compared to the IBRD, and has been providing about U.S.$5 billion per year in project funding. The third organization, set up in 1960, is the International Development Association (IDA), which provides loans on very favourable terms (essentially interest free) for periods of 35 to 40 years. These loans are made to governments in the very poorest countries for financing specific projects. The operations of the IDA provide a net subsidy to poor countries. These subsidized loans were separated from the IBRD loan portfolio so that the IBRD could maintain its overall creditworthiness by normal commercial standards. The IDA was providing about U.S.$8 billion per year in the late 1990s.

The fourth organization is the International Centre for Settlement of Investment Disputes (ICSID), founded in 1966. As its name suggests, it provides facilities for mediating and arbitrating disputes between governments and foreign investors. It is a small operation, dealing with a handful of cases per year. Finally, the most recent addition to the World Bank portfolio of organizations is the Multilateral Investment Guarantee Agency (MIGA), which was founded in 1988. It provides insurance against noncommercial or political risks in low-income countries, and will insure foreign investors against such contingencies as war, revolution, and expropriation. It will insure up to 90% of an investment and also helps governments find potential investors. It too is fairly small. In 1999 it approved 72 new contracts with a total liability of about U.S.$1.3 billion.

As described so far, the World Bank seems to combine the functions of a commercial bank (IBRD), an investment bank (IFC), an insurance company (MIGA), and an arbitrator (ICSID), with some direct foreign aid (IDA) added on. The World Bank does, however, have a policy role, which it has come to exercise more and more as time has progressed. Part of its policy role is to provide skilled supervision of projects. The more important aspect of its policy role is that it will often tie loans to economic policy reforms in the debtor country. For example, the World Bank will often require trade liberalization or a reduction in public sector control in return for a loan. In addition, the World Bank has a substantial research capacity that it exercises on a variety of relevant topics. Much of this research is published through an active publication series.

The organizational structure of the World Bank is much like that of a normal firm, except that its shareholders are the member countries. Countries vote in proportion to their financial contribution to the World Bank's portfolio, with the United States accounting for about 20%.

9.4.2 The IMF

Like the World Bank, the IMF arose from the Bretton Woods meeting of 1944, was formally set up in 1945, and has its headquarters in Washington, DC. It began operations in 1947 with 44 members and, like the World Bank, had 182 member countries by 2000. The basic purpose of the IMF is to support and promote the world trading system by providing relief for short-run balance of payments problems. In addition, the IMF charter contains articles of agreement between the member countries, so, like the WTO, the IMF maintains a set of international agreements.

The most important article of agreement is Article VIII, which requires that member countries maintain currency convertibility for current international transactions. What this means is that each country agrees to allow importers to exchange their local currency for the currency required to buy the product, and to allow exporters to exchange foreign currency for domestic currency at the same exchange rate (apart from transactions costs). In addition, each country stands willing to redeem its own currency at the same market exchange rate from foreign central banks that accumulate it.

For example, the Bank of Canada agrees to provide, at a market exchange rate, German marks to Canadian importers who wish to import German automobiles. In addition, the Bank of Canada stands ready to buy German marks, at (roughly) the same exchange rate. Suppose, for example, that the exchange rate is $0.72 per mark. If the Bank of Canada accumulates an excess of German marks it can then sell them to Germany's central bank (the Bundesbank) for Canadian dollars at the rate of C$0.72 for every German mark.

The importance of currency convertibility cannot be overstated, for without it international trade would be very difficult. In fact, the principal means by which imports are limited in many countries is simply by not allowing importers to purchase foreign currency, or by charging very high rates for foreign currency.

Perhaps the clearest way to see the importance of currency convertibility is to consider trade between two countries that do not maintain convertibility. Suppose that an exporter in Country A has arranged to sell a product to an importer in Country B. The easiest thing for the importer to do is to pay in its own currency. This will be fine for the exporter who can turn around and exchange the currency of Country B for its own currency. If, however, Country B does not stand willing to redeem its own currency, the central bank (and commercial banks) of Country A will not accept it from the exporter, so the exporter will not accept it from the importer. The exporter instead asks for payment in his own currency. If, however, the importer cannot convert his domestic currency into the currency of Country A, then that option is also closed. In the absence of a third currency to transact in, the deal with fall through: the trade will not take place.

The former Soviet bloc countries did not maintain currency convertibility in the past. As a result, no one was willing to hold their currencies, including the other countries in that bloc. Consequently, these countries traded much less than Western countries and had to forego the gains from trade. Most of the trade that did take place among these countries, and between them and the rest of the world, was either barter (directly exchanging, for example, Romanian petroleum for East German steel), or was financed in Western currencies such as German marks, Swiss francs, or even U.S. dollars. At present, the reforming countries of Eastern Europe are trying to establish convertible currencies and market-based trading systems. The extent of progress varies markedly across different countries.

As with the WTO, the IMF has little direct enforcement power. It cannot force members to abide by its articles of agreement. Only about one-third of the member countries actually maintain currency convertibility for current transactions, and only a handful maintain full currency convertibility: allowing convertibility at market exchange rates for any purpose, and allowing domestic residents complete freedom of choice to hold foreign financial assets. Canada and the United States were the first major countries to allow full convertibility following World War II.

The operations of the IMF are, as mentioned, focused on the balance of payments problems of member countries. The basic idea is that a country that is maintaining currency convertibility may occasionally run out of foreign currency. The country would then have to suspend redemption of its own currency in world financial markets, unless it could obtain a foreign currency loan. The IMF makes such loans.

The IMF was set up in connection with the Bretton Woods system of fixed exchange rates. Each country maintained a fixed exchange rate with respect to other countries, so, for example, the British pound was fixed at a value of U.S.$2.80 in the early Bretton Woods period. Occasionally, an exchange rate would be devalued or revalued. The pound, for example, was devalued to U.S.$2.40 in 1967. Trying to maintain a fixed exchange rate between countries with different monetary policies, different inflation rates, and in the face of balance of trade surpluses and deficits was difficult, and the fixed exchange rate system collapsed in 1973. Since then exchange rates between the major Western trading nations have (with some exceptions) been flexible: they are determined by market forces instead of by government decision.

The replacement of fixed rates by flexible rates would seem to reduce the need for developed countries to borrow from the IMF, at least for the purposes of defending an exchange rate. Flexible rate countries do not run out of foreign exchange. If one country needs to buy a lot of foreign exchange, it simply observes that the price it must pay for foreign currency rises in terms of its own currency. That is, its own currency depreciates. Depreciation determined by markets is a substitute for borrowing from the IMF. However, even under the current system, governments do like to manage their exchange rates and may borrow from the IMF on a short-term basis to smooth movements in their exchange rates.

Interestingly, the lending role of the IMF has actually increased in recent years. One reason is that many countries still try to maintain fixed exchange rates (usually in terms of the U.S. dollar), or rates that are pegged and change only occasionally, as determined by the government. Most of these countries are less-developed countries or middle-income countries in Latin America or Asia. These countries still need occasional loans for balance of payments reasons.

The second reason for recent IMF loans is to bail out governments of poorer countries that cannot pay their debts. The IMF intends to get its money back, but it is willing to provide short-term credit to struggling governments. Usually, however, the IMF attaches conditions to these loans concerning the domestic macroeconomic policy and exchange rate policy it expects the country to follow. This is referred to as IMF conditionality.

The use of conditionality can be illustrated by the case of Mexico, which was the IMF's biggest customer in 1995. In late 1994, foreign (and domestic) investors became very concerned about Mexico's rapidly accumulating foreign debt and about domestic economic policy and political events. The Mexico peso had been fixed to the U.S. dollar, but was freed to float in late December. The peso proceeded to fall sharply in value until it bottomed out in March of 1995. Meanwhile, in early 1995, Mexico came to an agreement with the U.S. government, other countries (including Canada), and private commercial banks that created a large exchange stabilization fund. This was not a loan to Mexico, just money that would be available to buy pesos if necessary. In addition, Mexico came to an agreement with IMF under which Mexico would cut government expenditures, establish a budget balance or a small surplus for 1995, restrain the growth of the money supply, restrain wage growth, and take other actions to restore stability. In return the IMF authorized a total loan package of U.S.$8.7 billion, and standby credit of up to U.S.$19 billion. Loan payments were provided in installments, following the achievement of policy targets by Mexican authorities.

Clients in 1999 include countries such as Pakistan, Russia, Thailand, South Korea, Zambia, Brazil and Mali. Like the World Bank, the IMF is controlled by the member countries, who have voting power in proportion to their contributions to the IMF's basic portfolio. The United States is the largest shareholder and has about 20% of the voting power.

9.4.3 The United Nations Conference on Trade and Development

The IMF, the World Bank, and the WTO form a triumvirate that regulates, coordinates, and, to some extent, controls international economic and business affairs. There is one additional international institution that should be mentioned: the United Nations Conference on Trade and Development (UNCTAD). This is the UN's contribution to the coordination of international trade policy. (The UN recognizes and has a loose affiliation with the IMF, the World Bank, and the WTO, but, at the practical level, all three institutions run completely independently of it.) The main point to make about UNCTAD is that it has very little influence on international trade policy. Most textbooks on international trade, international business, or international finance do not even mention UNCTAD.

The reasons for UNCTAD's lack of importance are worth understanding, for they apply to many UN activities. All international agencies, institutions, tribunals, courts, treaties, and agreements suffer from one great defect: they have no sovereign power to support them. If the Government of Canada chooses to levy taxes on textbook royalties, authors of textbooks must pay them or be carted off to jail. The Canadian government has sovereign authority over residents of Canada, and can back up that authority with physical force. International agencies, in contrast, must obtain voluntary compliance. The IMF might decide to impose a tax on member countries, but has no way of requiring payment and very little recourse if payment is not made, short of ejecting a member nation from the IMF, which it is not likely to do.

An international agency can offer financial or other incentives for compliance with its principles, as the IMF, the World Bank, and even the WTO do, and that is where much of their influence comes from. Someone or some country must, however, voluntarily provide the resources that are used to provide incentives. In the World Bank and in the IMF, policies are controlled by those who pay the bills: which, for the most part, is a handful of developed democracies consisting principally of the United States, Japan, Germany, Britain, France, Canada, and Italy, roughly in that order of importance. These countries comply with IMF principles and provide financial support, and that provides sufficient incentive for most other countries to voluntarily comply with IMF policies.

The power in the WTO is more decentralized than it once was and this is causing problems, as described in Section 9.3.6. Even so, bargaining power in the WTO is more or less proportional to economic power. If the United States, with the world's largest market, threatens to leave a negotiation or simply not comply with a regulation, the value of the regulation is much reduced for other countries. If Paraguay or Lesotho makes the same threat, it does not carry much weight. As a result, the principles formulated by GATT and now embodied in the

WTO have been in line with the views of the major trading nations, and these nations have therefore been willing to comply reasonably closely with the WTO principles. Other countries in turn then have an incentive to abide by these principles, so as to have the benefits of access to the markets and productive capacities of the influential countries.

The UN operates, instead, on the one country one vote principle. Needless to say, powerful countries like the United States and China have more influence than smaller countries, but UN and UNCTAD resolutions are dominated by the large number of relatively small low-income countries, and therefore do not have the significance as WTO or IMF articles.

9.5 Canadian Trade Policy Institutions

9.5.1 Responsibility for Trade Policy

Canada was a founding member of GATT and is a leading member of its successor institution, the WTO. Canada was also a founding member of the IMF and the World Bank. Its international policies are generally in line with the principles of these three institutions, and Canada is quite possibly the most scrupulous observer of these principles among major countries. (Even Canada has been found in violation of GATT codes, however, and Canada was a very early defector from the Bretton Woods system of fixed exchange rates.)

The conduct of trade policy in Canada is divided between several parts of government, and has been frequently reorganized in the past. At present, the main responsibility for international trade policy resides in the Department of Foreign Affairs and International Trade (DEFAIT). This department contains two ministers, one for foreign affairs (usually regarded as the more senior minister in the Department), and one for international trade. Important negotiations, such as the Uruguay Round and the North American Free Trade Agreement, are handled by special negotiating teams appointed directly by the Prime Minister's Office. Several trade promotion agencies are constituted under External Affairs, including the Export Development Corporation (EDC), the Canadian Commercial Corporation (CCC), and the Trade Commissions. The EDC and the CCC provide financing for exports, and the Trade Commissions, in cooperation with consulates and embassies, try to assist in market penetration for Canadian exports to foreign countries.

The Department of Finance is also strongly involved in trade policy and has its own International Branch. The Department of Finance has responsibility for setting tariffs. It may seem odd that tariffs are determined by Finance, while other issues are determined by the Department of Foreign Affairs and International Trade, but this reflects the historical importance of tariffs as a source of government revenue. In addition, the Department of Finance also houses the Canadian International Trade Tribunal, which makes final determinations on anti-dumping and countervailing duty cases. Another department, Revenue Canada, actually collects tariff revenue. Revenue Canada also makes preliminary judgements on countervailing duty and anti-dumping cases. The Department of Finance and Industry Canada share responsibility for international investment issues.

The Bank of Canada, through its control of the money supply and international currency transactions, has authority for exchange rate policy and international monetary issues. In addition, various other departments of government, including Agriculture, Consumer and Corporate Affairs (see Chapter 13), Energy, Environment Canada, and others have some jurisdiction over international issues. In fact, the economy of Canada is so open that it is hard to find any major policy area that does not have international implications. International policy is, however, the sole jurisdiction of the federal government. Provincial governments are consulted but have no statutory authority in this area.

9.5.2 Foreign Investment in Canada

Canada is a country with open financial markets as well as open commodity markets. As a result, many foreign individuals and foreign-based multinational firms, particularly from the United States, have invested heavily in Canada. Canadians invest heavily in other countries, especially the United States, and Canadian-based multinationals are very active in other countries. Per capita Canadian foreign direct investment in the United States exceeds per capita U.S. foreign direct investment in Canada. However, the asymmetry in size between Canada and the United States means that U.S. investment in Canada is much more conspicuous than Canadian investment in the United States.

During the early 1970s, concern that foreign investment was compromising Canadian national sovereignty reached a peak, and resulted in the passage of the Foreign Investment Review Act of 1973. This piece of legislation established the Foreign Investment Review Agency (FIRA), which was to review proposed direct foreign investments beyond a certain size, including takeovers, new ventures, and expansions by foreign firms already operating in Canada into new lines of business. The sole criterion for acceptance of investment was that the investment be likely to be of significant benefit to Canada.

Early in FIRA's life many investment proposals were rejected, but by the early 1980s, virtually all proposals were being accepted. Even in this latter period, however, FIRA proved to be a great irritation to foreign investors, mainly because of the paperwork and delays involved in the screening process. In 1984, FIRA was dismantled and replaced by a new agency called Investment Canada. The new agency was associated with a change in orientation and saw its role as being to attract foreign investment, rather than restrict it, although technically its functions included screening foreign investment. Investment Canada accepted virtually 100% of proposed investments. Finally, in 1993, Investment Canada lost its status as an independent agency and was absorbed into Industry Canada, which is a department of the federal government.

Many other countries, particularly low-income ones, have displayed a similarly schizophrenic attitude toward foreign investment. Even in the United States, political figures have expressed concern about Japanese and Arab ownership of U.S. industry. Does foreign investment represent exploitation of host countries, or does it generate net benefits for them? Fear about foreign exploitation has frequently led to various restrictions being placed on foreign investment, or even to outright expropriation. On the other hand, a desire to attract foreign investment has led to competitive bidding, in the form of tax holidays and direct subsidies, by political jurisdictions to obtain foreign investment.

Basic normative economics suggests that foreign investment is good for the host country, but only if the host country manages its tax policy and environmental policy appropriately, for the interests of the foreign shareholders are not the same as the interests of the host country. Subsidy and tax holiday bidding for "footloose" foreign investment is potentially very damaging to host jurisdictions, for they end up conceding the rents associated with their natural resources to foreign shareholders. In Canada, provinces often bid against each other for investments. Within Canada, this should certainly be controlled by the federal government, and at the international level, the WTO could be used to control the process.

This section focuses primarily on Canada's role as a host country for foreign investment. However, it should be emphasized that Canada is also a major supplier of foreign investment to other countries. In general, foreign investment outflows have attracted less public attention and less policy attention than inflows, except possibly in connection with the question of whether outflows of investment amount to exporting jobs. Some institutional lenders, including many pension funds, have restrictions on the amount of foreign investment they can undertake. In general, however, there is relatively little public policy activism directed toward outward investment flows.

9.6 Canada-U.S. Trade Relations

As has been indicated several times, Canada's most important trading partner is the United States. Therefore, Canada-U.S. trade relations are a very important part of Canadian public policy. The early history of Canada-U.S. trade relations has been outlined in Section 9.2. The early postwar period is subsumed in the development of GATT. Canada and the United States, as part of multilateral tariff reductions, lowered tariffs on each others' exports, resulting in a considerable expansion of trade between the two countries.

In 1965, Canada and the United States signed a special bilateral agreement, sanctioned under GATT, known as the Auto Pact. The Auto Pact removed tariffs and quotas on wholesale flows of North American-made motor vehicles and motor vehicle components, subject to certain safeguards requiring that Canadian production be at least equal to Canadian sales in the industry. As discussed in Chapter 8, this agreement generated substantial gains from trade, since each country was able to specialize in particular models and realize greater economies of scale. A current issue is whether, and how, to bring Japanese manufacturers who have set up plants in North America into the agreement.

FIRA was an irritant to Canada-U.S. trade relations, as was the National Energy Policy (NEP) of the late 1970s, which had as an objective the Canadianization of the energy industry, and induced several U.S. firms to sell out on what they felt were unfavourable terms. In 1985, the Royal Commission on the Economic Union and Development Prospects for Canada, under the direction of former Liberal cabinet minister Donald Macdonald, published a very influential report. The major recommendation of the report was that Canada seek a free trade agreement with the United States. Studies cited in the report indicated that Canada could expect substantial economic benefits from free trade with the United States.

Canada and the United States subsequently began a comprehensive set of bilateral negotiations aimed at substantially reducing trade barriers between the two countries. Within Canada, there was considerable debate over the desirability of a free trade agreement. There could be very little argument against the idea that economic gains from trade would result from freer trade with the United States. The most frequent objection was the claim that freer trade and the resulting increased economic integration between the United States and Canada would compromise Canadian sovereignty and/or Canada's national cultural identity. In addition, concern was expressed that the transition would be costly, dislocating large numbers of workers. Some people also objected that a bilateral agreement would undermine the multilateral trading system with the result that Canada would be placing all its eggs in one basket, the United States.

Proponents of free trade pointed out that the trade liberalization undertaken through GATT and via the Auto Pact over the 1950s and 1960s was far more substantial than the likely outcome of the 1986-87 free trade negotiations, and that these trade liberalizations increased economic welfare in Canada without reducing Canada's cultural identity or national sovereignty, and without imposing large transition costs on the economy. If anything, Canada's national identity was greatly strengthened in this period.

The long-standing free trade agreement between Ireland and the United Kingdom, and more recent free trade agreements in the EU and between Australia and New Zealand seem to have done nothing to undermine the political, cultural, and social independence of the participants. In Europe, this is regarded as something of a disappointment, since it was hoped by many that the EU would lead to much closer social and political harmony in Europe. National identities and nationalism generally have proved to be very robust.

The negotiating teams for Canada and the United States were able to conclude the Canada-U.S. Free Trade Agreement (FTA) in late 1987, and it was signed by Canadian Prime Minister Mulroney and U.S. President Reagan on January 2, 1988. Before the agreement became law, however, it had to be ratified by the Canadian Parliament and by the U.S. Congress. Ratification in the U.S. Congress was relatively straightforward, but Canadian ratification turned out to be more difficult.

The majority Conservative government in the House of Commons was able to pass the Canada-U.S. FTA, of course, but the (appointed) Senate was still dominated by Liberal appointees from previous Liberal governments. The Senate, which has the power to block legislation, refused to ratify the agreement without an election being called. The Prime Minister called an election for November 1988 and the resulting election campaign was devoted principally to the question of FTA ratification. Both the Liberals and NDP took positions against the FTA. During the campaign, elections polls and the stock market moved dramatically, as shown in Figure 9.1.

Stock market movements were closely related to the reported popularity of the Conservative Party, suggesting that investors, at least, believed that the FTA would generate economic benefits, although other concerns may also have contributed to these stock price movements. The Conservatives eventually won the election with a comfortable majority of seats, and the Senate dutifully passed the FTA, which went into effect on January 1, 1989.

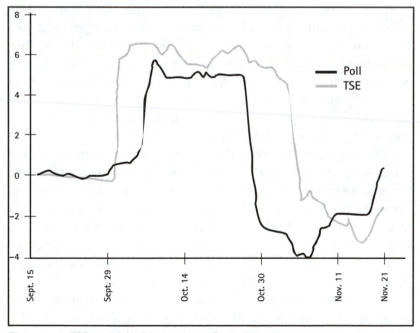

Figure 9.1 TSE and Poll Movements, Sept–Nov 1988
(Scaled deviations from starting values)
Source: Brander (1991), Figure 1.

After the FTA went into effect, Mexico indicated an interest in joining. Negotiations were completed in August 1992, and the North American Free Trade Agreement (NAFTA) was signed in December 1992. NAFTA was scheduled to go into effect on January 1, 1994, allowing approximately one year for it to be ratified by the legislatures of the three countries. In both Canada and the United States, however, new governments were elected before NAFTA went into effect. In the United States, the incumbent President, Republican George Bush, whose adminstration had negotiated NAFTA, was defeated by Democratic Party candidate Bill Clinton in late 1992, and the new Democratic administration took office in January 1993. The U.S. Congress (its legislative body) also became more firmly controlled by Democrats in the 1992 elections. The net effect was the emergence of additional NAFTA issues to negotiate, particularly relating to environmental and labour law issues, as strong forces in the Democratic party expressed reservations about how environmental and labour law issues would fare under NAFTA. The three countries were able to negotiate side agreements on these points. After a vigorous debate, the U.S. Congress did ratify NAFTA in 1993.

In Canada, the Conservative government also ratified NAFTA in 1993. Late in 1993, however, there was an election that the Conservatives (by then under the leadership of Canada's first female prime minister, Kim Campbell) lost to the Liberals, who were led by Jean Chretien. In the previous election, the Liberals had opposed the FTA, and some members of the Liberal party wanted the Liberal government to withdraw from NAFTA. However, the Liberal government decided to proceed with NAFTA, and Mexico also ratified the Agreement. NAFTA went into effect, as planned, in 1994.

9.7 NAFTA

9.7.1 General Objectives

NAFTA is essentially a minor modification of the Canada-U.S. FTA. The main objectives of NAFTA are:

1. to eliminate barriers to trade in goods and services among the three countries,

2. to facilitate conditions of fair competition within the free trade area,

3. to significantly expand liberalization of conditions for cross-bor-
   der investments,

4. to establish effective procedures for the joint administration of
   NAFTA and the resolution of disputes,

5. to lay the foundation for further cooperation to expand or
   enhance the benefits of NAFTA.

9.7.2 Elimination of Tariffs and Quotas

The most central and most important part of NAFTA is that it calls for
the gradual elimination of all tariffs and quotas on movements of qualified goods between the three countries. Qualified goods are those produced or substantially produced in the three countries. Such barriers to
trade are to be completely eliminated in five, 10, or 15 annual steps,
depending on the class of good. In some industries tariffs were eliminated immediately when the Agreement went into effect. Tariffs between
Canada and the United States had already been substantially reduced
under the FTA and, in many cases, had been eliminated altogether.

The qualification required that goods be substantially produced
within the NAFTA countries is intended to eliminate reexport of goods
from outside the region. Thus, for example, the United States would
not be able to import low-cost textiles from East Asia and reexport
them to Canada without paying normal Canadian tariffs for such
goods. The general requirement is that at least 50% of the value added
to a product must originate in the free trade area. There are some
exceptions, such as passenger automobiles, which have a 62.5% local
content requirement.

9.7.3 The Energy Sector

The energy component of the original Canada-U.S. FTA was one of the
most controversial areas, and this component carried over into NAFTA.
The agreement establishes what has been referred to as a continental
energy market. More specifically, the agreement eliminates import
restrictions and export restrictions on energy products. For example,
the United States agreed (under the FTA) to end its total embargo on
exports of Alaskan crude oil, and allow Canadians to import up to
50,000 barrels per day. In general, all countries will be required to treat

energy consumers (and producers) roughly equally, regardless of which country they are based in.

It is this latter provision that concerns economic nationalists. For example, many nationalists would like Canada to provide energy at low cost to domestic users and impose extra taxes on U.S. users. Such policies are ruled out by the agreement. Prices in the two countries may differ, but only as long as the price difference comes from normal commercial practice rather than as a result of government policy. Similarly, in the event of an energy shortage, the Canadian government may take action to reduce energy consumption, but is expected to do so on a proportional basis: consumption of Canadian oil, for example, would be expected to fall by the same proportion in both countries. Canada could not adopt a "Canada first" policy.

It is possible that Canada might be giving up something of value by agreeing to participate in a continental energy market. There are, as we shall see in Chapter 13, circumstances under which charging different prices to different users (called price discrimination) is economically beneficial to a seller, and Canada would apparently forego some of these opportunities. On the whole, however, most economists would argue that the agreement commits Canada to a policy that makes sense. One advantage is that it will prevent economically wasteful domestic subsidies to energy consumption of the type implemented under the National Energy Policy of the late 1970s.

9.7.4 Other Special Sectors: Agriculture, Services, Wine, and Beer

Several other sectors deserve special mention. Agriculture is a particularly important sector. Under NAFTA, trade in agricultural products is governed by separate bilateral subagreements, one between the United States and Canada, and one between the United States and Mexico. The Canada-U.S. bilateral agreement is the agriculture component of the FTA. Under this agreement, tariffs will be eliminated over a 10-year period (which began in 1989) in most agricultural commodities. The agreement also calls for the elimination of all agricultural export subsidies on exports between the two countries. This has only minor implications for overall subsidies, because most subsidies are general production subsidies or export subsidies for third markets. Much of the FTA and NAFTA treatment of agriculture was rendered moot by the Uruguay Round Agreement on Agriculture. As discussed in Section

9.3.4, all trade barriers are to be tariffied (i.e., converted to equivalent tariff values) and these initial tariffs are to fall over time. The total level of subsidization is to be significantly reduced.

Another important sector is financial services. In this sector, firms in all three countries will have more access to the other's markets, but will still not be treated symmetrically with domestic firms. As for other commercial services (such as computer services, accounting, architectural services, consulting services, some communication services, etc.), the three countries have agreed to the principle of national treatment, which means that any new regulations in either country will not discriminate in their effects among American, Canadian, and Mexican suppliers. This does not apply to health services, social services, educational services, transportation services, or basic telecommunications services.

Canadian governments have, in the past, exercised considerable control over the production and distribution of wine, spirits, and beer. This control, exercised mainly by provincial governments, has had the effect of restricting trade flows between Canada and other countries, and between provinces, usually with the intent of protecting local producers. NAFTA carries over the FTA provisions, which substantially reduced such intervention for wine and spirits, but left the status quo unchanged with respect to beer. However, a 1992 GATT panel (following a U.S. complaint) ruled that Canada must also reduce trade barriers in the beer industry.

9.7.5 Investment

U.S. investment in Canada has been a contentious issue in the past, as discussed in Section 9.6.2. NAFTA calls for national treatment for new businesses. This means that American, Canadian, and Mexican investors starting up new businesses in Canada would be subject to the same rules. The rules in the United States might be different from the rules in Canada, but whatever they were, they also apply equally to American, Canadian, and Mexican investors. The agreement also establishes national treatment for U.S.- or Mexican-owned firms operating in Canada and for Canadian-owned firms operating in the other two countries, with no restrictions on the repatriation of profits.

9.7.6 Dispute Resolution

One of the key items of the Canada-U.S. FTA, which carries over and is strengthened under NAFTA, concerns the resolution of trade disputes. In the absence of an agreement, disputes are resolved by unilateral government decisions in each country. Appeals to the WTO are possible, but WTO findings do not have the force of law in any sovereign country, such as Canada, the United States, or Mexico. Previous GATT findings (prior to the establishment of the WTO) were quite frequently ignored. The fact that trade policy disputes were decided nationally was of much more concern to Canada than the United States, because the United States is a much larger share of the total market than is Canada. In short, unilateral U.S. decisions could have major impacts on Canadian producers and Canada in general, whereas Canadian decisions would have at most a small impact on the United States.

The agreement established formal dispute settlement procedures. Disputes are submitted first to a bilateral Trade Commission, made up equally of representatives of both countries. If negotiation between the two parties and the Commission does not resolve the dispute, the matter is settled by an arbitration panel consisting of five members: two nominated by each country and a fifth member chosen by the Commission. If no agreement can be reached on the selection of a fifth member, that person is chosen by lot. The panel's findings are constrained to be consistent with the laws of each country and to be consistent with GATT, and the findings are binding on both countries.

Some Canadians have objected that the dispute resolution format is not strong enough, because it cannot overrule U.S. law. Thus, so the argument goes, the panel would be required to uphold a punitive law even if it were very unreasonable. It is not clear, however, how the panel would deal with a U.S. law that was clearly inconsistent with GATT or with some other aspect of the WTO, if such a law were passed. Such laws are unlikely in any case. Most trade policy disputes involve interpretation of laws that are supposed to be consistent with GATT. Concerns have arisen in the past when such laws were interpreted in a blatantly political way as a result of interest group activity. The panel should be able to partially correct such abuses, and would therefore represent a considerable improvement over the status quo.

Since the FTA went into effect, many trade disputes have started but only a handful had gone all the way to dispute resolution panels. Decision results so far are running about 50-50. Neither country is completely happy with the resolution system, but it does seem to be preferable to the previous system.

9.7.7 The Softwood Lumber Dispute

The characteristics of the dispute resolution process (and some of its problems) are well illustrated by its most high-profile case, the Canada-U.S. softwood lumber dispute. The economic background to the dispute arises from the fact the Canada and the United States have different forest management systems. In the United States, most timber rights are auctioned off to producers. In Canada, on the other hand, most lumber comes from land leased from the government. On leased land, forest products companies pay a tax, referred to as a stumpage fee on lumber that is cut. Thus, in the United States, producers pay the government for timber resources through their payment for timber rights, whereas in Canada most payment is through the stumpage fee system.

During the 1970s, the general prices determined at auction for U.S. timber rights turned out to be higher than justified by later lumber prices. Partly for this reason, the effective price paid by U.S. producers for the right to cut wood turned out to be higher than the price paid by Canadian producers through the stumpage system. A consortium of U.S. producers then argued that the low stumpage fees in Canada constitute a subsidy, and made a formal complaint to U.S. authorities. The initial complaint was made in 1982.

As described earlier, the countervailing duty provision of GATT allows for countervailing duties (i.e., tariffs) to be imposed on imports if those imports were subsidized by foreign governments. However, as of 1982, GATT did not clearly define what a subsidy was. The case of resource products was particularly ambiguous, and the softwood lumber case was unusual in that U.S. producers were claiming a subsidy even though no direct or indirect payment was made by any government in Canada to Canadian forest products producers.

In fact, many independent observers in Canada felt that Canadian stumpage fees were too low to be consistent with good management, and were primarily the result of successful lobbying efforts by lumber companies rather than sound public policy. However, it is hard to see how an insufficiently low tax (or stumpage fee) falls within the meaning of the term "subsidy" as used in international trade agreements.

U.S. countervailing duty cases are decided by agencies within the U.S. Department of Commerce (DOC). In 1983 the DOC decided against the complaint made by U.S. producers on the basis that the Canadian stumpage fee system did not constitute a subsidy. The U.S. producers appealed this decision to an appeal court called the U.S. Court of International Trade, which dismissed the appeal.

The major U.S. producers pursuing this case were located primarily in Oregon, Washington State, Idaho, and Montana. These firms had close associations with leading political figures in the Pacific Northwest, and sought to pursue their case through political intervention. In 1985, members of Congress from Oregon, Idaho, and Montana unsuccessfully proposed legislation in Congress to restrict imports of softwood lumber into the United States. In 1986, U.S. producers renewed their subsidy complaint to the DOC. Political leaders from Oregon, Washington, and elsewhere lobbied the DOC to take a more favourable view of the U.S. producers' subsidy complaint. In addition, political figures from these regions opposed beginning talks on a Canada-U.S. free trade agreement until the softwood case came to a satisfactory resolution. In 1986, the Department of Commerce made a preliminary finding in favour of the subsidy complaint, reversing its decision of 1983, even though the facts of the case had not changed. There was substantial controversy within the Department of Commerce over the high level of political pressure imposed on it.

As a result of this preliminary determination, a 15% countervailing duty (or tariff) was placed on imports of softwood lumber from Canada. In response, the Canadian government initiated high-level negotiations over the softwood lumber dispute with the U.S. Government. The result of these negotiations was the Softwood Lumber Agreement of 1986. Under the Agreement, the 15% tariff was converted immediately to a 15% export tax. Thus the Canadian government would collect the revenue rather than having the revenue accrue to the U.S. government. In addition, provision was made for the 15% export tax to be replaced by stumpage fee increases on a province-by-province basis.

Settlement of the Softwood Lumber Agreement allowed negotiations on the Canada-U.S. FTA to proceed. The FTA itself grandfathered the Softwood Lumber Agreement, which therefore became a subsidiary component of the FTA when it went into effect in 1989. Meanwhile, the major producing provinces had raised stumpage fees during the late 1980s so as to replace the export tax.

The effect of the Softwood Lumber Agreement was interesting. The Canadian share of the U.S. softwood lumber market, which had been about 30% through the early and mid 1980s, fell slightly, but prices of softwood lumber in the United States rose sharply. Thus, the profits of U.S. producers rose at the expense of lumber users, such as house builders, who faced higher prices. The biggest effect, however, was the substantially increased revenues flowing to provincial governments. In British Columbia, for example, additional revenues from higher stumpage fees were on the order of $500 million per year in the late 1980s. Thus, the main effect of the costly exercise in transfer-seeking by American producers was a transfer from U.S. lumber consumers to Canadian provincial treasuries, although U.S. producers did benefit and Canadian producers did suffer some lost profits. On the whole, the Softwood Lumber Agreement forced provincial government officials (especially in British Columbia, the major exporting province) to take action they should have taken anyway on purely normative grounds. This point was well understood within provincial governments. Public statements made by provincial governments were generally supportive of the Canadian producers' position, but private statements made by senior officials were very different in tone.

The next chapter of the story begins in 1991, when Canadian producers, through intense lobbying efforts, persuaded the federal government to unilaterally withdraw from the 1986 Softwood Lumber Agreement. Canada had the right to withdraw, but by withdrawing would no longer be immune to possible countervailing duty actions, since lumber would then be treated like any other good under the FTA. Canadian producers took the view that their position was much stronger with the FTA in force, and that a successful countervailing duty against them was unlikely.

When Canada withdrew from the Softwood Lumber Agreement in 1991, this action was viewed as provocative by various American interests, and the DOC immediately began a subsidy investigation without even waiting for a formal complaint from U.S. producers. The DOC very quickly imposed a preliminary 14.5% countervailing duty on softwood lumber imports from Canada. Thus, in late 1991, the situation was just the same as in 1986 immediately before the Softwood Lumber Agreement was negotiated.

In its final determination in 1992, however, the DOC reduced the countervailing duty to 6.5%. This was a fairly modest tariff that might have been viewed as a compromise outcome. Nevertheless, the Canadian producers and the Canadian government appealed the case to the binational dispute resolution panels created under the FTA. In May 1993, the FTA panel indicated preliminary concerns about the countervailing duty determination and asked the DOC to reconsider the case. The DOC did reconsider and concluded that the 6.5% determination was too low! The duty was raised to 11.5%. The FTA panel therefore continued its investigation of the case and in December 1993 concluded that the subsidy complaint was without merit and that the countervailing duty should be eliminated.

According to the FTA, and now embodied in NAFTA, FTA panels are normally supposed to be the final arbiter of trade disputes. However, there is the possibility that a country can make what is known as an extraordinary challenge to a ruling. The U.S. government made such a challenge in the Softwood Lumber case in early 1994. This challenge was then heard by a specially constituted binational extraordinary challenge committee. This was a NAFTA committee since NAFTA had gone into effect at the beginning of 1994. This committee decided against the U.S. challenge in mid-1994.

At this point, it appeared that the dispute might finally come to an end, but the U.S. producers decided to initiate a constitutional challenge within the U.S. legal system. They argued that binational panels constituted under NAFTA violated the U.S. Constitution because they violated the sovereign authority of the U.S. government. There is no question that NAFTA and other international agreements impose constraints on the sovereign authority of participating countries. That is the whole point of such agreements: to constrain countries so as prevent them from damaging each other. In particular, it is true that NAFTA panels do have the power to overrule domestic government decisions in all three NAFTA countries. As described earlier, NAFTA panels are supposed to make rulings consistent with national law in each country, but their interpretation of those laws can overrule the interpretation of domestic authorities. NAFTA panel decisions then have the force of law in each country. In this respect, NAFTA panels are more powerful than WTO panels, which do not have the power of law within any sovereign nation. This aspect of NAFTA was supposed to be one of its main strengths, in that it placed trade disputes in a relatively impartial legal framework. The constitutional challenge launched by the U.S. lumber industry therefore called into question the basic foundation of NAFTA and several other international agreements.

It is hard to see the merit in the constitutional position taken by U.S. lumber producers, since NAFTA was negotiated by the U.S. Administration and passed by the U.S. Congress, but one never knows how the U.S. Supreme Court (or any court) will rule. However, in late 1994, the U.S. producers abandoned their legal challenge. At this point, the DOC began refunding some $800 million dollars that had been collected in countervailing duties. In return for dropping this legal action, the Canadian government agreed to support a special consultation process to encourage cooperation in the industry. As a result, Canada and the U.S. reached another softwood lumber agreement in 1996, under which Canada would impose taxes and quotas that would have the effect of reducing exports of softwood lumber by about 14%. This agreement expires in 2001.

This example illustrates several important points. First, it gives a good sense of how long and complicated trade disputes can be, since this case lasted for 14 years before (apparently) drawing to a close. It also gives a good sense of how the dispute settlement process works. Perhaps most significantly, however, it shows the power of transfer-seeking incentives of the type described in Chapter 5. Firms in both countries were very successful in obtaining the active support of their respective national and state or provincial governments. They also persuaded these governments to spend very large sums of money pursuing these actions, even though each national government was almost certainly acting against the national economic welfare of its country by doing so.

9.7.8 Effects of NAFTA and the FTA

The big question arising from consideration of NAFTA and the FTA is whether these agreements have been good for Canada (and for the other two countries) overall. In the first few years after the FTA went into effect there was a great deal of public rhetoric about it. Various groups that had strongly opposed the FTA, such as the Canadian Labour Congress (CLC) and the New Democratic Party, argued strenuously that the effects of the FTA were very negative. On the other hand, groups that had supported the FTA, such as the Business Council of Canada and the Conservative government, argued equally strenuously that the FTA was having very positive effects. Both sides used a similar methodology: pick out all the bad things (or all the good things) that happened after the FTA went into effect and attribute them to the FTA.

For example, one line of argument used by opponents of the FTA was to attribute job losses to it. In late 1990, the CLC alleged that "226,000 jobs have been lost" since the FTA went into effect.[7] The basic method for arriving at this number was to add up job losses due to plant closures attributable, according to the CLC, to the FTA. One problem, of course, is that this count does not take account of new investments or new job opportunities created by the FTA. We expect some restructuring as a result of the agreement, which implies job losses in some areas but job gains in others. It is the net number that would be of more interest, but the CLC completely ignored any employment gains. Another problem is that the CLC may have attributed job losses due mainly to the recession of 1990-92 to the FTA instead.

The truth of the matter is that it was very difficult to tell what the effects of the FTA were for at least the first few years. One problem is that the primary restructuring effect of something like a trade agreement takes quite a few years to occur. In the short run, economic conditions are dominated by the business cycle and by the monetary policy that is used in an attempt to moderate the cycle. As it happened, the year the FTA went into effect was the last year of a long economic boom period. The following year, 1990, was the first year of a recession that lasted for three years. Thus, per capita real incomes fell in 1990, 1991, and 1992. In 1993 the macroeconomy performed well, yielding a modest increase in per capita incomes, and 1994 was a year of very strong economic growth and sharply declining unemployment.

It is very unlikely that the pattern of this recession and recovery was due to the FTA. Canada was due for a recession in 1990 and due for a recovery in 1993. This pattern matched the business cycle of other developed economies that, presumably, were not affected by the FTA. However, while the overall pattern of the business cycle was probably due to other factors, some specific aspects of the cycle may have been due to the FTA. For example, the performance of the export sector was relatively strong throughout this business cycle. Second, the 1990-92 recession was felt more strongly in Ontario than in the rest of the country, with British Columbia and Alberta not really having had a recession at all. This would be a plausible consequence of the FTA, since it was the import-competing industries of Ontario that would have faced the most difficult adjustment. It has also been argued, however, that Ontario's relative decline among Canadian provinces was more directly related to provincial government policy in Ontario.

Careful econometric analysis has shed light on the role of the FTA in Canada's recent economic performance. Gaston and Trefler (1994) note, for example, that manufacturing employment fell very sharply during 1990-92 (which is consistent with the relative decline of manufacturing-intensive Ontario). However, real wages of employed workers actually rose by 3% over this period. Furthermore, the industries where Canada suffered the most significant job losses were also industries where the United States suffered job losses, so the hypothesis that the FTA simply caused jobs to move south of the border does not seem right. Thus, the employment effect of the FTA was probably small compared to the effect of the business cycle. Head and Ries (1995) find that the industries that were doing well just before the recession were the ones that contracted most sharply during the recession. This suggests a regression toward the mean phenomenon, rather than an FTA effect. It is also worth remembering that the consensus estimate of the benefits of the FTA to Canada was only about 3% of GDP. Putting all this information together suggests that the FTA did not have a major impact on Canadian economic performance. A typical view among economists who have studied the effects of the FTA is that it had a small positive effect.

From Canada's point of view, NAFTA represents very little in the way of change. As previously mentioned, NAFTA essentially just brought Mexico into the FTA, along with a few other small changes. This required a substantial reduction in Mexican trade and investment barriers against U.S. and Canadian firms. Canadian trade barriers against Mexico were already low, so the required adjustments in Canada's trade policy structure were very minor. Furthermore, trade flows between Mexico and Canada are much too small for declines in trade barriers between Canada and Mexico to have much effect on Canada. The primary effect of NAFTA has been on Mexico, which has certainly suffered some adjustment problems as domestic producers have had to confront much more vigorous competition from U.S. exporters.

9.7.9 A Case Study: the B.C. Wine Industry [8]

Even if the FTA did not have a major impact on Canada as a whole, it did have a major impact on certain specific industries. One of the most strongly affected was the B.C. wine industry. Prior to the FTA, it was heavily protected by the B.C. Liquor Control Board, which charged high markups on foreign wines and allowed B.C. wines to dominate the low-price segment of the market. Dating from the 1920s, the B.C. wine industry used low-quality B.C. grapes, often mixed with grape concentrate from California, to produce cheap low-quality wine. Wine growers began planting better quality grapes during the 1960s, and some wineries experimented with high-quality wines in the 1970s and 1980s, but the vast majority of production was targeted at the protected low-quality segment of the B.C. wine market.

When the FTA was being negotiated, it was widely expected to cause the demise of the B.C. wine and grape industry, since it was felt that B.C. wines could not compete with superior California wines. Furthermore, a GATT ruling against Canada also reduced the protection that could be afforded against wines from other countries. When the FTA came into effect, quite a few growers of low-grade grapes sold their farms and received compensation under a special FTA adjustment assistance program. However, many grape growers dramatically increased their planting of high-quality grapes, and the major and minor wineries worked hard to develop high-quality wines in anticipation of more vigorous competition.

The net effect surprised almost everyone. The B.C. wine industry, now in direct competition with American wines, has done very well and has become a major exporter. Vintage B.C. wines have won a number of prestigious international competitions, and B.C. wines are doing better than previously in the domestic wine market. The industry has been growing rapidly, and has given rise a valuable side business, since the B.C. wine regions have become significant tourist destinations for those interested in touring wineries and tasting wines. This represents the effect of trade liberalization at its best. In a heavily protected domestic market, the B.C. wine industry did not perform well and had little incentive to improve. Once forced to compete, the industry did very well and greatly increased its value added.

We should not assume from this that all industries will prosper as a result of trade liberalization. Sometimes previously protected industries decline and disappear when forced to compete. The benefit of trade liberalization comes from allowing resources in an economy to flow to where they are most productive. As it happened, resources such as land and labour in the wine industry were being wasted on low-grade grapes and low-quality wines. After the FTA, these resources were put to much more effective use. We could not be sure that they would stay in the wine industry, but we could be confident that they would find a higher-value use somewhere.

9.8 Immigration Policy

Political parties in Canada have fought at least three national election campaigns in which international trade policy was the major issue. International investment policy has also played a significant role in political debate. Immigration policy, by way of contrast, has rarely entered into political discussion, and is a subject most politicians prefer to avoid, even though it is almost certainly more important than trade policy in influencing the long-run evolution of the country.

Perhaps the most salient fact concerning immigration is that many more people want to come to Canada than are allowed in by current policy. It is hard to estimate how many people would come to Canada if immigration were completely open, but there is little doubt that a policy of open borders would cause Canada's existing population to be swamped by migration flows, especially from relatively poor countries with high population growth rates. For example, at least 4 billion people live in countries with standards of living dramatically below Canadian levels. If only 1% of those people migrated to Canada, that would be about 40 million people, considerably outnumbering the current population of about 30 million.

This observation forces us to confront directly the question of whether immigration policy ought to be run for the benefit of current Canadians, or to what extent it ought to be run for the benefit of poor or disadvantaged people in the rest of the world. In most other areas of policy this question does not arise as a serious issue. It is taken for granted that trade policy, for example, should promote Canadian interests. In the immigration area, however, there is a strong humanitarian lobby that many Canadians find persuasive. The fact that immigration policy has a more important humanitarian element than trade policy contains a certain irony, for Canada could probably do a lot more good for poor countries by allowing free access for their exports than by accepting what is, from their point of view, only a small number of migrants.

A second salient feature is that, even with limitations on Canadian immigration policy, Canada has very high immigration rates by international standards. Canada has, for example, consistently maintained a per capita immigration rate more than double that of the United States. Immigration is a major part of overall population growth in Canada, and, in the 1990s, exceeded natural increase (births minus deaths) and therefore contributed over half of Canada's population growth in this period. Annual immigration levels were about 100,000 per year in the early part of the 1980s. During the late 1980s, Canada found it difficult, given various humanitarian objectives, to keep immigration levels down to existing targets. The government responded by increasing target immigration levels. In the 1990s annual immigration levels have averaged in the low 200 thousands.

Several aspects of immigration policy have become contentious. The first issue to address is simply the appropriate aggregate level of immigration. As indicated in Chapter 7, even without any immigration, Canadian population would continue to grow for many years because women of child-bearing age make up a relatively large share of the population. Assuming current fertility rates, natural increase alone would cause population to continue growing until about 2040, when it would peak at about 35 to 40 million. If, on the other hand, the government's current immigration target of over 200,000 per year were maintained, Canada's population in 2040 would be about 50 million and still growing. The Toronto and Vancouver metropolitan areas would be well over twice their current size: Vancouver would be similar to Toronto's current size, and Toronto would be similar in size to the present-day New York City.

Most of Canada, particularly the North, is ecologically very fragile and is capable of supporting only a very sparse population. On the other hand, Canada's southern arable regions are substantial and could certainly accommodate a population of 50 or 60 million and still not be nearly as crowded as, for example, the current Japan or India or even Western Europe. Fixed resources such as land, water, and oil would, however, have to be shared among a much larger population base. Benefits from renewable but finite resources such as forests and fish stocks would also have to be spread more thinly on a per capita basis. These effects would put downward pressure on living standards.

This downward pressure might, however, be more than offset by economies of scale, technological progress, or other sources of economic progress. In addition, of course, a growing population of humans raises a variety of ecological concerns, some of which are discussed further in Chapter 11.

The aspect of immigration policy that has received the most media attention concerns the fairness of the refugee system. Immigrants are allowed into Canada under a variety of separate programs. At the broadest level, there are three general categories of immigrants: family class, independent (including business class), and refugee (sometimes called humanitarian). Since signing the 1951 Geneva Convention relating to the status of refugees (and its 1967 Protocol), Canada has entered an international obligation to protect refugees. The technical definition of a Geneva Convention refugee is quite detailed, but the basic idea is that people who would be severely persecuted in their source countries as a result of their political beliefs, ethnic identity, religion, or for related reasons should be allowed to settle in other countries.

Prior to the 1980s, refugee immigration was a very modest part of total immigration and was carefully controlled by immigration authorities. Canadian officials would select a few thousand refugees per year from refugee populations around the world to settle in Canada, and, in addition, a small number of refugees made their own way to Canada and applied for immigrant status from within the country. As late as 1980 there were only 1,505 refugee claims made from within Canada.[9] A decade later refugee claims were running approximately 10 to 20 times this level.

There are several reasons for the dramatic increase in refugee claims from within Canada. First of all, the world is much more crowded than it was 25 years ago, or even 10 years ago, and there are, correspondingly, more potential refugees. Second, it is much easier to travel today than it was in the past. Canada, while still a prohibitively expensive destination for most potential refugees, is, nevertheless, only a day-long (or less) transcontinental flight away from anywhere in the world.

In addition, it has become known that Canada provides what is probably the world's most generous treatment of refugees. In 1985, the Supreme Court of Canada ruled that anyone who sets foot in Canada is protected by the Canadian Charter of Rights. This has been interpreted to mean that no one can be summarily expelled or deported from Canada. Instead, a refugee claimant has the right to publicly provided legal assistance, welfare payments, and other forms of support, and is allowed to stay in Canada while he or she goes through a slow but relatively generous refugee determination process. Since the current process was put in place on January 1, 1989, a large majority of refugee claimants have been granted immigrant status. Even when an application fails, many applicants still refuse to leave and remain in Canada illegally. This process is quite costly. As described by the Economic Council of Canada (1991, p. 25): "[The cost] is far beyond the value of any gains in scale economies or savings in tax and dependency costs that might accrue to Canadians from these claimants."

Most of the public debate over refugees has focused on whether particular claimants are legitimate refugees, or whether they are merely economic migrants who are jumping the queue. There are many stories of refugee claimants destroying identification papers while en route to Canada so that there is no way of checking whatever claims they make once they get to Canada. In the absence of evidence to refute a refugee claim, the claimant will usually be successful, especially if he or she is from one of the major refugee-producing countries. In order to stem the flow of refugees, the Canadian government has tried to make it harder for potential refugees from many countries to get to Canada by requiring them to obtain visas before being allowed to begin travel to Canada. (Airlines and other transport companies are required to check for appropriate visas or passports before transporting passengers.) This is an imperfect screening device, however, and once refugee claimants actually get into Canada, it does not matter whether they have an appropriate visa or not, they still have access to the Canadian refugee system and its attendant benefits.

There is some feeling that, although most refugee claimants who get to Canada are certainly needy and are much better off in Canada than they would be in their home countries, they are far from the neediest refugees, and certainly have not been selected on the basis of any systematic humanitarian or other criteria. They are simply the ones who have sufficient resources, knowledge, contacts, and luck to make it to Canada on their own, rather than waiting in their home countries for their claims to be processed. Observers have argued that, as a result of the Supreme Court decision, Canada has lost control of its borders.

Unfortunately, the debate over whether or not refugees are legitimate fails to address the main point. The point is that the world is full of legitimate refugees and getting fuller. UN estimates suggest that there are many millions of people who would meet UN refugee criteria, consisting largely of people threatened or displaced by civil wars and insurrection, political repression, ethnic violence, and related problems. It is, furthermore, not clear why we should restrict our attention to refugees created by political events as opposed to the millions more who are seriously disadvantaged for mere economic reasons. In addition, given the explosive population growth going on in much of the world, especially Africa, these problems are likely to get worse rather than better over the medium term.

The basic problem is that potential refugee flows are orders of magnitude greater than was envisioned when Canada and other Western countries designed their humanitarian refugee programs. The real question is whether Canada should guarantee immigration rights to all legitimate refugees and accept the consequence of very large and relatively uncontrolled immigration flows, and whatever social and economic costs would follow, or whether some compromise involving perhaps an annual numerical commitment to refugees should be adopted. It may be unrealistic to regard Canada as a potential haven for all legitimate refugees.

The increase in refugee immigration raises the question of the overall composition of immigration. Traditionally, the bulk of immigration into Canada was in the independent class, in which the applicant's potential value to Canada was the principal criterion for admission. The result was that immigrants filled important skill requirements in the labour force and in general contributed more than they cost. During the 1960s roughly 2/3 of all immigrants were in the independent class. By 1980 this had fallen to less than 1/3. This decline was due in part to the increasing share of the overall immigration target level being filled by refugees. More importantly, however, the independent class was squeezed out by expansion of family class immigrants (i.e., relatives of Canadian residents). Individuals, particularly recent immigrants who want to reassemble their families in Canada, and organized interest groups, lobby strongly for family-based immigration preferences. Family class immigration has become the major immigration category, along with the related assisted relative class. (Strictly speaking, since 1981, assisted relatives have been defined by the government as part of the independent class, but it would seem to make more sense to consider them as part of the family class.)

Neither family class nor refugee class immigrants are selected on the basis of benefit to Canada, and typically have a less attractive skill mix than would the independent class immigrants whom they displace. If one argues that Canadian immigration policy ought to be run for the benefit of current Canadians, then this pattern of immigration is a potential problem. Concern over the decline of independent class immigrants was one of the main reasons for the government's decision to expand immigration in the late 1980s. Their reasoning was that there was little that could be done to reduce the political demand for refugee and family class immigration, so the way to get more high-skilled immigrants was to expand the total. Even so, in 1998, independent immigrants (including business class, but not including assisted relatives) accounted for about 55% of the 174,100 immigrants who entered Canada. Family class and assisted relatives accounted for about 30% and refugees accounted for about 13% of the total.

A third issue related to immigration policy concerns the ethnic and racial composition of immigration. This is, understandably, a politically sensitive issue that is difficult to discuss openly. It is, however, sufficiently important that it is hard to ignore. The basic point is that the current ethnic composition of the immigrant flow is very different from that of the current population. This will, over the course of a generation, have a substantial impact on the ethnic and cultural composition of the overall population. Table 9.4 lists the regional sources of Canadian immigration in 1997.

TABLE 9.4 1997 Canadian Immigration According to Source Regions

Region	% of Immigrants
Asia and Pacific	54.2%
Europe and U.K.	17.9%
Africa and Middle East	17.5%
Latin America	8.0%
U.S.A.	2.3%

Source: Employment and Immigration Canada, *Quarterly Immigration Statistics.*

The policy question, put bluntly, is whether the ethnic mix of the immigrant flow should be considered in immigration policy. Officially, Canadian immigration policy is nondiscriminatory and multicultural.

In practice, of course, any immigration policy short of completely open borders acts to discriminate in some way. Shifting immigration policy in favour of refugees as opposed to business class immigrants (or vice versa) will certainly change the ethnic mix of immigration and have major implications for Canada's future.

Such issues are not, however, normally addressed openly or directly. Given the current delicate state of ethnic and race relations in Canada and throughout the world this might be the best approach. It would be hard to argue against the proposition, however, that the current character of Canada (or any other country) is due in large part to the ethnic structure of its past immigration flows. It also seems to be the case that different ethnic groups have very different experiences in Canada and elsewhere. The question is whether these considerations should be allowed to matter in evaluating future immigration policy.

A related issue concerns how immigrants should be treated once they arrive in Canada. Should they be encouraged to assimilate into the majority culture, or should they be encouraged to retain the cultural identity associated with their ethnic background or country of origin? Canadian governments have opted for the latter approach as part of a general policy of multiculturalism. Critics have questioned whether such policies serve the interests of the immigrants themselves or the interests of the broader community. The Economic Council of Canada (1991, p. 36), for example, argues that "immigrants to Canada should expect, and should be expected to subscribe to fundamental Canadian values," and advocates more expenditures on language training and socialization, and less on subsidization of multicultural activities.

9.9 Bibliographic Notes

An excellent source on the GATT system is Jackson (1999). A valuable discussion of the difference between NAFTA and the FTA is contained in Cadsby and Woodside (1993). A newsletter published by the WTO, called WTO Focus, is a very useful source of current information about international trade policy issues.

Notes

1. Data on average import duties is taken from Cuddington and McKinnon (1979), Figures 1 and 2.

2. *WTO Focus Newsletter* 1, January-February 1995, World Trade Organization, Geneva.

3. This discussion draws on Gleason (1987).

4. Statistical Office of the European Communities, *Yearbook of Agricultural Statistics.*

5. This is reported in Gary Horlick and Kristy Balsanek, "U.S.-GATT Anti-Dumping and Countervailing Duty Implementing Legislation," *Canadian Competition Policy Record* 15, Summer 1994, pp. 33-37.

6. *Canada's International Investment Position*, Statistics Canada Catalogue No. 67-202.

7. Virginia Galt, "226,000 jobs lost since pact, CLC says," *The Globe and Mail*, December 15, 1990, pp. A1, A6.

8. This subsection is based in part on a term paper entitled "The Impact of the Canada-U.S. Free Trade Agreement on the Grape and Wine Industry of British Columbia by Christian Ahlefeldt-Laurvig and Mark Tower.

9. See Economic Council of Canada (1991), p. 24.

On-line Sources

For the World Trade Organization, see: *http://www.wto.org/*

For the International Monetary Fund, see:
http://www.imf.org/external/index.htm

For information about NAFTA, see:

http://www.nafta-sec-alena.org/english/index.htm

10

Environmental Policy and Externalities

10.1 Environmental Concerns

In Canada, there is a vast array of regulation and government programs designed to protect the environment. Yet many Canadians
believe that governments in this country are not doing enough to
ensure a clean environment for future generations. In this chapter, we
focus on business practice and government policy affecting the natural environment. This includes such topics as air and water pollution,
handling of waste (especially toxic materials), ozone depletion, acid
rain, and global warming. In the next chapter, we take up the closely
related problem of managing major natural resources such as forests,
fisheries, soil, and water. Much of the debate over environmental issues
is confused, ideological, or purely emotional in its appeal. A useful first
step to take in understanding environmental issues is to understand the
market failure basis of many environmental problems. This, in turn,
requires an understanding of externalities.

10.2 Externalities: Definition, Analysis, and Examples

10.2.1 Defining Externalities

An externality can be defined as a nonpriced effect on a third party
arising as a by-product of the actions undertaken by another. This definition can be illustrated by example. Suppose that my next-door

neighbour throws monthly parties for which he hires a rock band. The band plays loud music that keeps the rest of the neighbourhood awake. From the neighbourhood's point of view, this is noise pollution.

My neighbour (the first party) and the rock band (the second party) have entered into an agreement or transaction that affects third parties, the neighbourhood residents. The (economic) welfare of neighbourhood residents is reduced by the actions of my neighbour. Furthermore, the cause of this welfare reduction (the loud noise) is not priced by any market: my neighbour does not have to pay a fee for the costs he imposes on others. In short, the loud music is a negative externality.

Externalities might also be positive and need not involve a second party. Suppose another neighbour is an avid gardener who maintains an exquisite rose garden. Other neighbourhood residents often stop and admire her garden (which they might, in other circumstances, be willing to pay to see). This neighbour (the first party) is conferring a benefit on her neighbours (the third parties) for which she receives no payment. This nonpriced benefit conferred on others is a positive externality.

These two examples do not have much to do with the world of environmental policy and corporate strategy. In fact, however, externalities are very important in the business world and represent the key to understanding environmental problems.

One of the leading current examples of an externality problem is acid rain. Canadian acid rain is produced principally by coal-burning industries (especially electric utilities) in the United States and Southern Ontario. The external effect is that acid rain damages forests, lakes, buildings, and wildlife (and possibly humans). Other forms of environmental pollution are also important examples: car exhaust, airborne emissions from toxic waste incinerators, waterborne emission of chemical waste into rivers and lakes, radiation from accidents in nuclear power plants, etc.

10.2.2 Externalities as Market Failure

Externalities cause market failure: they cause private markets to be inefficient. The nature of the market failure can be understood by noting that externalities cause a failure of the marginalist principle for social efficiency: social marginal benefit should be equated with social marginal cost. A negative externality creates a marginal cost of some activity (such as playing loud music or burning coal) that is not borne by the firm or person undertaking the activity (the first party), but is borne instead by others. This first party will equate his or her private or personal marginal cost to the marginal benefit of the activity, but will ignore the marginal costs imposed on others.

For example, suppose that a coal-burning electric utility in Ohio can choose between high-sulphur coal, which produces a lot of acid rain, and slightly more expensive low-sulphur coal, which produces less acid rain. Left to itself, it will choose the lower-cost high-polluting coal, even if the extra costs imposed on others are far higher than the savings to the utility. The result is an inefficient outcome: total costs to society (including the externality costs) are higher than necessary for producing electricity. Figure 10.1 illustrates the inefficiency associated with externalities.

Figure 10.1 Externalities as a Divergenge of Social and Private Cost

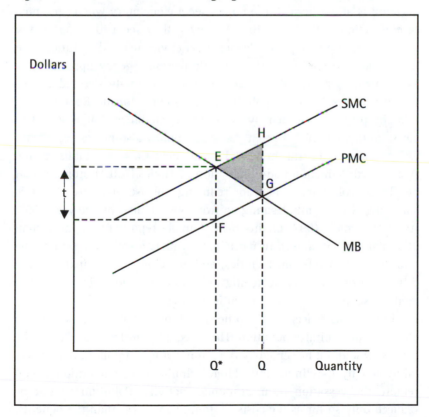

In Figure 10.1, the curve labelled *MB* is the marginal benefit of carrying out some activity (like using high-sulphur coal). This is taken to be both the private marginal benefit and the social marginal benefit (i.e., there is no positive externality). The curve labelled PMC is the private marginal cost, and the curve labelled SMC is the social marginal cost. (The PMC and SMC curves are drawn as linear and parallel to each other. This is just for convenience. In general they need not be either linear or parallel to each other.) Because of the negative externality, the social marginal cost exceeds the private marginal cost. The difference is called the marginal external cost. The socially efficient outcome would involve carrying out the activity up to point Q^*. However, the private individual or corporation would choose to carry out the activity up to point Q. The efficiency loss is given by area EGH.

This diagram illustrates two important points. First, activities with negative externalities will be carried out at too high a level if left to private incentives. Second, the socially efficient level of the activity in question is above zero. These points seem elementary when presented in connection with Figure 10.1. However, they seem to escape many participants in public policy debates over environmental pollution. The director of the U.S. Environmental Protection Agency appointed by President Reagan in 1981, Anne Burford, continually stressed voluntarism as the solution to pollution. Her general consul, Robert Perry, told the press "It's ultimately voluntary compliance that is going to clean up this nation."[2] Current Canadian policy also places significant weight on voluntarism. In 1991 Environment Canada established the Accelerated Reduction and Elimination of Toxics (ARET) program that developed voluntary targets for reducing the use of some 100 toxic substances by magnitudes ranging from 50% to 90% by the year 2000. As of December 1997, Environment Canada reported that more than 300 facilities had agreed to participate. This is a small fraction of the total number of relevant facilities, and agreeing to participate is very different from actually achieving pollution reductions. Evidence and analysis suggest that voluntarism is not the answer.

Environmentalists, on the other hand, often talk about seeking to eliminate or minimize pollution. This is equally misleading. The public interest would not be served by the minimization of pollution (and certainly not by its elimination). Literal elimination of pollution would require the cessation of most human activity. Pollution should be reduced only so far as the costs of doing so are less than the benefits.

10.2.3 The Simple Economics of Pollution Abatement

Figure 10.1 illustrates a situation where some economic activity (for instance driving, or producing paper, or using high-sulphur coal) has a fixed external cost associated with it. This is often the case, at least in the short run. If so, then the only form of externality reduction or abatement is to actually do less of the activity. Thus, for example, if a firm owns a pulp mill of a particular type, the only immediate way to cause less pollution is to run the mill less and therefore produce less pulp. In the long run, however, it is often possible to undertake other forms of pollution abatement. The firm could install scrubbers on the mill to remove pollutants, or install new cleaner machinery, or take other actions to reduce pollution. A diagrammatic analysis of pollution abatement is contained in Figure 10.2.

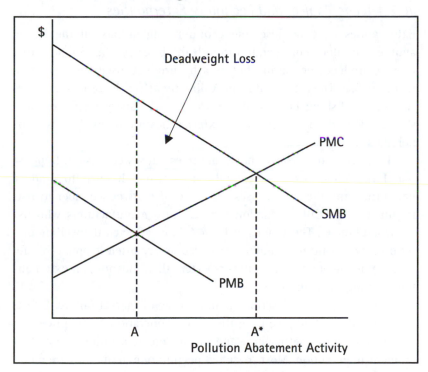

FIGURE 10.2 Externalities and Pollution Abatement

This diagram gives a very similar message to Figure 10.1. In this case, however, the horizontal axis measures abatement activity (e.g., extra scrubbers in pulp mills). The problem here is that the private marginal benefit of abatement is much less than the social marginal benefit of abatement. The private firm or consumer has an incentive to undertake abatement only up to the point where the private marginal benefit of abatement equals the private marginal cost of abatement, which occurs at point A. From the social point of view, these private incentives lead to too little abatement. The socially efficient level of abatement occurs where the social marginal benefit equals the social marginal cost, at point A*.

Abatement generates positive external benefits in that it generate benefits that are not captured by the party undertaking the abatement activity. As with any activity that generates positive externalities, pollution abatement will be underprovided if left to private incentives.

10.2.4 Technological and Pecuniary Externalities

Externalities arise because one economic agent has an impact on another that does not operate through the price system. Suppose that Firm A produces newsprint, but as a by-product discharges pollution that kills fish. The actions of Firm A directly affect the production possibilities of fishing boats and the welfare of fishery employees and shareholders (third parties). Such externalities are referred to as technological externalities.

There is a similar idea that sometimes causes confusion. Suppose that Firm A increases its demand for softwood lumber (to produce newsprint) and that this causes the price of softwood lumber to rise, raising the costs of production for furniture manufacturers who use softwood lumber. The actions of Firm A have affected the welfare of a third party: furniture manufacturers. People are often tempted to refer to this phenomenon as a pecuniary externality, meaning an externality operating through prices.

The example just described is not a case of market failure. Effects on third parties that arise from the normal operation of the price system do not cause inefficiency, and do not create a rationale for government intervention. Most so-called pecuniary externalities are merely examples of the marketplace allocating resources to efficient uses.

There are, however, cases where some underlying market failure is transmitted through price effects. One such example is the lemons problem described in Chapter 13 (Section 13.6). In this case, market failure is caused by asymmetric information, but the effect of the market failure operates through prices. After realizing that some market failures do operate through third-party price effects, it can sometimes be difficult to distinguish between a true market failure and pecuniary third-party effects arising from the normal efficient operation of the market system. The essential point is as follows. Pecuniary third-party effects may or may not reflect market failure. They do not cause market failure. Technological externalities do cause market failure.[3]

10.2.5 Property Rights and Fundamental Sources of Externalities

Why do externalities exist? Consider once again my neighbour who regularly hires a rock band to play at parties. If the music bothers me, why don't I just offer to pay him not to throw parties? If my other neighbours and I offer him enough, presumably he would stop, or rent some other facility in which to hold parties. In principle, this could solve the noise pollution problem. If the benefits of getting him to stop, as measured by his neighbours' willingness to pay, exceed the costs (the minimum amount he would accept to stop) then he will stop (or move) his parties. This would satisfy the marginalist principle and restore efficiency. This solution involves, in essence, the creation of a market for loud music.

In general, the creation of markets for previously unpriced external effects can solve externality problems. Externalities are interactions between people (or firms) that are not priced because they occur outside of markets. In short, externalities arise precisely because certain markets fail to exist. But why do certain markets fail to exist? Why are loud music externalities ever a problem if markets can spontaneously spring up to price the external effect? There are two basic reasons: high transactions costs and the absence of natural property rights.

Consider transaction costs first. In order to create the market for my neighbour's loud music, I have to go over and negotiate with him. So would the other neighbours. This is time consuming for all parties involved. In this case these costs are not prohibitive, but in many cases they are. Consider the problem of trying to set up a market for pollution caused by automobile exhaust. Are we to gather all polluters and breathers together to negotiate over how much will be paid to induce people to install pollution abatement equipment? If the costs of operating a market (transactions costs) are high compared to the potential gains from trade in the market, then the market will fail to exist.

The second issue concerns property rights. It may have struck many readers as unfair that I should have to pay my neighbour to stop having loud music played at his parties. Conversely, should my neighbour be required to pay me before being allowed to throw such parties? The ambiguity raised by these questions illustrates that there are no natural property rights over loud music. It is not clear whether I have a basic property right to quiet, or whether my neighbour has a natural right to loud music.[4] If the property right is mine, then my neighbour must pay me for the right to play loud music. He will be willing to do so only if his benefit exceeds the compensation he will have to pay me, which reflects my cost of having to hear the music. This is efficient (excluding the other neighbours from the issue).

Conversely, if the property right is his, then I must pay him if I want the music to stop, and the outcome will again be efficient. As was first pointed out by Coase (1960), it really does not matter, as far as achieving efficiency is concerned, to whom property rights are assigned. As long as they are assigned to someone, efficiency will result. (Assignment of property rights does, of course, affect the distribution of benefits between the parties.)

The problem in this case is that we could probably not agree on who has the property rights. If I did end up paying my neighbour to refrain from making noise, what is to stop someone else from starting up late night rock music sessions in the hope of attracting similar payment? Can anyone claim property rights in this "market"? If so, then the property rights are not really meaningful. In the case of environmental problems, the assignment of property rights is even more difficult. It is not feasible to assign property rights over the atmosphere or the ocean. If property rights cannot be agreed upon, or are hard to define, it is very difficult for markets to function.

10.3 Policy Solutions to Externality Problems

There are four basic policy solutions to market failure caused by externalities:

1. internalization of the externality,
2. quantity controls or standards,
3. taxes and subsidies,
4. market creation.

Perhaps the most obvious response to externalities is internalizing the externality. "Internalizing" means placing the economic agent generating the externality and the affected third parties under one management. For example, if a pulp mill damages a fishery, then having the firm that owns the pulp mill acquire the fishery would internalize the externality. This single firm would then have an incentive to reduce the emissions from the pulp mill to the efficient level.

Unfortunately, internalization is not likely to be feasible in many cases. For one thing, most efficiency-improving internalizations will be spontaneously undertaken by the private sector, leaving no particular role for public policy. The remaining cases are ones where internalization itself has very high costs. For example, to internalize the acid rain externality, it would be necessary to place under a single management most of the industries in the U.S. midwest and northeast, in Quebec, and in Ontario, along with responsibility for fish, forests, and wildlife in these areas. Aside from not being politically feasible, this kind of proposal would generate far more economic costs than benefits. Most current environmental externality problems are cases in which the costs of internalization would exceed the benefit.

Although it is difficult to solve externality problems by internalization, it is possible to create externality problems by what might be called "externalization." An example of this would be land tenure rights for logging in Canada. In much of Canada, substantial areas of forest are owned by governments (by the Crown), but are leased to forest products companies for logging. It is often argued that the level of reforestation carried out on such land is too low. This is not surprising, because the forest products companies cannot reasonably assume that they will definitely be the ones to benefit from the reforestation they carry out, especially as leases approach expiration. The company cannot be sure that it will obtain a new lease. Perhaps the land will be leased to someone else, or given up to a native land claim. Any reforestation has the character of a positive externality: it will confer benefits on the government (since it raises the value of the land) or on future users of the land. As with any activity that provides positive externalities, we expect that it will be underprovided.

The most common actual solution to externalities is quantity controls and standards. Factories are constrained to limit themselves to certain levels of pollution or to install specific types of pollution abatement equipment. It is possible, in principle, to achieve the efficient solution through quantity controls. In Figure 10.1, the efficient solution could be obtained simply by setting the activity level at Q^*. When acid rain is discussed, the suggested policy approach is to set targets for reduction of emissions, such as a 50% reduction in emissions by such and such a date. Emission standards are widely used in Canada.

Most economists would prefer to see less reliance on standards and quantity controls and more on taxes and subsidies. The appropriate response to a negative externality is to tax it. In Figure 10.1, if the activity were taxed at rate t, then the private marginal cost would rise (inclusive of the tax), so that it coincided with the social marginal cost at the efficient point, yielding activity level Q^*. (Subsidies would be used for activities with positive externalities.)

In Figure 10.1, taxes and quantity controls look like equivalent ways of achieving efficiency. Why, then, do economists favour taxes while policy makers (and the public) tend to prefer quantity controls? Economists favour taxes because of the incentive effects. If pollution is taxed, this gives the polluting firm a continuing incentive to reduce pollution. Taxes are a market-based solution; they exploit market-based incentives. In addition, taxes generate revenue that can be used to pay for environmental programs or for other purposes.

Standards are like a central-planning approach. If standards are used, even if they are enforced, the firm has an incentive to conform to the standard but go no further. Economists are also suspicious of the ability of policy makers to set sensible standards. Finally, obtaining compliance with pollution standards can be difficult.

Canada has had emission standards for pulp mills since 1971. One standard relates to the toxic effects of emission on fish. Sinclair (1991) reports that in 1985, of Canada's 122 direct discharge pulp mills, only 39 were in compliance with emission standards concerning effluent toxicity. The other 83 were not. The highest rate of compliance (43%) occurred in British Columbia, and the lowest (28%) in Quebec. It is worth noting, however, that actual toxic waste discharge was reduced by 31% between 1971 and 1985, despite (coincidentally) a 31% increase in annual industry output.

Pulp mills have been largely free from sanctions or penalties for noncompliance. The problem with criminal-based sanctions for noncompliance is that it is politically difficult to impose them and legally difficult to obtain convictions because of the reasonable doubt standard of proof. Governments in Canada are worried about employment in towns where pulp mills operate. They do not want to be in an adversarial position with pulp mills in such areas. Regulators of the industry tend to be close to the industry itself. When noncompliance occurs, as it usually does, it is politically much easier to get the firm to promise to try to do better in the future rather than impose penalties.

From the firm's point of view, the marginal incentive to comply is weak. Given that reducing emissions is costly, it is more attractive to hope that ex post bargaining with governments will protect the firm from prosecution. The advantage of taxes is that they are imposed ex ante and simply become a normal cost of business. Firms might not like them, but the scope for avoidance is much less than with standards. Taxes also provide a much more level playing field than standards that are honoured more in the breach than in the observance. Standards can, however, be effective in some areas. Compliance in auto emission standards, while far from perfect, has substantially reduced emissions, at least on a per car basis. It should also be emphasized that tax systems do require accurate monitoring technologies.

It is not entirely clear why politicians and most other people often favour standards. One possibility is that the idea of, in effect, selling pollution "rights" seems morally wrong. Simply taking higher taxes and allowing the firm to pollute the environment is likened to selling the right to commit rape or murder (and environmentalists are fond of using such analogies.) Politicians and most other people think naturally in terms of right and wrong; good and bad. If pollution is bad, we should try to reduce it, not sanction it. Julia Langer, executive director of the Ottawa-based Friends of the Earth, made the following statement[5]: "[it is] the wrong signal to give. If you say you can buy the right to pollute, then people will buy it. They won't strive for perfection." Adele Hurley observes "Some people believe clean air and water is a right. They say that if you make them a marketable commodity, it's dangerous. You're setting a price on a right." Wanting to recast a complex world in terms of simple absolutes, such as a right to clean air or water, is understandable. Unfortunately, it does not help much in actual policy formulation.

It is also likely that most people do not trust or appreciate the power of market solutions. They imagine that if pollution is taxed, then firms will simply pay the tax, pass the costs on to consumers, and not reduce pollution. (This is, of course, a misconception. The appropriate tax would reduce pollution by exactly the right amount.) Pollution taxes have not been used extensively in Canada, but they have been used in Europe, particularly in the Netherlands, where effluent charges were first imposed in 1969. Initially opposed by both business and environmental groups, effluent charges in the Netherlands are high and are increasingly used. They have resulted in a dramatic decline in effluent emissions, and have raised substantial revenues for environmental programs.

Taxes are a market-based approach to pollution control. Perhaps the fourth approach listed above, market creation, would be even more effective in exploiting market forces. The market creation solution requires assigning property rights and creating markets. This may be feasible in some cases. We could imagine a government bureau claiming property rights over the air and then selling pollution rights, which could be sold to others, in effect creating a market for pollution rights. In general, however, in cases where markets have not sprung up spontaneously, the costs of setting up markets are likely to be high.

There are, however, some creative ways of using markets in conjunction with standards to reduce the costs of achieving a given pollution control target. Consider, for example, the lead-trading approach adopted in the United States.[6] Lead compounds in auto emissions are very damaging to the environment, and have been linked to a variety of health problems in humans, especially children. Canada has simply banned leaded gasoline altogether. In the United States, rather than banning lead, the government has sought to reduce lead levels through the use of standards. Gasoline refiners are allowed to produce a certain amount of lead per unit of gasoline produced. The market innovation was to allow firms to trade lead rights. For example, suppose the lead standard were 5 grams of lead per every 10 litres of gasoline produced. A refinery that produced 10 million litres of gasoline would then have the right to produce 5 million grams of lead in this gasoline. This refinery might choose, however, to produce just unleaded gasoline, using up none of it lead rights. It would then be allowed to sell its lead rights to other firms. The right to include 1 gram of lead in gasoline might sell for 10 cents. The refinery could then sell its entire allocation of lead rights for $500,000.

The advantage of this system is that it minimizes the cost of achieving a given pollution target. Refineries that can eliminate lead from gasoline easily and cheaply will do so and will sell lead rights on the market to refineries that find it very costly to eliminate lead from gasoline. Over 50% of all U.S. refineries participate in the lead rights market. As refineries are re-equipped, there is an incentive to install new equipment that allows easy elimination of lead. For firms that must purchase lead rights, this purchase cost acts like a tax on lead, which tends to raise the price of leaded gasoline, which in turn provides a disincentive to use leaded gasoline.

Perhaps the environmental damage associated with lead is sufficiently high that an outright ban, as used in Canada, is the best approach. (In Figure 10.1, this would be represented by what is called a "corner solution": the *SMC* (social marginal cost) curve is so high that even at the point of zero pollution, *SMC* exceeds marginal benefit, implying that an outright ban is called for.) It is not feasible (or desirable), however, to ban all pollutants.

The United States has recently added new market-based programs. For example, in 1993 it held its first auction of SO_2 (sulpher dioxide) pollution rights. In this auction 150,000 SO_2 emission permits were sold for an average price of U.S.$150, with prices ranging from U.S.$122 to U.S.$450. Each permit purchased at auction allows the purchaser to emit a certain quantity of SO_2. Since these pollution permits are tradeable, this is an example of a tradeable pollution rights program.

A related system allows firms to earn credits that can be used to allow them to emit pollutants. Thus, for example, a firm that achieved pollution reductions in one production facility above and beyond some mandated requirement might be allowed to treat the difference as a credit that could be used to offset excess pollution in another plant. Usually these credits are not tradeable, but must be used by the firm that earns them. Credit systems are being tried in Australia, Germany, and the United States. Such systems have some valuable properties, but they would be even more efficient if the credits could be traded. The use of both credit systems and tradeable permit systems is still in its infancy, since only a handful are in place around the world, mostly in the United States. They may, however, become widely used if the U.S. (and other) experiments prove successful.

A market-based approach can take advantage of market efficiencies in achieving environmental objectives. At present, governments in Canada seem to be moving toward taxes and other market-based approaches to environmental problems, attracted in part by the possibility of raising much needed extra revenues. In particular, Canada's Green Plan (1990), produced by the federal government, suggests using market incentives. The Plan argues[7]: "Economic incentives can be used to harness powerful market forces to environmental ends. They have advantages over the traditional regulatory approach [standards] that Canada has relied on for decades." However, relatively little action toward harnessing this approach has been undertaken.

10.4 Specific Externality-Based Environmental Problems

10.4.1 Air Pollution

Air pollution is one of the environmental problems that will be fairly obvious to most readers of this book. Air pollution comes from two main sources: exhaust from motor vehicles and industrial emissions. The externality is very clear. Most drivers considering going out for a drive do not consider the cost that their car exhaust will impose on others. They will take a drive if the benefit to them is more than the cost to them as individuals. External costs will not be taken into account. Thus, we get too much car exhaust in accordance with the reasoning underlying Figure 10.1. The same reasoning applies to industrial emissions. A factory, or electricity generating station, or pulp mill is not going to take into account the external costs of its emissions.

Large cities tend to have particular problems associated with air pollution. In very large, highly polluted cities, such as Los Angeles, Mexico City, and Shanghai, urban air pollution is estimated to significantly reduce life expectancy. In major Canadian cities, air quality improved following the initial wave of environmental regulation in the 1970s, which consisted mainly of emission controls on cars and closing down or moving major industrial sources of air pollution. Air quality is falling again, however, because it is driven by increasing population and increasing densities, and there are few remaining low-cost fixes available. In particular, obtaining further reductions in car exhaust emissions will be difficult, and cities like Montreal, Toronto, and Vancouver are moving more toward trying to persuade people to drive less. This is difficult, however, since average commuting distances are rising and substitute forms of transportation, particularly urban rapid transit, are very expensive.

10.4.2 Acid Rain

Acid rain has been used as an illustrative example at several points in this chapter. Acid rain is created when sulphur dioxide (SO_2) and nitrogen oxides (NO_x) react with water to form sulphuric acid and nitric acid. These acids collect in clouds and fall to earth in the form of rain, snow, and fog, and in dry forms as well. Such precipitation raises the acidity of lakes and rivers, damaging and eventually eliminating fish and other life forms. It also damages and slows the growth of most species of trees and other vegetation, and speeds up corrosion of buildings, roads, and pieces of infrastructure.

About 70% of man-made atmospheric sulphur dioxides comes from (mostly coal-burning) electric power plants. Nitrogen oxides are created in approximately equal proportions by electricity generation and motor vehicle exhaust. Acid precipitation occurs throughout Canada, but the most seriously affected areas are in southern Ontario and Quebec where, according to Chiras (1994), at least 100 lakes have lost all wildlife and forest stocks are being seriously affected.

Most acid rain falling in Canada is believed to arise from sulphur dioxide and nitrogen oxide emissions originating in the United States, so, as indicated above, there is a classic externality problem that extends beyond any single political jurisdictions. This makes the problem particularly difficult to deal with, since there is always strong regionally based opposition to attempts to reduce acid rain. Opposition comes from coal-producing states such as Virginia, and from states where coal-based electricity is produced and used, such as Ohio. Lobbyists for these interests have gone so far as to argue that concern over acid rain has been promoted largely by Canadian energy producers who want to export energy products to the United States to replace energy currently provided by coal-burning electricity plants.

There has been considerable attention focused on attempts to control acid rain. In 1991 Canada and the United States signed the Canada-U.S. Air Quality Agreement, which requires a 40% reduction in emissions that cause acid rain, relative to 1980 levels, by the year 2010. Since much of this pollution comes from regulated or government-owned utilities, emission-reducing technology could be mandated fairly easily. The main method of emission abatement is through the installation of scrubbers in utility smokestacks. Canada achieved its required 40% cutback in SO_2 emissions in 1992 and the United States is on target to achieve its 40% reduction in SO_2 by 2010, as required. Reductions in NO_x are being achieved mainly through stricter emission controls for motor vehicles. As of the mid 1990s, total acid rain precipitation in Canada had fallen significantly from 1980 levels and some acidified lakes were recovering.

It would be interesting to do a calculation of the total cost of acid rain and compare this with the cost of reducing emissions of acid rain. Ideally, we would want to tax emission of sulphur and nitrogen dioxides so that the marginal private costs could be brought into line with social costs. Such calculations are difficult but not impossible, but do not seem to be available. It is estimated, however, that the cost of acid precipitation in the United States is about $5 billion per year.[8]

10.4.3 Ozone Depletion

The Earth's atmosphere contains a layer with substantial quantities of ozone, a variant of the oxygen molecule. Although high concentrations of ozone at ground level are considered a health hazard for humans, the atmospheric ozone layer provides very valuable protection against ultraviolet radiation from the sun. Prior to the 1980s, a number of scientists raised the theoretical possibility that a class of widely used industrial chemicals called chlorofluorocarbons (CFCs) might destroy atmospheric ozone. Various attempts to measure this effect were unconvincing until, in 1985, British scientists reported a hole in the ozone layer over the South Pole. This was a surprising finding, especially since very little CFC use occurs in that region.

Scientists have, however, finally worked out the chemistry of CFC-ozone interaction and predicted (correctly) the subsequent emergence of a hole in the ozone layer over the North Pole as well. It turns out that there are good (but complex) reasons as to why ozone depletion occurred first over the poles. It took many years of CFC use before there were sufficient atmospheric concentrations to materially affect the ozone layer, but measurable ozone depletion is now evident over temperate regions and is worsening quite rapidly. Some experts thought at first that ozone depletion might be a natural phenomenon, but there is now little doubt that CFCs are the principal cause.

Ozone depletion has direct effects on human health. It appears to be causing significant increases in skin cancer rates among Caucasians. People with very fair skin are particularly susceptible. In Australia, which has a large proportion of fair-skinned people, but is subject to both strong sunlight and significant ozone depletion, skin cancer rates have risen sharply in recent years. In the United States, skin cancer rates among whites increased by over 70% over the 1980s.[9] In addition, exposure to ultraviolet radiation causes cataracts, which cloud the lenses in the eyes. Left untreated, cataracts cause blindness, although surgical treatment is fairly simple, at least in wealthier countries. Finally, exposure to ultraviolet radiation apparently depresses the immune system, making humans more susceptible to viral and bacterial diseases of all types.

CFCs were regarded as wonder chemicals when they were first discovered in 1930. They are cheap, easy to produce, and nontoxic. They have been widely used as coolants in refrigeration and air conditioning, for foam packaging (including styrofoam cups), as propellants in aerosol cans, and for other purposes. Closely related gases (halons and other chlorine and bromine compounds) are also widely used and have similar ozone-depleting effects. Their effects on the ozone layer were completely unanticipated.

Surprisingly, a concerted international response to ozone depletion arose very quickly after ozone depletion was convincingly established. In 1987 a group of 24 countries signed the Montreal Protocol, calling for a 50% cut in CFC production by 1998. Another 11 countries signed in 1988. (Unfortunately, several major actual or potential producers of CFCs have declined to participate, including China. Having reached a stage of development where refrigeration is a rapidly growing industry, China is reluctant to impose extra constraints on the development process. Current officials there regard ozone protection and many other environmental objectives as a luxury that wealthy countries can afford but they cannot.) Canada was able to exceed Montreal Protocol objectives by achieving a 58% reduction in CFC production between 1987 and 1994, and expects to achieve virtual elimination of CFC production by 2003.

Current scientific understanding suggests that the ozone layer would slowly regenerate if ozone depleting emissions were dramatically reduced. More specifically, if CFC emissions were stopped in 2000, ozone levels would continue to fall for some period of time because of CFCs already in the atmosphere, but would regenerate to pre-1980 levels before the middle of the 21st century (i.e., in about 40 to 50 years). However, given the relatively slow decline in the worldwide use of

CFCs, readers of this book must reasonably expect ozone depletion to worsen over the course of their lifetimes.

The original ozone depletion problem arose in part from simple ignorance, since we did not know about the effect of CFCs on ozone until very recently. Now, however, this has become a classic externality problem. Any individual or firm or country that produces CFCs gets all the associated benefits, but suffers only a small portion of the costs. Social costs exceed private costs.

It is not obvious, however, what the appropriate policy response to ozone depletion should be. The unstated implication of most discussion of ozone depletion is that CFC production ought to be reduced to zero or as low as possible. While it appears likely that an appropriate marginal analysis of costs and benefits would imply a very substantial reduction of CFC production, there are some very high-value uses of CFCs (in computers and in health technology, for example) that probably should not be reduced to zero, at least until economically attractive substitutes can be developed.

10.4.4 Global Warming and the Greenhouse Effect

The earth seems to be warming up, partly as a result of the accumulation of carbon particles from fossil fuel combustion, and carbon dioxide and other greenhouse gases in the air. These materials trap heat in the atmosphere. This is referred to as the Greenhouse Effect. It is hard to predict the net effect of an appreciable warming of the earth's surface. It is possible that the world might, on average, benefit, as large Northern land masses become warm enough to sustain higher levels of economic activity. If, however, significant global warming does take place, it will certainly be very damaging for those parts of the world that are already hot, and it will accelerate the expansion of deserts. In addition, the polar ice caps may partially melt, flooding the world's low-lying coastal cities. Also, greenhouse effects may cause greater variability in weather patterns, resulting in more floods and droughts, etc.

Recent estimates, as reported on the World Resources Institute website (*www.wri.org*) suggest that temperatures have risen by about $0.5°C$ over the past century and will rise another $1°C$ to $2°C$ in the next century due to greenhouse emissions that have already occured. This could give rise to significant melting of polar ice-caps and an increase in sea level. Over the past century, average sea level has risen by 15-20°C (6-8 inches). Plausible but pessimistic projections suggest a rise in sea level on the order of 40 cm to 55 cm (16 to 22 inches) over the 21st century. Large parts of entire countries (e.g., Bangladesh and the Netherlands) are within 55 cm of sea level, as are parts of Canada, including much of the Maritime Provinces (New Brunswick, Nova Scotia, and Prince Edward Island) and heavily populated parts of Greater Vancouver. In some of these areas, a 55 cm increase in sea level could be defended (at considerable cost) using dykes, although flooding would become more frequent and more costly. It should be emphasized, furthermore, that these estimates are highly uncertain, and actual effects could either be much more serious or much less serious than suggested here. (See *www.fao.org* to access U.N. estimates.)

Once again, greenhouse effects represent classic externality problems. As we drive our cars or use electricity, we get full private benefits from such activities. We also impose global warming effects (i.e., we impose external effects, presumed to be negative) on the entire world. Thus we bear only a negligible share of any global warming costs of our own personal activity.

It has been suggested that carbon taxes could be used to address the greenhouse effect, but there is little reason to be optimistic about attempts to reduce these effects. At the international level, the externality problems are too great, given the central importance of energy production in economic development.

10.5 Siting of Hazardous Waste Facilities and the NIMBY Problem

One of the most intractable current environmental problems involves the siting of hazardous waste facilities, ordinary waste facilities, waste incinerators, etc. The most extreme aspect of this problem is the storage of nuclear waste, but storage and treatment of toxic chemical waste is a larger immediate concern. The traditional method of storing toxic chemical waste was simply to dump it into landfills on private or public land. Sometimes the waste would be in storage containers, sometimes not. In the late 1970s strong evidence emerged that communities living close to such landfills were suffering negative consequences. The most famous case concerned Love Canal, New York, where children appeared to suffer much higher than expected rates of birth defects, leukemia and other cancers, and various other health complaints.

While scientific and legal controversies continued over the exact links between toxic wastes and health hazards, it became clear that there was a serious problem in Love Canal.[10] The entire community was evacuated in 1980. The town of Times Beach, Missouri, was evacuated for similar reasons in 1982. In the aftermath of such incidents, various regulations have been passed in many countries, including Canada and the United States, governing the disposal and treatment of toxic waste. In addition, public concern and awareness over toxic waste has risen enormously, giving rise to the so-called NIMBY problem.

NIMBY stands for Not In My BackYard, and it refers to the problem that communities will usually strongly resist local siting of hazardous waste dumps or other facilities that might generate negative externalities. In the United States, some four years of work and $1.5 million were spent on a proposed (and much needed) treatment and storage facility for chemical waste in Sand Canyon in Los Angeles, but the facility was abandoned in the face of seemingly insurmountably negative public opinion. Construction of hazardous waste storage facilities remains inadequate to meet "need", with the result that wastes are being stored in unsuitable locations.

Hazardous waste needs to go somewhere. At the government policy level, it is possible to decide on relatively good locations for hazardous waste. They should be in geologically stable areas, away from major population centers, yet easily and safely reachable on major transportation routes, etc. Inevitably, however, proposed waste facilities are near someone, and such people are not usually persuaded by arguments that it is in the social interest for them to bear whatever risks are associated with hazardous waste facilities.

A fairly natural economic response would be to compensate local communities financially for increased risks associated with hazardous waste, but such approaches do not seem to go very far toward solving the NIMBY problem. In particular, many people view hazardous waste siting as an all or nothing issue, and are not amenable to discussing market-like transactions associated with hazardous waste. Second, in cases where a compensation approach has been tried, levels of compensation demanded tend to be prohibitively high.

Even if compensation can be used, there is a question of who should pay. Applying economic principles, the payment for waste disposal should be incorporated in the price of the products whose production gives rise to the waste. This is, however, hard to implement, giving rise to externality problems.

At present, there is a shortage of toxic waste incinerators in Canada. For example, there was a significant controversy at the University of British Columbia (UBC). UBC has had a small toxic waste incinerator for many years, but generates more toxic waste than can be accommodated and, so, has trouble disposing of this waste. Vancouver hospitals and other producers of toxic waste also have disposal problems. UBC proposed building a large toxic waste incinerator on campus that would be used to incinerate much of the toxic waste produced in the Vancouver area. The problem is that UBC is located at the western tip of Vancouver, just upwind of the densest population center in Western Canada, and arguably one of the worst places in Canada to put such an incinerator. Local residents protested vigorously. These protests were fuelled by findings linking various health problems to toxic waste incinerators in major U.S. cities, particularly the toxic waste incinerator run by the National Institutes of Health in Atlanta, Georgia. Largely as a result of local protest, the project was put on hold in 1994 and subsequently cancelled.

It should be noted that the NIMBY problem applies to areas other than toxic waste disposal, and is a powerful explanatory tool in understanding the operations of local government. Siting of halfway houses for paroled prison inmates, drop-in centers for drug users, and low-income housing projects are, for example, all subject to the NIMBY problem. Many people think such projects are a good idea in the abstract, but do not want them in their own backyard.

10.6 Cost–Benefit Analysis and Discounting for Environmental Projects

In evaluating possible environmental policies, cost-benefit analysis is often used. Consider, for example, the problem of sewage treatment. Private incentives for sewage treatment are too weak because each individual household bears only a small fraction of the total cost of its untreated sewage. Thus, individual households rarely invest in household-level sewage treatment technology (although it does exist) unless forced to do so by governments. In large cities that lack sewage treatment, water supplies are excessively contaminated with the bacteria that reside in human waste, causing excessively high levels of disease. Thus, there is a strong externality-based rationale for public provision of sewage treatment, possibly financed by mandated sewage connection charges or by general taxes.

Suppose a local city government is contemplating expanding its sewage treatment facilities. It could use cost-benefit analysis, as described in Chapter 3. It would add up the costs and benefits and see whether the total value is positive or negative. With construction projects such as sewers, the costs of the project come long before the major benefits. The main costs come during the years of construction, but the benefits do not even begin until after construction is completed and then continue for a long time. Thus, in comparing costs and benefits, the principal tradeoff is between current costs and future benefits.

In comparing costs and benefits that arise at different times, a discount rate is used. For example, suppose that our project is a very simple one, involving current costs and benefits that arise after 10 years. The net present value of the project would be

$$NPV = -C + B/(1 + r)^{10}$$

where r is the discount rate. Suppose that C (the cost) is 100 and B (the benefit 10 years hence) is 250. If $r = 0.1$ (or 10%), then $(1 + r)^{10} = 2.59$, and $NPV = -100 + 250/2.59 = -3.5$. The value is negative, implying that the project should not be undertaken. However, even a slight decline in the discount rate to, say, 9% would make the value positive and lead to a positive recommendation. Thus, the choice of the discount rate is very important. The longer the time horizon, the more important the discount rate. The selection of the discount rate is particularly important in the analysis of environmental projects, where we often consider projects that will have impacts for decades or even centuries.

How is the discount rate to be selected? One influential idea in public sector discounting is that the discount rate should equal the opportunity cost of capital, which is taken to be the pre-tax rate of return on investment projects in the private sector. The basic rationale for using the opportunity cost of capital as a discount rate is based on the assumption that the project (in this case the sewer) would replace an alternative private sector investment. Suppose this pre-tax annual rate of return is 10%. Thus we imagine that if we do not build the sewer, an alternative private investment with a 10% return will go ahead instead. Thus if we did not build the sewer, we could put the initial amount of 100 into the private investment and let it accumulate returns at the rate of 10% per year. At the end of 10 years the value would be $100(1 + 0.1)^{10} = 259$, which exceeds the environmental benefit of 250. Thus, if the group of people who would have received the environmental benefit of 250 instead get the private benefit of 259, they would prefer the private sector investment. Only if we had an environmental project that yielded more than 259 should we opt for it. This implies that using a discount rate of 10% would lead to the right decisions.

While this argument has a grain of truth, it is not quite correct. One point is that private sector returns may incorporate a risk premium. It has been argued (see Lind (1982)) that the appropriate risk premium that should be incorporated in public sector discounting is less than the risk premium embodied in private sector returns. More significantly, the entire argument for using the opportunity cost of capital rests on the assumption that the true alternative to the public project is a private sector investment. If the true alternative is to spend the money on a big party (or some other form of current consumption), then the private return to capital is not relevant. In this case, if we can assume that the current and future consumers are the same people, then the appropriate discount rate is determined by their willingness to trade off future consumption for current consumption, referred to as the consumer rate of time preference. The consumer rate of time preference is normally much lower than the private pre-tax rate of return on capital, perhaps on the order of 5%.

There is another complication. Suppose that 10 years from now there is a different group of consumers. Now we have a pure conflict of interest. Current consumers (who will not be here in 10 years) would prefer current consumption, since they get no benefit from the project. Future consumers prefer the project because they do not pay the cost but do receive the benefits. In this case, the discount rate is determined by the relative weights we put on future and current consumers. For projects with a duration of only 10 years, this intergenerational problem seems relatively minor. But for projects that will last 50 years or 100 years, the intergenerational conflict is really the key issue. If the government is the guardian of the future, it should place some weight on future generations. This implies a further reduction in the discount rate below current consumer's rate of time preference, at least for projects whose opportunity cost is current consumption.

There has been much debate over appropriate discount rates. In Canada, the official standing recommendation for public sector discounting derives from a 1976 Treasury Board document that suggests using a (real) discount rate of 10%. In practice, a real discount rate of 8% is more commonly used. However, as the analysis here suggests, there is no single discount rate that can be applied to all situations. The appropriate discount rate depends on the nature of the project. In particular, it depends on whether the alternative use of resources is an alternative investment or current consumption. (More precisely, it depends on the entire time path of the alternative consumption stream.) The appropriate discount rate also depends on the duration of the project, because this determines the extent to which intergenerational equity considerations arise.

For long-run environmental projects, a real discount rate of 8% or 10% is too high. Lind (1982) suggests 3% or 4% as reasonable discount rates for such projects. Harvey (1993) has made the sensible and interesting suggestion of using a declining discount rate. Thus, the first few years might be discounted at a rate of 10% or 12%, but a lower rate would be used for more distant years.

10.7 Jurisdiction for Environmental Policy

Some environmental externalities are purely local in nature, such as urban air pollution or sewage treatment, whereas others are global in their effect, such as global warming or ozone depletion. There are, in addition, environmental issues with an intermediate scope. This variation in the scope of environmental externalities and problems suggests that various different levels of government might reasonably be involved in environmental policy.

It is not surprising, therefore, that jurisdiction over environmental policy in Canada is divided among all three major levels of government: local, provincial, and federal. At the federal or national level, a department of government, Environment Canada, has jurisdiction over environmental policy. Most provincial governments also have separate environment ministries.

The global aspect of many environmental problems creates tensions at the international level, especially since there is no international body that coordinates and adjudicates international environmental disputes. As mentioned in Chapter 9, there is an environmental side agreement to NAFTA. This side agreement creates binational and trilateral panels to monitor and adjudicate environmental issues involving the three member countries. In addition, following the successful completion of the Uruguay Round of international trade negotiations, culminating in the formation of the World Trade Organization

(WTO), trade and environment issues have become the top agenda item for further negotiation within the WTO. Thus, some supranational institutions to deal with environmental institutions are emerging.

10.8 Bibliographic Notes

The theory of externalities is described in most public finance text-books, including those listed at the end of Chapter 1. Coase (1960) is the classic reference on the importance of property rights in external-ity problems. Dorfman and Dorfman (1993) contains a number of interesting readings on externalities and environmental issues. A very helpful survey of environmental regulation in Canada is contained in Nemetz (1986). As for sources on environmental issues, the World-watch Institute publishes an annual, *State of the World*, that provides a lot of valuable material on current problems. A similar but somewhat more technical regular publication is *World Resources*, produced by the World Resources Institute. The September 1989 special issue of *Scientific American* was devoted to environmental issues. Chiras (1994) is a very good introduction to environmental issues and Doern (1990) describes various case studies of Canadian environmental regulation.

Notes

1. Lorne Bozinoff and Peter MacIntosh, "Public Believes Government Not Doing Enough to Clean Up Environment," *The Gallup Report*, May 28, 1990.

2. Rhoads (1985), p. 115.

3. See Greenwald and Stiglitz (1986) for a discussion of pecuniary externali-ties.

4. Most cities have noise by-laws that provide some implications for proper-ty rights. Such rights are, however, hard to enforce.

5. John Fox, "Credit system could make pollution fight pay," *Financial Post*, April 23, 1990, p. 1.

6. This description is based on Robert W. Hahn, "Economic Prescriptions for Environmental Problems: How the Patient Followed the Doctor's Orders".; 1989. *Journal of Economic Perspectives* 3:95-114.

7. Government of Canada (1990), *Canada's Green Plan*, Ottawa: Supply and Services Canada, p. 156.

8. See Chiras (1994).

9. Cynthia Shea "Protecting the Ozone Layer," *State of the World*, 1989, p.820.

10. See Craig McInnes, "The Long Road Back to Love Canal," *Globe and Mail*, May 19, 1990, p. D5.

On-line Sources

For Canadian government information about environmental policy, see: *http://www.ec.gc.ca/cepa/index_e.html*

For Greenpeace's perspective see: *http://www.greenpeacecanada.org/*

For a perspective that gets much less media attention, see the Fraser Institute: *http://www.fraserinstitute.ca/publications/books/facts_not_fear/*

11

Natural Resource Management and Policy

11.1 Natural Resources and the Environment

This chapter is devoted to a set of environmental issues associated with natural resource use. We normally distinguish among three major types of natural resource: renewable resources (such as forest and fish stocks), nonrenewable resources (such as oil and natural gas), and land. These resources are important parts of the natural environment. In recent years, increasing concern has been expressed over the way in which such resources are used. Furthermore, in Canada, exploitation of natural resources is a very important component of business activity. In this chapter we consider some important principles of resource management and public policy toward natural resources.

11.2 Renewable Resource Management

The major renewable resources are fish stocks, forests, animal species, and, less obviously, soil. The key idea is that these resources regularly renew themselves through natural (primarily biological) processes. For the purposes of discussion, consider a particular renewable resource stock such as a particular species of fish. A key to understanding fisheries, or any renewable resource, is Figure 11.1.

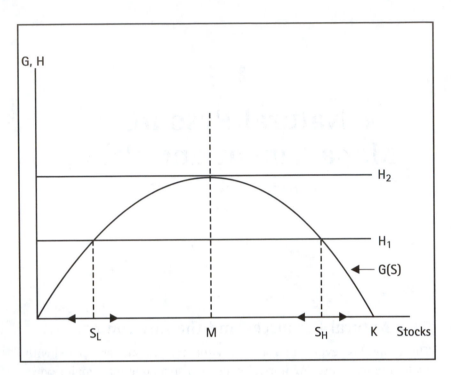

FIGURE 11.1 Renewable Resource Dynamics

The horizontal axis in Figure 11.1 measures the stock, S, of the renewable resource, in this case some species of fish. The curve labelled $G(S)$ represents the growth of the stock. As drawn in the diagram, the growth of the fish stock is zero if the stock itself is zero: if there are no fish to breed, then no additional fish will be added to the stock. If the stock is small but positive, the fish will breed and add to the stock, leading to positive growth. As the stock increases from low levels, growth also increases since there are more fish available to breed. At some point, however, indicated by stock level M, the fish stock is large enough to induce significant crowding effects, since newborn fish must compete with a large existing stock of adult fish for food, and therefore suffer reduced opportunities for survival. Thus, the growth of the stock declines as further increases in the stock occur. Left to itself, the fish stock would reach its maximum size, indicated by stock level K in the diagram, where growth would be zero. This is the carrying capacity of the fishery and represents the maximum stock that can be supported.

A commonly used mathematical function that captures this pattern of growth is the logistic function, which can be written as follows.

$$G(S) = rS(1 - S/K)$$

As can be seen from close inspection of this equation, if $S = 0$, the growth of the stock is zero. Similarly, if $S = K$, the growth of the stock is also zero. For intermediate levels of the stock, growth is positive, and it is maximized at $S = K/2$. The logistic function is often used in modelling renewable resources, although it is only an approximation and actual growth functions will differ for particular resource stocks. The general pattern exhibited in Figure 11.1 does, however, capture the essential elements of almost all renewable resources.

The horizontal lines on the diagram, denoted H_1 and H_2, are potential harvest rates. The key observation is that if harvest rate H is precisely equal to growth rate G, then the stock does not change in size, because the amount being harvested is exactly equal to the amount of extra growth. Thus, if $H = G$, we would say that the stock is in a steady state and the harvest is sustainable. If we consider harvest rate H_1, we can see that it can be sustained at a stock size of S_L or S_H, which are the stock levels where the harvest function intersects the growth function, implying that $H = G$. Given harvest level H_1, stock S_H is what we refer to as a stable steady state stock. This means that if the stock moves slightly away from S_H, it will tend to return. Consider, for example, a slight increase in the stock above S_H. This will cause the growth rate to fall slightly, in particular, below harvest rate H_1. Since harvesting exceeds growth, the stock will shrink in size and return toward S_H. Similarly, if the stock fell below S_H, the growth rate would rise above the harvest rate, leading to a self-correcting increase in the stock, moving it back toward S_H.

Similar reasoning shows that stock S_L is in an unstable steady state. Specifically, consider what happens if the stock is at level S_L and the harvest rate is H_1. This is a steady state, in that the growth of the stock exactly replaces the harvest as time proceeds. Suppose, however, that some shock lowers the stock slightly. Now the harvest rate exceeds the growth rate so the stock gets smaller. As the stock gets smaller, the excess of harvesting over underlying growth grows, so the stock declines even more rapidly. This continues until extinction occurs. Similarly, if we start at stock S_L and the stock is perturbed upward, the stock will continue to grow and never return to S_L. Thus, S_L in unstable in the sense that slight disturbances are not self-correcting. If the stock deviates from S_L, it quickly moves even further away and never returns. The possibility of unstable steady states has some interesting policy implications. It suggests that it does not make sense to try to manage a resource at an unstable steady state, even if this steady state appeared to be desirable, because a slight mistake can bring disaster. Especially if there is uncertainty about key parameters, such as the harvest or the stock, it is important to manage the stock with a considerable margin for error.

The maximum harvest that can be sustained (called the maximum sustainable yield) is H_2, which can be sustained at a stock size of M. Consider what would happen, however, if the stock happened to fall below M and harvesting continued at rate H_2. Now the harvest rate would exceed the growth rate of the stock and the stock would fall. Next period, the harvest, still H_2, would exceed the growth rate by even more, and the stock would fall even faster. Eventually, the stock would be extinguished and no fish would be left. Stock size M is a semi-stable steady state. As with the unstable steady state, it would be risky to try to manage the stock precisely at stock M with harvest H_2. A more conservative approach would be to adopt a harvest slightly below H_2 and let the stock settle at a stable steady state slightly above M. A harvest rate greater than H_2 would lead to extinction no matter what the initial stock size.

The basic economics of renewable resource management are fairly subtle. It is often taken to be self-evident that ideal management of a renewable resource implies harvesting at or near the maximum sustainable yield (H_2 in the diagram), and therefore requires maintaining a stock of size M. This is not necessarily true, however. First, it is possible that a renewable resource may be uneconomic. For example, if harvesting costs are high and demand for the resource is low, then it may be good management to simply leave the stock alone, in which case it would grow to carrying capacity K and remain there.

Second, it is also possible that a resource should be fully depleted. If, for example, the current value of resource product is very high, the harvest cost is low, and the growth rate is low, it might make sense to harvest all of the stock immediately, invest the proceeds, and earn more from the investment than could have been earned by managing the resource on a sustainable basis.

Another important possibility is cyclical management, in which the harvest level varies depending on economic conditions, subject to a requirement that the yield be sustainable on average. Thus, if prices of the resource good are high, a harvest exceeding the growth rate might be allowed, while if prices are low, a harvest less than the growth rate would be called for, leading to a sustainable pattern of harvesting overall, although in any one year the harvest might differ from the growth rate. There is also the possibility that optimal policy might call for variable harvesting, where the harvest would vary, depending on economic conditions, but with no overall sustainability constraint.

Finally, it is possible that optimal management calls for sustainable yield management, in which case there should be a positive harvest that is equal, on a year-by-year basis, to the growth rate of the resource. The appropriate level of this yield may or may not be the maximum sustainable yield.

One difficulty with resource management is that it is difficult to determine a fully optimal harvesting plan in a real situation because such analysis requires knowledge of the value of the resource in the future. Given the high degree of uncertainty about future values, there is strong sentiment in the resource management community toward sustainable yield management, so as to avoid the potentially serious mistake of depleting a resource that would have been very valuable in the future. Thus, sustainable yield management can be viewed as a type of insurance that is appropriate in the presence of uncertainty. Most major renewable resources are officially managed on a sustainable yield basis. However, as we shall see, sustainable yield is frequently not achieved and there is a strong bias toward excessive depletion in actual practice.

11.3 North Atlantic Cod and the Canada–Spain Turbot War

For much of the past 500 years, the Grand Banks cod fishery located off the coast of Newfoundland has been one of the world's most productive fisheries, and a major source of income for the province. This fishery was also intensively fished by European nations, particularly Spain. The current international Law of the Sea (dating from 1977) recognizes that countries have a right to control fishing and other forms of ocean use within 200 miles of their shores. Most of the Grand Banks fishery lies with the Canadian 200-mile limit. Some of it, however, lies outside this limit in international waters. Fishing in the international waters of the Atlantic is regulated by an organization known as the North Atlantic Fishing Organization (NAFO), of which Canada is a member.

Until the 1960s, fishing in the Atlantic cod fishery was not closely regulated. The fishery was very abundant, although the stock did not seem quite as large as it once had been. During the 1960s cod harvests rose sharply, reflecting progress in fishing technology and an increased number of boats. The harvest peaked in 1968 and then began to fall as a result of declining stocks. By the 1970s serious concerns were being expressed about the future of the stock, and efforts were made both within Canada and in NAFO to reduce catches to sustainable levels. In particular, the 1977 extension of the nautical limit to 200 miles (from 12 miles) allowed Canada control over much of the fishery. Fish catches were sharply reduced in the late 1970s and the cod stock began to recover.

The politics of this process led, however, to a bias in favour of overfishing. In Canada, it was always in the interest of politicians to use the most optimistic assessments of the stock in setting fishing quotas, and fishermen regularly complained the quotas were too restrictive. In addition, various other Canadian policies, especially regional development policies, had the effect of subsidizing the Canadian cod fishing industry. Also, Spanish and Portuguese fishing vessels increased the intensity of fishing efforts in areas outside the 200-mile limit.

As a result of overfishing, cod stocks started to fall again in the mid 1980s. The allowable harvest was reduced throughout the late 1980s as stocks fell, but the harvest consistently remained too high to allow stock recovery. The cod fishery remained commercially very important throughout this period, until 1992. In 1992, the stock had fallen to less than 5% of its level of a few decades earlier and was clearly in serious danger of extinction. In 1992, the Grand Banks cod fishery was closed for an indefinite period. The closure of the Grand Banks cod fishery was a major economic shock to Newfoundland and to fishing fleets from Spain and other countries. The stocks had been overfished by Canadian and European fleets to the point of near extinction. Figure 11.2 shows the evolution of the North Atlantic cod stock from 1962 to 1993. Note that in 1992, when the fishery was

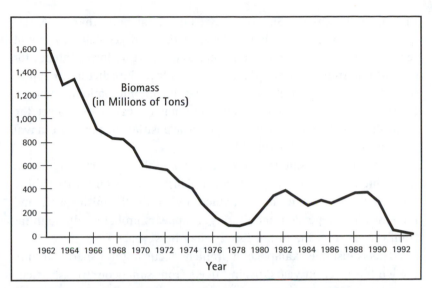

FIGURE 11.2 North Atlantic Cod Breeding Stock 1962–1993
Source: Lear and Parsons (1993) and Department of Fisheries and Oceans.

closed, stocks had fallen to less than 5% of the 1962 level. The fishery was re-opened for limited commercial fishing in July 1999. Total biomass did increase in the 1990s but was still marginal as of 1999.

Another important North Atlantic fish is the turbot. It was hardly harvested at all until the mid 1980s, when declining cod stocks combined with expanding fishing fleets induced a shift toward turbot, especially on the part of the Spanish and Portuguese fishing fleets. Like cod, turbot swim in and out of Canada's 200-mile limit. Overfishing occurred quickly: between 1984 and 1988, North Atlantic turbot stocks fell by 50% according to NAFO estimates.

By the late 1980s, NAFO was allocating quite low quotas for turbot in an effort to establish a sustainable yield, but Spain and Portugal objected to their low quotas and ignored them. Over this period, Spain and Portugal were catching at least 10 times their allocation. In 1995, it became clear that the turbot fish stock was also in danger of extinction and most fishing nations stopped catching turbot, except for Spanish vessels, which continued to be very active in the area just outside the Canadian 200-mile limit.

In early 1995, Canada seized a Spanish fishing trawler in this region. Upon seizure, Canadian authorities were able to demonstrate that not only was the Spanish vessel taking far more than its NAFO quota, but it was also taking undersized fish and keeping two sets of records, one true set and an additional set, reporting lower catches for official reporting purposes. Canada had no legal jurisdiction to apprehend the Spanish vessel, but received a lot of international support. Spain objected to the seizure and sent naval vessels to protect the Spanish fleet. Canada, however, was in a position to put more naval force into the area, which it did.

In the face of rising tensions, Canada and the EU (including Spain) were able to come to an agreement in April of 1995 on turbot fishing that would lead to dramatic reductions in the Spanish catch and increases in independent monitoring. It appears probable, although far from certain, that the turbot fishery may be saved.

This is just one example of a problem occurring in fisheries around the world. In recent years, fishing fleets from some countries, particularly Japan, Taiwan, and South Korea, have adopted drift net fishing, a process that involves stationing large nets that catch everything, rather than being tailored for specific types of fish. Drift nets, sometimes referred to as walls of death, represent a low-cost way of catching a lot of fish. (Japan has the world's largest fish catch.)

Drift nets create several problems, including the simple fact that current harvests are unsustainable. Another problem with drift nets is that they catch and kill a lot of species that are not commercially useful, including dolphins, which are supposed to be a protected species. The fishing boats treat this extra kill as being costless, but it may have substantial social costs arising from its effects on the overall ecology of the oceans, and for other reasons as well. Countries such as Canada, Australia, and the United States have been trying to get international agreement to ban, or at least to strictly limit, drift net fishing, so far without success. The world fish catch peaked in 1988 but, because of declining stocks, has been falling since then.

11.4 Open Access Resources and Congestion Externalities

Fishing stocks are not the only renewable resources that are under pressure. Forests, soil, and wildlife species are also being exploited at unsustainable levels. One reason for such problems is simple population growth: more people put more pressure on resource stocks. Population growth is discussed more fully later in this chapter. However, there is a very important market failure that contributes to renewable resource management. This is the open access problem (sometimes referred to as the tragedy of the commons[1]), which is actually a special type of externality problem.

The open access problem was first noted when sheep–raising was a very important economic activity in England. Most towns would have common areas where any sheep could graze, and, in addition, individuals would have private land. It was observed that common land was invariably overgrazed: grazed to the point at which the grass was damaged and its growth actually retarded, lowering the total yield from the common land. The question was: "Why was the common overgrazed when everyone knew that overgrazing was inefficient?" Only an incompetent sheep farmer would allow his private land to be overgrazed. The answer follows from the basic theory of externalities. Grazing the common creates an externality.

Consider first the management of private land. If Farmer A allows his sheep to graze on his own land, there is a cost: the grass is eaten, so it cannot be sold to other sheep farmers or fed to other sheep. If the farmer is foolish enough to allow his land to be overgrazed, he will bear the full costs. As a result he has an incentive to limit grazing to the efficient level.

Now consider the common. Suppose that Farmer A observes that the common has already been grazed as far as optimal management would suggest. What should he do? If he does not allow his sheep to graze, he gets no immediate benefit at all. If he allows his sheep to graze, he will get some benefit. He will also bear some cost in that his sheep will have less effective grazing land in the future. He might conclude that if his sheep do not graze, someone else's sheep will, so he has nothing to gain by restraining his sheep. More generally, he has an incentive to allow his sheep to graze just up to the point where his (private) marginal benefit is equal to his (private) marginal cost.

The social marginal cost, however, is much higher than the sheep farmer's private marginal cost, because when Farmer A allows his sheep to graze, he is reducing the capacity of the land to support the sheep of other farmers who also use the common. Therefore, the social marginal cost exceeds the private marginal cost, leading to excessive levels of grazing on the common. This conforms exactly to Figure 10.1.

The problem of common grazing land is dealt with fairly easily, at least conceptually. If grazing land is privately owned (or at least privately controlled), then a self-interested owner or user will have incentives to manage grazing efficiently. Thus, the solution is to convert common land to private control. This is in fact what happened to most common land in England. As population densities rose and the problem of the commons became more severe, particularly in the 17th and 18th centuries, common land was enclosed and converted to private control. This greatly increased agricultural productivity, although it also had the effect of reducing the real income of landless peasants who had formerly earned their living from common land.

Other open access resources, such as fisheries, are much harder to deal with, since it is often difficult to establish property rights. A fishing ground is like the common. In the absence of overall control, there is a tendency for waters to be overfished. There are really two externalities present. First of all, since the total number of fish is fixed at any one time, a fish taken by one fishing boat is a fish that cannot be taken by another. The social cost of taking an extra fish includes the loss to the other boats, raising the social marginal cost of fishing above the private marginal cost. Therefore, a negative externality is created.

Second, as with the common, taking too many fish today reduces the number of fish that can be taken tomorrow. However, if there are fewer fish tomorrow, this is a cost that is borne by all fishermen, not the one trying to decide whether to take another fish. Thus, the social marginal cost exceeds the private marginal cost for this reason as well. This intertemporal externality leads to an inefficiently small fish stock.

Referring back to Figure 11.1, the open access externality can lead to a harvest level above H_2, creating possible extinction of the resource, when optimal management might call for a harvest level like H_2. The response to externality problems in fishing has given rise to close regulation of the fishing industry in most countries. As can be inferred from Section 11.3, Canada has an active program of fishery management in which governments appoint regulatory authorities to set catch limits (quotas), restrict fishing seasons, and carry out other regulatory actions. However, this system, intended to address the basic open access market failure, has not been up to the task in either the Atlantic or Pacific oceans. In addition, as Section 11.3 emphasized, the biggest problem concerns the international externalities, since it is hard to develop international regulatory authorities. Such authorities (such as NAFO) do exist, but they have no legal authority or police power to require adherence to their regulatory determinations.

11.5 Other Renewable Resources

In addition to depletion of fish stocks, there is considerable concern over depletion of renewable resources such as forests. To some extent, concerns in these areas also reflect externality problems. It can be argued that the destruction of the Amazon rain forest, for example, may have costly global effects on climate. Only a small fraction of such costs are borne by the farmers currently cutting down the forests. However, even in cases where externality effects are minor, such as in those parts of Canada's forests that are privately owned, it is alleged that forests are being depleted too rapidly. The basic argument seems to be that simple mismanagement and myopia are the causes.

Soil depletion is also a very serious problem. The world's deserts are expanding, mainly in Africa, at the rate of 60,000 square kilometres per year, greatly compromising the capacity of many poor countries to feed themselves. The full explanation for this phenomenon is not known. It is due in part to changing rainfall patterns, which in turn are being altered by imperfectly understood human activities, including forest depletion. In addition, at a regional level, depletion of forests leads to soil erosion. Also, poor agricultural practice is in effect mining the soil in much of Africa. One of the problems is that in parts of Africa and in other poor regions much of the land is treated as common land, and is therefore subject to the problem of the common described in Section 11.4. However, even in Canada and the United States, where most agricultural land is privately owned, soil is also being lost rapidly. Presumably, when soil and arable land begin to rise in value, more soil conservation will be undertaken.

11.6 Ocean Use

Oceans are common property and are subject to standard common property problems. We have already considered the common property problems associated with fish stocks, and this applies to ocean-going stocks. Each fishing vessel and each country have an incentive to take fish beyond the economic value-maximizing harvest.

Oceans are also used for transportation of risky cargoes, particularly oil. We regularly read of oil spills. The basic point is that individual users of ocean transport have an incentive to under-provide safety. If an oil tanker spills its cargo, the owner of the tanker incurs some costs, but nothing approaching the full social cost of the spill. If owners of tankers did bear the full costs of oil spills, we would still have occasional oil spills, but far fewer than we have at present, since more resources would be devoted to preventing spills (stronger hulls, stricter standards about travelling in bad weather, etc.).

We do not have a good idea of whether oil spills cause long-term damage. It is worth noting that about half of the 3.2 million tonnes of oil that enters the ocean every year is natural seepage from offshore oil deposits. Oceans have apparently been handling this oil for many thousands of years. When oil is released into ocean waters, much of it evaporates, much of it is decomposed by bacteria, and the remainder eventually sinks to the bottom. There is no denying, however, that oil spills can have serious temporary effects on fish and other wildlife, not to mention lost human enjoyment of beaches where oil washes up.

A more serious threat to oceans comes from their use for garbage disposal. Huge quantities of garbage are towed out to sea and dumped. As a result, there are large quantities of long-lived plastics in the ocean. Some 160,000 tons of plastic are discarded into the ocean annually by American sailors and fishing boats alone.[2] Plastic bags in the water look like jellyfish, which are eaten by many animals, including sea turtles. Because plastic is indigestible, it gradually fills up a turtle's stomach, causing death by starvation. Balloons, plastic beads, and various other plastics either poison or starve much sea life. The plastic rings that hold together six-packs of canned beer and pop are particularly dangerous, and strangle large numbers of birds, seals, and other animals. Medical wastes, including containers of AIDS-infected blood, have been washing up on U.S. beaches, and discharges of human sewage have made many beach areas around the world unsafe for swimming.

Victoria, B.C., has been criticized by officials in the city of Port Angeles, Washington, just across the Juan de Fuca Strait. Victoria's large and growing discharges of untreated or only slightly treated sewage are making Port Angeles' beaches unsafe for recreation. Using the ocean for rubbish disposal is a very good example of the common property problem. Solving the problem will require some assertion of internationally agreed upon property rights. In 1988, 28 nations, including Canada and the United States, signed a treaty banning disposal of plastics in the ocean and banning dumping of other garbage between 12 and 25 miles from shore. However, compliance is hard to enforce.

11.7 Nonrenewable Resources and Intergenerational Equity

So far, we have discussed environmental problems arising from the open access aspect of many renewable resources. Open access externalities are less of a concern with major nonrenewable resources (although they can occur). The greater problem is simple resource depletion. Perhaps the most well-known example concerns oil, an apparently fixed resource that we are using up at a rapid rate. It has taken hundreds of thousands of years for oil deposits to accumulate, yet we could use most of them up in a matter of decades. At present rates of consumption, known reserves of oil would last for another 40 years, natural gas for 47 years, and coal for 204 years after 1995.[3] This problem arises even though oil production is not subject to externalities, property rights are well defined, and markets work well.

The basic fact is that use of nonrenewable resources cannot really be carried out on a sustainable basis. By definition, nonrenewable resources cannot be renewed on a time scale that is comparable to human time scales. A classic analysis of nonrenewable resource management carried by Hotelling (1929) shows that efficient exploitation of such a nonrenewable and nonaugmentable resource would, under otherwise stable economic conditions, lead to a gradual depletion of the resource and a real price for it that rose annually at a rate equal to the rate of interest, reflecting the increasing scarcity of the resource. This is known as Hotelling's Rule.

In 1973, a group of academics known as the Club of Rome published a widely read book called *The Limits to Growth* in which they argued that living standards would soon fall because we would run out of various nonrenewable resources such as iron ore, oil, etc. Their predictions, however, turned out to be very misleading, at least in the short run, for they failed to take into account the effect of changing prices. For example, even though current use levels would suggest depletion of oil reserves in 40 years, in fact price increases would prevent such depletion. If oil does become relatively scarce, its price will rise. The response will be just as it was in the early 1970s when oil

prices rose sharply. Individuals will have economic incentives to econ-
omize on their use of oil, to develop new technologies that conserve
energy, to find new sources of oil, and to switch to other energy
sources.

Countries with large oil deposits even have the concern that their
oil reserves might be rendered worthless by alternative energy sources.
When two scientists claimed (falsely, as it turned out) to have discovered cold fusion in 1988, oil producers feared that it would be very
damaging to their industry.

Does this mean that resource depletion is not a problem? Resource
depletion does not (necessarily) involve market failure. Given the population, and provided externality problems are either absent or appropriately addressed by policy, there is every reason to believe that fixed
resources will be allocated efficiently by markets. As population grows,
however, fixed resources get used up at a faster rate and have to be
spread over a larger base. It is quite likely that this resource depletion
effect could lead at some point to declines in living standards. This is
not a market failure, however, but simply the result of having to share
a fixed pie among more and more claimants.

Another aspect of resource depletion is intergenerational equity.
With any fixed resource, we have the option of using it now or saving
it for future generations. We can, of course, substitute other things for
used up resources. As we use up oil we can invest the resulting income
in factories and other productive assets, including alternative sources
of energy, that might be more valuable to future generations than the
oil would have been. The idea that a sustainable path of consumption
can be provided by investing rents from a nonrenewable resource in
alternative productive assets is associated with Hartwick's rule, named
after John Hartwick of Queen's University.

To the extent that current resources are simply consumed without
a corresponding replacement investment, this is purely a matter of
intergenerational distribution. Concerns about intergenerational equity are not easily dealt with, and do not yield obvious answers. To the
extent that we are concerned about future generations, using up
resources is a legitimate problem, even if there is no market failure.

Intergenerational equity arises as a concern because the preferences of future generations do not enter into current prices. If future
generations could bid for resources, current prices of exhaustible
resources might be much higher than they are and we would use them

up much more slowly. This is not quite a market failure, but simply a question about whose welfare is to be considered in our objectives. One response is that governments should be the guardians of the future, but just as the future does not bid for current resources, it does not vote either, nor does it march in demonstrations or make campaign contributions. Governments might be more sensitive to posterity than profit-maximizing firms, but we cannot expect such sensitivity to extend very far, as our experience with government debt accumulation and government fishery management suggests. There are, however, some examples of government attempts to provide a sustainable benefit from current use of nonrenewable resources. After the substantial increases in oil prices that occured in the 1970s, the government of Alberta set up the Alberta Heritage Savings and Trust Fund. The idea was that the profits or rents from the government share of Alberta's many oil wells would be put into the fund and used for investments that would provide an ongoing stream of benefits to residents of Alberta.

In considering the management of resource stocks, we should keep in mind the discussions of transfer-seeking or rent-seeking discussed in the Chapter 5. Resource stocks provide a pool of potential rents that many current claimants will compete for. Furthermore, since many of these resources are controlled by governments, there is a strong incentive for interest groups to lobby for public policies that will shift transfers in their direction. Future generations can be expected to have a hard time competing with current generations in this transfer-seeking game. Interestingly, however, some constituencies that seek to represent the interests of future generations have become very successful, including organizations such as Greenpeace (founded in Canada) and the Sierra Club.

11.8 Wildlife Conservation

As described in Chiras (1994, p.170-185), genetic diversity is being extinguished at a very rapid rate. Currently, one vertebrate (backboned) species goes extinct roughly every nine months, compared with a natural rate of one such extinction every 1,000 years. Most major mammals (except humans, their dog and cat companions, and farm animals such as cows, pigs, and sheep) now only have trace populations compared to what they once were. Populations of large primates (such as orangutans and baboons), elephants, lions, tigers, whales, etc. are certainly no more than 10% of what they were a century ago and continue to decline.

Most people shake their heads when presented with such data. In the case of elephants, blame is usually fixed on the ivory trade and the solution is to be found in banning ivory markets. Unfortunately, this misses the main point. Major primates and other species are simply being replaced by humans. It is estimated that approximately 40% of the current biological capacity of the planet earth is devoted to the human consumption chain. If population doubles in the next 50 years, as it well might, it is hard to see that much biological carrying capacity will be left for anything that does not enter the human food chain. In Kenya, population more than tripled between 1965 and 1998, and animal populations fell correspondingly.

It is not entirely obvious that this is a bad thing. Forced to make a choice between saving the life of a human or an elephant in Kenya, human ethics would lead us to favour the human. Current trends are simply making a similar choice on a much larger scale. It is true, of course, that saving an existing life is more compelling than planning new ones. Even so, we have to confront the issue of whether additional human lives are worth the opportunity cost of fewer animal lives and fewer animal species. In most economic analysis, we take human welfare as the objective that we try to maximize. In such calculations, other animals enter only as tools or instruments: their value is strictly related to their contribution to human welfare.

Some people will try to justify wildlife conservation on this instrumental basis. It is important to preserve major mammals so that humans can enjoy looking at them; it is important to preserve rain forests because we might discover medicines in them, etc. There is, however, another point of view: animals have value in themselves. Chimpanzee welfare, or elephant welfare, or dolphin welfare has significance, quite independent of what these species might contribute to humans. Many environmentalists hold strongly to this view, and as we learn more about these particular animals, it becomes increasingly clear that they share many of the attributes that we believe give humans intrinsic value.

A fairly extreme extension of this line of thought, referred to as the Gaia hypothesis, suggests treating the earth itself as a living entity with rights that humans should not be allowed to violate. While it is not entirely clear exactly what these rights might be, the idea has attracted considerable attention. Neither the Gaia hypothesis, nor valuing animals for their own sake have, however, been embraced at the public policy level in Canada or elsewhere, and would be difficult to implement.

11.9 Land Use, Waste Disposal, and Recycling

As mentioned at the beginning of this chapter, the other major resource to consider is land itself. As populations grow, land becomes scarcer, housing becomes relatively more expensive, and congestion increases. One major problem associated with land use is what to do with garbage. Hazardous waste raises particular problems, but even disposal of ordinary waste is becoming a major concern. Current North American lifestyles generate a lot of waste. The major method of waste disposal is through use of landfills, but landfills are becoming harder to find. Cities such as Montreal, Toronto, and Vancouver have had considerable trouble in recent years finding new landfill sites in which to dump garbage, and have expanded their use of incinerators. Incinerators also create local negative externalities, however, and are subject to the NIMBY problem. Nevertheless, Canada is a large country, and by going far enough away from the city (incurring high transport costs) it is still possible to find places to dump or incinerate garbage. As the costs of using landfill sites and other forms of waste disposal rise, it is natural to turn to recycling as a method of reducing waste.

The other force we would expect to operate in favour of recycling would be the increasing scarcity of the materials we discard. As basic materials become scarce, their prices should rise and incentives to recycle should increase. This effect has taken a long time to emerge, but may finally be having an effect. Over the past century, and especially in the past 25 years, technological progress has kept well ahead of resource depletion, with the result that the real cost of the basic materials that make up most garbage, including paper, wood, plastics, and glass, has actually been falling over most of this period. However, over the past couple of years such prices have been rising and, in addition, more effective ways of handling recycled products have been designed. In the early 1990s, for example, the glut of old newspaper had driven its price down to zero, but in 1994 its price fluctuated between $100 and $200 per tonne, far higher (in real terms) than at any previous time. The easiest major waste item to resell and reuse is aluminum, followed by plastic. Traditionally, glass has been a difficult item to deal with, and much glass put in recycling boxes has ended up in landfills. However, by 1995, even glass had a fairly active market in most parts of Canada.

Even so, the value of products for recycling pays only a small fraction of the cost of recycling. Most of the costs are still paid by taxpayers. There is an increasing attempt to use the polluter pays principle by making producers of products that generate garbage pay for the cost of recycling, but this has not yet gone very far. Some products are particularly costly to recycle. For example, according to legal counsel for the B.C. Paint Care Association,[4] the cost of recycling a can of paint is about $18, more than retail paint currently sells for. What this means, of course, is that the private cost of producing paint is less than half of the full social cost.

Efficient recycling is becoming an important area in corporate and public management. Designing products so that they can be readily recycled is a particularly interesting technical problem, as is designing products that make use of recycled materials. As for public policy, designing efficient recycling systems is a considerable managerial challenge, and many early attempts were abandoned. Local governments have learned, however, to take advantage of incentive effects. Providing subsidized compost boxes and providing door-to-door pickup of recyclable materials have proved to be useful techniques. Perhaps the most successful single public policy measure that can be undertaken, however, is the use of deposits as an economic incentive to recycle. If you examine public garbage bins (and public streets, parks, and beaches) you will rarely observe bottles that carry a deposit, while nondeposit bottles and other materials continue to be a serious waste problem.

11.10 Population Growth and the Environment

As is clear from other parts of this chapter, we might reasonably view the explosively growing human population as the underlying driving force behind environmental concerns. In the year 1 A.D., human population is thought to have been about 300 million, after which it required about 1,700 years to double to 600 million. By contrast, world population doubled from 2.5 billion to 5 billion in the 37-year period 1950-87 and, at current growth rates, would double again to 10 billion by about 2030. While the population growth rate has actually fallen slightly since its peak in about 1970, the absolute increase in population is very high, and in 1999 was roughly 78 million. At present, a population the size of Canada is added to the world about every four months. Figure 11.3 shows the growth of human population from 1600 to the present.

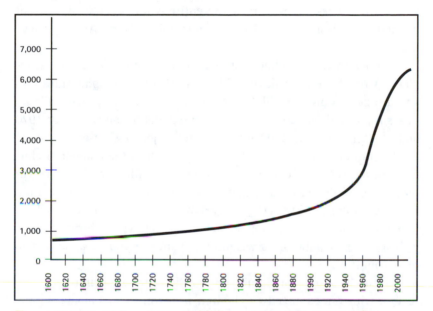

Figure 11.3 World Population in Millions: 1600 A.D.–2000 A.D.
Source: L. Collins, World Population in J. Ross, ed., *International Encyclopedia of Population*, Vol. 2. Free Press. New York, 1992. *World Population Prospects,* 1992 revised. United Nations, New York.

The tremendous increase in population that has taken place since the beginning of the Industrial Revolution (in the 17th century) is due mainly to technological progress in health care and food production. This progress has also allowed living standards to improve dramatically for most of the world's people, despite an exploding population. Until the 19th century, human impact on the global environment could reasonably be described as negligible. Humans could have significant local effects, but the earth was very large compared to the rather puny effects of human beings. Things have changed very rapidly, however, as human population has become so large that it threatens to engulf everything else on the planet.

Population optimists point out that wealthy countries have gone through a demographic transition that has put zero population growth in reach for them. The rapidly developing countries of Asia are following a similar pattern, and similar patterns may be emerging in Latin America. Perhaps, therefore, if economic development can get sufficiently far ahead, populations will naturally stabilize at reasonable levels. This is a real hope. It would, however, be difficult to provide sufficient resources to raise the entire world, even at its current population, to a standard of living comparable to North American levels.

Furthermore, the Middle East, the Indian subcontinent, and particularly Africa have been slow in following this demographic transition and are generating very high rates of net population growth. Figure 11.4 shows total fertility rates in major regions of the world for 1970 and 2000. (Total year 2000 numbers are projections based on actual fertility rates up to 1998.) Total fertility rates show the number of children an average women would have over her lifetime given current birth rates of all age groups. Long-run stabilization of the population requires a total fertility rate just over 2. However, it can take a long time for population stability to be achieved even with a fertility rate at or below 2 if population is weighted toward the young, as is true in most countries.

As can be seen from Figure 11.4, fertility rates vary enormously by region, with rates under two children per woman in Canada, China, Europe, and the United States. On the other hand, fertility rates still exceed five children per woman in sub-Saharan Africa. Until the 20th century, fertility rates in most parts of world were high (although not as high as current African levels), but high fertility was largely offset by high mortality, especially among young children. In the 20th century, there was a sharp reduction in mortality due largely to technological improvement in health care. In countries experiencing this combination of high fertility and low mortality (compared to historical standards) there has been unprecedented population growth that is not sustainable. In the absence of dramatic scientific and technological advances, population growth will probably be contained at some level not much exceeding about twice the world's current population. What is at issue is whether this will be achieved in a reasonable way or whether it will occur through nature's traditional methods of famine, disease, and war. After reaching an all-time low in the early 1980s, infectious diseases are making a comeback. AIDS and HIV get the most attention, but they are probably less important than the emergence of antibiotic resistant bacteria, which could well cause a major die-off in the 21st century.

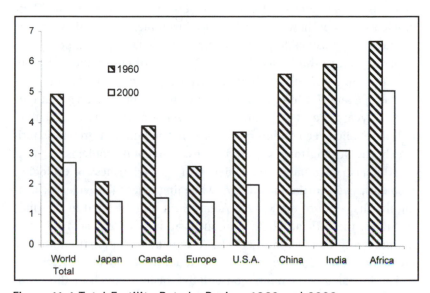

Figure 11.4 Total Fertility Rate by Region, 1960 and 2000
Source: *World Population Prospects*, 1998 Revision. United Nations, New York.

Most readers of this book will be aware of wars and famines in Africa in places like Somalia, Rwanda, and elsewhere. What is not emphasized in popular coverage is that these wars and famines are driven largely by population growth. For example, the main reason why the two tribal groups in Rwanda, the Tutsis and Hutus, came into conflict in the mid 1990s is that population in Rwanda more than quadrupled between the 1950s and the 1990s, bringing Hutus and Tutsis into conflict over land, and putting general pressure on traditional methods of agriculture.

For any given population, we can manage environmental resources poorly or well. We can attend to externalities and use the power of markets to promote efficient use of resources. We also need to understand the consequences of new technologies and deal with problems created out of past ignorance, such as ozone depletion and toxic waste disposal. These things can make a huge difference, but ultimately our growing demands on a finite resource base will have to be stabilized.

This discussion is not intended to sound sensational. Ecological problems are very serious and they are currently at very dangerous levels in many parts of the world. Some of the worst environmental problems are in the former state socialist countries of Eastern Europe, especially in some of the former members of the Soviet Union. These problems are not, however, technically insoluble, nor are they beyond the range of reasonable policy to improve. In fact, public policy has been very successful in dealing with the wave of environmental problems that emerged in wealthier countries in the early 1970s. In Western Europe and North America, air and water are both cleaner that they were 25 years ago. It is disturbing, however, that there is still relatively little explicit recognition of the fact that population growth is ultimately the driving force underlying environmental problems.

One also encounters simple denial of the seriousness of ecological problems, even in the face of overwhelming scientific evidence. During the first term of the Reagan Administration (1981-85) in the United States, the official administration position was that acid rain was not proven to have harmful effects. A (Canadian) National Film Board production on acid rain, entitled Acid Rain: Requiem or Recovery, which documented in rather conservative fashion much of the scientific evidence on acid rain, was temporarily banned in the United States during that period.

On the other side, as already indicated, one encounters naive and emotional appeals to end pollution, sometimes in combination with a generalized attack on Western technology as the source of all ecological evil. Some utopian notion of a natural lifestyle is sometimes held out as the objective. Unfortunately, mankind has had considerable experience with natural lifestyles and they were not very pleasant. As Hobbes observed, man in his (or her) natural state lives a life that is nasty, brutish, and short, and does not have much leisure for enjoying nature or anything else.

The best hope is to address environmental problems using the tools that have proved successful in the recent past in raising the quality of human life: application of a sensible economic policy based on an understanding of incentive effects, opportunity costs, and market forces, and, most importantly, ongoing development of scientific and technological knowledge. Furthermore, it is important to achieve reductions in fertility before the Hobbesian natural state is reached.

11.11 Bibliographic Notes

The annual *State of the World Report* edited by Lester Brown and the Worldwatch Institute is a valuable source on resource issues, as is the bi-annual *World Resources Report* from the World Resources Institute. The annual *World Development Report* from the World Bank also reports systematic information and provides in-depth analysis of issues relating to, among other things, the environment, resource use, and population and demography. The best source for the formal analysis of renewable resources is Clark (1990). Valuable textbooks on natural resources and environmental economics include Anderson (1991), Hartwick and Olewiler (1986), and Pearce and Turner (1990). A very useful collection of readings is available in Dorfman and Dorfman (1993). A good discussion of the concept of sustainability is provided by Pearce, Atkinson, and Dubourg (1994). Finally, there is a lot of material on resources and the environment available online at world-wide web sites maintained by Environment Canada, the Department of Fisheries and Oceans, and elsewhere.

Notes

1. A forceful statement of this problem can be found in Hardin (1968).
2. Chiras (1994), p. 392.
3. "Energy," in *World Resources 1994–95* (World Resources Institute), Table 9.2. New York.
4. The source for this and other material in this section is a *Globe and Mail* special report on Recycling, November 24, 1994, Section B.

12
Competition Policy

12.1 Introduction

Adam Smith and Karl Marx would not seem to have much in common. As discussed in Chapter 3, Smith (1776) offered the first systematic statement of the advantages of market-based free enterprise or capitalism as a form of economic organization. Marx, on the other hand, is history's most influential critic of market capitalism, and established the intellectual foundation of communism in his (1867) Capital. Interestingly, however, there is some common ground between Marx and Smith. Marx criticized the alleged tendency of private enterprise to concentrate economic power in the hands of a few owners of capital, and Smith was quite critical of monopoly power. Followers of both Smith and Marx would agree that monopoly power is a force that should be controlled by public policy.

In Canada, as in many Western countries, there is a body of legislation and a corresponding administrative apparatus charged with the tasks of promoting competition and ensuring that markets in Canada achieve acceptable levels of competition. This body of legislation and associated procedures is referred to as competition policy.

This chapter describes the law and institutions of competition policy as established by the Competition Act of 1986 and subsequent legal and legislative refinement. A historical review of competition policy leading up to the 1986 Act is also provided, as is a discussion of developments since 1986. Several significant cases are also discussed. The economic analysis of anti-competitive practices is provided in Chapter 13.

12.2 A Brief History of Competition Policy

12.2.1 Early Legislation

The late 19th century is often described as a period of robber baron capitalism in North America. Several individuals were able to put together highly profitable cartels, sometimes called trusts or combines, in areas such as oil, steel, tobacco, and railroads: the major industries of the period. Most of this activity occurred in the United States, but Canada had its own trusts or combinations in industries such as sugar, coal, and agricultural implements. Furthermore, the National Policy of 1879 (described in Chapter 9) erected high tariff barriers to protect Canadian manufacturing, greatly restricting the ability of foreign firms to compete with Canadian firms and therefore making it much easier for cartels in Canada to develop and to exploit monopoly power.

By the 1880s, cartels and industrial collusion had become significant political issues in Canada and the United States. In reaction, governments in both countries adopted policies to deal with them. The United States called it antitrust policy, while Canada referred to it as anticombines policy, though it has come to be called competition policy.

Canada's first anticombines law, entitled An Act for the Prevention and Suppression of Combinations Formed in Restraint of Trade, passed through Parliament in 1889 and was enacted into the Criminal Code of Canada in 1892. (The first U.S. anti-trust law, the Sherman Act, passed Congress in 1890.) The principal content of Canada's first anticombines law is reported in the following quotation:

Everyone is guilty of an indictable offence . . . who conspires, combines, agrees or arranges with any other person . . . unlawfully . . .

c) to unduly prevent, limit, or lessen the manufacture or production of any article or commodity, or to unreasonably increase the price thereof; or

d) to unduly prevent or lessen competition in the production, manufacture, purchase, barter, sale, transportation, or supply of such an article or commodity. . . .

The original legislators felt that this law gave legislative form to existing common law inherited from England, and that it would be used effectively in controlling monopoly power. Existing common law, however, was itself rather weak in its ability to control monopoly power, and the Canadian competition law of 1889 proved to be without useful content.

12.2.2 Weaknesses of the 1889 Competition Law

The weakness of the 1889 anticombines law arose from the following sources.

1. The use of the term "unlawfully" removed any substantive content from the original law. The legislation as it read in 1889 did not say that it was an offence per se to conspire to unduly raise price or lessen competition, only that it was an offence to unlawfully do so. In effect, insertion of "unlawfully" implied that there was such a thing as lawful undue lessening of competition, and meant that the legislation could not be read as defining unlawful acts. The logical content of the legislation was simply: It is an offence to unlawfully commit X. Since it is presumably an offence to unlawfully do anything, and since the legislation did not define the distinction between lawful and unlawful undue lessening of competition, the original law was logically without content.

   The original legislation was in fact completely unused until "unlawfully" was removed in an amendment in 1900. The amended legislation could then be read as actually defining illegal acts. The complete emasculation of the original law by the insertion of a single word seems too elegant to have arisen by chance. One suspects that at least one drafter of the original law was not sympathetic to the concept of competition policy.

2. The legislation contained no provision for administrative procedures to enforce the new competition law. In 1910, the legislation was amended to allow any six domestic residents to apply to a judge for an investigation into an alleged violation of the law. A 1919 amendment established a permanent investigative body, forerunner of the current Bureau of Competition Policy.

3. The word "unduly" in the original version of the law, and in subsequent versions, greatly weakened its application. Because of the word "unduly," any prosecution must not only establish that the accused parties are guilty of, for example, price-fixing so as to reduce competition, but in addition that this lessening of competition is undue. The problem is similar to that raised by the word "unlawful." If there is undue lessening of competition, then presumably there is also due lessening of competition, and it is up to the Crown (i.e., government prosecutors) to establish that the case at hand represents undue lessening of competition.

The force and meaning of "undue" rests very much on judicial intuition and precedent. In Canada, judicial precedent and practice developed a rather conservative interpretation of "unduly," making it hard to obtain convictions for the more serious offenses. In particular, judges have required that in order for lessening of competition to be regarded as undue, competition must be virtually eliminated. In effect, undue lessening of competition was taken to mean the establishment of a virtual monopoly. In the 1986 Competition Act, "unduly" was replaced in most instances by "substantially."

4. An early court decision established that the reference in the law to "articles and commodities" referred only to physical commodities, not to services. Thus, services were exempt from Competition Policy until an amendment in 1976 explicitly included them. In addition, banks and Crown corporations were exempt from Competition Policy until the Competition Act of 1986.

5. The final major weakness of the original law is more subtle than the others, but important. Until the 1986 Competition Act, most elements of competition law were part of the Criminal Code of Canada. (Some elements of competition policy had, however, been decriminalized in 1976.) On the surface, the status of criminal law might seem to make the competition policy more powerful, for criminal code convictions must be a stronger deterrent to violations of the law than convictions under civil law. While this may be true, the standard of proof required for conviction is higher for criminal law. Specifically, criminal law requires that guilt be demonstrated "beyond a reasonable doubt," whereas in civil law the standard of proof is only "the balance of probability." Using precise numbers to make the point clear, suppose a judge or jury in a criminal case subjectively believes that there is roughly an 80% chance that the accused party is guilty of the alleged offence. In such a case a verdict of innocent should be returned, because a 20% chance of innocence is more than enough for reasonable doubt. On the other hand, in a civil case, an 80% chance of guilt is more than enough to convict, so a guilty verdict should be returned. In addition, the cost of prosecuting cases, and, very probably, the reluctance of judges to convict are greater under criminal law than under civil law. In 1986,

major parts of competition law were placed under civil law. Some provisions remain under a strengthened criminal law.

As the preceding discussion indicates, there have been a series of revisions to competition legislation that have generally served to expand the jurisdiction and power of competition policy. The Combines Investigation Act of 1923 consolidated earlier changes to the law, and, as subsequently amended, formed the basis of competition policy until 1986. The addition of misleading advertising and deceptive marketing practices as anticompetitive practices in 1960 significantly expanded the enforcement activity of the Bureau of Competition Policy. In 1986, a new Competition Act came into force. While this Act was certainly the most significant revision to competition policy since 1923, it initially had to withstand considerable legal attack based on the Charter of Rights and related constitutional issues, but is now fairly well established. Significant amendments to competition law continue to be made. In 1999 a significant set of amendments came into force as Bill C-20.

12.2.3 Important Changes in Competition Law

Noteworthy extensions to competition law are indicated chronologically in the following list.

1889	first Canadian competition law: An Act for the Prevention and Suppression of Combinations Formed in Restraint of Trade
1900	removal of the word "unlawfully" as a modifier in the definition of indictable offenses
1910	complaint-based procedure to initiate investigations; specific reference to mergers placed in the law
1919	first permanent investigative machinery
1923	Combines Investigation Act of 1923
1935	price discrimination as an anticompetitive practice
1952	resale price maintenance as an anticompetitive practice
1960	misleading advertising as an anticompetitive practice
1976	service industries included under competition law and some decriminalization
1986	Competition Act
1999	Bill C-20 strengthens competition law

12.2.4 Objectives of Canadian Competition Policy

The primary economic interpretation of competition policy is that it is intended to reduce the inefficiencies associated with monopoly power and anticompetitive practices. This interpretation is a direct application of the analysis of monopoly power presented in Chapter 6. However, this interpretation gives a misleading view of the historical source of competition law, which has its roots in fairness considerations. Specifically, the historical public sentiment against monopoly power was due largely to the following two perceptions:

1. Cartels or combinations violated norms of procedural fairness in business practice. (For example, it might be viewed as simply unfair that large firms should conspire to put a small competitor out of business.)

2. The creation of market power through cartels led to the enrichment of a few owners of capital and the exploitation of consumers and smaller firms.

These concerns are important, but they have little to do with the inefficiencies of monopoly power. Instead they are based on notions of fairness or equity. The case against monopoly presented in Chapters 3 and 6 is primarily an efficiency argument. The possible transfers of wealth associated with monopoly power are not part of this efficiency argument. These transfers may be undesirable, but that assessment depends on a knowledge of who the shareholders in the affected firms are, and who the affected consumers are, along with a set of value judgements that allow determination of which individuals are more deserving than others.

Early perceptions of competition policy led naturally to a legalistic approach similar to existing criminal law. In fact, the original form of competition law did not use the word "monopoly" at all. Instead, the emphasis was on notions of conspiracy, by analogy with notions of conspiracy in crimes against the state or against individuals. As time has passed, however, the economic efficiency rationale for competition policy has become relatively more important, and the law has moved away from a focus on conspiracy, although anticonspiracy provisions still exist. As reformulated in the Competition Act of 1986, the primary focus of the law is now on promoting competition and economic efficiency.

12.3 The Competition Act of 1986

12.3.1 General Mandate and Organization

The Competition Act of 1986 (referred to hereafter as "the Act") consists of approximately 130 sections (as of the 1999 amendments in Bill C-20). The general mandate of competition policy, as described in Section 1 of the Act, is to "maintain and encourage competition in Canada in order to promote the efficiency and adaptability of the Canadian economy." Most of the operations and investigations called for under the Act are carried out by the Bureau of Competition Policy (referred to hereafter as the "Bureau") under the direction of the Commissioner of Competition (referred to hereafter as the "Commissioner"). (Prior to 1999 this person was known as the Director of Investigation and Research.) The Bureau is part of Industry Canada (a department of the federal government) and the Commissioner has the status of a Deputy Minister. The Commissioner reports directly through the Minister to Parliament. The position of the Commissioner has been vested with considerable independence, much like the Governor of the Bank of Canada. The Commissioner is, therefore, supposed to be largely free from political influences.

The Act specifies two general classes of business practice that constitute violations of competition law: criminal code violations and civil reviewable offenses. Both criminal code and civil matters are investigated by the Bureau. In the case of criminal code offenses, if a decision is made to proceed, the results of the investigation are communicated by the Commissioner to the Attorney General of Canada for prosecution. Civil matters are also investigated by the Bureau, but are adjudicated by a body known as the Competition Tribunal (referred to hereafter as the "Tribunal"). This tribunal was created by the Competition Tribunal Act, which passed into law at the same time as the Competition Act.

12.3.2 The Competition Tribunal

The Tribunal is composed of not more than four federal judges and not more than eight lay members, all appointed for terms of seven years, renewable for one additional term of another seven years. The Minister of Industry Canada appoints the lay members of the Tribunal. The judicial appointments to the Tribunal are the responsibility of the Minister of Justice.

For civil law matters, the Tribunal is a substitute for the normal court system. (Criminal law matters still go through the normal court system.) Most cases are heard by just three of the 12 tribunal members, at least one of whom must be a federal judge. The Tribunal has several advantages over the courts. First, the lay members of the Tribunal are experts in appropriate areas of economics and business, and the judges also have a chance to become expert in competition law and policy analysis, if they are not already expert at the time of their initial appointments. This contrasts with the standard court system in which competition law cases would often come up before judges with little specialized knowledge of competition policy. A second advantage is that the Tribunal is faster than the court system in dealing with cases. This was one of the objectives of the Act, because previously even cases of only moderate seriousness would drag on for six or seven years (including appeals). There is a well-known aphorism that justice delayed in justice denied. The Act states that "All proceedings before the Tribunal shall be dealt with as informally and expeditiously as the circumstances and considerations of fairness permit."

A third advantage is that the Tribunal has more flexibility in making decisions and in facilitating negotiated settlements with firms under investigation by the Bureau of Competition Policy. Finally, as will be described in more detail later on, the Tribunal allows competition policy to have more influence over merger activity than the previous system.

The Tribunal approach has precedents and, in particular, has some similarity to the Canadian approach to Worker's Compensation. Worker's Compensation in Canada is settled by adjudication, with one layer of appeal possible. Compared to the highly litigious U.S. system of legal suits, the Canadian approach seems far superior. In Canada settlements are fast, usually taking less than a year, and have little transaction cost associated with them: most of the money paid by firms actually goes to workers. The system is relatively uniform in its judgements, and uncertainty for injured workers and for firms is fairly low. In the United States, where injury claims go through the courts (and frequently involve jury trials), it is common for lawyers' fees to exceed the amount of money flowing to workers, cases frequently take several years to settle, and major cases often outlive many of the plaintiffs. Awards are sometimes enormous, and there is wide variation in the size of awards, so that the system as a whole resembles a slow-moving lottery more than anything else.

Despite the apparent advantages of the Tribunal system, it has been the subject of serious legal dispute. As described in Hunter and Blakney (1990), in 1990 Mr. Justice Philippon of the Quebec Superior Court ruled that the Tribunal was unconstitutional on the grounds of being contrary to the Canadian Charter of Rights and Freedoms. Specifically, Justice Philippon observed that the Tribunal carries out court-like functions. He then found that inclusion of lay persons (i.e., nonjudges) in a court-like body such as the Tribunal is inconsistent with Charter requirements for impartiality in the justice system. He argued that lay appointees may be insufficiently impartial to legitimately carry out judge-like functions. He also ruled that certain antimerger provisions violate freedom of association guarantees in the Charter. The government appealed this case to the Quebec Court of Appeal, which unanimously overturned the Philippon decision. The companies involved then sought to appeal this decision to the Supreme Court of Canada, but it declined to hear the appeal. Although the Supreme Court does not give reasons for declining the case, the decision to decline serves to solidify the constitutional legitimacy of the Tribunal.

12.4 Anti-competitive Practices
12.4.1 List of Anti-competitive Practices

Most of the activities of the Bureau are focused on a specific set of anticompetitive practices defined in the Act. In order to provide some perspective it is necessary to classify these practices into a small number of categories. The annual report describing the activities of the Bureau of Competition Policy[1] places its investigative activities in four categories:

1. mergers,

2. selected [other] civil matters,

3. misleading advertising and deceptive marketing practices,

4. selected [other] criminal matters.

Mergers (i.e., category 1) and other civil matters (category 2) are the civil reviewable or civil law offenses, while categories 3 and 4 are criminal offenses. There is, however, considerable overlap between civil and criminal offenses. From a policy analysis point of view it makes sense to categorize Bureau investigations into the following six areas:

1. mergers and abuse of dominant position (civil law),

2. conspiracy to lessen competition,

3. predatory pricing,

4. price discrimination,

5. resale price maintenance and refusal to deal,

6. misleading advertising and deceptive marketing practices.

As indicated above, mergers and abuse of dominant position are civil matters. Refusal to deal is also part of civil law. Conspiracy and misleading advertising and deceptive marketing practices remain in the criminal code. Predatory pricing, price discrimination, and resale price maintenance are also in the criminal code, but closely related offenses are dealt with under abuse of dominant position in the civil reviewable sections of the Act. Thus, a given offence involving, for example, abuse of dominant position through predatory pricing could, in principle, be dealt with either under criminal code or under civil sections of Canadian competition law.

12.4.2 Mergers and Abuse of Dominant Position

This category of anticompetitive practice contains two subcategories: mergers to reduce competition and abuse of dominant position, which, as mentioned above, entered civil law in the 1986 Act.

Mergers are acquisitions of whole companies or parts of companies by other firms. The Competition Act provides for taking action against a merger that "prevents or lessens, or is likely to prevent or lessen, competition substantially." Horizontal mergers are an obvious method of concentrating monopoly power. If there are three firms in an industry and they merge to form a single firm, then a monopoly position has been substituted for what may have been a reasonably competitive market structure.

Between 1910 and 1986 only nine merger cases were taken to court. Two accused parties pleaded guilty. In none of the seven contested cases was there a conviction. One of these cases, involving K.C. Irving's acquisitions of newspapers in New Brunswick, was won by the Crown at the original trial level but was lost on an appeal. Under the 1986 Act, the Bureau reviews all large mergers because of the prenotification requirement: firms planning a merger beyond a certain size must notify the Bureau of Competition Policy before the merger takes place, and allow the Bureau to review the merger. Normally about 20% to 25% of all mergers taking place in Canada in a given year will be reviewed. In a typical year this involves several hundred reviews. Over the period 1995-1999 the average number of reviews per year was 325. Of these, only a few are restructured or blocked in a given year. In 1998 a major review of proposed mergers in the banking sector was undertaken. The Royal Bank and the Bank of Montreal planned to merge, as did the Canadian Imperial Bank of Commerce and the Toronto-Dominion Bank. The Bureau recommended against these mergers. Because this involved the Banking sector, the Minister of Finance had overall jurisdiction, and he decided to disallow the mergers, based largely on the recommendation from the Bureau. While the number of mergers directly affected by Bureau activities is small compared to total merger activity, Bureau activities under the 1986 Act clearly have a much greater impact than pre-1986 merger policy had.

Two new defences for alleged merger violations were introduced in the 1986 Act. One new such defence is that international trade flows should be explicitly considered. Specifically, when a domestic merger is being examined, the level of competition afforded by imports is to be an important consideration, as described in Section 93 of the Act: The Tribunal may have regard to . . . the extent to which foreign products or foreign competitors provide or are likely to provide effective competition to the businesses of the parties to the merger or proposed merger.

In addition the 1986 Act allows for an efficiency defence. Specifically, Section 96 states:

> The Tribunal shall not [prevent the merger] if it finds that the proposed merger . . . is likely to bring about gains in efficiency that will be greater than, and will offset, the effects of any lessening of competition.

Abuse of dominant position arises if "one or more persons substantially or completely control, throughout Canada or any area thereof, a class or species of business," and if this dominant position is abused in certain specified ways. The abuse of dominant position sections of the law are intended to deal with market structures of the monopoly and dominant firm types. The law does not make monopoly illegal per se, but seeks to prevent various practices that might be used to establish or preserve monopoly or dominant firm market power.

The specific abuses of dominant position include the following (as defined in Section 78 of the Act).

a) squeezing, by a vertically integrated supplier, of the margin available to an unintegrated customer who competes with the supplier, for purposes of preventing entry or expansion in a market. For example, this means that the integrated petroleum producers must treat independent gasoline retailers basically as they treat their own gasoline retailing operations, as far as price and availability of product is concerned.

b) acquisition by a supplier of a customer who would otherwise be available to a competitor of the supplier, or acquisition by a customer of a supplier who would otherwise be available to a competitor of the customer, for the purpose of impeding or preventing the competitor's entry into, or eliminating the competitor from, a market;

c) freight equalization on the plant of a competitor for the purpose of impeding or preventing the competitor's entry into, or eliminating the competitor from, a market;

d) use of fighting brands introduced selectively on a temporary basis to discipline or eliminate a competitor;

e) pre-emption of scarce facilities or recources required by a competitor for the operation of a business, with the object of withholding the facilities or recources from a market;

f) buying up of products to prevent the erosion of existing price levels;

g) adoption of product specifications that are incompatible with products produced by any other person and are designed to prevent his entry into, or to eliminate him from, a market;

h) requiring or inducing a supplier to sell only or primarily to certain customers, or to refrain from selling to a competitor, with the object of preventing a competitor's entry into, or expansion in, a market; and

i) selling articles at a price lower than the acquisition cost for the purpose of disciplining or eliminating a competitor.

Only a few civil abuse of dominant position cases have gone before the Tribunal, and of those that have, several were appealed on constitutional grounds. For example, in 1989 the Tribunal found that Chrysler Canada was refusing to deal with a Montreal-based exporter and issued a supply order requiring Chrysler to supply parts to this exporter. Chrysler appealed this decision (on constitutional grounds) to the Federal Court of Appeal. This appeal was heard in 1991, and was unsuccessful. Chrysler then sought to appeal this case to the Supreme Court of Canada, but the Supreme Court decided, in 1992, not to hear the appeal, once again providing constitutional support for the Competition Act.

An important effect of the abuse of dominant position aspect of the Act is in resolving disputes before actually going before the Tribunal. For example, in one recent case the Bureau began an investigation concerning allegations that retail pharmacies in Ontario put pressure on manufacturers and wholesale suppliers of drugs not to supply mail order pharmacies. This would have violated point g on the above list. During the course of the investigation, the Ontario Pharmacists Association and the Canadian Pharmaceutical Association undertook actions to promote voluntary compliance with the Competition Act. Specifically, it informed members of the relevant provisions of the Act and, in particular, instructed retail pharmacies not to prevent mail-order pharmacies from getting access to drug supplies. The enquiry was then discontinued.

12.4.3 Conspiracy

The conspiracy section of the law, contained in Section 45 of the Competition Act, is the descendant of the original anticombines legislation of 1889. This section of the Act remains part of the criminal code. Its basic intent is to prevent the formation of cartels and to prevent any kind of anticompetitive collusion among firms. The most commonly prosecuted practice in this category is price-fixing: an agreement between producers concerning the level at which prices are to be set. The Act also specifically prohibits bid-rigging, the analogue of price-fixing for bidding situations. Other practices included under conspiracy are market-sharing arrangements (agreements to divide up a market along geographical or other readily identifiable lines), quota systems (agreements to limit production to certain fixed amounts per firm), and agreements to deter entry of potential rivals.

The Act explicitly allows coordination between firms for certain natural and obvious purposes, including definition of product standards and industry terminology, standardization of packaging and measurement, and measures to protect the environment. More surprisingly, the Act also allows cooperation among firms to restrict advertising or promotion, and for research and development.

Limited exemption from conspiracy sections of the Act is also allowed for firms operating in export markets, as stated in Section 45, subsection 5: "the court shall not convict the accused if the conspiracy . . . relates only to the export of products from Canada."

The enforcement of conspiracy provisions in competition law is subject to a number of difficulties. Explicit collusion over prices, or markets, or whatever, supported by written documents, makes a strong case for prosecution. But what about cases where explicit collusion is maintained without written documents? Such agreements are clearly illegal, but hard to prove. Even more difficult to investigate are collusive arrangements based on a tacit (rather than explicit) understanding between competing business firms. Tacit collusion means that firms are aware of the advantages of collusion and maintain a collusive outcome without direct communication between themselves. If one firm in an industry always announces its price list first, and other firms follow with similar prices based on an implicit understanding that no one firm should rock the boat, is this conspiracy?

Some analysts have suggested a third and still less clear layer of collusion, referred to as conscious parallelism, which captures the idea that firms might undertake similar actions, such as raising prices at more or less the same time and by the same amount, simply because they are similar and aware of their similarity. Firms may even copy each other on the grounds that what is good for one may be good for the others, but without exploitive intent. For example, the manager of some enterprise may simply adopt the rule that he or she will always charge the same price as a rival firm down the street. If this results in prices above the competitive level, are the firms guilty of conspiracy?

The conspiracy sections of the Act were strengthened in 1986, largely because judges had taken an extremely narrow interpretation of the previous law, rendering conspiracy cases hard to prosecute successfully. In 1980, a Supreme Court decision in the *Atlantic Sugar* case (discussed in more detail later in this chapter) rejected the use of circumstantial evidence as a basis for a finding of conspiracy, imposing the requirement that direct evidence of communication be obtained by the prosecution. Since conspiracies by their nature tend to be secretive and clandestine, there is often little documentary evidence to be found, especially in light of a subsequent Supreme Court ruling limiting the search and seizure powers of the Bureau.

This ruling certainly seemed to make conscious parallelism and even tacit collusion exempt from competition law, which was contrary to the intent of government legislators and officials responsible for competition policy. As stated by the Minister of Consumer and Corporate Affairs when the Act was introduced for discussion in 1985:

A number of recent Court decisions have created considerable uncertainty in the law and weakened its effectiveness . . . . It is the position of the Government that, in the interest of strengthening and clarifying the law, Parliament should restate its intention. . . .

The current law states explicitly (Section 45, subsection 2.1): "the court may infer the existence of conspiracy *with or without* [emphasis added] direct evidence of communication between or among the alleged parties."

Another weakening of the law that had occurred as the result of judicial interpretation prior to 1986 was that the Crown was required to prove not only that the accused had intended to enter a conspiracy, but also that they had intended to lessen competition unduly. Thus, even if the companies had intended to collude, and even if this collusion had reduced competition, they could still be found innocent if the Crown failed to prove that they actually intended to reduce competition unduly. A good analogy to pre-1986 conspiracy cases would arise in murder cases if conviction required a smoking gun [direct written evidence of conspiracy], a dead body [undue lessening of competition], and a demonstration that the person who shot the gun actually intended to murder the victim, over and above his intent to simply shoot the gun at the victim [double intent requirement].

The Act now states (Section 45, subsection 2.2): "it is necessary to prove that the parties intended to and did enter into a conspiracy . . ., but it is not necessary to prove that the parties intended [to reduce competition unduly]." This provision is referred to as the single intent requirement.

The double intent requirement has, however, re-emerged as the result of a legal challenge to a case begun before the 1986 Act. The Nova Scotia Court of Appeal ruled in 1991 that the pre-1986 law depended on the double intent requirement in order to be constitutional. Although the Court did not rule on the 1986 Act explicitly, by inference this ruling suggests that the single intent modification in the 1986 Act would be unconstitutional. This case was appealed by the Attorney General of Canada to the Supreme Court in 1992. The Supreme Court overruled the Nova Scotia Court of Appeal and affirmed that the single intent requirement is constitutional.

The penalty for price-fixing is normally in the form of a fine. Prior the 1990s, fines had been relatively modest, typically in the tens of thousands of dollars. In order to make fines a more meaningful deterrent, the Bureau and the Attorney General urged the imposition of higher fines, and the courts have, subsequently accepted this point of view. The first case establishing a much higher level of fines was the Abbott/Chemargo/Sumimoto pesticide case. The case involved market-sharing conspiracy directed by Chemargo Ltd. (a subsidiary of Bayer Corporation of Germany) and Sumimoto of Japan. As a result of this market-sharing arrangement, provincial governments in Canada paid unnecessarily high prices for pesticides used for forest protection. In 1993, when the case was ultimately decided, Chemargo was fined $2 million and Sumimoto was fined $1.25 million. Abbott was not prosecuted but agreed to pay $2.1 million in restitution to the provincial governments of Ontario and Quebec.

Two recent cases pushed fines to much higher levels. In 1999 VCAR Inc., a subsidiary of VCAR International Inc. was fined $11 million for fixing prices in the Market for graphite electrodes. (Graphite electrodes are primarily used in steel-making.) VCAR also agreed to pay an additional $19 million in restitution to victims of the price-fixing arrangement. In 1998, Archer, Daniels, Midland Company (ADM) and Ajinomoto Co Inc. were fined $19 million for price-fixing and market-sharing in the market lysine, an essential amino acid used extensively in the preparation of feed additives for hogs and poultry.

12.4.4 Predatory Pricing

Predatory pricing remains a criminal code violation under Section 50 Subsection 1c of the Act. The economic definition of predatory pricing is that it is the practice of charging a low price so as to drive a competitor out of business, with the hope of establishing monopoly power in the future. The exact wording of the law is:

> Every one who . . . engages in a policy of selling products at prices unreasonably low, having the effect or tendency of substantially lessening competition or eliminating a competitor, or designed to have such an effect, is guilty of an indictable offence. In addition to the criminal code section on predatory pricing, practice c listed above under abuse of dominant position (introduction of fighting brands) is a type of predatory pricing.

We do apparently see predatory pricing in the real world, but it is hard to distinguish from normal competition. The nature of competition is that some firms innovate, offer better price quality ratios than rival firms, and expand. Firms that cannot do as well go out of business. In addition, intermittent periods of price war are to be expected in oligopoly situations. Thus, the observation of low prices is usually just an indication that private incentives, channelled through competitive markets, are doing as Adam Smith would have hoped: serving the public interest.

In Canada, very few predatory pricing cases have been brought to court, largely because predatory pricing is so hard to distinguish from normal competition. In fact, the Hoffmann-Laroche case concluded in 1980 was only the second predatory pricing case to go to court, and the first successful case. The 1986 Competition Act has not greatly increased the frequency of predatory pricing court cases deriving from the criminal code sections of the Act. In fact, there have been no such cases between 1986 and 1999. What is more common, however, is application of the relevant abuse of dominant position sections of the Act under civil law to address predatory practices.

12.4.5 Price Discrimination

Like predatory pricing, price discrimination remains a criminal code offence (Section 50, subsection 1a), but is also covered by various provisions under abuse of dominant position. The economic definition of price discrimination is charging different prices to different buyers for the same good. For example, most telephone companies charge higher monthly telephone fees to business users rather than residential users. However, the price discrimination provisions of the Act do not deal with price discrimination at the level of final consumers. The principal intent of the law on price discrimination seems to be to establish procedural fairness in business practice. The exact wording of the relevant (criminal code) section of the Act is as follows:

> Every one engaged in a business who . . . assists in any sale that discriminates . . . against competitors of a purchaser . . . in that any discount, rebate, allowance, price concession or other advantage is granted to [one] purchaser [but not to another] is guilty of an indictable offence.

As this quote indicates, legal concern over price discrimination arises with respect to sales of inputs to other firms and in sales at the wholesale level, rather than with respect to sales to final consumers.
Very few price discrimination cases have been prosecuted; only one was contested prior to 1986 and the government lost that case. There is little prospect of dramatically increased prosecution of price discrimination cases under the 1986 Act, although there were a few cases in the late 1980s. From 1986 through 1999 a total of only 3 convictions were obtained.

One price discrimination case occurred in 1989, against a ski resort lodge that was the sole supplier of ski-lift tickets for the Mont Tremblant ski hills. This lodge offered discounts on ski-lift tickets to its own lodge guests. It did not, however, make corresponding discounts on ski-lift tickets available to guests staying at other lodges. The court ordered the lodge to make comparable ski-lift discounts available through other lodges.

Although the criminal code price discrimination provisions do not generate much activity, price discrimination also arises under the (civil law) abuse of dominant position provisions of the Act.

12.4.6 Resale Price Maintenance

Resale price maintenance arises in relationships between wholesalers, distributors or producers, and retailers. Specifically, if a supplier of some product tries to ensure that retailers sell that product at a particular price (or at least at prices no lower than some specified price), then the supplier is engaged in resale price maintenance. Resale price maintenance is part of the criminal code and is defined in Section 61 of the Act. The law reads as follows:

> No person who is engaged in the business of producing or sup-
> plying a product . . . shall . . . by agreement, threat, promise,
> or by any like means, attempt to influence upward, or to dis-
> courage the reduction of, the price at which any other person
> in Canada supplies or offers to supply or advertises a product
> within Canada; or refuse to supply a product to or otherwise
> discriminate against any other person engaged in business in
> Canada because of the low pricing policy of that other person.

Exceptions to this basic statement are made for formally affiliated companies (e.g., two companies that are subsidiaries of the same parent) and for formal principal and agent relationships (e.g., real estate agent and house builder). Suppliers are allowed to provide a suggested retail price, provided it is made clear that the retailer is under no obligation to sell the product at the suggested retail price.

Resale price maintenance has been and continues to be a reasonably active area. Over the period 1986-99, there have been an average of four to five resale price maintenance cases per year, with somewhat higher numbers in the early part of the period.

One recent resale price maintenance case was as follows. A real estate broker in Calgary, Alberta, known as Roberts Real Estate, was found guilty of price maintenance as a result of its relations with a discount real estate broker, Elite Real Estate Ltd., also located in Calgary. The general background to the case is that real estate brokers (and agents) in Calgary and in most other parts of Canada have a generally established pattern of commissions, such as 5% or 6% of the value of a property. (Commissions are often nonlinear: the percentage commission varies with the sale price of the property.) There are, however, discount brokers, who will offer lower commissions. If established real estate brokers are forced to compete with these lower commissions they would obviously be worse off. In an effort to prevent this erosion of commissions, established real estate brokers will often try to punish discount brokers in some way, perhaps by excluding them from multiple listing services, or through other means. Different real estate brokers are often forced to cooperate, as when an agent from one real estate broker has a listing and an agent from another broker finds a buyer. Normally, the broker with the listing will share the commission (which is paid by the seller of the property) with the broker who finds the buyer. Roberts Real Estate, however, offered lower commissions to Elite than to other real estate brokers on properties listed with Roberts. In addition, Roberts refused to show Elite's listings to potential buyers.

In March 1994, Roberts was fined $25,000 on a charge of resale price maintenance, although it could equally well have been charged under price discrimination. In a familiar pattern, this conviction was appealed to a higher court on constitutional grounds, but the appeal was dismissed. This ruling has undermined the ability of real estate organizations to maintain standardized commissions, although standardized commissions still dominate the industry.

12.4.7 Misleading Advertising and Deceptive Marketing Practices

This area is the most recent addition to the list of anticompetitive practices, having been added in 1960 and expanded in 1969 and 1976. It is the responsibility of a special branch of the Bureau, known as the Marketing Practices Branch. This area is sometimes referred to simply as marketing offenses. These offenses are part of the criminal code.

There were seven separate marketing offenses defined in the 1986 Act. Definitions from Sections: 52 through 55 of the Competition Act follow:

- *False or misleading representations*: "No person shall, for the purpose of promoting . . . any business interest . . . make a representation to the public that is false or misleading in a material respect." This includes claims about warranties, servicing, testimonials, and product tests.

- *Deceptive Telemarketing*: "No person who engages in telemarketing shall make a representation that is false or misleading in a material respect." In addition, various questionable telemarketing practices are carefully restricted by the Act.

- *Double ticketing*: If a product is marked (by the seller) with two prices, the seller must sell at the lower price. Selling at the higher price is illegal.

- *Pyramid selling*: A pyramid selling scheme is one in which one person pays a fee to participate in the scheme and receives a fee for recruiting others to participate, in chain letter or pyramid fashion. Such schemes are illegal. This provision of the law is not intended to interfere with normal franchising operations. It is intended to prevent schemes in which recruitment commissions become more important than the underlying product.

In addition, there are various provisions about multi-level marketing, which is a slight variation of pyramid selling. The difference is that in multi-level marketing actual materials for sale are exchanged. For example, suppose Person A obtains health food products then sells a franchise to Person B. Person B pays a commission to Person A and receives the health food products. Person B then sells franchises to Persons C and D, who pay commissions to B and, in return, receive the health food products. Thus, instead of the normal producer-wholesaler-retail chain, there is a potentially much longer chain of transactions before the product reaches final consumers (if it ever does). Multi-level marketing is not illegal per se, but the law requires that potential participants be accurately informed about compensation levels of those already in the plan.

Shortly after this provision went into effect, a multi-level marketing operation known as Lifestyles Canada Ltd. was convicted and fined $35,000 for violation of this provision on the grounds that recruitment procedures "misled many prospective participants into believing that it is easy to earn large amounts of money."

Quantitatively, misleading advertising and deceptive marketing cases account for the lion's share of competition policy cases. In the year ending March 31, 1999, there were 163 completed investigations, although only few would actually lead to prosecutions. In 1999 there were 5 convictions, resulting in fines totalling $1.4 million. The number of prosecutions was considerably higher in the late 1980s and early 1990s, although 1.4 million was a new record for total fines. In part this reflects a change in strategy by the Bureau to focus on a smaller number of cases, but to go for important cases and for higher fines. It also reflects improved compliance with the law by the business community. In late 1994, the first major case resulted in a $225,000 fine against Color Your World. Aside from using the American spelling "color" rather than the Canadian spelling "colour," Color Your World was convicted of misleading advertising because of a major advertising campaign claiming that products (paint, wallpaper, etc.) were being sold at dramatic discounts relative to after sale prices and regular book prices. In fact, these sale prices were little different from the prices that these products were normally sold at.

Following this case, the Commissioner of Competition stated that the intent of this case was to send a clear message to retailing that advertising of discount or sale prices must accurately convey the dis-

count and, in particular, that comparison prices must reflect that actual price at which the product is normally sold. In a similar case, wom-
ens' clothing retailer Suzy Shier Limited was fined $300,000. As part
of an advertising campaign Suzy Shier claimed that clothing was on
sale for 50% to 70% off original prices. Price tags on the clothing did
indicate very high prices, but it was established that clothing never
sold for these high prices and that the "special" tags indicating lower
prices were already attached to the clothing items before they even
entered the stores.

12.5 Significant Competition Policy Cases

12.5.1 Overview of Competition Policy Cases

The above description of anti-competitive practices yields the conclusion that the major areas of competition policy: those relating to mergers, monopoly power, and conspiracy, have relatively few cases. The
vast majority of cases are in the area of misleading advertising and
deceptive marketing practices, which have little to do with monopoly
power. Of the remaining cases, most are in the area of resale price
maintenance, which is only weakly related to the exercise of monopoly power. In both the marketing and resale price maintenance areas,
fines tend to be modest (although they are getting larger) and many
firms have, in the past, simply regarded the occasional fine as a cost
of doing business.

The following table shows the history of the distribution of prosecuted (i.e., criminal code) cases.

TABLE 12.1 Competition Policy Prosecutions
(number of criminal code prosecutions commenced)

Period	Other	MA/DMP
1890–1960	53	0
1961–1970	43	75
1971–1980	116	1,022
1981–1990	162	1392
1991–1999	39	182

Notes:

MA/DMP = misleading advertising and deceptive marketing practices

Sources: up to 1983: P.K. Gorecki and W.T. Stanbury (1984); 1983-99: *Annual Report*,
various years, Commissioner of Competition, Industry Canada.

Note that there were no mergers and monopoly (or abuse of dominant position) cases prosecuted before the courts after 1987, because these areas moved to civil law, where there has been considerable activity, as discussed earlier. Thus, anticompetitive mergers are no longer prosecuted; they are simply not allowed to proceed or are restructured.

It is noteworthy that in the 1990s, prosecutions were dramatically lower (in total number) than in the previous decade. This reflects in part a shift of resources away from criminal code investigations toward civil reviewable areas, and it also reflects a decision to initiate fewer but larger criminal code cases. The following subsections deal with specific cases that have been of particular significance in the development of competition policy.

12.5.2 The Gemini Airline Reservation Case

In 1989 the two major Canadian airlines, Air Canada and Canadian Airlines, formed a partnership to operate a computerized airline reservation system as a joint venture. (This joint venture was cleared by the Bureau of Competition Policy.) Canadian Airlines subsequently entered into an agreement to undertake a partial merger with American Airlines, a major U.S.-based carrier. In order for this merger to go through, however, Canadian would have to abandon the Gemini computer reservation system and join American Airlines' reservation system.

Accordingly, Canadian sought to leave the Gemini partnership, but this move was opposed by Air Canada which argued that Canadian was contractually bound to the partnership. This case was investigated by the Bureau of Competition Policy and considered by the Tribunal. In 1993, the Tribunal ordered that Canadian be allowed to exit from the Gemini Airline Reservation system, that it be allowed to take its database out of Gemini, and that the Gemini partnership be dissolved.

This was an interesting case because the central issue was the structure of the Canadian airline industry. In the early 1990s, it appeared that the Canadian commercial airline market might not be large enough to accommodate two full-service carriers, and there was considerable concern about the possibility of having a monopoly carrier. The partial merger between Canadian and American Airlines was seen as a way of ensuring continued competition in the Canadian market. Subsequently, this issue became somewhat moot through an agreement between Canada and the United States to allow airlines based in both countries to freely enter routes joining Canadian and U.S. cities, as described in Chapter 1.

This case illustrates the more flexible role of competition policy under civil sections of the 1986 Act. The Competition Tribunal was able to make what was essentially a public policy decision, based on economic analysis by the Bureau of Competition Policy, rather than focusing purely on legalistic issues in a criminal court. It is worth noting, however, that Air Canada began several legal suits against Canadian and American Airlines, most of which were settled out of court.

12.5.3 Mergers: The ERCO Case

The ERCO case was one of only two in which a firm was found guilty under the pre-1986 criminal code merger provisions of competition policy. The following description is based on McFetridge (1974).

In 1970, Electric Reduction Company (ERCO) pleaded guilty in criminal court to a merger charge and to two monopoly (now called abuse of dominant position) charges. The period in question was 1956-66. ERCO was a producer of industrial phosphates, used principally in the production of soap products. As of 1956, ERCO had a Canadian monopoly in the production of industrial phosphates, protected from U.S. competition by a tariff of 20%.

About 80% of ERCO's production was sold to three Canadian soap companies, all subsidiaries of U.S. parents. The rest was sold to a large group of small buyers. The three large soap companies were able to bargain with ERCO over prices. Proctor and Gamble, for example, paid a price equal to the U.S. price for phosphates plus 2.5%. The small buyers, on the other hand, paid prices equal to the U.S. price plus 20%: the exact markup allowed by the tariff. If ERCO had charged any more, the small buyers could have purchased more cheaply from the U.S., even after paying the tariff. Thus, small buyers paid much higher prices than large buyers for ERCO's product. It seems that the large buyers were in fact paying a price roughly equal to average costs (including a normal rate of return), and that small buyers were effectively paying prices high enough to allow ERCO to earn substantial excess or above normal profits.

In 1958, a second firm, Dominion Fertilizers, began producing phosphate fertilizers and announced its intention to enter the industrial phosphates market, where ERCO then held a monopoly position. ERCO decided that it could not tolerate a rival and purchased Dominion Fertilizers in 1959. ERCO also entered into arrangements with two other potential entrants, CIL and Cyanamid Corp., under which these firms agreed not to enter the industrial phosphates market.

ERCO then continued its practice of price discrimination, and continued to charge small buyers the full markup allowed by the tariff, earning the associated monopoly profits. ERCO was indicted in 1967 on merger and monopoly offenses, subsequently pleaded guilty, and was convicted in 1970. In addition to paying a fine, ERCO was required to end its practice of price discrimination and to refrain from "any arrangement designed to deter the entry of new phosphates producers." The merger was allowed to stand on the basis of ERCO's claim, uncontested by the Crown, that phosphates production had sufficiently large economies of scale that the Canadian market probably could support only one firm of efficient size.

12.5.4 Mergers: The Safeway Case

This was one of the first major merger cases considered by the Bureau under the 1986 Act. On December 12, 1986, Canada Safeway announced its intention to acquire 23 food outlets from Woodward Stores. Following an extensive enquiry, the Bureau identified six markets in Alberta and British Columbia where competition was likely to be eliminated or substantially reduced. These six markets were in the following cities: Edmonton, Lethbridge, Red Deer, Vancouver, Port Alberni, and Princeton (B.C.). As a result of the Bureau's concern, Safeway undertook to divest 12 stores in these markets within two years. As a result, the Bureau did not contest the merger, and the divestitures took place, with most of the outlets being sold to IGA, a smaller chain of food outlets. In addition the Bureau undertook to monitor Safeway for three years and reserved the right to apply further remedies if problems should arise.

This case illustrates the difference between the pre- and post-1986 approach to mergers. In the Safeway case, rather than contest a merger directly, the Bureau was able to restructure the merger so as to protect and, in this case, possibly promote competition.

12.5.5 Predatory Pricing: Hoffmann-Laroche

On February 5, 1980, Hoffman-Laroche (HL) became the first company convicted of predatory pricing in Canada. HL is a large multinational pharmaceutical firm that dominates the world's vitamin market (over 50% market share), and is the developer and marketer of the tranquilizer, Valium, which was for many years the world's best-selling prescription drug.

Most of the costs of the pharmaceutical industry are due to research and development. Actual production costs are small. Furthermore, once one company has discovered and tested a valuable drug, it is relatively easy for other firms to copy it. In 1970, HL was charging $42.50 per 1,000 tablets of Valium on the basis of operating costs of about $3 per 1,000. A small competitor, Frank Horner Limited, began producing a generic substitute for Valium, as allowed by Canadian drug patent law, and offered it for sale to hospitals at a price of $6.90 per 1,000 tablets. HL's response was to give Valium to hospitals free of charge, forcing Horner out of the market. In addition to this prima facie evidence of predatory pricing, correspondence was obtained outlining the plans to drive Horner from the market. Ten years later, HL was convicted of predatory pricing.

One wonders how HL could have expected to get away with such obvious and blatant predatory pricing. Presumably, company executives would point out (privately) that since no predatory pricing convictions had ever been obtained in Canada, and only one previous case had been taken to court, they could reasonably assume that the law on predatory pricing was inoperative. They were almost right.

12.5.6 Canadian Petroleum Industry

Perhaps the most widely publicized competition policy case is the Canadian Petroleum Industry case, which never even reached the courts. Prior to 1986, the Director of Investigation and Research would transmit the findings of the Bureau of Competition Policy on certain major cases to the (defunct as of 1986) Restrictive Trade Practices Commission (RTPC) for evaluation, before sending them forward for prosecution in the courts.

In 1973, a number of Canadian residents complained to the Bureau that the petroleum industry in Canada was acting in violation of competition policy. Complaints by six residents are sufficient, under the law, to warrant starting an investigation, and on this basis the Bureau went into action in 1973. A major investigation followed, culminating in a 1981 report consisting of 1,400 pages of printed text in seven volumes, and supported by 100 volumes of supplementary material, mostly seized documents.

The Director turned the report over to the RTPC and released some of its findings to the public. The principal finding was that Canadian consumers had been overcharged by some $12 billion by the oil industry. In addition, the major oil companies (including Chevron, Exxon, Shell, and Texaco, among others) were accused of a variety of practices that suggested collusion, although the report did not formally charge collusion, and were accused of predatory behaviour with respect to the independent gasoline retailers. An immediate outcry followed in Parliament, and newspapers ran headlines indicating that consumers had been "ripped off" by oil companies.

The RTPC evaluated the report and came to the opposite conclusion, as described in its report, published in 1986, and consisting of only three volumes comprising some 600 pages. The principal conclusions were that there was insufficient evidence that consumers had been overcharged and that there was "no evidence of collusion in any sector of the industry."

It is hard to know where the truth lies in this case. One complicating factor was that OPEC had had a disruptive effect on oil prices in the 1970s that created considerable consumer resentment against the oil industry. Nevertheless, many observers feel that the larger oil companies have been engaged in anticompetitive practices, particulary with respect to smaller retailers. Many of the issues that arose in the investigation of this case were incorporated in the abuse of dominant position section of the 1986 Act, so this case is of considerable historical importance even though it never went to court.

12.6 U.S. Anti-trust Policy and Microsoft

It is interesting to compare the U.S. and Canadian experiences. The first major point is that U.S. antitrust policy has been much more active than Canadian competition policy until recently. From 1890 to 1970, 564 cases of monopoly and merger were brought to court. In Canada, one might expect perhaps one-tenth as many, or about 50. In fact, nine comparable cases were brought to court in that period. Shepherd (1985, p. 312) states that in the United States, "mergers among direct competitors have been tightly constrained since about 1962." He also argues that price-fixing, while still common, has been substantially reduced by anti-trust action and that "anti-trust has had large positive effects."

Some of the more well-known U.S. cases involve dissolution of entrenched market power, which has never been done in Canada. The Standard Oil Case of 1911 had a major impact on North American industry. At the time, Standard Oil had over 90% of the U.S. oil refining market and exploited its monopoly power ruthlessly. The courts ordered the dissolution of Standard Oil into several smaller companies, which was achieved by 1913, greatly increasing competition in the industry.

In 1938, Alcoa, which had a monopoly in the North American aluminum market, was brought to court on the basis of entrenched monopoly power. The decision, rendered in 1945, required, interestingly from the Canadian point of view, that Alcoa sever its ties with its Canadian subsidiary, Aluminium of Canada (subsequently Alcan), and that it turn over government aluminum plants, built during World War II and operated by Alcoa, to new competitors, who turned out to be Reynolds Inc. and Kaiser Inc.

A very important recent case involved AT&T, which was an enormous regulated firm providing telephone services throughout the United States. The case ran from 1974 to 1984, when AT&T was forced to divest all of its operating companies, which provide local telephone service, and some of its other operations as well. AT&T was, however, freed from price regulation and freed from regulatory constraints on entry into other lines of business. One of the reasons for this decision was to allow AT&T to use its technological sophistication to enter other high-technology industries, increasing competition in those areas as well.

Perhaps the largest U.S. anti-trust case, as measured by the resources consumed, resulted in defeat for the anti-trust authorities. This was the IBM case, which began in 1969 and ended in 1982. IBM was accused of a variety of anti-competitive practices. This case involved the full-time efforts of hundreds of individuals, including many lawyers, economists, and accountants, for several years. It generated several *million* pages of documentation, and cost IBM many millions of dollars, including one out of court settlement concerning an associated private damage suit launched by Control Data Corporation, costing IBM roughly U.S.$100 million. IBM was able to avoid conviction on the government's case, and defeated some 20 other associated private damage suits in court.

More recently, U.S. anti-trust authorities undertook a substantial investigation of Microsoft, the world's leading producer of computer software.

As of mid-year 2000, computer software producer Microsoft was found guilty in the U.S. court of various anti-trust offenses. The trial judge accepted the remedy suggested by the U.S. Government, which involves breaking up Microsoft into two arm's length companies. One company would produce the Windows operating system and the other would produce "applications" software, including the suite of products in Microsoft Office. The case is currently being appealed by Microsoft and is likely to go to the U.S. Supreme Court.

This case illustrates several important issues. If we were to use Canadian terminology, we would say that the Microsoft case is primarily about abuse of dominant position. The first issue to establish was that Microsoft had a dominant position, and this depended very much on what is referred to as "market definition". Microsoft lawyers argued that the relevant market was the market for all computer software. While Microsoft was the biggest single producer of software in the U.S. and the world, the lawyers argued that there was sufficient competition in the overall software market. The U.S. government lawyers argued that the relevant market should be more narrowly defined as "operating systems for personal computers". The judge decided that the more narrow definition was appropriate and that Microsoft, as the producer of "Windows", had a virtual monopoly in this market. The rest of the case is then based on the idea that Microsoft used its dominance in the operating system market to restrict or prevent competition in the markets for other software products. In particular, the judge found that Microsoft sought to prevent purchasers of the operating system from having competitive access to Internet browsers, word processors, and other products produced by companies other than Microsoft. Microsoft used several mechanisms to achieve this, including changing the Windows operating system in ways that made it difficult for other producers of application software to achieve compatibility with the underlying Windows operating system. In addition, Microsoft insisted that vendors of computer systems who purchase the Windows operating system sign restrictive contracts that gave preferential treatment of Microsoft applications.

As with any legal case, the dynamics of the trial process were important. In this particular case, the judge found that the testimony of Microsoft founder and CEO Bill Gates and the testimony of Microsoft's consulting expert economist, Richard Schmalensee, was seriously lacking in credibility.

There were several possibilities for remedies suggested, including breaking up Microsoft, making the underlying Windows code freely accessible, or imposing detailed restrictions on the contracts used by Microsoft in selling the Windows operating system, possibly combined with other restrictions on Microsoft's conduct. The judge felt that the third of these options would require too much continuing legal oversight of Microsoft and that Microsoft has already largely ignored previous restrictions of this type imposed on Microsoft in an earlier and narrower anti-trust case. The judge felt that making the underlying Windows software "open" would be insufficient to open up competition in the relevant markets, and therefore opted for the breakup option. As a result of the breakup, the new "applications" company would compete on a more level playing field with other producers of applications software, and it is even possible that the operating system market might become more competitive as well.

Shepherd (1985) concludes that U.S. anti-trust policy has been very worthwhile. He estimates that the ratio of economic benefits to costs for the Standard Oil case was 67 to 1, and for the Alcoa case 19 to 1. Perhaps the most important benefit, however, has been in preventing anti-competitive practices that might otherwise have been attempted.

12.7 Competition Policy: Past Performance and Future Prospects

Without doubt, competition policy in Canada has had a restraining effect on price-fixing and overt collusion, and has certainly more than paid for the costs of operating the policy on that basis alone. The operations of the Bureau of Competition Policy required a budget of approximately $25 million in the fiscal year ending March 31, 1999, and fines generated approximately $41 million in revenues. In addition, there are costs associated with use of the courts. On balance the fines generated by competition policy enforcement were probably roughly equal to the direct cost of operating competition policy in the late 1990s. Those costs and revenues are, however, small compared to the overall economic impact of competition policy. For example, the mergers evaluated are frequently worth hundreds of millions or even billions of dollars. The comparatively recent extension (in 1960) of competition policy to include misleading advertising and deceptive marketing practices also generates clear benefits. In the areas of mergers to reduce competition and abuse of monopoly power, policy does not seem to have had much effect in the pre-1986 era, but the post-1986 ability of policy to restructure mergers to protect competition seems to have had positive effects.

On the whole, competition policy was not applied very effectively prior to 1986. In trying to fit complex economic issues into one of two boxes, guilty or innocent, the legal process often ignored the fundamental economic considerations at issue. Those considerations usually involve tradeoffs between degrees of competition, realization of scale economies, and other subtle but important aspects of business. By focusing on the guilt or innocence of a defendant, the overriding normative concern of the overall public interest is neglected. A strictly correct legal decision could easily be a bad policy decision. In short, economists would argue that a courtroom may be a good place to make decisions of criminal guilt or innocence, but not a good place to formulate economic policy.

Successive amendments to competition policy have gradually brought the law more and more into line with normative economic reasoning, but the entire progress along these lines was modest until the passage of the Competition Act of 1986.

The 1986 Act changed the structure of competition policy significantly. In the areas of mergers and abuse of dominant position, because civil law has replaced criminal law and cases are dealt with by the Tribunal rather than by the courts, it is possible to use economic criteria as the basis for making decisions. The Tribunal has the power to order the parties to refrain from certain actions, or undertake other actions, without having to convict the parties of a criminal offence. This allows the Tribunal to focus on making the economy more competitive, rather than on questions of criminal guilt or innocence.

In those areas of competition law that remain in the criminal code, various criteria for convictions were stated more clearly and more forcefully, allowing prosecutions to be obtained more easily. Several other important changes were introduced by the 1986 Act. One change was to clarify and modify investigative procedures. This change resulted from a finding by the Supreme Court of Canada that previous procedures were in violation of the protections against unreasonable search and seizure guaranteed by the Charter of Rights. Other important changes were that banks and Crown corporations were brought under the jurisdiction of competition policy by the 1986 Act.

In addition, since 1986, the Bureau placed much more emphasis on information and compliance programs. Specifically, it devoted substantial resources to producing easily understood guidelines that explain in detail which kinds of business practices are acceptable and which are not, and what businesses should do to comply with the law. It has also sought to distribute and discuss these guidelines actively in order to raise awareness of appropriate business practice, rather than simply react to complaints that come in. This is the competition policy equivalent of preventive health care. In the future, the Bureau will increase its focus on proactive encouragement of compliance with the law, rather than simply coming in after the fact to impose punishment.

Another important role of the Bureau lies in the area of regulatory intervention. The Commissioner of Competition makes submissions to regulatory bodies on the competitive effects of actual and proposed regulatory practices. This area of work has turned out to be significant in its use of resources and in its influence on policy. The Commissioner has taken a particular interest in regulation in the telecommunications sector, making a substantial number of representations to regulators in this area.

The future of competition policy will be affected by the increasing internationalization and globalization of the world economy. In particular, many of the firms under investigation nowadays are large multinationals whose entire international operations might be relevant in a given case. As a result, Canadian competition policy authorities have started to cooperate with their counterparts in the United States and Europe. In August of 1995, the United States and Canada signed a the Canada-U.S. Competition Policy Agreement that establishes closer formal ties between the Bureau of Competition Policy and its U.S. counterparts (the Antitrust Division of the Justice Department and the Federal Trade Commission). There was a time when a lawyer or economic consultant who worked on competition policy cases would expect never to leave Canada. Today, such people might fly to London or Washington or Tokyo to investigate cases. There are also increasing attempts to harmonize competition policy across countries, and several countries that have lacked coherent competition policy in the past, especially in Eastern Europe and Latin America, are trying to develop competition policy institutions modelled partly on the Canadian model. In addition, the World Bank (discussed in Chapter 9) has taken an interest in the development of competition policy infrastructure as part of the development process. There have also been suggestions in the WTO that competition policy issues might be linked to trade policy issues.

12.8 Bibliographic Notes

The basic source for competition law is a document produced by Consumer and Corporate Affairs (1986) entitled *Competition Law Amendments: A Schematic Presentation of Bill C-91* and the *Present Act*. The modifications of competition law introduced in 1986 are contained in Bill C-91. Another valuable primary source is the *Annual Report of the Director of Investigation and Research: Competition Act*, which reports the activities of the Bureau of Competition Policy. A valuable general source for competition policy material is the journal, *Canadian Competition Policy Record*. A good textbook on U.S. antitrust policy is Viscusi, Vernon, and Harrington (1992), while Green (1990) is a valuable industrial organization textbook containing much information on Canadian competition policy. In 1998, the *Review of Industrial Organization* (a U.S.-based journal) published a special issue (edited by Thomas Ross) on Canadian competition policy. Now a days, the best source of current information about Competition Policy is the Internet.

Note

1. Commissioner of Competition, Director of Investigation and Research, Competition Act, Industry Canada.

On-line Sources

For the Canadian Competition Bureau, see:

http://strategis.ic.gc.ca/SSG/ct01254e.html

For information about Canadian competition, see: *http://csgb.ubc.ca/ccpp/*

For information about U.S. anti-trust policy, see:

http://www.antitrust.org/site/tableof.htm

13

Anti-competitive Practices: Economic Analysis

Chapter 12 provided an institutional and historical discussion of competition policy in Canada. In this chapter the corresponding economic analysis of competition policy is presented. Each section is devoted to the analysis of one the six anti-competitive practices listed in Chapter 12: collusion (or conspiracy), mergers, predatory pricing, price discrimination, resale price maintenance, and misleading advertising and deceptive marketing practices.

13.1 Collusion

Collusion is the normal term used for business practices that fall under the conspiracy sections of competition policy. The most common collusive practices are price-fixing, bid-rigging, and market-sharing arrangements (usually through quotas). Collusion normally arises in oligopolistic industries, although it sometimes also arises in the dominant firm and monopolistic competition market structures.

The basic objective of collusion is to allow the firms involved to earn monopoly profits. Perfect collusion would imitate the pure monopoly outcome: joint profits would by maximized. In the days before the development of competition policy, collusion was sometimes maintained by explicit contract. Firms would sign contracts with each other, limiting the amount of output each would sell or the geographical area in which each would operate. Successful instances of collusion, in which the firms succeed in acting much like a single monopoly firm, are sometimes described as cartels.

Since the development of competition policy, collusive contracts have been in violation of the law. Even if the legal system failed to actively prosecute a collusive agreement, no such contract would be enforced by the courts. Thus, actual collusive contracts are of limited value to the firms (since they are not enforceable) and create a potential legal liability.

Firms that engage in collusion confront two basic problems: first, how to ensure that the colluding firms maintain the collusive agreement in the absence of a legally enforceable contract, and, second, how to avoid prosecution. These two basic problems present a tradeoff to the firms involved, since actions that increase the chances of maintaining the collusive agreement typically make the prospect of prosecution more likely.

The basic incentive problem of collusion is as follows. The collusive agreement will, by its nature, require that each firm restrain output below normal (noncollusive) production levels. Restraining output will allow the industry to move up the industry demand curve and charge a higher price. The collusive price and output levels occur where industry marginal revenue is just equal to industry marginal cost, as with monopoly pricing.

From the point of view of any one firm, however, its own marginal revenue is above marginal cost, meaning that it has a unilateral incentive to expand output. This is best illustrated using the following equations.

$$MR^f = P + (\Delta P)q \qquad (13.1)$$
$$MR^I = P + (\Delta P)Q \qquad (13.2)$$

where ΔP is negative, representing the price fall that is required if sales are to be increased by one unit. MR^f is a single firm's marginal revenue, MR^I is the industry's marginal revenue, P is price, q is the output of a single firm, and Q is the industry's output.

Recall from Chapter 6 that marginal revenue is the extra revenue resulting from a one-unit increase in output. If a single firm increases output, it gains the price charged for the extra unit of sales, but industry selling price falls, reducing the revenue of the firm by the change in price, ΔP, times its output, q. These two effects are reflected in the two terms of Equation 13.1. Industry marginal revenue is similar, except that the second term is industry output, Q, times the fall in price, as shown by Equation 13.2. Since industry output exceeds the output of any one firm, the subtraction for the effect of the price decline is larger for the industry than for a single firm. As a result, industry marginal revenue is less than the marginal revenue of a single firm that increases output.

An increase in output by one firm causes revenue to fall in other firms. The industry marginal revenue associated with an increase in output by one firm is that firm's marginal revenue minus the losses to other firms. Industry marginal cost is, however, just the same as a firm's marginal cost. If industry marginal revenue is set equal to marginal cost, the firm's marginal revenue must be above marginal cost. Consequently, the firm faces an incentive to expand output.

The following stylized example sets out the incentive problem clearly. Suppose there are several firms in an industry. In the absence of collusion, each would earn profit N annually. This level of profit might still exceed normal competitive profits, but it will be less than full monopoly profits. Profits under full collusion, if divided up among the firms, would yield an annual profit of M to each firm, where $M > N$. The annual benefit to each firm from collusion is $M-N$.

In effect, the colluding firms are in a situation like the Prisoner's Dilemma described in Chapter 6. If they cooperate, they all do well, but, given the output levels of the other firms, any one firm has an incentive to defect by producing more output. A defecting firm raises its own profits, but reduces the profits of the other firms by more than its own gain. By defecting, a single firm can earn even more than M, at least temporarily. In most cartels this proves, sooner or later, to be an irresistible temptation.

Nevertheless, periods of collusion have been frequently observed in many industries. Cartels tend to be most stable when the firms involved can communicate with each other easily and when the relationship is likely to last a long time. If a collusive arrangement has been reached, and the firms are likely to interact for many years, the incentive to defect on the agreement is partially offset by the idea that defection today will be matched by retaliatory defection next period by the other firms. The defecting firm must trade off the short-term gains from defection against the long-term losses from disintegration of the collusive agreement: the firm will give up the benefits of collusion, $M–N$, for (at least some) future periods.

Economists have considered how this threat of retaliation can be most effectively used by firms in the industry to promote collusion. Like Ulysses confronted by the sirens, the firms would like to collectively bind themselves to a course of action they would otherwise stray from. The firms would like to be able to commit themselves to the collusive agreement. One way of trying to generate an environment in which collusion is maintained is by establishing the expectation that defection will be met by damaging retaliation or punishment. The strongest form of punishment would be that any defection would result in defection by others forever. Presented with such a prospect, firms would face a strong incentive not to defect from collusion.

But what if defection did take place? Is the industry to be locked forever in punishment mode, with firms foregoing potential monopoly profits? In fact, this so-called grim strategy of threatening to defect forever if a rival defects does meet minimal tests of consistency: it is what economists refer to as a Nash equilibrium, which means that each firm is maximizing its profit, given the strategies selected by rival firms. In addition, these strategies are credible or sequentially rational in that it is not irrational for an individual firm to actually carry out the punishment threats if called upon to do, given that it expects other firms to do so also. A more favourable outcome, however, from the firms' point of view, might involve more limited trigger strategies that require only short periods of retaliation following a defection.

Axelrod (1984) has shown in laboratory experiments that so-called tit-for-tat strategies are good at maintaining collusion without sacrificing too much during retaliation. Tit for tat involves following any defection by a single period of retaliatory defection, then returning to the collusive strategy. Thus, if one firm raised its output and undercut other firms in period 1, rival firms would respond by producing more, leading to further price reductions in period 2, reducing the profits of all firms. After this punishment period, however, the retaliating firms would return to the collusive output and price levels, expecting the initial defector to have learned its lesson. The firms' hope is that the expectation of such punishment, or at least the experience of punishment, will deter further defections.

In any circumstance, collusion is made particularly difficult if there is considerable uncertainty in demand, so that firms have a hard time distinguishing between defection and bad luck. If so, any one firm's temptation to defect is increased, because it may not even be found out.

Collusion is one way for a small group of firms to try to achieve monopoly profits (at the expense of consumers). Even in jurisdictions where collusion is illegal, and even granting that collusion is usually unstable, it is still an important business phenomenon and warrants public policy to restrict it. The rationale for anticollusion laws therefore has a solid normative foundation.

13.2 Mergers

Merger is a more direct method of trying to increase monopoly power than collusion. A merger brings control of previously independent operations under one management. Unlike collusion, however, mergers are not focused exclusively on increasing monopoly power. Most mergers, in fact, can be easily justified on efficiency grounds. Even in the United States, only a small fraction of total merger activity is contested by policy authorities, and in Canada, as discussed in Chapter 12, only a handful of cases have been prosecuted in the entire history of competition policy. Since merger provisions were shifted from criminal to civil law in 1986, competition authorities have had more influence in opposing or modifying proposed mergers, but the overwhelming majority of mergers are uncontested by authorities.

13.2.1 Some Definitions

A merger is the amalgamation of two firms, or parts of two firms, into a single firm. Most mergers are takeovers: one firm (the bidder or acquiring firm) buys and absorbs another firm or part of another firm (the target). The difference between a merger and a simple (nonmerger) purchase of physical assets is that a merger involves the purchase of a business unit as a going concern.

It is normal to distinguish between three types of mergers: horizontal mergers, vertical mergers, and conglomerate mergers. Horizontal mergers are mergers between two business units that produce essentially the same product. For example, in 1999, Sears, a major department store chain acquired Eatons, another a major Canadian department store chain, and merged operations of the two chains. Both firms were in the department store business, so the merger was of the horizontal type.

A vertical merger takes place between two firms that would otherwise be in a potential buyer-supplier relationship: a merger between firms carrying out adjacent steps in a production process. If, for example, a producer of jet aircraft, such as Boeing, were to purchase a major airline such as Air Canada, this would be a vertical merger. A conglomerate merger is a merger between firms carrying on different lines of business, as, for example, if Eatons had been bought by Alcan Aluminium. Many mergers have both vertical and horizontal elements, so the distinction among the three types is not always clear in practice. This distinction is, however, conceptually useful.

The merger process is often referred to as the market for corporate control, reflecting the idea that the important aspect of mergers is that they transfer control of business units from one set of owners and managers to another. This buying and selling of business units is a market like any other. One can then apply standard normative economic analysis of markets to this market for corporate control. For example, if this market satisfies the conditions of perfect competition, then control over business units should wind up in the hands of those who can most effectively use the units. If, on the other hand, market imperfections are important in this market, then we might expect it to perform poorly from the public interest point of view.

13.2.2 Horizontal Mergers

The debate over merger policy is most acute with respect to horizontal mergers. The standard analysis of horizontal mergers focuses on the tradeoff between the reduction in competition caused by a merger and the increase in allocational efficiency due to the exploitation of the advantages of size or economies of scale.

Consider an extreme case. Suppose there are two firms in an industry and that production is characterized by very strong economies of scale (as in the production of wide-body jet aircraft), so that both firms have downward-sloping average cost curves over all reasonable ranges of production. If the firms merge, the new firm could, if it chose, produce the same output as the two firms had previously, and at lower average cost. There is an obvious efficiency gain arising from realization of economies of scale.

Unfortunately, the new firm would not choose to produce the old level of output. If the new monopoly firm wishes to maximize profits, it will restrict output, raise price, and cause an increase in the standard allocational inefficiency associated with monopoly power. Depending on the nature of competition in the original duopoly situation, the monopoly outcome resulting from the proposed merger might be welfare-improving or welfare-reducing.

It is worth emphasizing that the firms themselves should do well. If stock markets behave rationally, both target firm and bidder firm should be able to get an excess return. That excess return may be based, however, on a transfer from consumers, not on a net improvement in efficiency.

Suppose, on the other hand, that despite substantial economies of scale, there were many firms in the industry, as if producers of wide-body jet aircraft were as prolific as corner groceries. At this extreme it seems obvious that a few mergers would be in the social (and private) interest. Where should the line be drawn? In some countries there has been an effort to use concentration ratios as a guide. The four-firm concentration shows the fraction of sales accounted for by the largest four firms. One simple rule would be that if this ratio were to go above a certain level, then a merger should not be allowed.

Unfortunately, the use of concentration ratios is not well grounded in economic analysis. Whether a horizontal merger is welfare-reducing or welfare-improving depends crucially on the nature of demand in the industry, on the structure of costs, and, perhaps most importantly, on the mode of competitive rivalry among firms in the industry. Interestingly, Canada's current Competition Act explicitly states that concentration data should not be the sole basis for finding that a merger substantially lessens competition.

Considerable research has focused on the gains to firms resulting from mergers, usually using financial stock market data. Most of this work, unfortunately, does not directly address the social costs and benefits of mergers. These papers ask whether mergers generated net gains to the firms involved, as measured by changes in the stock market prices of the shares of bidder and target firms around the merger announcement date. The general conclusion of this work is that there are private gains to mergers, and that most of the gains go to shareholders of target firms: there is a significant increase in share prices of target firms during the merger process, and a smaller increase in share prices of bidder firms.

The problem with trying to use these results for an evaluation of merger policy is that even if there are gains to firms involved in the mergers, it does not follow that the public interest is necessarily being served. As mentioned above, the gain to the firms might arise either from efficiency gains, or from an increase in monopoly power, or from some combination of the two. If the gains come from an increase in monopoly power, then social welfare is probably being reduced, not increased.

13.2.3 Vertical and Conglomerate Mergers

The basic economics of vertical mergers is much less clear than the theory of horizontal mergers. The natural reaction to a proposed vertical merger is that it may reduce competition. There is, however, a well-known line of argument that runs in exactly the opposite direction. Suppose that firm A is a monopoly supplier of some important input to Firm B, which is in turn a monopolist in consumer markets. If the two firms are separate, then Firm A charges a monopoly markup on the input sold to Firm B, raising Firm B's costs. Firm B then charges a monopoly markup in the consumer market. If Firm A and Firm B were to merge, then the distortion associated with charging a monopoly price for the transaction between Firm A and Firm B disappears, and overall allocational efficiency may rise. In effect, vertical mergers reduce the number of steps at which monopoly power is used, and may, therefore, reduce the total social cost of monopoly power.

The case just described is the case of bilateral monopoly. Moving to other market structures greatly complicates the analysis. Public discussion of competition law and competition policy suggest that vertical mergers are of greatest concern in oligopoly situations. Suppose there is one firm in an upstream industry and there are several firms in a downstream industry. The downstream industry buys essential goods or services from the upstream industry. The fear seems to be that if one downstream firm merges with the upstream firm, the merged firm will discriminate against the rival downstream firms. If it refused to deal with the downstream rivals altogether, then it could, in the absence of entry, establish a monopoly in the downstream industry.

In more complex situations, such as bilateral oligopoly (oligopoly in both upstream and downstream industries), economic theory is ambiguous concerning the effects of vertical mergers on performance.

One important idea is that such mergers facilitate the transfer of assets that are difficult to transfer on an arm's length basis (i.e., through asset markets).

As for conglomerate mergers, economic theory has relatively little to say. Presumably, the basic rationale for such mergers is that there is some advantage to carrying out two separate activities in the same firm. (Such advantages are referred to as economies of scope.) For example, it is often suggested that the marketing network in place to market one line of products can be effectively used to market another line of products acquired by the firm through a merger. In any case, conglomerate mergers have no obvious effect on the competitiveness of particular markets because, by definition, they involve firms producing in different markets. As with vertical mergers, one of the gains might be that it is easier to transfer assets from low-value uses to higher-value uses through mergers than by selling assets on an arm's length basis through used-asset markets.

Some critics have argued that conglomerate mergers lead to undesirable concentrations of political power. This concern focuses on aggregate concentration: the fraction of total economic power (usually measured by sales or by total assets) accounted for by some small subset of large firms, such as the largest 10 firms or largest 50 firms.

13.3 Predatory Pricing

Predatory pricing is the practice of charging a low price with the intent of driving a rival out of the market and increasing monopoly power. Predatory pricing should be distinguished from a normal price war that may be the punishment phase (as described in Section 13.1) of a generally cooperative industry, or that may simply be the normal process of competition, in which more-efficient firms gradually drive less-efficient firms out of business.

Even if we assume that predatory pricing does occur, the normative effects are ambiguous. Charging low prices is, in the first instance, good for consumers, and is exactly what we want competition to achieve. If, as a result, the predator is able to drive competitors out of business, establish monopoly power for some period of time, and then raise prices, consumers may be worse off. It is necessary, however, to compare the benefits to consumers during periods of low price with the costs during the period of monopoly power. It is entirely possible that consumers might benefit on the whole from such pricing patterns.

Furthermore, some economists have argued that predatory pricing is essentially irrational: the costs of predatory pricing almost always exceed the gains. They believe, therefore, that we do not need to worry about predatory pricing, because it should (almost) never happen. The difficulty with understanding why predatory pricing should occur is that, if there are monopoly profits to be earned, then both (or all) firms involved should recognize this and be unwilling to leave the market.

Some firms might be better able than others to withstand a prolonged period of low prices, and might therefore hope to win a war of attrition with smaller or more heavily indebted rivals. Still, this period of attrition is likely to be very costly. In order to benefit from predatory pricing, the predator firm must enjoy a sufficiently long subsequent period of monopoly profits to offset the losses incurred during the predatory phase.

If the predator firm did establish a lucrative position of market power, however, new rivals would be expected to enter. If they entered fairly soon, the predator would not have time to recoup its earlier losses and might, if it repeats the predatory strategy, incur even greater losses. Belligerent ice hockey players generally have short careers, and the same may be true of firms.

What determines whether new firms will enter after an episode of predatory pricing? That depends on their expectations concerning future predation. If they believe that the predator will not persist in predation, they will enter. If, in turn, the potential predator knows that potential rivals do not expect future predation, then it knows they will enter, and predation would indeed be a poor strategy. This set of expectations is a consistent equilibrium in which predation would not occur. This line of argument has sometimes been referred to as the chain store paradox, because despite its persuasiveness, we apparently do occasionally see predation, especially in chain store situations.

A recent line of research has argued that predatory pricing can best be viewed as a reputation-building exercise. The basic idea is that certain attributes of the predator firm, such as its costs or the preferences of its managers, are unknown to actual or potential rivals. In essence, the firm might be either a tough firm (i.e., a firm with low costs and very aggressive management) or a weak firm (i.e., with high costs and an acquiescent management). Predatory pricing could then be interpreted as an attempt to establish a reputation for being a tough firm. If successful, the firm may not only drive its current rival out of business, but it may also deter future entry, which is the crucial requirement for actually getting net benefits from predation.

As discussed in Chapter 12, very few predatory pricing cases have been prosecuted in Canada. This probably reflects the reality that pure predatory pricing is not very common. We do, however, not infrequently see a partial version of predatory pricing, especially, as already mentioned, in chain store industries, such as gasoline retailing or supermarkets.

In a particular geographical area, there might be a major chain and a small independent. The large chain will tolerate a certain level of rivalry from the independent, but if the rival begins to expand, the chain will undertake predatory action, either by offering very low prices at its nearest store, or by putting up a new retail outlet very close to the rival. In part, this is to discipline the wayward small firm, but, in addition, it is intended to send a message to all other small independent rivals who compete with the chain in other geographical areas. The chain is presumably trying to establish a reputation for toughness so as to restrain all of its (actual or potential) rivals, and might well be prepared to take losses at the store actually engaged in the predatory action.

13.4 Price Discrimination

Price discrimination is the practice of charging more than one price for the same product. For example, regulated telephone companies normally charge higher prices (for local service) to business users than to residential users. (They receive explicit permission to do this from the regulatory authority, as will be described in Chapter 14.) Price discrimination is common at the retail level: movie patrons are charged different prices for the same film depending on age, bus fares also vary by age, and various products are offered at discounts to students.

Price discrimination does not include peak load pricing, which means charging higher prices for use in peak periods than in off-peak periods (as with hotels, air fares, and long distance telephone calls). The point here is that a hotel room, for example, during a very busy period is a different (and more valuable) commodity than an otherwise identical hotel room in the off-season.

Canadian competition policy is not directed at retail price discrimination. The intent of competition policy is to ensure that rival firms have access to the same prices for their inputs, so that a supplier firm cannot affect the competitive positions of firms in the downstream industry.

13.4.1 Perfect Price Discrimination

The basic point is that price discrimination can allow a firm to increase its profits. This is most easily seen for the case of monopoly. Figure 13.1 illustrates an extreme version of price discrimination, called perfect price discrimination or complete price discrimination. Perfect or complete price discrimination occurs when the firm is able to extract all of a consumer's surplus.

Curve D is the demand curve and the line denoted AC represents the firm's average cost, which is assumed to equal marginal cost. Recall, as described in Chapter 2, that the demand curve shows consumers' willingness to pay for the product. The intercept on the vertical axis, denoted A on Figure 13.1, shows the maximum willingness to pay for the first unit of the product. In other words, A is the maximum

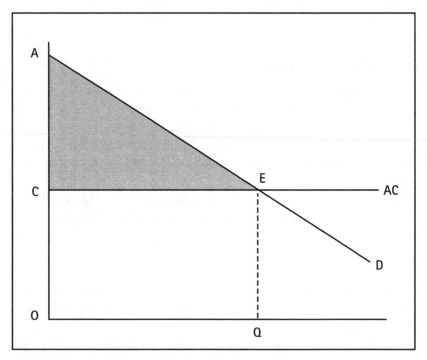

FIGURE 13.1 Perfect Price Discrimination

amount that any consumer will pay for the first unit. If, for example, the product is a particular movie, then A represents the maximum amount that the person most eager (and most able) to see the movie would be willing to pay. Suppose this person is named Mr. Eager, the firm would like to charge Mr. Eager price A. The ideal price for this consumer, Mr. Eager, from the firm's point of view, would be A.

If the general price were A, no other movie tickets would be sold. But if the firm could charge a separate price to each consumer, it would charge A to Mr. Eager, capturing all of Mr. Eager's consumer surplus. The person with the next-highest willingness to pay, Ms. Keen, is willing to pay at most B to see the movie, so the theatre would like to charge her B, capturing all her surplus, and so on. If the firm could charge a different price for every unit of the product (including when Mr. Eager and Ms. Keen return to see the movie again), then it would keep charging each consumer his or her maximum willingness to pay, as far as point E. At E the willingness to pay of the marginal consumer is just equal to marginal cost. The firm could extract the entire area $AEQO$ as revenue. Paying costs $CEQO$, it would be left with an above-normal profit equal to triangle ACE.

This represents the absolute maximum that the firm could earn from this industry. Its profit would considerably exceed the standard monopoly profit, which involves only a partial extraction of consumer surplus. In this case, all surplus is extracted. Interestingly, however, the socially efficient output level, Q, is produced. At this point, the marginalist principle for social efficiency is satisfied: marginal social benefit, as measured by marginal willingness to pay, is just equal to marginal cost. Perfect price discrimination may seem unfair, but it is not inefficient.

13.4.2 Two-Market Price Discrimination

In practice, perfect or complete price discrimination will not occur. For one thing, firms do not have sufficient information about the willingness to pay of individual consumers. A less extreme version of price discrimination is two-market discrimination, in which the firm segments its market into two submarkets. This is illustrated in Figure 13.2.

Figure 13.2 is drawn so that the market demand and marginal revenue curves in the two markets share the same vertical axis. We also

assume, for simplicity, that marginal cost is constant. The profit-maximizing decision requires that the firm equate marginal revenue and
marginal cost in each market separately, producing amounts Q_1 and
Q_2, and charging prices P_1 and P_2 in markets 1 and 2 respectively. This
pricing strategy is more profitable to the firm than charging the same
price in both submarkets.

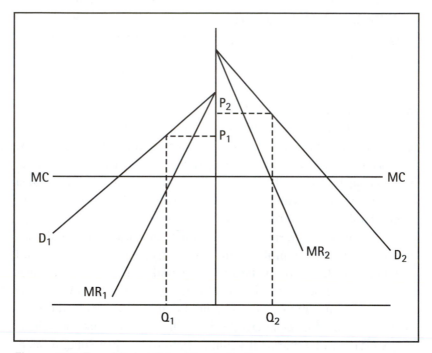

Figure 13.2 Two–Market Price Discrimination

13.4.3 Limits on Price Discrimination

There are limits on price discrimination. One limit is created by competition. If Firm X is earning potential surplus from Ms. Keen, another firm has an incentive to offer Ms. Keen a similar product at a slightly lower price because it can still earn a net profit on her purchase.
Some degree of market power is required for price discrimination. A
second limit is created by arbitrage. If a shoe store is trying to sell the
same pair of shoes to Ms. Indifferent for a lower price than the price
charged Ms. Keen, then Ms. Indifferent has an incentive to buy the

shoes and resell them to Ms. Keen. Price discrimination requires the ability to prevent or at least limit arbitrage.

The welfare effects of price discrimination are not clear. Price discrimination may (depending on demand, cost, and the type of discrimination) actually increase efficiency. Admittedly, the efficiency gains will go principally to the shareholders of the firms, but who is to say that they are less deserving than consumers, especially given the importance of pension funds as equity holders. Price discrimination is not necessarily a bad thing. It may even allow a firm that could not otherwise stay in business to survive, benefitting consumers and the firm. Price discrimination is frequently used by regulated firms. (The problem of meeting a minimum profit constraint using price discrimination leads to what is called Ramsey Pricing, which will be discussed in Chapter 14.)

13.5 Resale Price Maintenance

Resale price maintenance (RPM) occurs when a manufacturer or wholesaler tries to insist that a retailer sell a good at a stipulated price (or, more generally, at a price no lower than some stipulated price). As indicated by Table 12.4, RPM is frequently prosecuted. It is also well known that RPM is a common business practice, despite the law.

The intuition supporting laws against RPM is that RPM helps firms maintain market power. Restricting RPM, so the argument goes, should increase overall competition. It should certainly lower retail prices. There are, however, two counter-arguments that have been presented.

One counter-argument relates to consumer search behaviour. If consumers see, or even hear about, a particular product being offered at a particularly low price, they will be unwilling to pay a higher price for the product at other retail outlets, possibly reducing overall sales. This is referred to by the firms involved as spoiling the market. If, furthermore, the discount price represented a marketing attempt to get people in the store, and was not high enough to cover normal costs, overall sales at other outlets might fall to the point where the product could not be continued, and overall social welfare could decline.

A second, and more persuasive, argument in favour of RPM is that many products have a high service component, and that service will decline without RPM. The standard example is computers, and Apple Computer Inc. successfully fought an RPM charge in the United States. Personal computers are a product with a fairly high service component.

Especially when personal computers were first introduced, most potential buyers knew very little about them. A buyer might spend several hours with a knowledgeable salesperson before making a choice. Furthermore, the buyer might expect to return for advice about software or hardware additions, for training, and, of course, for any repairs or other problems that might arise. The retail price of the computer must cover the cost of all these ancillary services, which were and are important to the product.

Consider the incentives facing a potential discounter. The discount firm can buy the product for the same wholesale price as the full-service outlet (as required by laws against price discrimination), then offer it for sale for a lower retail price, but not offer much in the way of services. It might even operate as a mail order house, offering no ancillary services. Consumers would have an incentive to do all their learning at full-service outlets, essentially consuming costly services free of charge, then buying from a discounter. Consumers would benefit, discounters would benefit, but full-service outlets would suffer.

The question, of course, is not whether discounting is fair to full-service dealers. The public policy question is whether discounting is against the overall public interest. Apple was able to argue successfully that this discounting process would lead to the reduction, and, in some areas, the elimination of full-service outlets, and that this was counter to the public interest. In effect, the argument is that there are positive externalities associated with ancillary services, and that these positive externalities cannot be supported at socially efficient levels without RPM. (This argument presumes that the services in question cannot efficiently be priced and sold separately from the physical good.) On the whole, however, the welfare effects of RPM are ambiguous, and the case for an active policy against RPM does not have a strong normative foundation.

13.6 Misleading Advertising and Deceptive Marketing Practices

13.6.1 Normative Rationale

In Canada, laws against misleading advertising and deceptive marketing practices have been in force only since 1960, but they have grown into a major area of competition policy. As a result, the marketplace is no longer dominated by the *caveat emptor* (buyer beware) philosophy. Sellers are responsible for ensuring that products meet advertised standards and also that products meet certain standards that are not explicitly advertised, but are taken to be implicit conditions of sale.

What is the normative economic rationale for such policy? Unlike the other anti-competitive practices, misleading advertising and deceptive marketing practices are not related to monopoly power. In fact, the industries where such practices occur most frequently are relatively competitive, such as general consumer retailing.

General public support for competition policy in this area is very strong, and very few complaints are heard that enforcement should be reduced, even among business lobbyists. The basic economic rationale for such policies, has, however, not yet been fully worked out. As mentioned, such a rationale would have little if anything to do with monopoly power, and externalities and public good considerations do not seem relevant. Where then is the market failure?

By process of elimination (recall Chapter 3), the remaining cause of market failure is imperfect information. If buyers had full information about products and sellers there would be very little need for legislation concerning misleading advertising and deceptive marketing practices. Consumers would not be misled or deceived. If a consumer had full information about, for example, a used car, it would not matter what the salesperson said. In fact, however, buyers do not usually have full information about the products they buy. In particular, they are usually less well-informed about the nature of the product than the seller.

13.6.2 Informational Market Failure: The Lemons Problem

The normal buyer-seller relationship is therefore one of asymmetric information. In the past 25 years, economists have come to understand that asymmetric information is an important source of market failure. Perhaps the most important result of asymmetric information is the so-called lemons principle, first articulated by Akerlof (1970).

Akerlof first advanced the lemons principle to explain certain features of the used car market, in particular, why the market seemed to be dominated by lemons or poor quality items. Suppose there are good used cars and lemons. The problem is that good used cars and lemons do not look any different: the essential characteristics of the car are hidden under the hood and can be inferred only by an expert or through experience. As a result, the buyer of a used car typically knows much less about it than a seller. This is a situation of asymmetric information.

Suppose that an appropriate price for a good used car is P, and an appropriate price for a lemon is X. What price would the seller of a used car charge? The seller of a good used car would certainly want to charge P. However, the seller of a lemon also has an incentive to charge P! After all, the buyers cannot tell good cars from bad, so why should the seller reveal he has a poor quality car? He has just as much chance as the owner of a good car of selling at price P. Buyers, however, could be expected to realize that not all cars offered for sale at price P are worth P. A buyer must expect that there is some chance he or she will purchase a car of value X, and will reduce his or her willingness to pay accordingly. In fact, if there are an equal number of good cars and lemons available, the appropriate market price is $(P + X)/2$, reflecting the average quality.

But owners of good used cars will be unwilling to sell their good cars for less than they are worth, so most owners of good used cars will simply keep them, and the market will be dominated by lemons. The price will adjust accordingly, so that in the end market price does not differ much from X, and very few good used cars will change hands. This is the lemons principle, sometimes called adverse selection: under conditions of asymmetric information, low-quality items will tend to dominate the market. (This adverse selection or quality degradation argument has been used as an argument for a wide range of licensing restrictions.)

Market failure occurs because Pareto-improving transactions are foregone. There may be someone who would be very pleased to buy a good used car for price P, and someone else who would be very pleased to sell a good used car for price P. There are potential gains from trade if these two people could get together. However, in a market suffering from adverse selection, such trades will not take place. This is the market failure.

The lemons problem is a very important problem in many markets. Consider, for example, medical services. In the days before the medical profession was carefully regulated to maintain standards, it was plagued by quacks: doctors who would promise much more than they could deliver. This was a successful strategy because patients had no way of judging quality of care, certainly not before treatment, and frequently not after treatment either. Standards regulation in many areas can be viewed as a response to market failures caused by asymmetric information.

13.6.3 The Lemons Problem and Misleading Advertising

What do marketing and advertising have to do with differential information and the lemons problem? Advertising is implicit in the lemons story. In effect, sellers of lemons are advertising their cars as high-quality cars. This is misleading advertising. In general, a buyer's main source of information about a product is what the seller says, either through advertising or directly. If the seller is free to misrepresent quality, then the lemons principle will apply. If, however, the seller is constrained to tell the truth, and has an incentive to tell the truth, created by the possibility of prosecution, then market failure will be reduced. In short, making misleading advertising and deceptive marketing practices illegal is an effective policy response to the market failure created by asymmetric information.

In addition, of course, such legislation appeals to notions of procedural fairness. Many of us regard misleading advertising and deceptive practices as unfair, quite apart from any associated market failure or efficiency losses.

13.7 Bibliographic Notes

The use of punishment strategies to maintain collusion is examined in Porter (1983), Axelrod (1984), and Brander and Zhang (1993). The performance of mergers is analyzed in Eckbo (1986) using stock market data, and in Ravenscraft and Scherer (1987) using accounting data. The basic tradeoff between the efficiency and monopoly power effects of horizontal mergers is presented in Williamson (1968), and the theory of vertical mergers is explained in Williamson (1971). The reputation effects of predatory pricing have been analyzed formally by Kreps and Wilson (1982). An empirical investigation of the chain store paradox using Canadian supermarket data is in West (1981). Important papers in the general theory of entry deterrence are Dixit (1980) and Eaton and Lipsey (1981). For an application to merger issues see Ross (1993). RPM theory is reviewed by Mathewson and Winter (1985). The analysis of the lemons problem is due to Akerlof (1970). Other fundamental contributions to the theory of informational market failure include

Pauly (1974), Spence (1973), and Rothschild and Stiglitz (1976). Many of the theoretical issues considered here are examined in more detail in Carlton and Perloff (1994) and Viscusi et al. (1992).

14

The Theory of
Price and Entry Regulation

14.1 The Meaning of Regulation

At the most general level, all business activity is regulated. Environmental policy, discussed in Chapters 10 and 11, consists largely of regulation, and competition policy, discussed in Chapters 12 and 13, can also be viewed as regulation. In addition, all firms are controlled or regulated by the legal system and the tax system. When we speak of the regulated sector or regulated industries, however, we mean something much more specific. We are referring to a specific group of industries that are subject to price and entry regulation.

Price and entry regulation are usually thought of as being applied to private sector firms, but Crown corporations, which are owned by government, also make up a large part of the regulated sector. Each regulated industry is under the jurisdiction of some government-appointed regulatory board or commission. These regulatory boards have authority over both private firms and some Crown corporations. Crown corporations not subject to regulatory boards or commissions are subject to review by Cabinet or by legislative committee, and may carry out a regulatory function themselves. The basic theory of price and entry regulation presented in this chapter is intended to apply to Crown corporations and to privately owned regulated firms.

Electric power is the traditional or standard regulated industry. It provides electric power and light, which are known as utilities. (Provision of water is also called a utility.) As a result, the subject of price and entry regulation is often referred to as public utility regulation, and the term "public utility" has been used by some analysts to refer to any firm subject to price and entry regulation. In this book, however, public utilities refers strictly to regulated provision of true utilities as given in dictionary definitions: power, light, and water.

The major industries subject to price and entry regulation are electric power, telecommunications, radio and television, and parts of the transportation sector. In addition, oil and natural gas have been subject to some price and entry regulation, and the operations of marketing boards in agriculture also involve price and entry regulation. Provision of electric power in Canada is carried out mainly by Crown corporations, rather than by regulated private firms. The two largest suppliers of electric power in Canada are Hydro Quebec and Ontario Hydro Services Company, both of which are provincial Crown Corporations.

An important point concerns the meaning of the term "public." When discussing regulation, public, as in public enterprise, refers to ownership by government. Government enterprise means the same thing as public enterprise, just as the terms "government policy" and "public policy" are synonymous. Crown corporations are public enterprises. A private firm or privately owned firm is simply a firm that is part of the private sector (i.e., not government owned). A firm that is partly owned by government and partly by the private sector is referred to as a mixed enterprise.

Unfortunately, this usage does not match standard terminology in financial circles, where a public firm is one that is owned by the private sector but publicly traded (i.e., its shares can be bought and sold by anyone). A private firm or privately held firm, according to this usage, is one whose shares are not publicly traded, i.e., it is owned by a private group in the sense that outsiders can be excluded. In policy discussions, confusion over this point can and does arise, although the context will usually make the meaning of the term "public" clear. In this book, we use the regulation terminology: public ownership means government ownership, and private ownership means ownership by the private sector, whether or not the shares are publicly traded.

14.2 Natural Monopoly as the Rationale for Price Regulation

As suggested above, the theory of price regulation is sometimes referred to as public utility regulation. Certainly, public utilities are the industries we should keep in mind as we discuss price regulation. The basic rationale for public policy intervention in public utilities arises from market failure caused by natural monopoly.

Natural monopoly, as described in Chapter 6, is most obviously caused by economies of scale that are large compared to the size of the market. In particular, natural monopoly is said to occur when any feasible level of demand can be met at lower cost by a single firm than by two or more firms: there is room in the market for only one firm of minimum efficient scale (MES). Natural monopoly is also related to economies of scope, which are advantages of carrying out related activities in the same firm. The general definition of natural monopoly is that it arises when a single firm can produce an output, or a set of related outputs, at lower cost for the relevant levels of output than two or more firms can. Natural monopoly is, in general, caused by both economies of scale and economies of scope.

For a single product, natural monopoly means that the firm's average cost curve is downward sloping over most of the relevant range, as illustrated in Figure 14.1. The most normal reason for this kind of cost structure is that fixed costs are very large compared to marginal costs. Fixed costs are costs that do not vary with amount of output produced. Sometimes fixed costs are avoidable if the firm shuts down, but they must be incurred before any output is produced. Thus, to achieve efficient scale, the fixed costs must be spread over a very large output.

For example, there is room for only one James Bay hydroelectric project in Quebec. The costs of the project were enormous, and require a large annual interest payment (a fixed cost) on the loans taken out for construction. Even the annual fixed cost of maintaining the project is enormous. Given the project's existence, however, producing a few more kilowatts of power requires only turning on a few switches, thus marginal cost is almost nothing until the maximum yield is approached. It would make no sense to have two separate firms trying to operate two James Bay projects, with two sets of transmission lines, etc. Having two firms would very nearly double the cost of getting the same output, at least with current technology.

Similar arguments could be made about local telephone service: putting in local telephone lines represents a large fixed cost. Adding a new customer to the network is very inexpensive. Once again, it would make no sense to have two separate companies (in a single area) putting in two sets of telephone lines.

Technologies do change, however. Long distance telephone service was once a natural monopoly, when long distance calls were sent through wires. Now that long distance calls are bounced off satellites, or sent through fibre-optic cables, this service is no longer a natural monopoly. In the United States, several firms have entered the long distance market, although the original incumbent, AT&T, remains the dominant supplier of long distance services. In most parts of Canada, consumers now have access to more than one supplier of long distance services. In addition, cellular telephones are also a new technology that greatly reduces the natural monopoly aspect of telephone communications.

An unregulated natural monopoly provides a dangerous opportunity for the exploitation of monopoly power, especially given the nature of demand for the services in question. Power and even telephone services are often referred to as necessities. An economist would say simply that these are products whose short-run demand is inelastic, meaning that if the price of power or telephone service were to rise sharply, most people would, in the short run, simply pay the extra cost rather than significantly reduce usage.

Because of the dangers of monopoly exploitation and the resulting inefficiencies, most natural monopolies are subject to price regulation: they are not free to set their own prices but must get permission for price changes either from a government appointed regulatory board of some sort, or, in the case of some Crown corporations, from cabinet or legislative committees.

14.3 Average and Marginal Cost Pricing

The first regulatory question to confront is simply: "How should the price be set?" The two most natural approaches to price regulation are average cost pricing and marginal cost pricing. Average cost pricing means that price should be set so that, at the level of demand forthcoming at that price, the firm just covers its costs, (including a normal rate of return on capital). Marginal cost pricing means that price should be set so that, at the corresponding level of demand, marginal cost is just equal to price.

The first point to make is that marginal cost pricing and average cost pricing are not equivalent in general. It is possible that average cost and marginal cost prices could be the same but, depending on demand and cost, marginal cost pricing may lead to either higher or lower prices than average cost pricing. Figure 14.1 illustrates the more common situation: the marginal cost price is less than the average cost price.

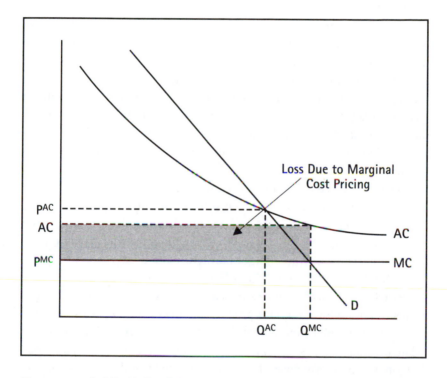

Figure 14.1 Public Utility Pricing

The rationale for marginal cost pricing follows from the application of the marginalist principle for the normative analysis of public policy, as described in Chapter 2. Recall that demand is a measure of marginal willingness to pay for the service, which we take as our best measure of marginal benefit. Therefore, price equals marginal benefit. The marginalist principle says that marginal benefit should be equated with marginal cost. Thus, setting price (marginal benefit) equal to marginal cost is the implied solution.

If price were above marginal cost, then an extra bit of the service is worth more to some consumer (as measured by his or her willingness to pay) than the extra (or marginal) cost of producing it. Net surplus can be generated (i.e., allocational efficiency can be improved) by increasing output. On the other hand, if price were below marginal cost, this means that the cost of producing the last unit was above the value of that unit, so production should be decreased. Only if marginal cost is equal to price is allocational (or Pareto) efficiency achieved.

This reasoning seems persuasive, and it is logically sound. Marginal cost pricing is the efficient solution. Unfortunately, this is not the whole story, for marginal cost pricing can cause problems. In particular, in the situation illustrated in Figure 14.1, marginal cost is below average cost at the quantity produced, implying that price will be below average cost if marginal cost pricing is used. In the diagram, the marginal cost price, P^{MC}, is below average cost. Therefore, the firm will be unable to cover its costs and will require a subsidy from the government.

There are three objections to requiring a subsidy. First, such subsidies can be viewed as unfair. If the services of public utilities are subsidized by taxpayers' money, this means that people who are heavy users of public utilities are, in effect, receiving a transfer from taxpayers at large, some of whom might hardly use the utility's services at all. Why should people who have a taste for goods that happen to be characterized by increasing returns to scale be subsidized by people whose tastes run more toward goods produced with constant returns to scale?

The second objection is that the regulator is very unlikely to know what marginal cost is. Our previous argument for marginal cost pricing obviously presupposes that the regulatory authority knows the level of marginal cost, so that it can insist that price be set at that level. If the regulator simply says to the firm: "Set price equal to marginal cost and the government will cover your losses," then very serious incentive problems are created.

Specifically, if the firm (and its unions) knows that losses will be covered by taxpayers, and no one outside the firm has enough information to really understand its cost structure in detail, then the firm has very little incentive to keep costs down. If the firm is required to cover its costs, then at least some discipline is imposed on the firm. In short, many people distrust, after much painful experience, any policy approach that involves having the government write blank cheques.

The third problem is simply that the cost of subsidies might be higher than is commonly realized. An extra dollar paid in subsidies has to come from somewhere, either from current taxes, from borrowing (creating a tax liability for the future), or from printing money (which, as will be described in Chapter 17, creates an inflation tax). Raising this dollar of extra revenue costs more than one dollar. There are administrative costs in doing all the paperwork, and there are efficiency losses caused by the distortionary effects of taxes, not the least of which is all the effort that goes into tax avoidance by taxpayers.

It is hard to get reliable estimates of the full cost of raising a dollar of tax revenue, but reasonable calculations[1] suggest that this cost is probably between $1.30 and $2. In short, the cost of a $1 million subsidy is much more than $1 million to the economy as a whole; the cost is more like $1.3 million or $2 million.

The implication of this extra subsidy cost is that we should be prepared to trade off inefficiencies in regulation (or in any policy area) against the inefficiencies caused by raising revenue. For this reason alone, a small departure from marginal cost pricing is perfectly reasonable, if it economizes on the use of government revenue.

These problems with marginal cost pricing all arise from an insufficiency of marginal cost prices. The opposite problem is less likely, but it can arise: a natural monopoly may have marginal costs substantially above average cost at the market clearing output level. (Ontario Hydro is probably in this position.) If so, then marginal cost pricing would generate large profits for the regulated firm. It seems inappropriate, on equity grounds, for shareholders or workers in public utilities to earn large above-normal returns. If, on the other hand, these profits were turned over to the government, then consumers of the utility's services would be subsidizing general government programs, which also seems unfair.

This leaves us with the conclusion that if we were forced to choose between average cost pricing and marginal cost pricing, average cost pricing would be preferred. There, are, however, some more complex but very useful pricing practices, which are described next.

14.4 Nonuniform Pricing

Normal or uniform pricing means that the same price is charged for each unit of the product, independent of the quantity purchased by a single buyer. Most products are priced in this way: if one MacDonald's hamburger costs $3, then 10 MacDonald's hamburgers cost $3 each, or $30 in total, and 100 MacDonald's hamburgers cost $300 (should anyone actually want to buy 100 hamburgers).

It is also fairly common, however, for products to be sold at nonuniform prices, which means that the price per unit varies with the amount purchased. The most common type of nonuniform pricing in the private sector is probably quantity discounts. For example, a 20-piece order of Chicken McNuggets costs less per McNugget than a six-piece order. Nonuniform pricing is sometimes referred to as second degree price discrimination.

Nonuniform pricing can also be used in the regulated sector to obtain increased pricing efficiency while still allowing the regulated firm to cover its costs. The simplest form of nonuniform pricing is two-part pricing. A more complicated version of the same principle is multipart pricing. The following equations show the algebraic form of uniform pricing, two-part pricing, multipart pricing, and general (uniform or nonuniform) pricing. In these equations, E represents total expenditure, P represents price, Q represents quantity, and L represents an access or licence charge.

(14.1)	$E = PQ$	(uniform pricing)
(14.2)	$E = L + PQ$	(two–part pricing)
(14.3)	$E = L + P_1Q_1 + P_2Q_2 + ... + P_NQ_N$	(multipart pricing)
(14.4)	$E = f(Q)$	(general)

Equation 14.1 is self-explanatory. Under uniform pricing, total expenditure, E, is simply price times quantity consumed. Equation 14.2 illustrates two-part pricing. Total expenditure consists of two parts: an access fee, L, and a usage fee, P. In essence, this is like uniform pricing with the addition of an access fee. The basic idea is that anyone who wants to consume the product must pay the access fee to begin with. Once the access fee is paid, each unit of consumption costs P. Consumption is not allowed if the access fee is not paid.

The access fee is sometimes referred to as a licence fee or a membership fee, depending on the context. Local telephone service is priced using two-part pricing, with the usage fee (for additional local calls) being zero in most parts of Canada. Some fitness clubs have a membership fee and additional user fees for some services.

Equation 14.3 illustrates multipart pricing, which is commonly used in the pricing of electricity. In this case, there is an access fee, as with two-part pricing, but instead of having a constant usage fee, the customer is charged some price, P^1, for the first Q^1 units of consumption, a different usage fee, P^2, for the next Q^2 units of consumption, and so on. If successive blocks of consumption have progressively lower usage fees, this system is called a declining block pricing system. We could also imagine a rising block pattern, but this is less common.

In general, it is possible to generate pricing schemes that do not fit conveniently into any of the first three categories. The general form for a pricing system is given by Equation 14.4, which indicates simply that expenditure is some function of quantity consumed, presumably with expenditure never decreasing as quantity consumed rises. Equation 14.4 includes the other three equations as special cases. Figure 14.2 illustrates various pricing systems diagrammatically.

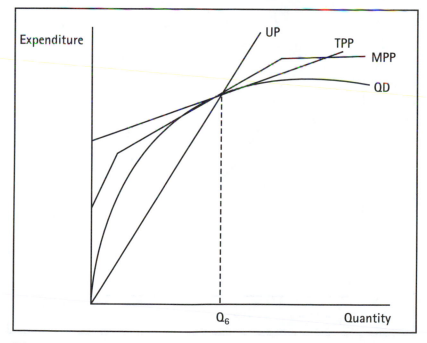

FIGURE 14.2 Nonuniform Price Schedules

The line representing uniform pricing is denoted *UP*. The two-part pricing curve is denoted *TPP*, and curve *MPP* represents a multipart pricing schedule of the declining block type. The fourth curve, denoted *QD*, shows an example of a smooth nonuniform pricing scheme incorporating quantity discounts. Note that uniform pricing produces a straight line from the origin. Two-part pricing produces a straight line from the access fee on the vertical axis. Other types of nonuniform pricing produce nonlinear curves (or at least functions that are only linear in pieces). For this reason, nonuniform pricing is sometimes called nonlinear pricing. In Figure 14.2, the slope of the expenditure schedule is equal to the usage fee.

Why is nonuniform pricing used? In the unregulated private sector, it is used, presumably, because firms find it advantageous. But why do they find it advantageous? And what is the normative or public interest rationale for allowing nonuniform pricing in the regulated sector? Figure 14.3 represents an extreme case that helps make the point that nonuniform pricing, in this case a simple two-part tariff, can improve efficiency.

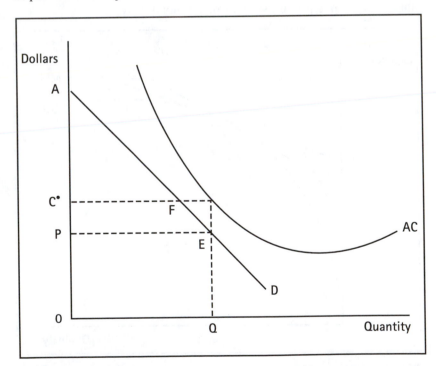

Figure 14.3 Two-Part Pricing

In the case of Figure 14.3, the average cost curve for the product, *AC*, lies entirely outside the demand curve, *D*. With uniform pricing, the firm cannot cover its costs, no matter what the price. About the closest it can come to covering costs is by charging price *P*, producing quantity *Q*, and incurring average cost *C**. Its loss would then be *(P–C*)Q*. An ordinary private firm simply could not stay in business. A public enterprise would require an ongoing government subsidy.

Note, however, that this product is socially desirable, because the total value to consumers exceeds the total cost of production at output level *Q*. Recall (from Chapter 2) that the height of the demand curve shows the marginal value of the product as measured by willingness to pay. Adding up all those marginal valuations for each unit of output produced gives the total value of the product. This total value is given by the area under the demand curve,[2] up to the production point. Thus, the total consumer value of *Q* is area *OAEQ*. The total cost is only *OC*BQ*, which, as drawn, is clearly less than the total value.

The product is socially worthwhile, in the sense that consumers are more than willing to pay for the cost of production, but it will not be provided under uniform pricing if the firm must cover its costs. The value of nonuniform pricing is that it can extract more revenue from consumers, without discouraging them altogether. If the firm charges *P* as a usage fee, and in addition charges an access fee or licence fee, *L*, it will be able to cover its costs. This licence fee comes out of the consumer surplus that consumers would enjoy at price *P*.

A private firm would want to maximize profit. A public enterprise should want to maximize social welfare, as given by total benefit minus total cost. In either case, the actual calculation of the appropriate usage fee and access fee is difficult, because increases in the access fee may induce some people to stop consuming. (They will do so if their personal surplus at the chosen usage fee is less than the access charge.)

Even for a regulated firm or public enterprise that could cover its costs with uniform pricing, a two-part or multipart scheme would allow a usage fee closer to marginal cost to be charged and could increase efficiency. However, being able to use nonuniform pricing does increase the ability of firms to extract surplus from consumers, and can enhance the exploitation of monopoly power, if the firm wishes to use it for that purpose.

14.5 Price Discrimination

Nonuniform pricing is not the only pricing variation that can be used by firms. Price discrimination, which means charging a different price (or different price schedules) for the same product to different consumers, has been discussed in Chapter 10. The basic economic effects of price discrimination are similar to those of nonuniform pricing. Like nonuniform pricing, price discrimination increases the power of firms to extract revenue from consumers, and, also like nonuniform pricing, this power can be used to increase the overall contribution of the product to general economic welfare, or it can be used to enhance the exploitation of monopoly power. Nonuniform pricing is often thought of as a type of price discrimination. Thus, if a firm charges different nonuniform price schedules to two different consumers, it is using two types of price discrimination at the same time.

Price discrimination is common in regulated industries. In the case of both telephone service and electricity, residential users are presented with a different price schedule than are business customers. These industries therefore make use of both price discrimination and nonuniform pricing.

14.6 Peak-Load Pricing

Another pricing variation that is important in price regulation is peak-load pricing. Peak-load pricing is used for long distance telephone service, electricity, and various transportation services. In addition, it is commonly used in the private sector. Peak-load pricing involves charging different prices (or different nonuniform price schedules) at different times.

During times of heavy use, users are charged higher rates than at times of light use. For example, long distance telephone rates are higher in the middle of the day than during the night. The normative rationale for peak-load pricing is very clear. The basic point is that the marginal cost of telephone service at night is less than the marginal cost during the day. For example, as has already been mentioned, most of the costs of the telephone system are fixed costs, associated with the cost of the overall network. Given the network, the production cost of putting a call through is very low, until capacity is approached. As capacity is approached, however, sound quality declines, and, when capacity is reached, no more calls can be handled and callers must wait, incurring waiting costs.

The principle cost associated with a call during busy periods is the congestion cost imposed on the system, as manifested in delays and poor sound quality. This is part of the social marginal cost of the call, and should be included in the price paid by the customer, if efficiency is to be achieved. Put simply, if the network has some probability of being used to capacity, only those long distance calls that are most valuable, as measured by the amount people are willing to pay for them, should be made. If a higher price is charged, then only calls with a value at least equal to that price will be made. This is the peak-load principle, and it is important in achieving efficient use of scarce resources.

Looked at slightly differently, when a system is being used to capacity, the marginal cost of an extra unit of output is the cost of building and operating additional capacity. Therefore, the price charged in such periods should include a contribution to capacity costs. During periods of underutilized capacity, the only marginal cost is the marginal operating cost; no capacity charge should be levied.

Peak-load pricing bothers some people. More than one consumer advocate has complained that peak-load pricing is not very useful because the low prices are offered at inconvenient times. In fact, it is hard to imagine any coherent idea of fairness would conflict with the use of peak-load pricing. One reasonable idea of fairness is that users of economic services should pay in proportion to marginal cost, which implies that peak-load pricing is desirable, because marginal cost varies depending on the time when the service is used.

14.7 Multiproduct Firms and Cross-Subsidization

So far we have discussed price regulation as though each regulated firm produced only one product. In fact, many firms produce several products. For example, Canada Post, which is a Crown corporation regulated by Parliament, provides several classes of mail service, and delivers mail between many pairs of origins and destinations.

The following question has been posed: if a regulated private firm has been instructed to set prices so as to cover its costs, how should those prices be set? In the case of a single-product firm, the answer is obvious: price must be set equal to average cost. (Even so, however, actually measuring cost can be very difficult for a regulatory authority.) With a multiproduct firm, additional complications arise. For example, there may be several different ways of setting prices so as to cover costs. Trying to extend the idea of average cost pricing is not very helpful, because it is hard to assign the costs of general overhead to specific products. For example, how much of the cost of the giant mail sorting machine in Toronto should be allocated to first class mail?

Accountants and economists have come up with various ways of making such shared cost allocations, and some of them could be (and are) used in actual pricing in both regulated and unregulated firms, but these average cost allocations do not maximize efficiency. The efficient solution, known as Ramsey pricing,[3] has been worked out, but seems to violate norms of procedural fairnes and therefore has not been widely used, although it has been applied in some cases.

Actual regulatory practice makes fairly general use of cross-subsidization, which involves using revenues from one product or service to subsidize another product or service. For example, long distance telephone service subsidizes local service (although this cross-subsidy is declining and may soon be eliminated), and first class mail subsidizes other classes of mail. Interestingly, these two cases indicate that cross-subsidization in practice tends to run in the opposite direction to the cross-subsidies suggested by the Ramsey formula.

14.8 Rate-of-Return Regulation and the Averch-Johnson Effect

One important problem that has only been touched on briefly so far is that regulators do not have nearly as much information about the firms they regulate as the firms themselves do. Even if the firms are required to provide large quantities of documentation, the regulators will not be able to interpret or appreciate what the documents say as well as the management of the firm can. Managers always have inside information to which others do not have access. (This is, incidentally, a classic example of the asymmetric information problem discussed in Chapter 13.)

Specifically, the regulator cannot really be expected to know the cost curves or the demand curve of the firm as well as the firms themselves do. The management of the firms does not know this information perfectly, of course, but it will have a better idea than others. The regulator cannot, therefore, impose the efficient pricing scheme directly. All a regulator can do is allow the firm to propose prices, and then agree that the pricing proposal seems reasonable or else reject it.

The basis for acceptance or rejection of pricing proposals is usually a rate-of-return criterion. The regulated firm is allowed to set prices so as to earn a reasonable rate of return on a portion of its assets. (This portion is referred to as the rate base and consists of most assets.) The rate of return is an accounting variable that can be observed by the regulator. The allowable rate of return varies from time to time and region to region depending on market conditions. The regulator can find out whether, in the previous year, the firm earned a reasonable rate of return. If not, the firm will be allowed a general price increase, which will normally increase revenue, assuming the firm is charging something less for its services than the monopoly prices.

Subject to the regulator's notions of fairness, and to the lobbying of interested parties, the firm will normally be allowed a considerable amount of latitude in determining the exact composition of its price increases. One hopes that the firms will use this flexibility to maximize efficiency, given their budget constraints, through appropriate non-uniform, price discriminating, peak-load, and cross-subsidized price structures.

Unfortunately, there are several problems created by rate-of-return regulation, one of which is the Averch-Johnson (AJ) effect, first analyzed by Averch and Johnson (1962). They observed that the assets used to compute the rate of return consist mostly of physical capital: buildings, dams, nuclear reactors, etc. If the allowable rate of return is, say, 10%, and the firm has $1 billion in the rate base, then the firm is allowed to earn $100 million in net earnings, which is supposed to correspond to normal profits. Note, however, that the firm can increase its allowable earnings by increasing its asset rate base. If the firm doubled its rate base to $2 billion, it would be allowed $200 million in earnings rather than only $100 million.

The source of the inefficiency is the asymmetric treatment of capital and other factors of production (notably labour) in determining allowable earnings. Labour is deducted as a cost, but it is not in the rate base. The cost of capital, as reflected by interest charges, depreciation, and other charges, is also deducted as a cost, and capital is in the rate base. The following algebra shows how the rate-of-return calculation works. Letting N represent net earnings and R represent revenue, we obtain Equation 14.5.

$$N = R - wL - \delta K - OC \qquad (14.5)$$

where w is the wage rate, L is labour, δ is the annualized cost of capital, K is capital, and OC is other costs. Rate-of-return regulation places the following constraint on earnings,

$$N = rK \qquad (14.6)$$

where r is the allowed rate of return. If the firm is interested in its shareholders, it will strive to maximize the rate of return on equity. Letting E represent equity, this rate of return is N/E. If the firm holds equity constant, increasing the rate base by borrowing money to purchase capital, it can increase N (in accordance with Equation 14.6) and increase its rate of return to shareholders.

This provides the firm with an incentive to use an inefficiently high capital to labour ratio, raising the firm's average cost curve. This is illustrated in Figure 14.4.

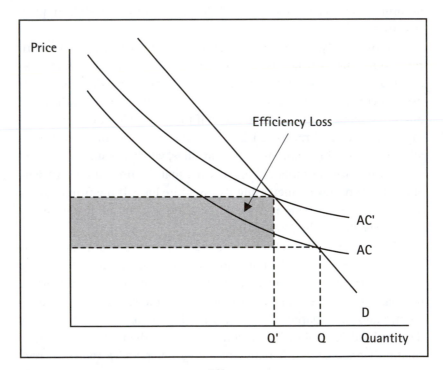

Figure 14.4 The Averch–Johnson Effect

As a result of using an inefficiently high capital to labour ratio, the firm experiences an upward shift in its average cost curve from AC to AC'. Assuming output falls from Q to Q', the efficiency loss is shown by the shaded area in Figure 14.4. This is an example of production inefficiency, as described in Chapter 2. The AJ effect is sometimes called rate-base padding.

In addition to the AJ effect, rate-of-return regulation also allows the management of regulated firms considerable insulation from market discipline. Management errors, inefficient labour contracts, thick carpets, or whatever, simply get reflected in higher prices. The management of a regulated firm or public enterprise is in much the same position as the bureaucracy described in Chapter 5, and can extract slack in much the same way.

There is considerable debate over the actual importance of the AJ effect and related inefficiencies in public utilities. Overall, there is some evidence of rate-base padding, but the apparent cost is not so high as to warrant giving up on rate-of-return regulation altogether. Nevertheless, some modifications of rate-of-return regulation have been applied.

One successful alternative to rate-of-return regulation is price-cap regulation. The basic idea of price-cap regulation is that the regulated firm is allowed a certain maximum price increase each year. This price increase equals the relevant measure of inflation minus expected productivity improvements (which may be estimated using data from a range of jurisdictions). The firm may charge less than this price cap if it wishes. The advantage of this method is that the firm has an incentive to reduce costs and operate as efficiently as possible, because it will be able to keep the extra profits. The difficulty with price-cap regulation is that it may be difficult to determine an appropriate maximum price.

14.9 Price-Cap Regulation

Price-cap regulation has been used in Britain in recently privatized industries such as telephones, natural gas, and water. It has also been widely used in the United States, particularly in regulating local telephone service. In an interesting study of long distance telephone pricing, Mathios and Rogers (1989) compare U.S. jurisdictions that had adopted price-cap regulation to those that had maintained rate-of-return regulation and found that price-cap regulation led to lower prices for a given service level.

14.10 Entry Regulation

In most industries where there is price regulation there is also entry regulation. The extreme case, which is quite common, occurs when one firm is given a mandate to serve a particular market and other firms are excluded. The natural question to ask is why entry restriction should be necessary in industries characterized by natural monopoly.

The major point is that even a natural monopoly may be subject to competitive entry. Furthermore, this entry can be efficiency reducing. We normally believe this problem applies in multiproduct firms, but it can arise even with a single-product firm, as first pointed out by Panzar and Willig (1977). Figure 14.5 illustrates this possible problem.

Curve *AC* represents the average cost curve of a public enterprise. Given its mandate to satisfy all demand forthcoming at the price charged, and constrained to price at average cost, the public enterprise would produce at Q^*, and charge price P^*. Note that the firm is actually producing on the upward sloping part of its average cost curve, beyond the point of minimum efficient scale. Nevertheless, the firm is a natural monopoly, for no way of dividing up output Q^* between two

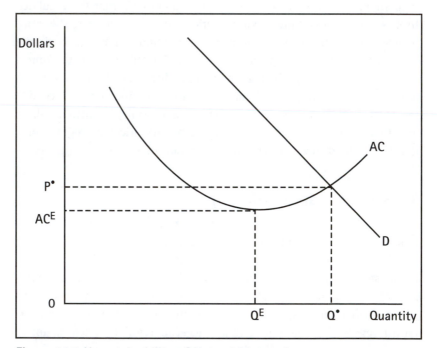

Figure 14.5 Unsustainability of Natural Monopoly

different separate firms would result in a lower total cost, assuming both firms had the same cost curve. Therefore, the efficient solution is to have a single firm in the market.

Despite the fact of natural monopoly in this industry, an unregulated entrant would enter if allowed to do so. An entrant could enter the market, produce up to output level Q^E, which is the minimum efficient scale, incur average costs of AC^E, and charge a price below P^*, undercutting the incumbent public enterprise.

The difference between the unregulated entrant and the public enterprise is that the entrant is not forced to price at average cost, or to serve all demand forthcoming at the price charged. The entrant can serve just a portion of the market if it wishes. It can therefore skim off the most fruitful level of production, leaving the public enterprise to serve the rest of the market. As drawn, the public enterprise would only have a small market left, and would be forced to incur high average cost, raising the overall cost of supplying a given level of output, Q^*.

A numerical example will make the point more clear. Suppose that the minimum point of the average cost curve occurs at an output of 9,000 units (point Q^E in Figure 14.5), and suppose that this minimum average cost is $9 per unit. Suppose further that demand crosses the average cost curve at an output of 10,000 units (point Q^* in Figure 14.5) where average cost is $10 per unit. Finally, suppose that the average cost at output level 1,000 is $30 per unit. A regulated monopoly should produce 10,000 units of output (under average cost pricing) at a total cost of $100,000. However, an entrant would have an incentive to come into the market, and produce and sell 9,000 units at a total cost of $81,000. If the regulated firm then produced 1,000 units, in an effort to make sure that all original customers were served, it would incur total costs of $30,000. The total cost of producing 10,000 units under the new arrangement, with both the entrant and the regulated firm in the market, would be $111,000, or $11,000 more than with just the regulated monopoly.

The situation just described is not likely to arise. A very similar, and more empirically important problem can, however, arise with multiproduct firms. For example, Canada Post must serve a number of different routes, some of which are more profitable than others. If other firms could enter the mail delivery business in direct competition with Canada Post, they would have an incentive to skim off the profitable routes, such as intra-city mail in Toronto, Montreal, and Vancouver, depriving Canada Post of economies of scale (and economies of scope) and leaving it with unprofitable routes such as the Inuvik-Yellowknife run. Either low-density routes would be abandoned completely, or they would be served at high cost, either to the taxpayers, or to the mail users.

This particular case mixes issues of equity and efficiency. Much of the public debate over postal service focuses on some notion of fairness in providing mail service in high-cost areas. The point being made here, however, relates to efficiency. The argument is that allowing entry in areas where a public enterprise or regulated private firm has a mandate to provide service may actually reduce efficiency, because of the skimming problem. In Chapter 16 we will discuss the problems confronting Canada Post and regulation of mail delivery more fully. One point worthy of note is that Canada Post has had significant competition from couriers, despite the fact that couriers are restricted by regulation to providing high-end service rather than regular mail. However, Canada Post recently acquired Purolator Ltd., one of the major couriers operating in Canada.

14.11 The Capture Hypothesis: A Positive Theory of Regulation

So far our discussion of price regulation has been normative. We have focused on how regulation should operate, and looked at some of the pricing techniques that regulators might allow in their enthusiasm to serve the public interest. There is also a more cynical view of regulation, associated particularly with Stigler (1971) and Posner (1974), and known as the capture hypothesis. This hypothesis is a suggestion about the positive theory of regulation. It argues that regulators tend to be captured by the industry they are supposed to be regulating, and serve the interests of the industry at the expense of the public interest. Stigler and Posner maintain that we would be better off doing away with most price and entry regulation.

An amusing hypothetical account of how a regulator becomes captured is provided by Carr, Mathewson, and McManus (1972). They consider an eager young regulator, law degree or public administration degree in hand, off to some unnamed regulatory agency, determined to serve the public interest. The young regulator is in for some hard years. The objective is to allow the firm a fair rate of return while ensuring that it serves the public interest. But the young regulator finds that neither determining a fair rate of return nor identifying the public interest is easy.

For one thing, the regulator never has enough information. The only source of information is in fact the regulated industry. Our regulator ends up spending a lot of time with industry people, and finds that they are not a bad lot. They treat regulators well, and frequently hire ex-regulators. Outsiders, such as politicians and consumer groups, on the other hand, do not understand the industry or the problems of regulators. In fact, after a few years on the job, our regulator is surprised by how frequently he or she sees things eye-to-eye with the industry, and is no longer disturbed by frequently taking the side of the industry when making regulatory decisions. Thus, the regulator is gradually captured by the regulated firm.

14.12 Bibliographic Notes

General references on the normative theory of regulation are Brown and Sibley (1986) and Viscusi, Vernon, and Harrington (1992). Ramsey (1927) is the original source on Ramsey pricing. Analysis of the AJ effect is due to Averch and Johnson (1962). A primary source on the rationale for entry regulation is Panzar and Willig (1977). The capture hypothesis is associated with Posner (1974) and Stigler (1971). An interesting attempt to use regulatory outcomes to infer the objectives of regulators is described in Ross (1984).

Notes

1. In fact, this discussion ignores some of the subtleties of welfare measurement. The area under the market demand curve is only an approximation to a more exact measure of welfare changes. This approximation is very close as long as the product absorbs only a small amount of any consumer's overall budget so that income effects are small.

2. The efficient solution was first determined by a young mathematician named Frank Ramsey in 1927. The basic formula is $(P - MC)/P = A/E$, where P is the price of a particular product, MC is the marginal cost of the product, A is a constant that is the same for all products produced by the firm, and E is the elasticity of demand. Not surprisingly, the formula links price to marginal costs. The additional element in the formula is that the markup of price over marginal cost is higher if the elasticity of

demand is lower; that is, if demand is inelastic. This is a characteristic we associate with necessities. What the Ramsey formula says, therefore, is that markups should be highest for the most essential services! This is a situation where intuitive ideas of procedural fairness conflict with efficiency objectives.

15

Major Areas of
Private Sector Regulation

15.1 An Overview of Canadian Regulation

In this chapter we examine some of the major areas of price and entry regulation in the Canadian economy, focusing mainly on private sector firms. Table 15.1 lists the major regulated industries and the regulatory authorities responsible for them.

Table 15.1 lists the industries that comprise what might be described as the regulated sector in Canada. These are the industries in which price and entry regulation are important. This list contains some industries that are not normally thought of as belonging to the regulated sector, even though they are subject to substantial regulation. Specifically, agriculture, the financial industry, oil, and the postal service would not normally appear on a list of this sort. It is true that regulation in these industries is different in intent and in character from regulation in the classic public utilities, as later sections in this chapter will make clear. Nevertheless, if one is interested in an overview of price and entry regulation, it would be a serious omission to ignore these industries.

The narrowly defined list of regulated industries, including electric power, telephones, airlines, radio and television, railways, trucking, pipelines, and water carriers accounted for about 10% of GDP in 1999. Agriculture accounted for another 3.5%, and the financial sector, together with real estate industry services (which is not closely regulated), accounted for about 14% of GDP.

TABLE 15.1 Regulated Industries in Canada

Industry	Regulatory Authority	Federal or Provincial
Electric power	CC*	Provincial
Telephone	Canadian Radio–Television and Telecommunications Commission (CRTC)	Federal
Airlines	Canadian Transportation Agency (CTA)	Federal
Agriculture	Various marketing boards	Federal and provincial
Financial	Office of the Superintendent of Financial Institutions (OSFI) and Provincial authorities	Federal and provincial
Railways	CTA	Federal
Radio	CRTC	Federal
Television	CRTC	Federal
Trucking	Highway transport boards	Provincial
Pipelines	National Energy Board (NEB)	Federal
Oil and gas	NEB, complex array of national, provincial, and municipal authorities	Federal and provincial
Water carriers	NTA	Federal
Postal service	CC*	

* CC means that the industry is dominated by one or more Crown corporations that are, in essence, self-regulating, subject to government review.

Most of this chapter is devoted to an industry by industry discussion of the major areas of regulation, including sections on telecommunications, airlines, agricultural marketing boards, and the financial industry. Electric power is not discussed here since it falls naturally into Chapter 16's examination of Crown corporations.

Over the past 15 years there has been considerable dissatisfaction expressed over the extent of regulation in several countries, including Canada, the United States, and Britain. As a result, the term "deregulation" has come into vogue, and was a major part of the platforms of the government in power in all three of these countries during the 1980s. Both Britain and the United States have gone much further in undoing regulation than Canada has, but all three countries have made substantial changes. A general discussion of deregulation is contained in Section 15.7. Also, some firms in the regulated sector are Crown (i.e., government-owned) corporations. Such corporations are taken up in Chapter 16. The Crown sector has been shrinking over the past 15 years, primarily because of privatization, which is the sale of Crown corporations to the private sector. Several examples and an overview of privatization are provided in Chapter 16.

15.2 Telecommunications Regulation

Canada's telecommunications industry is dominated by Bell Canada, which provides telephone service to Ontario, most of Quebec, and the Northwest Territories. It provides about 60% of all telephone service in Canada. Bell Canada is 100% owned by a holding company, Bell Canada Enterprises (BCE), which was created in 1983 to hold Bell Canada and Northern Telecom as separate corporate entities. Prior to 1983, Northern Telecom had been a wholly owned subsidiary of Bell Canada. The reason for the 1983 reorganization was to free Northern Telecom, which manufactures telephone equipment, from coming under de facto regulatory control by the CRTC, which regulates Bell Canada. In early 2000 Northern Telecom (by then renamed Nortel Networks) was divested by BCE and became fully independent. BCE is a widely held company, which means it is owned by a wide range of private shareholders, none of whom has a controlling interest. BCE is Canada's largest corporate employer and second-largest company (after General Motors) by sales.[1] Taken by itself, the Bell Canada component is among Canada's largest 20 companies by either of these measures with assets of about $20 billion and 1999 revenues of $12.7 billion. Bell Canada has also been one of Canada's most profitable companies for most of its history.

One question that comes to mind immediately is why a regulated firm, which is protected from entry, should be allowed to earn high profits. In 1986 the CRTC did take the very unusual step of ordering Bell to reimburse its customers some $206 million, arguing (convincingly) that Bell was charging higher long distance rates than would prevail if competition were allowed, and was earning a rate of return above normal levels. Bell CEO Albert Jean de Granpré fought this regulatory ruling in court.[2] De Granpré argued that Bell has little incentive to undertake good investments if the CRTC was simply going to take away its profits.

The Other major firm providing telephone service in Canada is TELUS Corporation, which was launched in 1990 to privatize Alberta Government Telephones (AGT). Ownership of AGT was transferred to TELUS, and shares in TELUS were then sold to the public. In 1995, TELUS bought ED TEL (Edmonton Telephone) from the city of Edmonton and therefore expanded its service area to the entire Province of Alberta. In 1999, TELUS merged with B.C. TEL (British Columbia Telecom) to form a large western-based telecommunications company. The merger was described as a "merger of equals" but the merged entity adopted the TELUS name. As of 2000, TELUS is acquiring QuebecTel, which has a minority share of the Quebec telephone market. (Bell Canada has the majority share of the Quebec market.) TELUS is seeking to become a major national telecommunications firm with a large cellular telephone service and various Internet and multi-media products in addition to standard telephone service. In 1999, TELUS had annual revenues of about $6 billion and assets of about $8 billion.

There has also been a major recent consolidation of telecommunications in Atlantic Canada as the four major telecommunications firms in the area merged in 1999 to form Aliant. The four underlying firms were NB Tel (New Brunswick Telephone), NewTel Enterprises (of Newfoundland), Island Tel (of Prince Edward Island) and MTT (Maritime Telephone and Telegraph of Nova Scotia). There will be an attempt to retain the identities of the underlying firms, but they are all part of Aliant, which in turn is 53% owned by BCE. The two other large telecommunications companies in Canada are Manitoba Telecommunications Services, which is now a regulated private sector firm, and Saskatchewan Telecommunications, which is owned by the Government of Saskatchewan, and is the one remaining significant government-owned telecommunications firm in Canada. Following a 1989 Supreme Court of Canada ruling establishing exclusive federal jurisdiction over telecommunications regulation, all of these companies are regulated by the CRTC. Prior to this ruling, the prairie companies were regulated by provincial regulatory boards. The rationale for local monopoly power is that local telephone service has been regarded as a natural monopoly. The main point is that it is inefficient to have parallel transmission lines and other capital equipment in any given area. This natural monopoly characteristic is the main normative rationale for regulation in the telephone industry.

However, in the 1990s cellular telephone technology emerged as a major part of the telecommunications market. The cellular sector is unregulated in that any firm can enter the industry and can charge whatever prices it likes. Cellular phones use high-frequency radio (i.e., electromagntic) waves. They do, however, piggyback on the pre-existing local telephone systems in that they must access these systems to allow cellular phones to make calls to noncellular phones. The relatively high cost of cellular telephone use implies that it is not really a competitor for standard telephone service, but is a complementary service. Thus, people who have cellular telephones have them in addition to regular telephones, not instead of regular telephones.

The long distance market has undergone a dramatic change in recent years and is now very different in character from the local service market. In order to understand this market it is necessary to know something about telephone technology. Local telephone service is routed through copper wires that are either in the ground or supported by telephone poles. These telephone lines are owned and maintained by local telephone companies such as Bell Canada, Saskatchewan Telecommunications, etc. The signals in these copper wires are electronic (i.e., they consist of moving electrons). Long distance telephone calls travel by microwave relay (line of sight electromagnetic signals that are transmitted from one relay station to another), or by satellite (using electromagnetic signals) or, increasingly, by fibre optic cable using laser-based signals. Microwave relay is the oldest of these technologies, and became widely used in the 1950s. Satellite technology experienced its period of rapid growth in the 1970s, and fibre optic cable developed commercially in the 1990s.

A long distance call using satellite technology works as follows. A phone call from Vancouver to Halifax could travel by telephone lines in Vancouver to a transmission point, then be converted into electromagnetic signals and beamed to a communications satellite that would redirect the signal to a receiving station in Halifax, which would convert the signal back to electronic form and transmit it via local telephone lines to its destination in Halifax. Alternatively, the signal could be sent by the older microwave relay system at approximately the same speed, or by fibre optic cable. Fibre optic cables can carry information faster, in much larger volumes, and more reliably than conventional copper wires, microwave relay, or satellite transmissions. The first Canadian fibre optic cable connecting Canada with Europe was completed in 1994.

The local telephone companies jointly provide long distance services through a fairly complicated arrangement involving three other companies. First, the local companies jointly own a company now named Stentor (after a Greek warrior with a loud voice), which provides long distance service within Canada and between Canada and the United States, using microwave relay, satellite transmissions, and optic fibre. Prior to 1992, Stentor was known as Telecom Canada. In addition, a company known as Telesat Canada owns and operates the satellites used for long distance telephone transmissions. When this company was set up in 1969, it was jointly owned by the federal government and by the local telephone companies. It's ownership envolved through several phases and Telesat is currently owned by BCE. In addition, a third company, Teleglobe Canada, handles long distance traffic to other countries (i.e., aside from the United States). Teleglobe was a Crown corporation until 1987, when it was sold to the private sector. Bell's parent, BCE, has a substantial minority share in Teleglobe. As of late 2000 Teleglobe will merge with BCE, which purchased 73% of the company. Teleglobe had a monopoly granted by the CRTC to handle overseas long distance services until 1997. In 1998 the overseas long distance market was opened up to competition.

The local telephone companies (through Stentor and Telesat, and with the cooperation of Teleglobe) were able to act as a monopoly provider of long distance service in most of Canada until 1992. (Any one user would interact only with his or her local telephone company, who therefore had monopoly power with respect to this user.) As satellite transmission capability grew during the 1970s and 1980s, it became obvious that there was no need for long distance service in Canada to be provided by a monopoly. There is no economic reason why two different companies could not pick up local signals in Halifax, transmit them by satellite to Vancouver, and have them picked up by B.C. Tel for local transmission. However, the local companies strongly resisted allowing long distance competition, since they did not want to give up their (very profitable) joint monopoly in the long distance market.

One argument against allowing competition was that the long distance market was used (with the support of regulators) to cross-subsidize basic access to local service. Charges for basic access (i.e., for providing and maintaining a telephone line for a given user) are much lower than the actual cost of providing such access. Profits on long distance service have been used to cover these costs. The industry has traditionally defended its practice of cross-subsidization on both equity and efficiency grounds. The equity argument is simply that it is socially important for everyone to have access to basic telephone service, and therefore that basic service should be inexpensive. Images are presented of poor elderly people in need of emergency ambulance service, but unable to phone for it because they cannot afford a telephone.

The efficiency argument is based on what are referred to as network externalities. The basic idea is that when Ms. A joins the telephone network, she confers a benefit on herself, but she also confers an external benefit on others who might want to communicate with her. Ms. A will take only her own benefits into account and might therefore fail to join the network if the cost is higher than her personal benefit, even if the total benefit to society, including her own benefit and the benefits to others, exceeds that cost. This kind of positive externality calls for a subsidy to improve efficiency: people should be subsidized to join the system.

Both of these reasons for cross-subsidy were important in the 1950s and 1960s when the telephone system was trying to increase market penetration, and the relative cost of telephone service was fairly high in comparison to average incomes. Nowadays, however, the telephone system has reached close to 100% penetration in Canada, so these reasons are much less compelling, and the actual cost of providing telephone service has fallen dramatically relative to average incomes. Very few people are likely to go without basic telephone service today, even if local service is required to pay its own way. Thus, both the equity argument and the efficiency argument for cross-subsidy from long distance to local access are no longer very persuasive.

The United States had to respond to basically the same set of issues, starting from a very similar industry structure. The United States has, however, taken much more dramatic action than Canada. The major telephone company, AT&T, was in 1984 forced to divest the local service companies or operating companies. The operating companies are still subject to regulatory control, but are no longer subsidized by long distance service.

AT&T continues to provide long distance service, but the long distance service has been deregulated, which means that anyone is free to enter the long distance market and that companies in the market are free to set whatever prices they choose. In addition, AT&T has been allowed the freedom to enter other lines of business (such as personal computers). The net effect of these changes has been a sharp decline in long distance charges and an increase in the range of quality of long distance services offered. Local service charges, on the other hand, have risen somewhat. In addition, some operating companies have introduced what is called measured service on local calls, which means that customers pay for local calls on a per call and per minute basis.

In Canada, a company known as CPCN Communications applied for permission to compete in the long distance market in the mid-1980s but was turned down by the CRTC. CPCN was jointly owned by the railway companies, Canadian National (a federal Crown corporation) and Canadian Pacific, which had their own trunk system of microwave relays for railway communication purposes and were therefore well placed to enter the market.

In the late 1980s, CP bought out CN's share in CPCN (reflecting the federal government's privatization agenda) and CP subsequently sold a substantial share to Rogers Cable. CPCN also renamed itself Unitel and reapplied for permission to enter the long distance business. In 1992, the CRTC finally decided to allow Unitel to enter the Canadian long distance market as a provider of basic service. The 1992 CRTC ruling required local service companies to allow Unitel access to their local telephone networks.

However, long distance service was not fully deregulated, and Unitel was required to pay a contribution margin to the local service companies to cover their share of the access subsidy. With Unitel and other companies competing with the local companies (through Stentor), the long distance market has became quite competitive. In 1995 Unitel reached near-bankruptcy and was essentially absorbed by AT&T Canada. AT&T Canada is a distinct corporate entity that is affiliated with AT&T. In the late 1990s AT&T Canada emerged as a major "player" in the Internet and other telecommunications markets.[3]

A primary policy issued that has emerged in the telephone markets concerns "rate rebalancing", which refers to the idea that the local service charges should rise and long distance charges should fall to reflect actual costs for these services. One popssible adjustment would be to increase the basic monthly access fee. Another alternative would be to introduce measured service: charging by the call and by the minute for local telephone calls. Moving to measured service could even allow a reduction in the monthly access charge (although only a few of the U.S. operating companies that use measured service have gone this far).

The economics of the problem are clear cut. Rate rebalancing and the introduction of measured service would improve efficiency in the telephone industry. The basic point is that such changes will bring actual prices (and marginal benefits) more into line with marginal costs, and that will increase efficiency, in accordance with basic marginalist principles. Consumers would be made better off, not worse off, by such changes. It is sometimes argued that the costs of measuring local telephone calls may exceed the benefits of increased efficiency, but this seems unlikely because modern technology has made the measurement of phone calls relatively easy.

In addition, such changes would be in line with another principle of fairness: the users of an economic service (as opposed to a social service like welfare) should be the ones to pay for it. As things currently stand, people who make only the occasional telephone call pay the same price as those who use the phone constantly. For example, someone who makes only a few short local telephone calls per week pays the same fee as someone who has a computer modem turned on and uses a telephone line 12 or 14 hours per day (as many people do). Thus, the infrequent user is subsidizing the heavy user. In all probability, it is high-income people who use local telephone service more, so the current direction of subsidy is regressive in that low-income people subsidize high-income people on average.

Despite these clear economic arguments, there is strong consumer resistance and some political resistance to rate rebalancing and to measured service. Many people argue that such local measured service charges are unfair, and some seem to regard the right to free local calls as a fundamental principle on a level with free speech and freedom of the press. This is one of the areas where ideas of fairness seem to be nothing more than what people are used to. The once popularly held idea that it was unfair for a woman to take a job that a man could do has come to seem absurd. Similarly, it is likely that at some point in the future the idea that a normal economic good like local telephone calls should be free will seem foolish and old fashioned.

In telecommunications, regulatory events have been driven largely by technological change, as should be clear from the discussion of long distance service and cellular service. More substantial changes are on the way. In particular, new techonologies may soon make local telephone service open to competition. One possibility is extension of cellular technology to allow direct house-to-house communication without use of telephone lines. Another possibility is having telephone calls come in in conjunction with cable T.V. signals, either in cables of the current type or in fibre optic cables. On the other hand, if local telephone companies can replace existing copper wires with fibre optic cable at the level of household connections, local telephone companies could provide T.V. signals in competition with cable companies. Thus, it is likely that cable and telephone companies will soon be in competition for a generalized telecommunications market.

Another important technological development is improved satellite technology. U.S. companies are planning so-called death stars that will have the capability to provide several hundred television channels via satellite directly to homes in North America (i.e., including Canada), using small inexpensive satellite dishes that can sit unobtrusively on top of a T.V. set as receivers. This technology could also be used for voice communication. This is one area where regulators may have kept up with technological capability, since regulatory provision for direct home reception from satellite did precede industry capability.

Finally, in the past few years there has been tremendous growth of the so-called information highway, which is a largely noncommercial set of interlocking computer networks. Networks are connected using telephone wires, fibre optic cables, satellite transmissions, and other mechanisms. It is now possible to sign on to a computer in Whitehorse in the Yukon and gain immediate access to data and visual images in Europe, Australia, Japan, or potentially almost anywhere.

One of the most interesting aspects of the information highway is the Internet. The Internet is a particular computer network that started as a spinoff of a U.S. military network and was adopted by many universities and research organizations during the 1980s. With the development of effective video-imaging capability, the Internet has in the 1990s become a major force in the world of telecommunications. The commercial online computer services have found it necessary to provide Internet access to their subscribers. Anyone who is connected to the Internet can obtain access to a huge array of information contained at the vast number of Internet sites now online. Much of the information in this book was obtained from the Internet.

At present, this Internet system is largely unregulated, but it creates quite a few potential regulatory issues. One important issue relates to copyright and intellectual property rights, especially of software, because it is relatively easy to pirate computer software through the information highway. A related regulatory concern is national and personal security; fairly significant leaks of highly confidential information have already occurred. Maintenance in the form of making sure the system is reliable, doesn't break down, doesn't get excessively congested, etc. is also a problem. Finally, censorship is a major issue, since much of the traffic on the information highway contains material that some people find offensive, and there is concern that commercial interests may fill up the communication lines with advertising. In addition, of course, if the system becomes more commercialized and natural monopolies seem to exist in certain functions, regulation of pricing and entry will be considered.

15.3 Airline Regulation and Deregulation

For most of its history, the airline industry in Canada was dominated by two large firms, Air Canada and Canadian Airlines International (and its forerunners). Air Canada was a Crown corporation until 1988, when a large part of it was sold to the private sector, and the corporation was fully privatized in 1989. Canadian Airlines International was created in 1987 by Pacific Western Airlines' takeover of CP Air. In 1999 Air Canada acquired Canadian Airlines International. There are also regional, federal, and commuter airlines in the Canadian market.

The Canadian airline industry continues to be partially regulated, although the extent has diminished markedly over the recent past. Historically, the development of the Canadian airline industry has been a major area of government involvement in business. The legacy of World War I was that early responsibility for air transport resided with the Department of Defence. In 1936, responsibility was transferred to the newly created Department of Transport, and in 1938, the new Transport Act gave jurisdiction over air transport to a regulatory board, the Board of Transport Commissioners, forerunner of the Canadian Transport Commission, which in turn gave way to the National Transportation Agency, subsequently renamed as the Canadian Transportation Agency. Throughout most of this history, and up to the present, the industry has been subject to price regulation, entry regulation, route restrictions for existing carriers, and a variety of other regulations.

In the early days of air transport, including the early post-World War II period, transcontinental air transport was probably a natural monopoly. The relatively low level of demand in that period implied that economies of scale were not fully realized by the single full-service airline of the time, Crown corporation Trans-Canada Airlines (renamed Air Canada in 1964). CP Air was allowed its first transcontinental route in 1959, ending the Crown carrier's monopoly, although it is likely that neither firm was able to operate at minimum efficient scale. There was, in any case, a plausible natural monopoly or perhaps natural duopoly rationale for regulation of airlines until fairly recently.

In reality, however, the natural monopoly rationale was less important in determining the nature of regulatory policy than was another objective: opening up Canada's North. This was seen as an extension of the nation-building policy pursued through the extension of rail transport throughout the West. Air transport was to have a similar role in Northern development. Regulation and government ownership were, therefore, used to force airlines to offer Northern service, usually in return for being given Southern routes.

This reason does not fit readily into the normative framework for policy described in Chapter 3, except in the category of other social objectives. There is no underlying normative reason to try to speed up Northern development beyond the rate that natural (i.e., free market) forces would suggest, unless Northern development can be taken as an end in itself. (Many environmentalists would take exactly the opposite view: that preservation of the natural environment of the North is an end in itself, and they would oppose even natural economic development.)

The Northern development rationale for regulation has subsequently given way to a fairness argument. Many people argue that it is fair that small communities, particularly in the North, but also in other areas, should have adequate air service, and regulation is seen by many as the best way of ensuring this service. Airlines can be forced to fly certain routes, and they can be forced to offer what seem to the regulator like reasonable prices for travel on these routes.

There was a brief flirtation with deregulation in 1957 when a Conservative government took office, but this policy trend was reversed under subsequent Liberal governments that were more inclined to distrust market forces. Interestingly, the strongest lobbyists against deregulation were the incumbent firms in the industry and the regulators, who seemed to see eye to eye on this and many other points.

Throughout the 1960s and 1970s, there were many critics of airline regulation. They argued that prices were far too high, that service was poor, and that the principal effect of regulation was to enable the airlines to exploit consumers and to waste resources. If there had been a natural monopoly argument for regulation in earlier years, the validity of that argument had disappeared as a result of increasing density of air traffic and technological innovation. The airline industry was regarded by many as an important example of the capture hypothesis described in Chapter 14.

These critical voices were stronger in the United States, which like Canada, had a long history of tight regulation of the airlines. In 1978, the U.S. airline industry was deregulated, over the protests of the major firms in the industry. The outcome was a sharp reduction in fares. Bargain fares dropped by about 20%.[4] Regulation had been keeping prices above competitive levels. Under regulation (in Canada and in the United States) each carrier had to get permission to fly a particular route. Many routes had only one carrier, so a pure monopoly existed. Major routes might have two carriers, but these carriers would have long histories of implicit collusion. Regulators would not permit entry on existing routes by new potentially aggressive competitors.

In addition, prices were regulated, so that even if one carrier was possessed by an urge to compete aggressively, it was prevented from doing so because it could not get permission to offer lower prices. Furthermore, many airlines in the United States had become inefficient, for if their costs rose, they could always just ask the regulator for higher prices, which would, of course, be justified by the higher costs.

Deregulation allowed new firms to enter existing routes, and allowed firms to charge whatever prices they wanted. New firms did enter. A company called People's Express became a corporate folk hero, offering no frills fares of less than 50% of pre-1978 levels on many domestic routes. (People's went out of business, but the most successful U.S. airline company of the past decade, Southwest Airlines, has followed the People's strategy.) The news was not all good, at least not for everyone. The intense competition, combined with an increase in 1979 in the price of oil (which is a major cost for airlines), placed many firms in financial difficulty. The following years saw several bankruptcies and many takeovers. In the process, many workers lost jobs (and found new ones) and occasional groups of passengers were left stranded. Management staffs were trimmed and the real value of wages in the industry fell. Opponents of deregulation in Canada argued that the U.S. situation was chaotic, and not to be emulated.

In fact, however, the U.S. experience made it obvious that regulation of airlines had been very inefficient. The aftermath of regulation simply indicated the extent of the previous rents that had been extracted from consumers and either paid out to workers, management, and shareholders in above normal returns, or simply consumed in pure waste. To become efficient again, the industry had a lot of restructuring to do. That restructuring entailed some costs, but those costs were less than the benefits.

The U.S. experience created enough momentum in Canada for deregulation of the airlines to be taken seriously. In 1984, a limited deregulation was proposed by the Liberal government of the day. This deregulation allowed unlimited freedom to reduce fares on Southern domestic flights, and freedom to exit from routes served by another carrier. In addition, freedom of entry into charter services was established.

This deregulation had a major impact, and fares did fall sharply in Canada. Major regulatory intervention still existed after 1984, however. In particular, free entry was not established on regularly scheduled service. Thus, even though Air Canada and CP Air competed against each other on most important routes, there was little opportunity for additional entrants, although quite a number of small independent charter airlines and feeder airlines did enter the market. One small airline, Pacific Western Airlines, grew to become a significant regional carrier based in Alberta, and actually acquired CP Air in 1987, forming Canadian Airlines. A fairly substantial charter airline, Wardair, sought to become a full service national carrier in the 1980s, but struggled financially and was taken over by Canadian Airlines in 1989.

The privatization of Air Canada that occurred in the late 1980s also contributed to a withdrawal of government influence in the industry, since Air Canada was able to focus on business objectives rather than having obligations to pursue government policy objectives. Even as of the early 1990s, however, entry regulation remained important in the industry, particularly with respect to foreign carriers. Specifically, no foreign carriers were allowed to fly domestic routes, and even international routes were carefully regulated, mostly through so-called bilaterals under which the Canadian government would grant a particular route to a foreign carrier. In return, the foreign government would allow a Canadian carrier access to a comparable route. Thus, for example, Canada might agree to allow British Airways a daily flight on the Toronto-London route, and in return the British government might allow Air Canada daily access to the same route.

During the early 1990s, the two major carriers in Canada suffered from significant financial pressure, caused in large part by the prolonged recession of 1990-92. Major doubts were expressed about whether two major carriers could continue to exist in Canada. The possibility of having a monopoly carrier seemed unattractive and two possible contingency plans were hotly debated in policy circles. One possibility was to allow a Canadian airline to combine in some way with a major U.S. carrier. The other possibility was to allow U.S. carriers direct access to the Canadian market. In fact, both possibilities came about, at least in part.

In 1993, American Airlines was allowed by Canadian competition policy authorities and by Canadian regulators to purchase a substantial minority share in Canadian Airlines International, and to amalgamate certain functions, particularly the computer reservation system.

Furthermore, in 1994, Canada and the United States signed an agreement creating an open skies policy between the two countries. This agreement allows carriers based in either country to fly freely between the two countries. Thus, for example, Air Canada can now decide to fly between, for example, Saskatoon and Minneapolis without requiring special permission from U.S. authorities. Similarly, U.S. carriers can freely establish routes between U.S. and Canadian cities. The primary remaining bottleneck is the ability of carriers to obtain airport space, which is at the discretion of local airport authorities. Despite the "open skies" term, however, a carrier from one country is still not allowed to fly domestic routes in the other country. Thus, United Airlines (the largest U.S. carrier) cannot, for example, decide to enter the Vancouver-Montreal route.

In 1999, Canadian Airlines International was acquired by Air Canada. It surprised some observers that the Competition Policy authorities were willing to "sign off" on this acquisition, as it created a near monopoly in the Canadian airline industry. However, Canadian was in severe financial difficulty and may have closed down in the absence of a takeover. The other major alternative would have been to allow an American (or other) airline carrier to take over Canadian. One concern arising from the takeover was the possibility of a sharp escalation in airfares, notwithstanding regulatory oversight by the Canadian Transport Agency. In the immediate aftermath of the takeover, Air Canada did reduce the number of flights and raise airfares in many categories. However, the takeover of Canadian has created room for regional carriers to grow and possibly provide reasonable competition in the market. One small regional carrier, Westjet (based in Western Canada) was able to establish itself as a significant presence by mid 2000.

It is also possible that restrictions on international carriers will be further relaxed. The international airline business has undergone a significant rationalization through the development of "strategic alliances" which consist of groups of airlines that cooperate on route planning and in other areas. Air Canada belongs to one of the major strategic alliances. Given the development of large international strategic alliances, the rationale for having a protected "national carrier" (i.e., a domestically-owned major airline) seems to be weaker than in the past.

One important additional point about deregulation is that price and entry regulation should not be confused with safety regulation. When deregulation of the airline industry is discussed, no one is suggesting doing away with safety regulations. There is a strong normative rationale for safety regulation on the grounds of informational market failure. Consumers cannot reasonably be expected to understand the safety features of airlines; it is much more sensible simply to have safety standards enforced by a single central authority. Both the United States and Canada maintain rigorous safety regulation regimes.

15.4 Marketing Boards and Supply Management

Marketing boards are very different in origin and structure from regulation in transportation, telecommunications, and public utilities. Agricultural industries are highly competitive. In fact, they are often taken as the classic example of perfect competition. There are many producers, so no single producer has any influence on product prices: he or she just takes the price as given by the market. As a result, there is little apparent reason for governments to intervene in agriculture. However, there has been extensive government intervention. The reasons given for regulation in agriculture[5] are to ensure ample and secure food supplies and to stabilize farm incomes.

The secure supply reason is presumably based on the idea that ordinary insurance markets cannot deal with certain types of undiversifiable risk associated with wars or natural disasters. Therefore, the government must correct for market failure. This might be important in some countries. However, since Canada is arguably the world's most efficient and productive food producer, and is a large net exporter of agricultural products, it seems likely that Canada's food supply would be as secure as that of any country even without intervention.

The income stabilization motive arises from the high volatility of world prices in agricultural products, and from the volatility of farm output due to variability in weather patterns. Farmers have very uncertain incomes and, although crop insurance exists and agricultural futures markets are large and important, private markets do not seem to have done an adequate job of insulating farmers from risk.

In addition, the actions of marketing boards, in addition to trying to stabilize income, in fact seek to increase farm income generally. In many countries, including both Canada and the United States as well as the EU, farmers have proved to be very effective transfer-seekers. (Recall the discussion of the Common Agricultural Policy in Chapter 9.)

Marketing boards are composed of groups of producers formed for the purpose of marketing their products. This in itself confers no regulatory power and need not involve governments. However, some marketing boards have been given broad powers of supply management by governments and have control over price and entry in certain areas. The discussion of regulation here is concerned strictly with marketing boards that have supply management powers. These supply management boards are similar in many ways to standard regulatory agencies: they are responsible to either the federal government or to a provincial government, and have broad authority to regulate the industry in question.

The major supply management boards operate in milk, eggs, poultry, and tobacco, accounting for about 20% of total farm revenue.[6] In addition, the Canada Wheat Board, which is constituted as a Crown corporation, but does not have supply management powers, has a very important role as the monopoly agent for Canada's wheat exports.

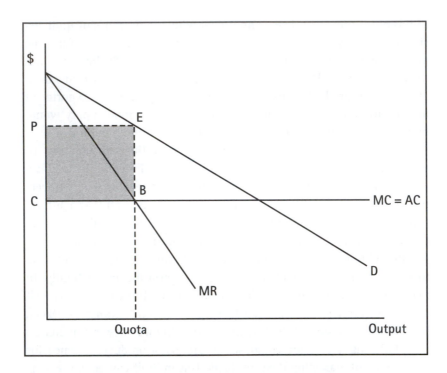

FIGURE 15.1 Creation of Economic Rent Using Quotas

The most important economic function of the supply management boards is to restrict output through a quota system. The Board allows a producer to sell milk only if that producer has a quota. If a producer wants to expand production, he or she must obtain a quota, usually either by buying it or by inheriting it. Quota systems are the perfect collusive arrangement. Entry is irrelevant, because no one can sell without a quota, and total output can be set easily. Total output is simply equal to the total quota. By setting the quota equal to the monopoly output, the industry can earn monopoly profits.

If quotas were set at the output level that would prevail in competitive markets, the quotas would have no value. If quotas are set at the monopoly level, then the quota has value equal to the present value of the monopoly rent, because that is what someone would be willing to pay for the quota. This is illustrated in Figure 15.1.

Area PEBC is the monopoly rent created by the quota. The present discounted value of this monopoly rent is therefore the value of the quota. In Ontario, dairy quotas in 1999 could be purchased for about $830 for the right to produce and sell one litre of liquid milk per day.

The total quota value of the average dairy operation was about $800,000, representing several years of gross revenue that the quota allows the producer to earn. This implies that a substantial share of revenue (perhaps 25%) is monopoly rent. In chicken production, the average value of a single farm's quota was over $1 million in 1999 leading to chicken prices that were substantially higher at the wholesale level in Canada than in neighbouring U.S. states. In British Columbia, the 1999 quota price allowing a producer to produce one chicken per cycle (5 chickens per year) in perpetuity was about $35.

The quota values represent the extra prices that consumers pay for the products controlled by supply management boards. Farmers who received quotas free when they were first set up, or farmers who realize appreciation on their quotas, do well from the quota system, but farmers who must pay for the quota to enter the business receive no expected net benefit from supply management. The amount they pay is exactly equal to the expected excess return, so the two effects cancel each other out, leaving only normal profits. The new farmer would do just as well if there were no supply management. Prices for output would be lower, but this would be offset by lower costs, due to not having to buy quotas. The quota system is an example of the transitional gains trap discussed in Chapter 5.

In fairness to the quota system, it should be pointed out that the relative price of agricultural products fell through the 1960s, 70s and 80s, (on average), mainly because of technological improvement. The development of supply management systems dates principally from the 1960s, and has helped ensure that farmers on the land at that time receive some of the benefits of technological innovation in the industry.

Supply management has also allowed the restructuring of major agricultural industries, particularly dairy production, without imposing hardships on the small farmers. As of the 1950s, it was clear that a large number of small dairy farmers would have to be replaced by larger operations. Between 1951 and 1976 the number of dairy farms in Canada fell from 455,000 to 91,000. Introduction of supply management in 1967 under the Canadian Dairy Commission essentially gave producers then on the land a property right to the dairy industry. Instead of going out of business through bankruptcy because of being below minimum efficient scale, small producers who received quota allocations were able to continue farming and eventually sell their quotas to larger operations when they chose to retire.

Consumers paid for this policy, of course, but paying for it through monopoly markups was probably cheaper than paying for it through large scale subsidies, as have been used in Europe. The time has come, however, to put an end to the policy, for it now serves very little purpose, since the monopoly profits are capitalized in quota prices and must be paid by new entrants. Consumers are now paying unnecessarily high prices, and the barriers to interprovincial and international trade erected by marketing boards are causing gains from trade to be foregone.

As discussed in Chapter 9, as part of the Uruguay Round on International Trade Negotiations, Canada agreed to abandon the international aspects of its supply management system. Foreign supplies were simply prevented from entering Canada because foreigners did not have quota rights. Under the Uruguay Round Agreement this restriction was eliminated and replaced by very high tariffs that will diminish somewhat over time and may allow some foreign competition.

15.5 Financial Regulation

There were 22 failures of financial institutions between 1980 and 1985, including two chartered banks. A few additional failures have occurred since (up to 2000). In several of these cases, suspicion was expressed about questionable practices, and in many cases the portfolios of the firms were insufficiently diversified.

The total cost of these failures is not available, but it should be emphasized that this is a very disturbing record, representing substantial costs to depositors, to the Canadian Deposit Insurance Corporation, and to taxpayers, and representing serious economic disruptions in various regions of Canada. This recent record suggests that improvement in the regulatory environment is called for. The following sections describe the nature of current financial regulation, examine the market failure basis for regulation, and suggest some areas for regulatory improvement.

15.5.1 Current Financial Regulation in Canada

The traditional basis of financial regulation in Canada was the division of the industry into four sectors, referred to as the four pillars: chartered banks, securities (or investment) dealers, insurance companies, and trust companies. The four pillars were kept separate by legislation that envisioned each pillar as having a particular function. Chartered banks took in deposits and made loans; securities dealers dealt with the buying and selling of bonds, stocks, and other securities; insurance companies dealt with insurance; and trust companies managed estates. In addition, there are other financial firms that do not fit into these four categories, including credit unions, mortgage loan companies, loan finance companies, and independent pension funds. Entry into these industries, especially banking, was carefully regulated.

While these functional definitions seem separate, the functions of the four pillars have come to overlap more and more as a result of changes in technology and increasingly sophisticated demands from customers. In July 1987, restrictions separating chartered banks, trust companies, and securities and investment dealers were substantially relaxed. In particular, there have been several mergers between chartered banks and investment dealers.

All financial firms perform the basic function of intermediation: they take assets in some form from one party and reinvest these assets with another party. The basic process is that these firms take savings from savers and allocate these savings to those who wish to make use of them. In the process of intermediation, liquidity is created: the pieces of paper generated by the financial sector act as a medium of exchange for buying and selling goods and services.

The chartered banks are still the largest part of the financial industry, at least as measured by total assets. Table 1 reports the assets of financial institutions in Canada as of 1998.

Table 15.2 Assets of Financial Sector, 1998

Type of Firm	Assets ($ billion)	Share
Chartered banks	946	62%
Insurance companies	237	15
Credit unions	140	9
Trust companies	54	4
Investment and securities firms and other consumer and business intermediaries	110	7
Other	41	3
Total	1,528	100%

Source: Statistics Canada Catalogue 3968, 1999.

Investment and securities firms seem relatively unimportant in this table, but much of their importance is not reflected in asset holdings. Much of their activity is brokerage: bringing together buyers and sellers of stocks and bonds (and making the trades), without actually holding large volumes of assets themselves. Investment firms are therefore far more important in channelling financial capital than their asset share would suggest.

Regulatory jurisdiction for the industry is divided between federal and provincial governments. Chartered banks are under the exclusive jurisdiction of federal legislation. However, insurance companies, trust companies, and mortgage loan companies are all subject to both federal and provincial legislative authority. Credit unions, the caisses populaires of Quebec, and investment dealers are all under provincial jurisdiction. The outcome of this institutional background to financial regulation is a very complex regulatory system.

Chartered banks are regulated by the Office of the Superintendent of Financial Institutions (OSFI), who reports to the Department of Finance (Finance Canada), and by the Bank of Canada. Banks are subject to capital adequacy regulation by the OSFI, which ensures that the ratio of liabilities to equity capital is not excessively high. They are also required by the Bank of Canada to maintain some of their assets in highly liquid form. Prior to 1993, chartered banks were also required to maintain some fraction of the deposits they took in as reserves with the Bank of Canada (i.e., some fraction of deposits would be redeposited in the Bank of Canada). As of 1994, this reserve requirement was reduced to zero. Trust companies are much like banks in their operations, as are credit unions. Insurance companies may invest in stocks, bonds, real estate and mortgages, subject to various limitations. They may not take deposits or underwrite securities.

In addition to these regulations, financial firms are subject to a wide variety of restrictions concerning the way in which they do business. Firms are supposed to avoid self-dealing, to avoid excessive risk-taking, to avoid taking advantage of inside information, and to treat clients fairly. All deposit-taking institutions may also belong to the Canada Deposit Insurance Corporation (CDIC), which insures certain types of deposits up to certain limits. If the institution goes bankrupt, the insurance reimburses depositors up to the applicable limit. This is intended to eliminate the phenomenon of bank runs, which occur when many individuals try to simultaneously withdraw money from a single bank, rendering the bank illiquid. However, one problem with the CDIC is that because it provides security to individual depositors, these depositors do not have an incentive to be concerned about the overall riskiness of the institutions where they make deposits. This problem is thought to have contributed to several financial failures in Canada, particularly the failure of the Canadian Commercial Bank in 1985.

15.5.2 Conventional Rationale for Financial Regulation

Sometimes the need for regulation in the financial sector is taken as self-evident, arising from the importance of the financial markets. However, the implication that just because a sector is important it should be closely regulated has no basis in evidence or theory. Dale (1984) offers the following four reasons for regulation of the financial sector.

1. The liabilities of banks and near-banks are money, the quantity of which national authorities seek to control for stabilization reasons.

2. Because financial institutions play a key role in channelling financial resources to the rest of the economy, governments may seek to control the direction of their lending.

3. The financial sector's role as a repository for the public's savings makes it a prime target for consumer protection legislation.

4. Because they are considered to be vulnerable to financial collapse, financial firms are subject to extensive prudential regulation designed to minimize the risks and to reduce the costs of failure.

Dale's description of the reasons for regulation are undoubtedly correct from a positive or historical point of view. They accurately describe the concerns of legislators and regulators that have led to the regulation we now have. Note, however, that only the first of Dale's reasons relates directly to the basic economic rationale for policy described in Chapter 3.

Dale's second reason is particularly suspect from a normative point of view. It is true that many governments exercise control over the movement of financial resources. In the few remaining centrally planned economies such as Cuba and North Korea, this control is complete: the state completely determines the disposition of financial resources. In many low income and semi-developed countries, including India and many South American countries, the allocation of financial capital is controlled largely by governments. This is also true of the reforming or transistional economies of Central and Eastern Europe. In general, it is the most productive economies in which financial markets are able to operate the most freely: the United States, Canada, Germany, Japan, Hong Kong, etc.

Proponents of market-based economic principles emphasize, and even opponents of free enterprise concede, that what private markets do best is allocate scarce resources to the areas where they are of high economic value. This does not mean that private capital markets operate perfectly, only that they operate a good deal better than any alternative system of allocating financial capital. From a normative point of view, the fact that financial markets are in the business of channelling financial resources to various uses is not in itself a justification for government intervention.

It is, of course, a great temptation for governments to intervene in capital markets to ensure low-cost financing of projects that are politically expedient. In many countries, for example, banks are required to fund government housing projects. The problem is that funds devoted to government projects are funds withdrawn from higher-value projects. It sounds great for governments to force banks to finance low-income housing. Unfortunately, such projects take funds away from business investments that would generate higher real incomes, and these projects undermine the private housing market as well. In short, such regulations have a very high opportunity cost.

Dale's third and fourth reasons for intervention are also suspect as fundamental principles. Reason three is just a version of the idea that economic services that are important should be regulated by government. This only makes sense if there is some reason to expect government regulation to perform better than private markets. A similar comment is true of Dales fourth reason: the mere presence of risk does not in itself justify government intervention. Risk is part of normal business activity, and markets have natural ways of responding to risk, notably insurance and diversification. Only if the government can improve upon the performance of such markets (i.e., only if there is market failure) is intervention warranted on these grounds.

15.5.3 Normative Principles and Financial Regulation

An important instrument of stabilization policy is control of the money supply, and bank liabilities are the largest component of the money supply. Therefore, the Bank of Canada exercises considerable influence over the banking sector. There is, however, no basic economic reason why banks should be treated differently from other deposit-taking firms. Macroeconomic control depends on total liquidity, not just on bank liabilities. In practice, the liabilities of credit unions and trust companies are money just as much as bank deposits are. Asymmetries between banks and functionally similar financial institutions have been reduced in recent years but not eliminated.

Capital adequacy requirements are a response to the high leverage associated with financial firms. In most nonfinancial firms, the amount of debt is comparable to the amount of invested capital. Some firms (such as IBM) carry almost no debt, using retained earnings and stock issues as the only source of finance. Firms with more debt than invested capital would, in most industries, be considered highly leveraged. The equity capital in the firm acts as a cushion to creditors.

Financial firms, on the other hand, tend to be very highly leveraged by the nature of their business. Deposit-taking institutions in particular are in the business of taking on debt: deposits are liabilities. It is normal for banks to operate with ratios of debt to invested equity capital of between 20 to 1 and 40 to 1. Such levels of leverage would be unheard of in most industries.

The implication of high leverage is that the shareholders of the bank have a relatively small investment compared to creditors of the bank. Furthermore, firms that are this highly leveraged have very little cushion against unfavourable market conditions. If a small portion of the portfolio of a bank fails, this can wipe out the entire value of equity.

As already indicated, banks are subject to capital adequacy regulation requiring them to maintain adequate capital in relation to their operations and to comply with any regulations or directives that may be issued by the OSFI in this connection. What form of market failure is capital adequacy regulation based on? Financial firms are highly leveraged, but is there any reason to believe that unregulated firms would choose levels of leverage that were too high from the public interest point of view? The major rationale for capital adequacy requirements is based on informational asymmetries and pecuniary externalities.[7]

The argument is that the failure of a bank can disrupt the economic activities of creditor and debtor firms. These disruptions are not something that will impose direct costs on the management and owners of the bank. The bank, therefore, will not take into account these costs in choosing its capital structure and will choose a capital structure that is too highly leveraged from the public interest point of view. In essence, there is a pecuniary externality associated with banking activity that calls for government regulation of the capital adequacy type. However, pecuniary externalities only represent market failure when they arise as a result of informational asymmetries. Thus, the fundamental source of market failure in financial markets must be related to informational market failure.

It might be argued that the pecuniary externality associated with banks applies to any large firm. For example, if GM Canada[11] were to go bankrupt, many creditors would be forced into bankruptcy as well. In fact, the pecuniary externality argument does apply to nonfinancial firms as well as to financial firms. The main difference is that the problem is much more severe for financial institutions because of their very high leverage. In addition, the informational asymmetries that lie at the root of market failure due to pecuniary externalities are probably more significant in the financial sector than in other areas. (There are credit rating services that are in the business of providing information about credit risk to depositors and creditors, but such services do not fully eliminate informational asymmetries.)

Concern about excessive risk-taking and self-dealing also has its foundation in informational market failure. The idea that financial institutions might be prone to excessive risk-taking arises from the following intuition. Because of high leverage, most of the money at stake in investments undertaken by financial firms is borrowed money. For every $1 of the owners' at stake, there might be $25 of depositors' money at risk. High-risk strategies are attractive because the benefits associated with the strategy (i.e., the returns when things work out well) go to the owners, while the costs (i.e., the losses in bad states of the world) are borne mostly by depositors. The incentive created by high leverage is sometimes described as the "heads I win, tails you lose" effect.

If depositors understand the environment in which they operate, and if they bear the downside risk of investment strategies, they will be reluctant to invest in an institution that does not have a safe, well-diversified portfolio. Unfortunately, for this buyer beware approach to work, depositors must be as well informed about investment opportunities as the managers of the financial firms, in which case they would not need the services of such firms anyway.

There is an inevitable informational asymmetry between customers and managers of financial firms. As discussed in Chapter 3 and elsewhere, informational asymmetries create market failure. This market failure is manifested in excessive failures of financial institutions, excessive investments of time and energy by customers in an attempt to monitor the decisions of financial firms, and in other ways as well.

Because of informational asymmetries, there is a strong case to be made for having the government gather and provide much more information about the transactions of financial firms. Monitoring agencies such as the OSFI should be extended more broadly in the financial industry and should make frequent public reports of the activities of firms in the industry. In addition, the legal power of government should be used to require disclosure of financial transactions by the firms involved. These are natural policy responses to market failures caused by informational asymmetries.

15.6 Other Regulated Industries

Some mention should be made of major areas of regulation that have not been covered in detail, such as broadcasting. The CRTC controls entry into radio and television broadcasting. Since the early 1970s, much of the regulation in this area has been focused on the objective of promoting Canadian culture, but this objective seems to have weakened in recent years.

Another major area of regulation is trucking, which is often alleged to be the clearest demonstration of the regulatory capture hypothesis discussed in Chapter 14. Other significant areas of regulation include natural gas pricing, railroads, and taxicabs. Professional occupations such as doctors and lawyers are self-regulating and are able to restrict entry and influence prices. This self-regulation may serve the public interest by enforcing standards, and may be viewed as a reasonable response to market failures created by informational problems, but such groups also have cartel-like characteristics.

15.7 Deregulation

The preceding sections have raised the issue of deregulation. Substantial deregulation of long distance telephone service and airlines has occurred in Canada over the past two decades. The agricultural supply management system is also suggested as a likely candidate for dismantling, especially in light of the Uruguay Round agreement on agriculture. Financial deregulation is proceeding: entry restrictions that kept the four pillars of the financial sector separate have been relaxed to a substantial extent. Deregulation in other areas has also been proposed, and no major new regulatory initiatives have been suggested in recent years.

These observations reflect Canada's policy history. Regulation had accumulated over the years, with left-of-center governments expanding the range of government intervention, and right-of-center governments acquiescing under pressure from the interest groups created by the policies. Many extensions of regulation were undertaken under the Liberal governments of Pierre Trudeau in the late 1960s and 1970s, particularly in the energy sector, but also in agriculture, health care, and broadcasting. Many of these regulatory adventures proved disappointing, and the tide in the 1980s was against regulatory expansion, partly as a result of accumulating evidence of inefficiencies created by regulation. In addition, lobbying efforts by potential entrants also contributed to the momentum for deregulation. Enthusiasm for deregulation seemed to have diminished by the mid-1990s, however, so we may be reaching something of a political equilibrium.

The most important question to ask with respect to regulation or deregulation is whether a normative foundation for regulation still exists. The basic conditions that made regulation a good idea at one time may no longer exist. This is true of long distance telephone service and airlines, and is probably true in rail transportation as well, and may become true in television broadcasting with the expansion of cable and computer technologies. Many people would say the same of agricultural supply management and entry restrictions in the financial sector.

Regulations should not be expected to stay in place forever. Industries go through life cycles, influenced by technological change, changes in the rest of world, and changes in other industries. We should expect that tight regulation would be appropriate at some stages of the industry's life cycle, but not at others. The general policy approach of imposing regulation and simply leaving it in place forever is certainly wrong. A very important task of any regulatory authority should be to ask frequently whether the regulations in force are still a good idea, or even whether they were ever a good idea.

While there has been considerable such discussion in the past 15 years, relatively little actual deregulation has taken place until recently. In some sense, the 1980s was the decade of talk about deregulation, but it was not until the 1990s that major regulatory changes came into force. At present, regulation is evolving quite rapidly in transportation, telecommunications, and financial services.

There is a good reason why regulation took a long time to dismantle. Regulation creates interest groups, and not least among the interest groups are the regulators themselves. A recommendation from a regulatory agency in favour of deregulation is a recommendation to do away with one's own job. It is little wonder such recommendations are rarely forthcoming. In addition, regulation typically creates monopoly rents for the industry concerned. For all their talk about the value of the private sector and sound business principles, firms like Bell Canada and Canada Post do not want competition and have fought very vigorously against its expansion within their areas of activity. Support for deregulation, if it is to come from anywhere, must come from outsiders: small business groups like the Canadian Federation of Independent Business, or consumers' groups. For the reasons mentioned in Chapter 5, it is much harder for such groups to recognize their interests and focus their efforts than it is for the interest groups that benefit from regulation.

Regulation has an important role to play. Indeed, in Chapter 10 it was argued that environmental regulation is not extensive enough. However, it is clear that price and entry regulation should be used sparingly, and that these tools have probably been overused in the past.

Notes

1. As reported in *Canadian Business*, "Performance 500," June 1995, p. 104.

2. Eric Reguly, "De Granpré keeps Bell ringing," *The Financial Post 500*, Summer 1987, pp. 16-20.

3. This information is taken from Robert Crandall "Managing the Transition to Deregulation in the United States." (1995), p.67-82.

4. Robert Dodd, Joanne Bonnyman, and Jody Shore (1982), *The Low-Priced Air Fare Review: A three year perspective*, Canadian Transport Commis-

sion Research Branch, Passenger and Aviation Economics, Report No. 1982/02E.

5. See, for example, the Economic Council of Canada (1981), Chapter 6.

6. John Spears, "Guardians of Farm Prices Face Critics," *Toronto Star*, November 9, 6. 1986, p. F1.

7. A very interesting experimental investigation of the performance of simulated financial markets in the presence of informational asymmetries is described in Cadsby, Frank, and Maksimovic (1990).

16

Public Enterprise and Public Goods

16.1 An Overview of Crown Corporations and Public Enterprise

In Canada, as in most Western countries, an important part of business activity is carried out by public enterprises. These enterprises are structured like private sector corporations, with boards of directors, chief executive officers, and so on. However, these firms are not owned by private shareholders, but by governments instead. In Canada, these public enterprises are generally referred to as Crown corporations.

Before proceeding, it is important to emphasize that the Crown corporation sector in Canada has been shrinking since the mid-1980s, after a vigorous expansion of public enterprise in Canada that occurred during the 1960s and 1970s. The main reason for this shrinkage is *privatization*. Many federal and provincial Crown corporations have been sold to the private sector. An overview of these privatizations is provided in Section 16.5

The term "public enterprise" lacks a precise definition, and some firms that we think of as public enterprises are not formally Crown corporations. In addition, some Crown corporations are not sufficiently independent from government departments to be called public enterprises, and some are more like regulatory authorities than producers of economic goods and services. In this book, however, we do not focus on these rather subtle distinctions. In general, the set of firms that are

Crown corporations and the set that might be referred to as public enterprises are almost the same. The terms "Crown corporation", "public enterprise," and "public corporation" will therefore be used interchangeably. A firm that is partly owned by government and partly by private shareholders is referred to as a mixed enterprise.

A public enterprise has more autonomy than a government department, is technically responsible to Parliament or to a provincial legislature as a whole, rather than to a particular minister, and operates from a more specific mandate than a government department. Its employees are not part of the civil service, and its management is in the hands of a board of directors and a group of executives who are much more independent of government than are the senior bureaucrats who manage departmental affairs.

Public enterprises differ from the private sector in that their directors and senior management are appointed by government, they are exempt from many taxes paid by private sector firms, and their debt is ultimately a liability of the government, which is therefore no more risky than a government bond. Public enterprises will normally have a mandate that involves some objective other than profit maximization, and as such are direct instruments of government policy.

The public enterprise form can be thought of as an attempt to achieve some of the efficiencies of the private sector in the pursuit of government policies. Public enterprises are more important in Canada than in the United States, Japan, and even Australia, but they have been declining in importance. The 1999 Annual Report to Parliament on Crown Corporatons recorded 85 federal Crown Corporations with total assets of 67 billion and 71,000 employees, down from 112,000 in 1994. (There are also a large number of provincial and small municipally owned enterprises.)

The following three tables provide lists of the major public enterprises under the categories of electric power, general, and financial. Tables 16.1 to 16.3 indicate several patterns about Canada's public enterprises. The largest nonfinancial public corporations are in the electric power sector, accounting for over 95% of assets in that sector. Alberta is the only province served principally by a privately owned (but closely regulated) firm. The large electric power companies are among the largest firms of any type in Canada (as measured by assets). The other major public enterprises are largely in transportation, energy, communications, and financial services.

The assets of the financial firms are not comparable to the assets of nonfinancial corporations. The essential activity of the financial industry is the creation of financial assets and liabilities. The firms borrow money from savers (liabilities) and loan the money to others (assets). Consequently, the assets (and liabilities) of a financial firm will be very high in relation to shareholder's equity or fixed investment. Thus, an industrial firm with assets of $1 billion will typically be much larger in economic size than a financial institution with assets of $1 billion.

The larger financial public enterprises are of significant size and importance compared to most private sector financial institutions. The largest four corporations in Table 16.3 are all among the largest finan-

TABLE 16.1 Major Public Enterprises—Electric Power

Corporation	Assets (1998 $ billion)	Ownership
Hydro Quebec	57.3	Government of Quebec
B.C. Hydro	11.7	Government of British Columbia
Ontario Hydro Services Co.	9	Government of Ontario
Ontario Power Generation	8.3	Government of Ontario
Manitoba Hydro	7.7	Government of Manitoba
New Brunswick Electric Power	3.6	Government of New Brunswick
Saskatchewan Power Corp.	3.2	Government of Saskatchewan

Source: *Annual Reports.*

TABLE 16.2 Major Public Enterprises—General

Corporation	Assets (1999 $ billion)	Ownership
Canadian Wheat Board	8.1	Government of Canada
Canada Post Corp.	2.8	Government of Canada
Canadian Broadcasting Corp. (CBC)	1.5	Government of Canada
Saskatchewan Telecom.	1.2	Government of Saskatchewan
Atomic Energy of Canada	0.9	Government of Canada
Via Rail Canada Inc.	0.6	Government of Canada

Source: *Annual Reports.*

TABLE 16.3 Major Public Enterprises—Financial

Corporation	Assets (1999 $ billion)	Ownership
Caisse de dépôt	83.3	Government of Quebec
Bank of Canada	33.8	Government of Canada
Canada Mortgage & Housing	21.1	Government of Canada
Export Development Corp.	15.2	Government of Canada
Alberta Treasury Branches	9.3	Government of Alberta
Insurance Corp. of B.C.	5.9	Government of British Columbia
Federal Business Development Bank	5.0	Government of Canada

Source: *Annual Reports.*

cial institutions in Canada. The largest financial firm in Canada by assets is the Royal Bank of Canada, with 1999 assets of roughly $272 billion.

16.2 Normative and Positive Reasons for Crown Corporations

The most important normative rationale for Crown corporations in the public utility area is natural monopoly. A Crown corporation is an alternative to price and entry regulation of a private sector firm, although the Crown corporations are themselves either regulated or have an internal regulatory process. There is, however, much more behind the development of public enterprise in Canada than just natural monopoly.

Some of the other reasons for public enterprise are related to more general problems of market failure. For example, even if the extent of economies of scale is not great enough to cause natural monopoly, an industry might still be imperfectly competitive, and might be able to earn above normal or excess returns. Crown corporations have been introduced in such industries to try to reduce these rents, either by taking the rents themselves and turning them over to taxpayers, or by charging low prices and forcing the rest of the industry to compete and reducing its rents. This was part of the rationale for the development of Petro-Canada, which was ultimately privatized.

Another market failure reason for the development of public enterprise is the alleged inability of financial markets to finance very large scale projects, even if those projects are worthwhile. Crown corporations are able to borrow more easily than a private firm, because their debts are assumed to be guaranteed by the government. In addition, the government can simply loan (or give) money to the Crown corporation outright. This reason for the development of Crown corporations has been important in the electric power industry, where the required investments have been largely compared to the size of any potential set of private financial sources.

Public corporations may be used to supply public goods, although this is rare, and they may be used to subsidize the development of activities with positive externalities. Public enterprises may pursue distributional or equity objectives, and, in addition, some public enterprises, such as the CBC and the Canadian Film Development Corporation, are focused on other social objectives, notably cultural ones. Similarly, Crown corporations have been set up in liquor distribution and to run lotteries, presumably to protect the public from anticipated excesses that would result from allowing liquor and gambling to be provided by the private sector.

In short, public enterprise in Canada has been targeted at almost the entire array of normative rationales for government intervention. Some people, moreover, would like to see Crown corporations applied more as a tool of macroeconomic stabilization policy, essentially as employers of last resort.

Public corporations have also been based on the following rationales: regional development, bridging gaps (undertaking economic activities that the private sector will not undertake), bailing out a failing firm, creating infrastructure, and outright nationalism (the desire to have a national presence in some industry). These rationales are at best questionable if taken as ends in themselves. Only if they fit into the basic normative rationale for policy intervention are they valid.

For example, the bridging gaps rationale can hardly be taken as a reason in itself for a public enterprise. There are many investments that the private sector will not undertake, and usually this is a good indicator that an investment is not worthwhile. The private sector does not grow bananas in the Yukon; this is not a reason to create a Crown corporation to grow bananas in the Yukon. If, on the other hand, the private sector fails to provide a service because of public good problems, or externality problems, then public enterprise may be appropriate to fill the gap.

If the private sector is unwilling to finance a particular project, it is, of course, hard to tell whether this represents market failure, and therefore justifies intervention by a Crown corporation, or whether the project itself is not good. A politician's usual definition of a good project is one that helps win votes, and this does not necessarily coincide with the market's definition of a good project, where people vote with dollars. There is, therefore, often a strong temptation for politicians to use Crown corporations to undertake economic adventures that the market would not support. Experience suggests that, on the whole, the market's judgement tends to be better than that of visionary politicians, as some of the examples to be discussed in Section 16.3 will indicate.

One reason for the development of Crown corporations is ideological. The basic ideology of socialism is that the state should own the means of production. Not many modern Canadian socialists would hold rigidly to this traditional ideal of socialism, and in 1991 the national NDP officially abandoned nationalization of key areas of the private sector as part of its policy platform. Still, many socialist elements in Canadian politics have been, and still are, very sympathetic to a general expansion of state ownership in the economy, and are happy to seize on any reason to promote the expansion of Crown corporations, although this sentiment is much weaker in the early years of the 21st century than it was in the 1960s and 1970s.

In addition, of course, the creation and promotion of public enterprise is due in part to the (by now familiar) interest group activity described in Chapter 5. Crown corporations have constituencies. Many public enterprises, such as the Farm Credit Corporation and the Export Development Corporation, provide subsidies to interest groups. The subsidized groups then become voices in favour of expansion of the public enterprise.

16.3 Major Crown Corporations

16.3.1 The Electric Power Industry

The electric power industry has already been discussed at several points. Of all areas of public enterprise activity, this is the one where the formation of public enterprise rests on the strongest normative foundation. On the whole, these firms have performed reasonably well. The industry has gone through a similar history in most parts of Canada, beginning as an unregulated private industry, becoming regulated as a response to concerns about the exploitation of monopoly power, and eventually being nationalized.

The formation of Hydro Quebec was completed in 1963, apparently because the province was unhappy with its experience in trying to regulate the prices and profits of privately owned companies, and also to promote a francophone management presence in Quebec. In addition, the government felt that a public enterprise would be better suited to undertake the very large scale nature of subsequent hydroelectric development, presumably for reasons related to market failure in the financial sector of the economy.

B.C. Hydro was also created by the nationalization of the privately owned B.C. Electric Co. in 1961, and its merger with the existing (but small) public enterprise, the B.C. Power Commission. Interestingly, the only publicly given reason for this policy was that B.C. Hydro, as a provincially owned utility, would not have to pay income tax. In addition, however, the government of the time believed that a public enterprise could more easily handle the financing of large-scale hydro developments.

In both Ontario and Quebec, the provincial governments have directed the relevant Crown corporations (Ontario Hydro and successors, and Hydro Quebec) to undertake policies that private firms probably would have been unwilling to undertake. In particular, these firms have been forced to assist in regional development by providing subsidized electricity prices for certain regions, and by locating major production facilities in targeted areas. In 1999, the old Ontario Hydro was broken up into three new organizations, each of which took over one or more previous responsibilities of Ontario Hydro. The production of electricity was taken over by Ontario Power Generation, Inc. The transmission and distribution activity was taken over by Ontario Hydro Services Company (OHSC). These two corporations remain Crown corporations. At the retail level the electricity market has been opened to general competition under the administration of the third successor to Ontario Hydro—the independent Electricity Market Operator.

16.3.2 Petro-Canada

Petro-Canada was created in 1975. The confluence of several historical forces combined to establish conditions conducive to the formation of such a company. First, as a result of OPEC, in 1973-74 the price of crude oil jumped sharply, as shown in Table 6.2, creating large windfall profits in the industry. Second, the early 1970s was a period of strong Canadian nationalism, during which much criticism was directed at foreign ownership, particularly in the energy sector. (Recall from Chapter 9 that FIRA, the Foreign Investment Review Agency, was created in 1973.) Third, general attitudes toward business fluctuate over time, and the early 1970s was a period when general mistrust of business was at something of a crest. In addition, the Liberal government of the time under Pierre Trudeau contained a fairly strong (by Liberal Party standards) ideological socialist element. An additional factor was that the government had an independent concern about Northern development.

While none of these reasons fits very easily into the market failure rationale for government intervention, one additional rationale given at the time for the formation of Petro-Canada may be related to a legitimate market failure. Specifically, this was described as a "window on the industry" rationale. This term referred to the problem that Canadian energy policy authorities had a difficult time finding out the state of exploration and development in the industry, and, in particular, had been badly misled about existing reserves by the (mostly foreign-owned) private sector firms in the industry. Arguably, therefore, Petro-Canada might have addressed some informational market failure.

In any case, given these various concerns and historical conditions, the creation of a Crown corporation was a natural and fairly popular response. Petro-Canada was to establish a major Canadian presence in the industry, provide the government with information about the industry, assist in Northern development, promote competition at the consumer level, and help bring the energy sector under the control of Canadians. The initial purchase of assets by Petro-Canada is still shrouded in a certain amount of mystery, but it seems that Canadian taxpayers paid far more than they should have.

From a modest beginning, Petro-Canada grew at a remarkable pace through the late 1970s and early 1980s, mainly by swallowing up other firms, although it did some subsequent efficiency-related downsizing. As of the mid-1990s, it is one of the three dominant firms in the Canadian oil and gas sector (along with Imperial Oil and Shell) and among the 30 largest nonfinancial corporations in Canada as measured assets or sales. It also holds the lion's share of permits to explore Canadian frontier areas. Some of Petro-Canada's acquisitions have been financed from earnings, but most have been financed with government money.

From the consumer's point of view, the industry is much as it always was. Petro-Canada does not seem to have had much impact on the retail performance of the industry, despite its very large presence at the retail level. Critics argue that, while Petro-Canada is doing nothing particularly wrong, and is operating much like a private firm, it is serving no legitimate policy purpose. Peter Foster[1] made the following summary statement about Petro-Canada:

> Of the three key prongs of Petrocan's original mandate, "Canadianization" has been achieved by spending taxpayer's money; the Crown corporation's "window on the industry" has revealed primarily that the company itself was not necessary; and its mission to ensure "security of supply" through . . . frontier exploration, has largely been a failure.

The performance of Petro-Canada is, by ordinary business criteria, certainly sub-par. Over the 10-year period 1980-89, Petro-Canada's return on shareholder's equity was 1.43%, compared with 10.8% for Imperial and 9.46% for Shell. A return of 1.43% is also well below the opportunity cost of government funds, and indicates that the taxpayers were gradually losing the value of their investment. The fact that Petro-Canada was able to grow rapidly in the early 1980s despite poor financial performance is attributed to the political skills of CEO Bill Hopper. He is regarded as one of the most successful public entrepreneurs of Canadian business history. It is not clear, however, that publicly funded entrepreneurship is in the public interest.

In 1991 the Minister of Energy, Jack Epp, announced that Petro-Canada served no public policy purpose and should be privatized. NDP Energy Critic Lorne Nystrom had previously argued against privatization, saying:[2] "Most of the oil industry is owned by foreigners and owned by private interests. We intend to drag this thing out and to try and mobilize public opinion against [privatization]." Liberal Senators also opposed privatization. In 1992, the Conservative government undertook a 20% privatization of Petro-Canada, selling off a block of 39.5 million shares at $13 per share, a somewhat lower price than had been anticipated. Subsequently (in 1993) an additional 10% was sold.

Privatization was on the agenda of the Conservative government of Brian Mulroney over its two terms of office, running from 1984 through 1993, and was a frequent debating point between the Conservatives and the NDP. The performance of Petro-Canada is sufficiently ambiguous that either side of the privatization case can be argued, depending on one's ideology. The NDP tends to distrust big business, and is suspicious of the oil companies. Conservatives tend to distrust intrusive government. Both sides have good reason for their distrust. If there is some market failure in the oil industry, however, normative reasoning suggests that competition policy, together with judicious use of the tax system, is probably the best approach, rather than using a Crown corporation. In its 1995 budget, the Liberal Government of Canada announced its intention to sell off its remaining 70% share in Petro-Canada. All but 20% was sold in 1995 at which point Petro-Canada became, essentially, a private sector corporation.

16.3.3 Canada Post

Canada Post began operations as a Crown corporation in 1981, replacing the Post Office Department.[3] Canada Post was formed as an attempt to remedy three serious problems with the Post Office: large deficits, poor service levels, and poor labour-management relations. Canada Post was granted the same legal monopoly status held by the Post Office. Specifically, the Canada Post Corporation Act states that "the Corporation shall have the sole and exclusive privilege of collecting, transmitting, and delivering letters within Canada." There is a provision to allow private sector competitors to carry letters of an urgent nature, but they must a charge a rate of at least three times the comparable first class postage rate.

The rationale for having postal service in the public sector is that postal service is a natural monopoly. In addition, Canada Post is seen as promoting some social objective by cross-subsidizing its operations, so that sending mail over high-cost mail routes costs consumers the same as intra-city mail in dense urban centers. The principle objection to allowing free entry into the mail delivery business is that the low-cost routes would be skimmed off by the private sector, leaving Canada Post with only the high-cost routes. As discussed in Chapter 14, it is possible that skimming can actually raise total costs. The more important political objection to skimming is that it is perceived as unfair to those who live in isolated communities.

When Canada Post began operations in 1981, it raised the price of a first class stamp from 17 cents to 30 cents. Since then the price has risen at about the rate of inflation, keeping the real cost roughly constant. In August 1995, first class stamps rose from 43¢ to 45¢, and 46¢ about mid-2000. As a result of the dramatic initial increase in price, and some improvements in productivity, Canada Post has been able to eliminate their deficit. Using Canada Post's financial statements to determine its deficit (or net subsidy from taxpayers) is difficult because it receives three separate government subsidies. Second class mail is subsidized as a matter of policy. Canada Post therefore treats this subsidy simply as a fee for service that is included in revenues from postal operations. Canada Post also receives subsidies for infrastructure, which it also treats as part of revenues. Finally, any difference between costs and revenues is reported as a deficit, and is paid as a subsidy by the government.

In the 1981-82 fiscal year, the first part of which was served by the Post Office, Canada Post and the Post Office had a residual subsidy of $588 million from the government. By 1985-86 this residual subsidy had fallen to $210 million, and it fell further to $38 million in 1987-88, the last year of deficit. In 1990-91, Canada Post reported a positive net income of $14 million on total revenues from operations of $3.7 billion. In 1993, Canada Post recorded a modest $18 million loss, and in 1994 reported a rather large loss of $270 million. However, this loss included an estimated cost of $282 million, so it would be reasonable to believe that Canada Post is in an approximate break-even position. In 1995 a modest loss of $69 million was reported, then throughout the late 1990s Canada Post was able to report modest net income (profits) which are turned over to the Government of Canada.

Price increases made a substantial contribution to reducing the postal service deficit in the early years, but in the late 1980s, improvements have come about mainly through improvements in efficiency. The real cost per piece of mail more than doubled between 1964 and 1981. Between 1981 and 1984 this real cost fell by about 5%, but then fell by about another 20% by 1990-91. In 1973, the volume of mail handled was about 93,000 pieces per full-time-equivalent employee. Despite substantial investments in labour saving machinery over the following decade, the volume of mail handled actually fell to about 89,000 pieces per employee in 1983-84, but rose to about 169,000 pieces per employee in 1990-91 and has continued to rise.

Quality of service continues to be something of a problem, although what little objective evidence there is suggests that quality has improved in recent years. Many users make a routine practice of using couriers to deliver important mail. Service between Canada and the United States is a particular problem.

What conclusions can be drawn about the role of Canada Post as a Crown corporation? The first conclusion is that the performance of the Post Office as a government department was poor, much worse than private sector standards, but also much worse than postal services in the United States and other developed countries. It is not clear why the Post Office had such problems. It has been suggested that one source of problems was a post-World War II decision to hire a lot of ex-military personnel into management positions in the Post Office, creating a rigid and inflexible bureaucracy that led to poor labour relations. The transition to Crown corporation status has clearly caused considerable improvement. Productivity has risen, the net cost to the taxpayers has fallen dramatically, labour relations are somewhat improved, and strike activity has been reduced. While there is still room for improvement in the Post Office, the transition to the corporate form would have to be regarded as a success.

16.3.4 Via Rail

Via Rail was established in 1977 to take over passenger service from CN Rail (a Crown corporation) and CP Rail (a private firm). Via pays rent to CN and CP for the use of stations, tracks, and locomotives. It maintains its own fleet of passenger cars; assumes direct responsibility for marketing, ticketing, and onboard services; and owns some of its own stations. Via Rail was created because of concern over mounting subsidies to passenger service. Both CN Rail and CP Rail were reluctant to cross-subsidize passenger service from the profits on freight, and the government hoped to avoid paying large direct subsidies. This hope has not been realized fully although progress has been made. Table 16.4 reports the financial performance of Via Rail.

Table 16.4 Via Rail Financial Statistics, 1980 to 1998 ($ millions)

Year	Operating Cost	Operating Revenue	Loss	Subsidy	Subsidy (2000 dollars)
1980	359	141	218	320	680
1981	581	168	413	412	786
1982	602	179	423	432	743
1983	642	194	448	451	733
1984	595	201	394	397	619
1985	725	205	520	524	784
1986	689	209	480	462	665
1987	696	263	433	452	623
1988	790	279	511	509	674
1989	775	249	526	471	593
1990	540	143	397	441	533
1991	541	150	374	393	449
1992	532	156	376	389	439
1993	547	164	383	348	384
1994	509	176	333	318	344
1995	418	174	243	255	271
1996	392	184	208	224	236
1997	393	190	202	212	219
1998	461	200	261	178	182
1999	440	220	220	170	172

Source: Economic Council of Canada (1986), various Via Rail Annual Reports.

In 1998, Via Rail carried 3.85 million passengers. This implies a subsidy of roughly $47 per passenger trip. The average fare was about $48 per passenger trip. In other words, an average 1998 trip cost about $95, of which the passenger paid only half. Perhaps the most extreme example of subsidization occurred on the Hearst-Nakina run in Northern Ontario in 1984. This route was travelled by 384 passengers in 1984, and the subsidy per passenger trip was $2,125[4] (or over $3,000 in 2000 dollars). It would have been cheaper to supply chauffeur-driven limousines. The share of total operating costs covered by operating revenues even in 1999 was an alarmingly low 50%. However, in fairness to Via Rail, it should be noted that this represents substantial improvement, since the 1999 subsidy was down (in real terms) to less than 25% of its 1981 peak.

It is hard to see a normative reason why rail transport should be so heavily subsidized. It is a private good in competition with air transport, bus transport, and private cars. Some people argue that the road and highway system is subsidized and that rail should be comparably subsidized to avoid distorting the system toward motor vehicles. It is also argued that negative externalities associated with motor vehicle transport might justify a subsidy to rail transport. However, the empirical analysis that would support these assertions has not been done, and most economists remain highly sceptical about the value of passenger rail subsidies.

The principal reason for the poor performance of Via Rail is interest group activity. Whenever Via Rail tries to rationalize its services by dropping uneconomic routes, a public outcry led by local politicians in the affected area follows. The federal government usually reacts by ordering Via to maintain service. Most politicians would prefer to spend several hundred million dollars (which most voters will never even hear about) rather than be accused on the evening news of callously closing down local railway stations.

The unfortunate fact is that passenger rail service is no longer economic in most parts of the country. For most purposes, rail travel is inferior to air travel, bus travel, and travel by private car on a cost per mile basis. In general, travel by rail consumes more resources than travel by air or bus for the same distance. If passengers were charged the full cost of rail transport, they would stop using it. This would, incidentally, greatly boost air and bus service demand and air and bus service levels for many small towns. The main exception is the Quebec-Windsor corridor, where the high density of rail traffic might make full cost service feasible at competitive prices. If left to the private sector, passenger rail service in most parts of the country would have disappeared. This is the kind of allocational decision that the private sector is good at. The principal effect of government intervention in this case has been to use taxpayers' money for the benefit of the small group of people who use rail passenger service frequently.

16.3.5 Caisse de dépôt

One very interesting public enterprise is the Caisse de dépôt of Quebec. The Caisse was established in 1965 primarily to administer the contributions to the Quebec Pension Plan. The Caisse also took on the management of several other Quebec pension plans. The Caisse was given the joint mandate of maximizing returns, subject to risk considerations, and of supporting the economic development of Quebec. Since 1965, pension funds in general have grown very substantially, and the Caisse has grown rather more than anticipated, and, as reported in Table 16.3, is now a very large financial firm.

In managing its assets, the Caisse invests in a variety of securities, including shares of private sector firms. However, if the Caisse buys a significant portion of the stock of any firm, it automatically (by definition) turns that firm into a mixed enterprise, and brings it, in principle, under the partial control of the Quebec legislature. As it has grown, the Caisse has, as a byproduct, extended the range of government control into the private sector. Some people view this as a cause for concern. The Economic Council of Canada (1986) recommended that the Caisse be restricted to at most a 10% share in the voting stock of any private sector company.

It should be pointed out that the government of Quebec has not used its indirect control of firms through the Caisse to influence their actions. The Caisse, as with most pension funds, is generally a passive investor.

16.3.6 Cape Breton Development Corporation and Sydney Steel Corporation

In 1967, the Dominion Steel and Coal Corporation (DOSCO), already the recipient of substantial subsidies on the order of $3,000 per employee (about $17,000 per employee in 1995 dollars), stood in imminent danger of bankruptcy. Because DOSCO was the main primary employer in Cape Breton, its bankruptcy was perceived as a local crisis, and both federal and provincial governments felt it necessary to take action. The action taken was to create Crown corporations. The federal government created the Cape Breton Development Corporation (DEVCO) to take over DOSCO's coal operations, and the Nova Scotia government created a provincial Crown corporation, the Nova Scotia Steel Corporation (SYSCO), to take over the steel operation.

The financial performance of DEVCO is reported in Table 16.5.

TABLE 16.5 Performance of DEVCO, 1970 to 1999

Year	Employees	Sales ($ millions)	Subsidy ($millions)	Subsidy (2000 $millions)
1970	4,441	26.1	35.0	159
1975	3,752	31.5	51.2	163
1980	4,270	115.1	99.2	185
1985	3,470	165.1	96.9	142
1986	3,580	183.2	110.6	155
1987	3,651	184.6	153.3	207
1988	3,410	206.4	90.8	117
1989	3,336	195.2	28.0	34
1990	2,983	238.4	14.9	17
1991	2,852	216.3	31.9	35
1992	2,554	253.9	31.0	34
1993	2,335	266.0	31.0	33
1994	2,279	231.8	38.5	41
1995	2203	235.4	25.4	27.2
1996	2091	188.4	unknown	unknown
1997	1894	167.3	43.5	45.1
1998	1738	167.9	22.1	22.7
1999	1635	98.9	40.6	41.0

Source: Economic Council of Canada (1986); various DEVCO Annual Reports.

The mission of DEVCO is officially described as one of developing the local economy. In fact, its mission is simply employment protection. As early as 1957, a Royal Commission on Coal had concluded that coal mining in Cape Breton was not economic, and suggested that the government should assist people seeking to relocate in other areas, but not try to support the industry in Cape Breton. Hundreds of millions of dollars later, DEVCO is still a substantial net burden on taxpayers, and during some periods an alarmingly high one. The subsidy was, for example, about $42,000 per job in 1987—more than the employees got paid! It would have been cheaper to pay the workers to do nothing. In effect, DEVCO had negative value added in 1987, as it has over much of its life.

If the price of energy rises sharply again, as it will sooner or later, mining coal in Cape Breton could become profitable. Instead of waiting until the coal can be sold at a profit, however, the government chose to deplete this exhaustible resource in order to sell it off at a loss.

Devco continued to suffer poor performance in the late 1990s. In 1999 the Government of Canada announced plans to close part of Devco and sell off the rest, accompanied by a large additional subsidy to compensate workers and for "regional development."

16.4 Regulation, Crown Corporations, or Direct Government?

So far in this chapter we have described some of the more important public enterprises in Canada, and we have pointed out that the main normative rationale for Crown corporations should be based on market failure considerations. However, direct government ownership and regulation of the private sector are alternative policy tools that can be used to respond to the same market failure that might justify public enterprise. The natural question that arises is: having identified a role for government intervention, should that role be assigned to a government department, to a Crown corporation, or to a regulatory authority?

Unfortunately, although much has been written on this subject, we lack a clear consensus on what the important normative considerations are. All three types of government action involve what are sometimes called "agency" problems: some responsibility for the public interest is delegated to a particular set of people whose actions cannot be easily monitored and who have considerable discretionary power. Since the self-interest of such people may conflict with the public interest, we cannot always be confident that the public interest will be served.

The theory of bureaucracy described in Chapter 5 is an example of the agency or delegation problems that can arise if tasks are allocated to a department of government (i.e., to the bureaucracy). The capture hypothesis described in Chapter 14 is the agency problem that arises with regulation. Public enterprises have similar agency problems, in that the managers of public enterprise, and individual politicians, can be expected to use public enterprises partly as tools of their own interests.

16.4.1 Public Enterprise and Government Departments

A public enterprise has several advantages over a government department. One advantage is that the functions of the public enterprise are insulated to a greater extent from day-to-day political pressures. It was argued, for example, that this was an important reason for setting up Canada Post. When postal service was under the control of a cabinet minister, the principal objective of the minister was to survive the six months or one year in the portfolio without destroying his or her political career. In pursuit of this objective it was much easier to provide subsidies to the post office than to make difficult management decisions.

The creation of a Crown corporation, on the other hand, allows someone (the CEO) to be held accountable for its long-run performance. This gives the CEO and the senior management an incentive to make decisions that are difficult in the short run in the hope of getting long-run benefits. In addition, the government of the day is not held accountable at the political level for these decisions. A Crown corporation can take a tough line with its employees over some contract provisions, without the government being accused of being anti-labour. It can more easily cut back uneconomic areas of service, without being subject to the intensity of interest group lobbying that arises over department-level decisions in government.

A Crown corporation has more flexibility in the use of its workforce (and in its ability to hire and fire) because its workers are not part of the civil service. Workers in Crown corporations feel, for the most part, that they are part of the business community, rather than part of government. The question, of course, is whether these differences have any effect. As the experiences of VIA Rail, the CBC, and other high-profile Crown corporations suggest, the activities of Crown corporations do spill over into the political arena, and managers of Crown corporations are subject to at least some of the same pressures as civil servants to serve the short-term political interests of senior politicians.

16.4.2 Public Enterprise, Mixed Enterprise, and Private Sector Regulation

The choice between a public enterprise and regulation of a private firm, is, as has already been indicated, somewhat arbitrary, since these two

Table 16.6 Privatization of Federal Crown Corporations and Mixed
Enterprises, 1984 to 1999 (selected)

Company Privatized	Percent Sold	Transaction Date	Assets* ($ millions)
Northern Trans. Ltd.	100	1985	75
Canada Development Corp.	47	1985–87	6,324
de Havilland	100	1986	346
Pecheries Canada	100	1986	16
Canadian Arsenals	100	1986	126
Nanisivik Mines	18	1986	65
CN Route	100	1986	40
Canadair	100	1986	478
Northern Canada Power Commission (Yukon)	100	1987	269
Teleglobe Canada	100	1987	502
Fisheries Products Int.	63	1987	224
Varity Corp. Warrants	100	1987	N/A
CN Hotels	100	1988	136
Northern Canada Power Commission (NWT)	100	1988	143
Air Canada	100	1988–89	3,084
Northwestel	100	1988	152
Terra Nova Telecomm.	100	1988	112
CNCP Telecomm.	50	1988	352
Nordion	100	1991	N/A
Cameco	20	1991	97
Petro-Canada	20	1992	7,278
Westcoast Energy (37% owned by Petro-Canada)	37	1992	342
	37	1992	342
Telesat (54% owned)	54	1992	155
Petro-Canada	60	1995	7,864
Canadian National Railway	100	1995	7,624
Nav Canada	100	1996	1,574

* Assets as of previous year to privatization transaction

Sources: W.T. Stanbury (1994), annual reports, various years.

organizational forms are, to some extent, substitutes for one another. In the case of mixed enterprises, which are owned partly by government and partly by private investors, the distinction becomes blurred altogether. The presence of private shareholders should, in principle, impose additional discipline on a firm to make decisions on a business rather than political basis. But this may either enhance or impair the effectiveness of a corporation in pursuing a public policy objective.

16.5 Privatization

Just as deregulation has become an important part of policy debate, so has privatization, which refers to the practice of selling off public enterprises to the private sector. Table 16.6 provides a list of Canadian Crown corporations that have been privatized in recent years. Table 16.7 shows the major provincial privatizations.

Most of these firms have made an apparently successful transition to the private sector, although it is still too early, and generally rather difficult, to assess their performance from the public interest point of view.

In undertaking privatization, the main question to be asked is simply: "Is there currently a strong normative rationale for keeping the corporation in question in the public sector?" In cases where the rationale is based fundamentally on bridging gaps, regional development, employment protection, or simple nationalism, but cannot be linked to more fundamental market failures, it is likely that the corporation would serve the public interest better in the private sector.

16.6 Public Goods

Much of this book has been devoted to market failure caused by imperfect competition. In addition, some attention has been paid to informational market failure and to externalities. The other cause of market failure is public goods. Public goods are not the same thing as publicly provided goods, although public goods usually are publicly provided. Normally, provision of public goods is carried out by departments of government rather than by Crown corporations. A public good has the following two characteristics:

1. A public good is nonrival in consumption: even though one person consumes the good, others may consume it also.

TABLE 16.7: Major Provincial Privatizations, 1983 to 1999 (selected)

Company	Province	Percent Sold	Date
Pacific Western Airlines	Alberta	98	1983–84
Sugar Refinery	Quebec	100	1986
Saskatchewan Oil & Gas Corporation	Saskatchewan	100	1986–89
SOQUEM	Quebec	100	1986
Prince Albert Pulp Co.	Saskatchewan	100	1986
Donohue Inc.	Quebec	56	1986
Fisheries Products International	Newfoundland	26	1987
SOQUIP Alberta	Quebec	100	1987
Oil & Gas of Saskatchewan Power	Saskatchewan	100	1988
BC Hydro's Gas Division	B.C.	100	1988
BC Second Mortgage Program	B.C.	100	1989
Manitoba Forestry Resources	Manitoba	100	1989
Potash Corporation of Saskatchewan	Saskatchewan	100	1989
Alberta Government Telephones	Alberta	56	1989
Saskatchewan Oil (10 million shares)	Saskatchewan	60*	1989
Alberta Government Telephone	Alberta	98.5	1990
Novatel systems/cellular phones	Alberta	100	1992
Nova Scotia Power Corp.	Nova Scotia	100	1992
Toronto Sky Dome	Ontario	100	1994
SunCor	Ontario	25	1992
Syncrude Canada	Alberta	16.7	1993
Alberta Energy	Alberta	100	1994
Ven Cap Equities	Alberta	31	1995
Manitoba Telecom	Manitoba	100	1997

* Province's interest reduced from 25% to 10%.

Sources: W.T. Stanbury (1994), annual reports, various years.

2. A public good is nonexclusive: it is impossible (or at least very costly) to exclude anyone from consuming the good.

In Chapter 3, this definition was illustrated using the example of a lighthouse. The services of a lighthouse are not used up when one ship is warned by the light; other ships will simultaneously receive such warning. Therefore, a lighthouse is nonrival. In addition, it is impossible to prevent anyone from seeing the light from lighthouses (without turning the lighthouse off). If anyone is to benefit from the lighthouse, all will have access. A lighthouse is nonexclusive.

It is possible to imagine goods that are nonrival (up to a point), but from which people can be excluded. A painting is a good example. You may enjoy looking at a painting. Another person could simultaneously enjoy the painting (subject to limitations imposed by crowding). It is, however, relatively easy to exclude someone from seeing a painting, simply by putting the painting in a room to which admission is controlled. It is, on the other hand, hard to imagine a good painting that is nonexclusive but rival.[5]

Other public goods include national defence, public parks, police services, and the court system. Most public goods are provided directly by government. (Construction or maintenance of a public good might be contracted out, but the payments and managerial decisions are made directly by government.) Crown corporations and regulation of the private sector are not used for public goods.

The basic point to make about public goods is that they are a source of market failure. The problem is that, because a public good is nonexclusive, no one can be prevented from consuming it. Most consumers, therefore, would not pay, and no private firm could make money from providing the service, even if the service were very valuable.

The efficient outcome, as implied by the marginalist principle, is that a public good should be produced up to the point where the marginal social benefit equals the marginal social cost. Because a public good is nonrival, the marginal social benefit is equal to the sum of private marginal benefits. Equation 16.1 expresses this condition.

(16.1) $SMB = \Sigma PMB = SMC$ (efficiency condition for a public good)

The fact that it is hard for the private sector to provide public goods is manifested in the so-called free rider effect. Suppose that a private organization proposes to provide a public good (such as public noncommercial television), and asks for contributions. Many people might recognize that they would value such a service, but they also recognize that their own private benefit is small compared to the total cost of such an exercise. A contribution of $50 or $100 is not going to make much difference to the product delivered.

Furthermore, the consumer will be able to consume the good whether or not he or she provides a contribution. Many people intend to pay, of course, but just never get around to it. Each viewer has an incentive to be a free rider; to enjoy the product produced by the contributions of others. The Seattle station of the U.S. public broadcasting system (PBS) estimates that about 10% of its viewers contribute to the station, meaning that 90% are free riders. This contribution rate of 10% is considered relatively high by the standards of other PBS stations.

Even when public goods are provided by the public sector, it is hard to determine the right amount of the public good, because the government does not know the marginal benefit placed on the good by consumers. Getting people to reveal their preferences is difficult, and is fraught with various preference revelation problems, in that people have incentives to misrepresent their preferences.

If people think they will get something for free (i.e., that other people, or taxpayers at large, will pay for it), then, if they place any positive valuation on the good at all, they have an incentive to overstate their preference for it. Conversely, if people believe they will be asked to pay in proportion to their announced interest, they will have incentives to understate their preferences.

Many situations have elements of public good considerations. If, for example, a group of firms is trying to undertake generic advertising to increase overall demand for their product, each firm has an incentive to try to free ride on the contributions of others. This is probably why generic advertising is rare.

16.7 Bibliographic Notes

A useful survey of Crown corporations in Canada is Economic Council of Canada (1986). Frequently cited collections of articles on Crown corporations are Pritchard (1983), Tupper and Doern (1981), and Kierans and Stanbury (1985). A very interesting analysis of the effect of government ownership using data generated by the takeover of Domtar by the Caisse in 1981 is Boardman, Freedman, and Eckel (1986). A valuable discussion of Canadian bailouts of corporations is Trebilcock (1986). A discussion of privatization is contained in Walker (1988).

Notes

1. Peter Foster, "Hopper's Folly," *The Globe and Mail Report on Business*, August 1991.

2. Drew Fagan, "Minister says Petrocan shares unlikely to be sold this year," *The Globe and Mail*, October 20, 1990, p. A1.

3. The following discussion is based in part on the *Report of the Review Committee on the Mandate and Productivity of Canada Post Corporation* (1985) (report commissioned by the Minister of Consumer and Corporate Affairs) (Ottawa: Supply and Services Canada).

4. Dunnery Best, "Little progress being made on solving Via's problems," *Financial Post*, May 24, 1986.

5. For this reason, some people define a public good simply as a good that is nonexclusive, arguing that this condition implies or subsumes nonrivalry.

On-line Sources

For information about specific Canadian public firms, Sedar is a good place to start: *http://www.sedar.com/homepage.htm*

For details about specific American public firms, Edgar is a good place to start: *http://www.sec.gov/edgarhp.htm*

17
Macroeconomic Policy

17.1 The Basic Principles of Macroeconomic Stabilization

This chapter focuses on one of the basic normative rationales for government intervention discussed in Chapter 3: macroeconomic stabilization. This is a very substantial topic in itself, about which many books have been written. Macroeconomic stabilization policies are very important in conditioning the general environment in which business firms operate. Interest rates, exchange rates, inflation rates, liquidity conditions, unemployment rates, the public debt, and other aspects of the macroeconomic environment are strongly affected, if not controlled, by macroeconomic stabilization policy. Such policies do, in addition, bear on other areas of policy.

17.1.1 Objectives of Macroeconomic Policy

The basic objective of macroeconomic policy is to stabilize the pace of economic activity and encourage economic growth. Before the development of active macroeconomic policy, market economies were subject to violent and damaging swings in overall activity, the most dramatic of which was the Great Depression of the 1930s. Because of this stabilization objective, the terms "stabilization policy" and "macroeconomic stabilization policy" are frequently used as synonyms for macroeconomic policy.

Macroeconomic policy seeks to stabilize the rate of unemployment, and, in addition, policy authorities would also like to keep it low. Thus, a stable unemployment rate of 6% would be viewed as better than a stable unemployment rate of 12%. Another major focus of macroeconomic policy is inflation. As with unemployment, policy authorities would like to keep inflation rates stable, and, beyond mere stabilization, would like to keep them low. In fact, many observers view the appropriate target not as stabilization of *inflation*, but as stabilization of the *price level*, which would imply an inflation rate of zero! (Canada last achieved zero inflation rates in the first part of the 1950s, although the inflation rate in 1999 was, at 2.0%, not far from zero.)

The record of macroeconomic stablization policy has a major impact on the long-run growth path of the economy. One of the subtleties of macroeconomic policy is that it is often tempting to take actions that might increase the temporary growth rate of the economy and therefore redress short-run cyclical problems, even though such policies might be damaging to future growth. It is important for macroeconomic policy authorities to simultaneously consider the short-run (cyclical) and the long-run (growth) effects of their policy decisions.

Long-run economic growth is the most important measure of change in an economy's performance. A few decades of rapid economic growth can have a dramatic effect on human welfare, raising a typical person from near subsistence to comparative comfort. Thus, for example, the general quality of life in economies such as Singapore, Taiwan, Hong Kong, and China has been completely transformed in the past 30 years. Even in Canada, despite poor per capita growth in the first half of the 1990s, the average Canadian was still considerably better off in the year 2000 than in 1960. In 2000, real living standards in Canada were at, an all-time high, albeit only slightly higher than a decade earlier.

17.1.2 Monetary Policy and Fiscal Policy

The basic tools of macroeconomic policy are monetary policy and fiscal policy. Monetary policy refers to control over the supply of money, or, more generally, over the general liquidity of asset markets. When we refer to the liquidity of a particular asset, we are referring to how easily it can be converted into cash or some other asset. For example, cash itself is completely liquid, government bonds are highly liquid, real estate is less liquid, and machines in place in a factory are very illiquid. At the macro level, market liquidity refers to how easily cred-it can be obtained and to the ease with which assets can be exchanged for other assets.

It is, in most countries, the responsibility of a central bank to con-trol market liquidity. Central banks are part of the public sector, although senior officers have a certain amount of independence from the elected government of the day. In Canada, the central bank is the Bank of Canada. In the United States, the central bank is the U.S. Fed-eral Reserve System, usually called the Fed. Aside from the Fed, the other central banks that have the most influence on the world mone-tary system are the German central bank (the Bundesbank), the Japan-ese central bank (the Bank of Japan), and the British central bank (the Bank of England).

A central bank acts a banker to other financial institutions. Thus, other financial institutions, such as commercial banks, can have accounts with the central bank and can make deposits in those accounts. Com-mercial banks can also borrow money from central banks. There are sev-eral ways that a central bank can increase liquidity in the economy. One very direct method is by literally printing money. It can then give or loan the printed money to the government or to a client financial institution. An equivalent but more sophisticated alternative is for the central bank to create a deposit. If the central bank simply credits an account held by a commercial bank with an extra $1,000, it has just created $1,000. Sim-ilarly, a central bank can create money by writing a cheque drawn on a deposit it creates for itself. If the Bank of Canada writes a cheque, drawn on itself, for $1,000 and gives it to you, it has just created $1,000. The main recipient of central bank largesse is usually the federal government, which is able to use the central bank's power to create money as a way of (partially) financing government deficits.

When the Bank of Canada creates money, it increases the amount of money in the economy that can be loaned or used to buy other assets. This is why increasing the money supply causes market liquid-ity to increase. Aside from creating money directly, a central bank can also influence market liquidity by undertaking so-called open market operations, which involve the buying and selling of bonds on ordinary markets. Thus, for example, if the Bank of Canada purchases an out-standing government bond, it takes a low liquidity asset (a bond) out of the hands of the private sector, and replaces it with a high liquidity asset (money in the form of a cheque drawn on the Bank of Canada). This increases total liquidity in the system.

In addition, central banks provide loans to banks at a rate of interest known as the bank rate. Changing the bank rate also affects the amount of liquidity in the economy. For example, if the Bank of Canada lowers the bank rate, then commercial banks will be more likely to borrow money from the Bank of Canada and use this as a basis for loaning money to their clients, raising total liquidity in the system. The bank rate also acts as a signal of the Bank of Canada's intentions, and this signalling effect alone can often affect market liquidity.

The money supply is not a clearly defined concept. In fact, there are many different measures of the money supply. The monetary base is defined as the liabilities of the Bank of Canada, which consist mainly of currency and deposits in the Bank of Canada. This monetary base provides the foundation for a broader concept of money that is created through the banking system according to the money multiplier process. If, for example, the government is credited with an account in the Bank of Canada, and writes a cheque on that account, the recipient of that cheque will probably deposit it in a bank. The bank then loans out most of that money to someone else, keeping only a small fraction of the deposit in the form of reserves.

The recipient of the bank loan will then deposit that money in another bank. Most of this money is lent out again, except for reserves, and so on. At each step, liquidity is created. When the process ends, total deposits in commercial banks will have risen by many times the initial increase in the monetary base. The sum of chequing account deposits in banks plus currency outside banks is referred to as M1. If savings accounts are added in, we have M2. There are many more increasingly broad measures of the money supply.

The important macroeconomic variable is market liquidity, but it is far from clear exactly how market liquidity should be measured. The amount of bank deposits available to be loaned is very relevant, but so are deposits in other (i.e., nonbank) financial institutions, credit card lines of credit, and even short-term bonds. However, not all these financial instruments are of equal liquidity, so one cannot simply add them up. Whatever liquidity is, however, it is influenced by the monetary base, which is under the direct control of the Bank of Canada. If the monetary base rises, liquidity tends to increase; if the monetary base falls, liquidity tends to decrease.

The Bank of Canada has its impact by affecting the supply of liquidity. In addition, liquidity conditions are influenced by the demand for liquidity. We occasionally have situations when demand for new loans falls sharply and banks have trouble finding customers to take on loans. In such situations we say that financial markets are highly liquid. The increase in net liquidity arises, in this case, from a decline in demand rather than an increase in supply.

Fiscal policy refers to aggregate government expenditures, aggregate taxes, aggregate borrowing, and the net level of aggregate demand for good and services that the government sector contributes to overall economic activity. One important fiscal indicator is simply the net deficit (or surplus) position of the government. For many purposes we focus on the deficit position of all governments combined: federal, provincial, and local, although we might also consider just some subcomponent, such as the federal deficit. Traditionally, provincial and local budget deficits have been small compared to the federal budget, but they grew rapidly in the early 1990s, led by alarmingly high deficits in the Province of Ontario. In 1994 and 1995, however, provincial budget deficits fell sharply, and several provinces had nearly erased their budget deficits as of the 1995-96 fiscal year. The Province of Ontario also elected a new government in 1995 that reduced the provincial budget significantly. By the turn of the century, the provincial budgets were in reasonable balance overall, with British Columbia being the one province with notably poor budgetary performance over the late 1990s.

If the federal government has a deficit, it has two alternatives: it can borrow from the public (domestic or international), or it can pay its expenses by having the Bank of Canada create money.[1] Provincial and local governments can only borrow. Federal government expenditure is equal to taxes plus net borrowing plus net monetary base creation, and provincial government expenditure is simply equal to revenues plus net borrowing.

The overall budget deficit is not the only important fiscal indicator. Economists frequently subdivide the overall deficit into two components: a structural deficit and a cyclical deficit. The cyclical deficit is that component of the deficit that is attributable to the economy being in a cyclical downturn. The structural deficit is therefore the component that would remain even if the economy were performing at some neutral or reference level. The fact that there is a cyclical deficit reflects what are sometimes referred to as automatic stabilizers, which are automatic changes in the tax-expenditure balance that occur as the cycle proceeds. For example, when the economy moves into a down-turn and unemployment rises, income tax revenues will tend to fall and expenditures on unemployment insurance will tend to rise, caus-ing the cyclical and overall deficits to rise also. Thus, the deficit will change over the cycle even without explicit government action.

17.1.3 Controlling Interest Rates

Interest rates are simply the cost of money. Consider the following exam-ple. Ms. A wants to buy a $300,000 townhouse, but does not have enough money herself to buy the house. She does have $200,000 on hand, but would need to borrow (i.e., obtain a mortgage) for the additional $100,000. Suppose the interest rate that she could obtain on a one-year mortgage was 10%. She would then need to pay $10,000 in interest dur-ing the first year of the mortgage. Now suppose that interest rates sud-denly rise and it turns out that the mortgage rate faced by Ms. A is 20%. In this case she would need to pay roughly $20,000 in interest during the first year of the mortgage. It is quite possible that Ms. A would find it fea-sible to pay $10,000 in first year interest but not $20,000. She would then decide not to take out the loan and defer her housing purchase. In effect, the interest rate is the cost or price of the loan, and if this price rises too high people will demand fewer loans (i.e., less money).

Interest rates may be affected by both monetary policy and fiscal policy. If the Bank of Canada creates extra money, it puts downward pressure on the cost of money: interest rates tend to fall. Thus, expan-sionary monetary policy puts downward pressure on interest rates and contractionary monetary policy puts upward pressure on interest rates. If the government increases its deficit, and does not cover the deficit with money supply creation, it must borrow money. This increases the demand for loans and puts upward pressure on the interest rate, unless increased borrowing from outside the country fully offsets this increased demand for loans. Holding monetary policy constant, and assuming that foreign borrowing does adjust to fully offset the increased or decreased demand for loans in Canada, then decreasing deficits (or increasing surpluses) tend to make interest rates fall, and increasing deficits tend to make interest rates rise.

In public policy discussions, people often tend to assume that low interest rates are good and high interest rates are bad, largely because low interest rates stimulate economic activity. It is also important to recognize, however, that changes in interest rates have a significant redistributive effect, and that some people are made worse off by interest reductions. Specifically, people who receive much of their income from interest earned on investments will have lower incomes if interest rates fall. (More precisely, their real interest income will fall if the real interest rate, net of inflation, falls.) The largest category of people with interest incomes is retired people, most of whom depend heavily either on their own investments, or on investments made on their behalf in pension funds.

Public policy discussions also sometimes exaggerate the extent of control that the Bank of Canada has over the state of liquidity and over interest rates. The Bank of Canada is a very important actor in the system, but liquidity conditions and interest rates are also affected by the actions and decisions of commercial banks, other financial institutions, investors, savers, and various foreign participants in financial markets, including foreign investors and foreign central banks. Suppose, for example, that the Bank of Canada wants some broad measure of money to increase. It can undertake an expansion of the monetary base, but unless commercial banks are willing to use that expansion as a basis for increasing loans, then broader aggregates will not be much affected. Similarly, the Bank of Canada cannot just choose an appropriate interest rate. It can usually move interest rates up or down from current levels, but it is constrained in its influence by all the other forces in the monetary system.

17.1.4 Aggregate Economic Activity and Keynesian Policy

In order to stabilize economic activity, the government must stimulate activity when the economy is operating too far below capacity and restrain activity when the economy gets overheated. As first emphasized by Keynes (1936), stimulating the economy requires increasing aggregate demand, which is the total demand for goods and services. Aggregate demand has four main components: consumer demand, investment demand, net exports, and government demand.

Increasing government spending tends to increase the government's demand for goods and services directly, but if the increased spending is financed by taxes, then consumers or business firms have less to spend. If taxes are held fixed, and government spending rises, then the government deficit rises and aggregate demand unambiguously increases. Consequently, net increases in aggregate demand are associated with increases in the deficit. Deficits therefore represent expansionary fiscal policy, and surpluses represent contractionary fiscal policy.

Investment demand is responsive to interest rates. Investment demand refers to the demand for investment goods: new buildings, equipment, etc. If a business has cash on hand, it can loan out the money, earning the going interest rate, rather than undertaking new real investments. In this case the opportunity cost of new investment projects is the interest rate. Most businesses must borrow to undertake new projects, in which case the interest rate is a direct out-of-pocket cost associated with investment. In either case, if interest rates are high, the cost of investment is higher, and less real investment will be undertaken than if interest rates were lower. The reasoning is very similar to that presented in Section 17.1.3, where we considered Ms. A's decision of whether to invest in buying a house. Higher interest rates lead to lower investment demand and lower aggregate demand.

Since both monetary policy and fiscal policy may influence interest rates, this is a second channel for aggregate demand to be affected by policy. (The first was direct government spending.) In particular, expansionary monetary policy puts downward pressure on interest rates, which tends to increase investment, which in turn increases aggregate demand and tends to increase economic activity. Contractionary monetary policy has the reverse effects.

Expansionary fiscal policy creates a complication, for while its direct effect on government demand is expansionary, it also tends to put upward pressure on interest rates. This is contractionary, because investment tends to fall. In effect, government spending tends to crowd out private investment. This is referred to as the crowding out effect. If there is slack in the economy, the crowding out effect does not fully offset the expansionary effect of increased deficits, and so-called expansionary fiscal policy is indeed expansionary. If however, the economy is operating at capacity already, increased government spending must come at the expense of less spending elsewhere—usually by crowding out private investment.

Equation 17.1 summarizes this reasoning concerning the determination of aggregate demand.

$$AD = C + I(r(M,G)) + G + NX \qquad (17.1)$$

AD stands for aggregate demand, C for consumption demand, I for investment demand, r for the interest rate, M for the money supply, G for government spending, and *NX* for net exports. As indicated, investment demand depends on both *M* (monetary policy) and *G* (fiscal policy).

If the economy is operating at a low level, then it can be heated up by an expansionary monetary policy and/or an expansionary fiscal policy. Conversely, if the economy is expanding too quickly, it can be restrained with contractionary fiscal policy or contractionary monetary policy. This approach to policy was first systematically analyzed by Keynes (1936), and is therefore referred to as Keynesian policy. This view of policy has considerable insight, but there are complications, as the following sections will show.

17.2 Macroeconomic Policy in an Open Economy

17.2.1 Effects of Exchange Rate Changes

So far we have discussed macroeconomic policy without much discussion of the international environment. In fact, the international environment is very important for the conduct of macroeconomic policy. The starting point for discussing international effects is the exchange rate. Recall from Chapter 8 that the exchange rate is the rate at which one currency can be exchanged for another. Thus, if one Canadian dollar can be exchanged for 70 cents of U.S. currency, then the exchange rate is 0.70. If the value of the Canadian dollar were to rise to 75 cents per U.S. dollar, this would be an appreciation. A decline in value, correspondingly, is a depreciation. There is an exchange rate between every pair of currencies.

The exchange rate is a very important variable to an exporter. If the Canadian dollar appreciates relative to the U.S. dollar, a Canadian producer who is selling in the United States and earning U.S. dollars suddenly finds that the Canadian dollar value of those U.S. earnings has fallen. Typically, the producer's costs are primarily denominated in Canadian dollars. With stable Canadian dollar costs and falling Canadian dollar revenues, the producer's profit margin will fall and perhaps turn negative. The producer may raise U.S. dollar prices so as to restore some of the lost Canadian dollar value of the exports, but Americans would then purchase fewer goods, reducing the overall quantity of exports from Canada. Alternatively, the producer might simply cut back or even abandon exports to the United States. From the point of view of an American importer who buy goods denominated in Canadian dollars and brings them to the United States, an appreciation of the Canadian dollar implies that the effective U.S. dollar price of those goods has risen. This importer will also tend to reduce the quantity and value of Canadian goods purchased. Therefore, the Canadian dollar value of export earnings and the real volume of exports will both tend to fall as appreciation occurs.

In addition, as American goods become cheaper to Canadians through appreciation of the Canadian dollar, Canadians will buy more of them. Thus imports from the U.S. rise. When we consider the macroeconomic or aggregate effects of these individual incentives, we realize that the net export term in Equation 17.1 will tend to decline following this appreciation. Therefore, aggregate demand for Canadian produced goods tends to fall, which is contractionary. Thus, exchange rate appreciation is a contractionary macroeconomic force, whereas depreciation is expansionary.

The exchange rate, especially the Canada-U.S. exchange rate, is an important macroeconomic variable for Canada. If policy authorities in Canada could put downward pressure on the Canadian dollar, this would tend to stimulate economic activity. However, a depreciating currency also has a cost. A country that lowers its exchange rate is just lowering the price at which it sells its goods and is therefore lowering the return to the underlying factors of production that produce those goods. In effect, a depreciation is like a wage cut. As Canadians, we can generate more demand for our services in the international marketplace if we collectively take a wage cut. Thus, if depreciation occurs, we find that the price of foreign goods rises relative to our incomes. Even domestic prices may rise as foreigners bid for our domestically produced goods. Domestic real estate looks like an increasing bargain to foreign investors, and domestic residents may find it harder to buy homes as local currency prices of domestic real estate are bid up, etc. The wage cut makes us work harder to achieve a given consumption bundle. If we do not have enough work (i.e., if the economy has high unemployment and idle capacity) then a wage cut through depreciation may be a good response. However, being in a position where such wage cuts are needed is a symptom that the economy has not been performing well.

Canada has a flexible exchange rate. It is not targeted to any particular value in terms of another currency but can move in whatever direction international forces push it. Most countries have flexible exchange rates, although some countries peg their currencies to major international currencies (usually the U.S. dollar). For example, Hong Kong pegs its currency to the U.S. dollar. This is referred to as a fixed exchange rate system. One important and interesting development has occurred recently in the European Union (EU). Prior to 1999, the countries of the EU sought to keep currencies in close alignment with one another. This was not a pure fixed exchange rate system but it was close. As of January 1, 1999, eleven of the fifteen members of the EU adopted a new common currency. This new currency unit is called the "Euro" and it was introduced with a value similar to the U.S. dollar. The underlying currencies continued to exist, with a strict fixed relationship to the Euro. For example, there are 6.56 French francs to the Euro and 1.96 German marks to the Euro. Initially, Euro coins and physical currency were not introduced, but they are scheduled to be introduced on January 1, 2002. The four members of the EU who did not join the currency union were the United Kingdom, Sweden, Greece, and Denmark. These countries may join subsequently, and EU itself may expand in the future. Shifting to a common currency is really one step further than having a fixed exchange rate.

17.2.2 Determinants of Exchange Rates

We have established that exchange rates are important macroeconomic variables, but how are they determined? And how can domestic policy authorities influence exchange rates? The answers to these questions are based on the idea that an exchange rate is simply a price. A currency is like any other asset such as a bond, a stock, or a piece of machinery. Its price is therefore determined by supply and demand. Canada's exchange rates vis-à-vis U.S. dollars, Japanese yen, the Euro, etc. are determined in international currency markets. If fewer people seek to buy Canadian dollars with Japanese yen, then demand for Canadian dollars in the yen-dollar market will fall and the Canadian dollar will tend to depreciate relative to the Japanese yen.

This pushes our question a step further back. We now know that exchange rates are determined by supply and demand in currency markets, but how are these supplies and demands determined? One source of demand for Canadian dollars in international currency markets arises from foreign consumers who want to buy Canadian goods and services. If a Japanese consumer holding yen wants to purchase Canadian-made furniture, somewhere along the line those Japanese yen must be exchanged for the Canadian dollars that are used to pay the furniture makers. Even more obviously, if Japanese tourists want to take vacations in Canada, they will need to buy (or will demand) Canadian dollars with their Japanese yen. These transactions contribute to the demand for Canadian dollars in the dollar-yen market.

Conversely, if Canadians wish to buy Japanese goods, or take holidays in Japan, they will need to sell some of their Canadian dollars to obtain Japanese yen. This contributes to the supply of Canadian dollars in the franc-dollar market. Thus, part of the supply and demand for Canadian dollars arises from trade in goods and services.

However, only a small part of short-run fluctuations in exchange rates can be linked to changes in trade flows. A more important source of short-run variation in supply and demand for currencies comes from investment activities. For example, suppose that a Japanese investor wishes to purchase a Government of Canada bond denominated in Canadian dollars. That investor must exchange Japanese yen for Canadian dollars before buying the bond. Investment demand of this type is an important part of the demand for Canadian dollars. Thus, the demand for Canadian dollars is determined in large part by the desire of foreign investors to make investments in Canadian investment instruments.

But what would make an investor want to purchase Canadian bonds? The return on holding a bond is the interest rate. If the interest rate is attractive, then the foreign investor will be more inclined to purchase the bond and will therefore be more inclined to demand Canadian dollars on international currency markets. This creates an important link between exchange rates and interest rates. When Canadian interest rates rise, this makes Canadian bonds and other debt instruments more attractive. This in turn makes investors want to buy Canadian dollars so as to invest in these instruments. As these investors enter currency markets demanding Canadian dollars, they put upward pressure on Canadian exchange rates.

We can now infer one method by which Canadian policy authorities can influence the exchange rate. Specifically, by putting upward pressure on domestic interest rates through contractions in liquidity, it is possible for the Bank of Canada to put upward pressure on the exchange rate.

This interest and exchange rate mechanism strengthens the contractionary effect of tight monetary policy. Not only does the associated increase in interest rates tend to reduce domestic investment in

Equation 17.1; in addition, the exchange rate tends to appreciate, putting downward pressure on net exports. Thus, in the presence of flexible exchange rates, and provided international investment flows are mobile across countries, the international environment tends to strengthen the effect of monetary policy. Developing a formal theory of this mechanism was one of the contributions for which Canadian Robert Mundell received the 1999 Nobel Prize in Economics.

So far we have indentified two sources of supply and demand in currency markets. One source is the net effect of trade in goods and services; the other is the net effect of private investment flows. There is one other major source of demand and supply in currency markets: direct purchases and sales of currencies by governments. The vast majority of these official international reserves are held in the form of U.S. dollars.

17.2.3 Fiscal Policy in an Open Economy

So far we have argued that the effect of international openness is to increase the influence of monetary policy on macroeconomic activity, and to introduce a new instrument, direct currency transactions, as a tool of macro policy. What about the effect of fiscal policy. If international investment flows are highly mobile and exchange rates are flexible, we would expect the impact of fiscal policy to be weakened by open economy considerations. To see this, assume that the government undertakes a pure fiscal expansion. That is, it increases government expenditures (as represented by G in Equation 17.1), using additional borrowing to finance the extra expenditures. As the government borrows money, it puts upward pressure on the interest rate. However, as interest rates rise, foreign investment flows in, attracted by these interest rates. Foreign investors must obtain Canadian dollars, so they enter currency markets, demanding Canadian dollars, and putting upward pressure on the Canadian exchange rate. The rise in Canadian exchange rates in turn tends to reduce the net export component of Equation 17.1. This contractionary effect tends to offset the expansionary effect of the increase in government spending. Thus, fiscal policy loses some effectiveness in an open economy with flexible exchange rates and capital (i.e., investment) mobility.

We might note in passing that if there is a very elastic supply of foreign investment (i.e., if large investment flows will be induced by even small interest rate increases), then increased goverment borrowing will have little effect on interest rates. It is as if the government simply borrows directly from foreigners without disturbing domestic financial markets. Fiscal policy still loses its effectiveness in this case, because the highly responsive capital inflows put strong pressures on the exchange rate.

17.3 Inflation

17.3.1 Meaning of Inflation

Inflation is the general rate of price increase. If all prices rise at 10% per year, then the inflation rate is 10% per year. High and variable levels of inflation can be very damaging. In the first place, high inflation levels seem to be psychologically unsettling; most people simply do not like high inflation. In addition, high and variable inflation makes it more difficult for people to make good consumer decisions, since information about prices gets out of date rapidly. When they buy something they have to spend more time and effort searching the market to obtain price information than they otherwise would. In addition, for reasons that are not yet fully understood, high inflation rates seem to interfere with the operation of financial markets. For example, when inflation rates in North America were in double digits during the 1970s (recall Table 7.4), long-term bond markets stopped operating.

We have discussed the inflation rate as though it were easy to observe. In fact, measuring the aggregate level of price change is not easy. In Canada, the principle measure of aggregate inflation is the Consumer Price Index (CPI) as calculated by Statistics Canada. Statistics Canada selects a representative bundle of consumer goods—food items, clothing items, transportation items, etc. The prices of these items are then sampled over time in various locations in Canada. If all individual prices rise by 10% over a given year, then the CPI would also rise by that amount too, indicating 10% inflation.

The CPI slightly overstates increases in the cost of living (and therefore slightly overstates inflation). One important reason is that it does not fully adjust for changes in product quality or for the introduction of new goods. Thus, for example, it does not fully capture the idea that a personal computer that costs $2,000 in 1999 is a much better product than a personal computer that cost $2,000 in 1990. Second, the CPI also does not fully adjust for the fact that consumers change their consumption habits as relative prices change. Statistics Canada is always looking for ways to improve its procedures, and does make a reasonable but conservative attempt to deal with both of these effects. It is generally conceded that the upward bias still exists, but it is small. For the purposes of this textbook, we take the CPI as the appropriate measure of inflation.

17.3.2 The Fisher Effect

Inflation diminishes the value of money. If inflation is 10% per year, and Ms. Prudent has $100 under her mattress, then by the end of the year, the value of that money has declined by about 10%. More to the point, if she loans $100 to someone else at the beginning of the year, and is paid back $100 at the end of the year, she will have lost 10% of the value of that money. It can, at the end of the year, purchase only 90% of what it could at the beginning. In order to protect the value of the money, Ms. Prudent would have to earn an interest rate of at least 10%. If the interest rate is exactly 10%, she is no further ahead at the end of the year than at the beginning. Her real rate of return or real interest rate is zero.

In general, the real interest rate is equal to the nominal or actual interest rate minus the expected rate of inflation. If expected inflation suddenly rises, then, to keep real interest rates constant, nominal interest rates must rise by the amount of the increase in the expected inflation rate. This is referred to as the Fisher Effect.

$$i = r + E(\text{infl}) \qquad (17.2)$$

Equation 17.2 is the Fisher equation, which expresses the Fisher Effect in algebraic form. Variable i is the nominal interest rate, r is the real interest rate, and $E(\text{infl})$ is the expected rate of inflation.

Focusing on the Fisher equation allows us to understand why government policy authorities may have only limited power to control long-run real interest rates. Specifically, if the government takes energetic policy action to change the nominal interest rate, it is possible that such changes might be offset by changes in inflationary expectations. The real interest rate may be harder to change, especially in the long run. The determinants of real interest rates include fundamental factors such as individual attitudes toward time preference, the expected return on real investments and, especially in an open economy, the willingness of foreigners to borrow and lend in domestic financial markets. Government policy can influence these things, but not easily.

17.3.3 Inflation and the Money Supply: the Quantity Theory

Inflation is controlled mainly by monetary policy. High rates of money supply growth lead to high rates of inflation. Suppose, for example, that real output remains fixed, but that money supply doubles. This means that there are more dollars chasing the same goods. The real purchasing power of the expanded money supply cannot rise if real output is not rising. In order for real purchasing power to stay constant when the nominal money supply doubles, the purchasing power of each dollar must fall. An inflation rate of 100% will cut the value of each dollar by half, keeping purchasing power constant, as required. Thus, if real output is fixed, inflation should equal the rate of growth of the money supply, other things equal.

Expansionary monetary policy increases aggregate demand. If the supply of goods and services can respond to the increase in demand, which will be possible if the economy is operating at less than capacity, then inflation need not increase commensurately with the increase in the money supply. If, however, the economy is operating at full capacity, aggregate supply cannot increase to match the increase in aggregate demand, and inflation will result instead.

In practice, an increase in the rate of expansion of the money supply will have both output effects and inflation effects. Some economists have argued that the inflation effects always dominate, at least in the long run. The extreme version of this view is the so-called quantity theory of money, which holds that monetary expansion has no long-run effect on real output, and translates directly into inflation. In this view of the world, monetary policy is described as neutral with respect to real output.

Real output will normally be growing, and increases in the money supply will be required to accommodate this growth if deflation (a general decline in prices) is to be avoided. Additional monetary expansion, according to the quantity theory, will lead to commensurate increases in inflation. Table 17.1 shows some inflation and money supply data from several countries.

It is clear from Table 17.1 that the correspondence between money supply (as measured by M1) and inflation is far from exact. Nevertheless, it is also clear that there is a very strong approximate relationship

Table 17.1: Money Supply and Inflation

(all figures are percentage changes from the previous year)

Country	1975 M1	1975 Inflation	1985 M1	1985 Inflation	1998 M1	1998 Inflation
Chile	275	371	14	30	-13	5.0
Argentina	218	100	572	672	.03	1.0
Israel	22	29	246	371	11	5.4
S. Korea	30	25	11	2	2	7.5
Britain (U.K.)	19	24	18	6	4	3.4
Italy	8	17	11	9	5	2.0
Japan	10	12	3	2	5	0.6
Canada	19	11	31	4	6	1.0
U.S.A	5	9	12	4	3	1.5

Source: International Monetary Fund, International Financial Statistics, July 1994, 1992, 1988 issues, 1999.

between money supply growth rates and inflation. Roughly speaking, single digit money growth rates will normally produce single digit infla- tion, double digit money supply growth will normally produce double digit inflation, and triple digit money supply growth will normally pro- duce triple digit inflation. As the table indicates, this lesson has gradu- ally been absorbed into central bank practice, since many countries that had problems with inflation in the 1970s and 1980s managed to bring inflation under control by the 1990s. However, several of the major transitional economies of the former Soviet bloc continue to have seri- ous problems with inflation, as do some other countries as well.

In Canada, as can be seen from Table 7.4, there seemed to be major regime shifts in the early 1980s, and again in the early 1990s. Specif- ically, there was a downward shift in inflation between 1982 and 1983, when inflation fell from double digits to about 5%, where it stayed for about eight years. Then, between 1991 and 1992, inflation seemed to rachet down once again to the 2% range. In both cases, the decline in inflation was the result of a conscious policy effort within the Bank of Canada to contract liquidity so as to reduce inflation, and in both cases, the monetary contraction did reduce inflation while also appar- ently contributing to sharp recessions.

The 1980s monetary contraction had fairly broad support, since many people felt that inflation had gotten out of control in the late 1970s and early 1980s. There was some doubt about whether inflation could be reduced back to the 5% range without inflicting intolerable damage to the economy, but the policy was maintained and the economy did recover. The further reduction in inflation that occured in the early 1990s was more controversial. The Governor of the Bank during that period, John Crow, was a proponent of price stability and wanted to reduce the inflation rate to zero or close to it. The Government of Canada, not to mention the opposition parties, provinical governments, and many public critics, expressed concerns about the Bank's zealousness in pursuing price stability and felt that the resulting high real interest rates and protracted recession were excessive costs to pay for trying to achieve price stability. Utlimately, the question over whether the reduction in inflation achieved in the early 1990s was worth the costs is empirical in nature. The Bank of Canada argued that low inflation contributes to the long-run growth of the economy and that the short-term costs of the policy were relatively low.

17.3.4 Inflationary Expectations and the Effectiveness of Monetary Policy

Some economists argue that monetary policy is a very ineffective tool for expanding output, even in situations of excess capacity, and that it should be targeted principally toward keeping inflation at low levels. Others have argued that monetary policy is very useful in influencing output. As mentioned earlier, we usually observe that expansionary monetary policy has some inflationary effects, even in the presence of excess capacity. What determines the effectiveness of monetary policy as an output expansion tool?

The answer is what expectations largely determine the effectiveness of monetary policy. Recall that monetary policy has its effect by reducing interest rates, which increases investment. The first point to add is that it is the real interest rate that is relevant for determining the real cost of investment. Expansionary monetary policy will increase investment demand only if it can decrease the real interest rate.

Suppose, however, that when an expansionary monetary policy is adopted, most people believe that monetary policy is neutral and that inflation will rise accordingly. If they believe this, then participants in financial markets will need to raise nominal interest rates so as to keep real interest rates at the going level, in accordance with the Fisher Effect. If nominal interest rates do rise so as to keep real interest rates constant, then no increase in investment demand is forthcoming, output stays constant, and inflation corresponding to the increase in the money supply results. Expectations turn out to have been correct and monetary policy has been neutral in its effect on output, translating only into higher inflation.

This description embodies consistent or rational expectations, and it demonstrates that monetary policy will be neutral if people expect it to be. People who hold this view are associated with a school of thought that goes by several different names: the monetarist school, the quantity theory school, the rational expectations school, and the policy neutrality school. Proponents of this view are opposed by Keynesians or neo-Keynesians, who believe that the monetary policy mechanism described in Section 17.1.4 is very important.

Keynesian effects can arise if expectations differ from expectations of policy neutrality. Monetary policy can then have real output effects. In the early 1980s, the U.S., Britain, and Canada all embarked on tight money policies to try to reduce inflation. Economists of the rational expectations school argued that a reduction in monetary expansion could reduce inflation without much lessening of real economic activity.

In fact, real economic activity did fall quite sharply, so the pure policy neutrality view was certainly off target. However, this policy experience was something of a success for the policy neutrality school, for inflation was brought down quickly, and was followed by a long sustained economic recovery that brought real levels of economic activity well beyond the levels of the late 1970s, and with lower levels of inflation. One interpretation is simply that the long run took a little longer to materialize than the policy neutrality school anticipated.

This discussion of expectations also suggests another point: the credibility of announced government policy has a major effect on the effect of government policy. Suppose, for example, that the government announces that it will bring down inflation through contractionary monetary policy. If people believe this then they will respond by lowering nominal interest rates, lowering wage demands, and so on, and the transition to lowered inflation will be achieved quickly and painlessly. If, however, people do not believe it, then they will not lower nominal interest rates or wage demands without a prolonged period of painful government restraint. Faced with such a prospect, the government may abandon the policy, proving the sceptics right. The effectiveness of government policy depends in part on credibility.

17.3.5 The Inflation Tax

As Table 17.1 indicates, many countries have experienced very high rates of money supply growth and inflation. If, as argued earlier, inflation is costly, why do countries adopt such policies? The answer to this question is that inflation has value to governments, essentially as a tax. This is particularly true in many less-developed countries that do not have effective income tax systems. Consider the following thought experiment. Suppose that real output in some country is 100, that the money supply is 100, and that the price level is 1. There are no income or commodity taxes and all money is held by private citizens.

The government wishes to consume real resources (presumably for public benefit). Suppose that the government (through the central bank) creates 100 new units of money, to be spent by the government. (The government deficit is therefore 100, paid for by an expansion of the money supply.) Assuming real output stays fixed at 100, there is twice as much money demand as before for each unit of real output. At the old prices, both the private sector and the government could claim the entire GDP, but there would not be enough real output to go around. Prices must be bid up. The new equilibrium occurs after an inflation of 100%. The new price level is 2, in keeping with the larger money supply of 200.

Since the government has half the money supply (100), it can consume half the country's GDP. Private citizens are left with the other half for consumption and investment. What has happened? The real value of the private money supply has diminished by 50%, reflecting exactly the government's claim over resources. This government has, in effect, confiscated or taxed half of private sector income. This confiscation or taxation was achieved through inflation. The inflation was a tax on the private sector, just as if the government had taxed all citizens 50% of their income directly. This is described as the inflation tax or seniorage.

In many countries, the inflation tax is the most important single source of government command over resources. It is easy to collect, and it is politically appealing, because most people do not understand it or even see it as a tax. When governments want to spend much more than they collect in direct taxes (i.e., when they run large deficits), the inflation tax is the tax of last resort. Most economists argue, however, that it is a very inefficient form of taxation, and is therefore indicative of bad government.

17.4 Unemployment

17.4.1 Types of Unemployment

So far, we have not discussed the major focal point of macroeconomic policy: unemployment. When politicians think about macroeconomic policy, they think first about unemployment, reflecting public concern. The first task in discussing unemployment is to be clear about terminology. The following list defines some of the relevant concepts.

Unemployed worker: a person who is actively looking for work but not actually working, or who is on temporary layoff.

Labour force: the sum of employed and unemployed workers.

Unemployment rate: the ratio of unemployed workers to the labour force.

Participation rate: the ratio of the labour force to the overall population.

Discouraged worker: a person who would like to be employed but who is not actively looking for work, and who is therefore not counted as unemployed.

There will always be some people leaving old jobs and looking for new ones, or seeking first time jobs. Similarly, there will always be some firms that find it necessary to reduce their labour force, or that go out of business entirely, releasing unemployed workers onto the labour market. Unemployment associated with normal job turnover of this type is called *frictional unemployment*.

In addition, some workers who would like jobs lack the skills necessary to make it worthwhile for a firm to hire them at going wage levels. Some workers may live in regions of low labour demand, and may be unable to find local firms to hire them, even if they have useful skills. Unemployment arising from the mismatching of skills or location is referred to as *structural unemployment*. It has been argued, for example, that the Canada-U.S. Free Trade Agreement (subsequently expanded to the North American Free Trade Agreement) may have temporarily produced increased structural unemployment as parts of the economy were forced to restructure, rendering some old skills obsolete and creating demand for a different mix of skills.

Finally, unemployment that arises principally from swings in aggregate demand is referred to as *cyclical unemployment.* The distinction between frictional, structural, and cyclical unemployment is not absolutely clear in practice. In times of low cyclical aggregate demand, the time spent between jobs for workers involved in normal turnover will increase, and the problems of regional and vocational mismatching will appear more severe.

17.4.2 The Natural Rate of Unemployment

Because of frictional and structural unemployment, even a perfect macroeconomic policy would not reduce unemployment to zero. Nor would we want unemployment to be zero. The task of matching workers to jobs is complex, and we can expect it to consume resources, including some time spent by unemployed workers searching for new jobs. Workers do not necessarily accept the first job offered to them, and firms do not always hire the first person to apply for a job. Similarly, it takes time for workers to realize that their skills might be out of date, or that they might have to move to find a new job. In any dynamic economy, where skill requirements are evolving and the geographic pattern of activity is changing, there will be some natural frictional and structural unemployment.

There is, therefore, a natural rate of unemployment. This natural rate is determined in part by the size of new entry into the labour force, and in part by the rate of change of skill requirements and locational requirements in the economy. Most importantly, however, it is determined by the willingness of workers to be unemployed.

Most workers are voluntarily unemployed in the sense that they could find jobs at some wage. Understandably, however, a worker who has been earning $25 an hour or more might be unwilling to accept a job paying $10 an hour. University professors who lose their jobs might be unwilling to accept jobs driving taxis (although many have), or working at MacDonald's. In the short run, at least, they would prefer to look for a new job resembling their previous one, rather than accept a much less attractive job. Such a situation is very hard on the person involved, of course, but in a strict sense such unemployment is voluntary.

Time spent in job search will be higher if unemployment insurance is higher, if family income is higher (i.e., if there is a working spouse), or if the worker retains some hope of direct government policy to save his or her job. The natural rate of unemployment is sensitive to all these factors.

The importance of the natural rate of unemployment is that we should not try to use macroeconomic policy to reduce it. If we incorrectly judge that the natural rate is lower than it actually is, and try to use increased aggregate demand to lower the imagined cyclical unemployment, then, instead of reducing unemployment and raising output, we will tend to induce inflation and increase the government debt. Macroeconomic stabilization policy is best in dealing with cyclical departures in unemployment from the natural rate. It is not effective in pushing the natural rate down.

It should be emphasized that there is nothing particularly good about the natural rate of unemployment. The natural rate may well be too high, as it certainly is in Canada. The point being made here is simply that macroeconomic policy is not a good tool for dealing with the natural rate. If the natural rate is too high, this is most likely due to government policy itself, which has created too many rigidities in labour markets. For example, the policy of supporting depressed regions through money-losing Crown corporations, rather than reducing unemployment, actually increases the natural rate. This arises because it prevents workers in those regions from recognizing the market's signal to change their skills and/or locations.

Using unemployment insurance to subsidize high unemployment industries also increases the natural rate. For example, in Atlantic Canada, it has been common practice for some fishermen to work for nine or ten weeks of the year and collect unemployment insurance for the rest. In some communities in Canada, it is common for workers to work for the minimum time required to be eligible for unemployment insurance, and then give up the job to someone else who will do the same thing. In this way four or five people can be employed doing the work of only one full-time worker, receiving a subsidy from the rest of Canada to support them when they are not working.

If an excessively high natural rate of unemployment is created by other areas of policy, operating at the level of individual incentives and then applying incentive-based microeconomic policies is the correct response. For example, instead of subsidizing uneconomic industries, it would make more sense to subsidize the acquisition of new skills, or to subsidize relocation costs, or even to subsidize the job search process itself.

17.5 The Public Debt

It would not be appropriate to discuss macroeconomic policy without considering the public debt. The public debt acts as a constraint on the major tools of macroeconomic policy. A government's debt is nothing other than the accumulation of (properly measured) net fiscal deficits. The amount of aggregate debt a government can accumulate is limited; therefore its capacity to carry out fiscal policy is also limited. In addition, the aggregate level of public debt may have an impact on economic growth and may therefore be viewed as an instrument of macroeconomic policy itself.

17.5.1 Sources of the Public Debt

Using fiscal deficits to stimulate economic activity, and therefore expand employment, has an important budgetary consequence: it tends to lead to an accumulation of debt. In principle, application of Keynesian macro-economic policy should not result in increasing debt. The original idea was that the governments would run deficits in times of low aggregate demand, and run surpluses in times of high aggregate demand. While there was no absolute requirement that deficits and surpluses would be exactly offsetting, it was presumed that no large net accumulations of surplus or debt should result. Roughly speaking, the basic innovation of Keynesian policy was that budgets should be balanced over the business cycle rather than insisting on budget balance in each year.

In fact, rather than achieving budget balance over the business cycle, virtually all Western governments that have applied Keynesian principles have experienced a bias toward deficit spending. In Canada, the federal government ran a surplus in the 1973-74 fiscal year. It then ran 34 consecutive deficits before posting a small surplus in 1997-98, followed by surpluses in the subsequent two years as well. Between 1974 and 1997 Canada went through four complete business cycles without running a surplus.

There are two basic reasons why deficits are more common than surpluses. The first relates to the positive theory of government. It is very easy for governments to spend money and very hard for them to reduce expenditure. Citizens want expensive social programs like medicare, subsidized higher education, generous welfare programs, and universal pensions. They also want low taxes. The benefits of higher spending come immediately; the costs come later, to be dealt with by other governments. For these reasons there is a natural bias toward excessive spending.

Second, there has been a systematic underassessment of the natural rate of unemployment. Throughout the last four business cycles, even at the most vigourous peak of the cycle, unemployment has seemed too high, and was a policy priority. There have been strong calls for expansion of aggregate demand throughout the cycle. The worst misdiagnosis was in the late 1970s under the Liberal government of Pierre Trudeau. Unemployment was in the 7% range, which was interpreted as representing high cyclical unemployment. The government ran very high deficits, entrenching very high expenditure commitments. Subsequently, the economy moved into a downturn in the early 1980s, and the level of deficit spending rose again.

In retrospect, it seems that the unemployment rates of the late 1970s represented increases in the natural rate, reflecting rapid rates of labour force growth, high levels of technological change, the growth of the two-income family (making it easier for one member of the family to remain unemployed longer), and the increased generosity of government programs making it less costly to be unemployed. The appropriate policy would have been to try to improve the efficiency of labour markets at a microeconomic level, rather than undertaking large fiscal deficits.

In the late 1990s, the federal government, also a Liberal government, sought to establish fiscal responsibility as a top priority and, as already noted, managed to run three consecutive surplus budgets at the end of the century, and looked likely to run surpluses or at least balanced budgets into the early part of the 21st century. This required significant political courage, although enough concern about mounting debt had been expressed to make the policy politically successful in the end. The basic argument made by the Finance Minister, Paul Martin, and the Prime Minister, Jean Chrétian, was that fiscal responsibility actually did more to promote improved real incomes and employment opportunities than deficit spending. From an economist's perspective it made sense for the government to run surpluses in the late 1990s in view of the robust performance of the economy, but it had been a long time since a federal government had been able to achieve that.

17.5.2 The Burden of the Public Debt [3]

The result of continuing deficits was a rapidly accumulating federal debt. In 1974, interest on the federal debt used up about 9% of federal revenues and was, much smaller than government expenditures on goods and services. In 1996, interest on the federal debt peaked at 36% of federal government revenue and, at over $45 billion, was greater than expenditures on goods and services. Interest on the debt, over the single decade from the mid-1970s to the mid-1980s, changed from being a modest portion of revenue to being the single most important broad category, taking dollars away from government services like health care and education. In the years following 1996, debt charges (i.e., interest) have fallen as a share of revenues and were 27% in the fiscal year ending in 1999. Table 7.12 provides some basic data on deficits and on debt service for all levels of government combined.

As of 1999, the net federal debt was $577 billion. Total net public debt (combined federal, provincial, and local debt) in 1998 was over $800 billion. On a per capita basis, total public debt amounted to over $27,000 per person in Canada in 1999.

It is important to have a clear understanding of exactly what the burden of the debt is, especially since this subject is the source of much confusion. To start with, there is an important distinction between an internally held debt and an external debt.

The easier subject is the external debt. An external debt is a debt owed by a domestic government to foreign citizens. This debt has two significant characteristics. First, it is owed to people who are not subject to taxation by the domestic government, and, second, it is usually denominated in a foreign currency.

An external debt is much like a debt owed by one individual to another. If large debts are undertaken now, this represents a burden in that the debts must be paid back later. If the debts are used to finance projects with a higher rate of return than the interest rate, then the benefits will exceed the burden. If not, the burden will exceed the benefits. During the early 1980s, an international debt crisis arose because many countries, especially in South America and Africa, undertook debts that could not be easily repaid. Much of this borrowing was used to pay for sharply increased international oil prices (that occured in 1973-74 and again in 1979) and therefore reflected current consumption. Few long-term real assets whose earnings could be used to repay the debt were put in place.

In any case, an external debt represents a clear burden or liability for future taxpayers. Even if a country defaults on debt, there are very high costs, since this will compromise the ability of a country and its citizens to participate in international financial markets. Specifically, if a national government either fails to pay or is late in paying it debts to international creditors, then firms and citizens in that country will typically find it difficult to borrow money in international markets. This is because lenders might fear that the government's financial problems might reduce the prospects that private borrowers could repay loans. Even if these private borrowers earn enough foreign exchange to pay back these loans, they might find that the government wishes to tax or simply confiscate a large share of it. Also, a government that cannot pay its debts creates uncertainty about the long-run economic climate and increases the likelihood that domestic businesses will fail. In the late 1990s about 25% of Canada's public debt was externally held and this percentage was falling slowly.

A domestically held debt is somewhat different. In fact, there was a considerable controversy in the 1960s over whether a domestically held debt was a burden at all. The basic argument supporting the idea that an internal debt imposes no burden on the future is that an internal debt is a debt that "we owe to ourselves." The future reshufflings of income between taxpayers and bondholders are just transfers and, so the argument goes, do not impose real resource costs on the economy. Unfortunately, however, this argument is false.

Speaking pragmatically, if a debt is denominated in domestic currency and is owed to domestic residents, the government always has two feasible options that it does not have with external foreign currency debt. It can simply print money to pay off the debt, or it can tax recipients of interest income a substantial part of that income.

Common sense, however, suggests that there is a burden on the future created by a public debt, even if it is internally held. Common sense is often wrong in economic matters, but in this case it is right. The burden of Canada's internally held debt, accumulated largely since the mid-1970s is, as previously mentioned, already being felt. This burden is represented by the increasing fraction of government revenue that must be allocated to paying interest on the debt, reducing real expenditure levels in areas of government services, and increasing the real tax burden on the economy.

The burden arises because, when the government borrows money, it is exchanging something of equal value: a bond promising command over resources in the future. This is a liability on taxpayers at large. Nonbondholding taxpayers in particular, suffer an increased future liability with every extra dollar the government borrows. While it is true that the government will not go bankrupt over an internal debt, it is also true that someone will bear the burden.

If the government prints money to pay off the debt, then inflation will result, and, in effect, an inflation tax will extract wealth from citizens. If, alternatively, the government taxes interest income at high rates, it is confiscating from bondholders some of the payment that had been promised to them. In short, the government has sufficient power over internal debtholders that it can always find a way to meet its budget requirements by imposing the burden of the debt on them if it chooses to. With external debts, the burden cannot be imposed on the recipients of the interest payments, short of actual default. Thus, while an internal debt can be dealt with more easily than an external debt, it is no less a liability for future taxpayers.

Debts may still be worthwhile. If the debt is used to pay for an asset that generates returns in excess of the interest payments, then the burden of the debt should be gladly accepted, for this burden will be less than the benefits. If borrowed money is used to pay for schools and hospitals that greatly increase the quality of life and/or increase the productive capacity of the population, or if it is used to pay for roads and bridges that improve private sector productivity greatly, then this borrowing is a good investment.

Public borrowing must, however, be viewed as an investment. If government borrowing is used to fund uneconomic Crown corporations, or if it is spent on current consumption that does not generate future benefits, then that borrowing will impose a net burden on the future.

Critics of the federal government point out that program expenditures (expenditures on government programs) and transfers to provinces to fund higher education and medical care fell as a fraction of GDP from 1984 through the late 1990s. This is presumably to be taken as evidence of government tightfistedness and mismanagement. What is true is that approximately the entire increase in federal government debt since 1984 is attributable to deficits created by the need to pay interest on prior debt. In short, if there had been no federal debt in 1984, and therefore no interest payments to be made, the federal government would have run significant surpluses throughout the 1990s. The cascading effect of borrowing money to pay interest on previous borrowings created a growing problem of increasing debt. This is much like the problem confronted by insolvent individuals or private firms who find themselves borrowing money just to pay interest.

If it is possible to turn the corner and get to a point where debt actually starts to fall, then this "vicious cycle" can be reversed. As debt levels fall, less money has to be spent on interest payments on that debt and more money is available to pay off the underlying debt principal—and of course more money is available for other uses. The federal government and Canada as a whole (i.e., the federal government plus the provinces) may have turned this corner.

In the late 1990s, a combination of strong economic growth and fiscal restraint allowed the federal government to move Canada's fiscal position to a surplus position. This creates a more comfortable fiscal situation that might allow room for modest tax reductions. In the short run, tax reductions would tend to reduce the surplus or move the budget toward a deficit, but if these tax reductions served to boost economic growth (and therefore boost the tax base) significantly, that would be a further bonus. It is still too early to be sure that Canada's fiscal position has become sustainable, as an economic contraction would put serious pressure on Canada's finances. One thing we can say is that the prognosis is positive as we enter the 21st century.

One potential cloud on the horizon concerns provincial budgets. As of the 1998-99 fiscal year, two large provinces, British Columbia and Ontario, were in considerable deficit positions. The good news is that the other eight provinces were in positions where the ratio of debt to provincial income was declining. Furthermore, Ontario appeared to be on a trajectory toward establishing fiscal balance. Therefore, the only province with a clearly unsustainable fiscal position was British Columbia, which therefore would require some structural readjustment. Aggregating the provinces and the federal government together, the Canadian public sector as a whole was in a surplus fiscal position in 1998-99 and appeared likely to maintain a modest surplus in at least the subsequent few years.

There is a strong political incentive in favour of deficit spending, as the benefits occur in the short run and costs are long-run costs that may be borne by future governments. However, governments in many jurisdictions, including most Canadian jurisdictions, have learned the lesson that these costs are usually not worth incurring. Another short-run incentive that governments face is to attempt to present misleading information about the budgetary position. At the federal level and in most provinces in Canada changes have, in contrast, been in the direction of providing more accurate and more helpful information. The only outlier again was British Columbia, where the NDP government of the late 1990s adopted the practice of leaving certain classes of capital expenditures (on such things as roads, schools, and hospitals) out of the official provincial deficit. This created the very odd situation where the "deficit" and the "increase in debt" were two very different numbers. It is reasonable to distinguish between the capital and operating expenses for some purposes, but any accumulating debt that is ultimately supported by taxes, including debts incurred for roads, schools, and hospitals, should be reported in the aggregate deficit.

17.5.3 Government Deficits and Current Account Deficits

One noteworthy aspect of Canada's recent experience with deficits is that the pattern of government deficits (all levels of government) is similar to the pattern of something called the current account deficit. The current account consists essentially of the sum of export earnings on goods and services plus Canadian earnings from foreign investments minus imports of goods and services and investment earnings flowing to foreigners from Canadian investments. If this account is in surplus, Canada would be building up financial claims on the outside world, because earnings from the outside world would exceed payments to the outside world. Conversely, if the current account is in deficit, this means that Canada is becoming increasingly indebted to the rest of the world.

In fact, the current account in Canada was in very substantial deficit from the early 1980s through the late 1990s, but turned positive in the first quarter of 2000. Current account deficits imply that foreign claims on Canada were growing. If the current account is in deficit, this means that foreigners are earning Canadian dollars from exports to Canada and repatriated interest payments and profits from Canadian investments that exceed the amount Canada earns from foreign sources. Thus, if Canada converted its foreign earnings to Canadian dollars in international markets, foreigners would still have Canadian dollars left over. What happened to those extra dollars?

The answer is that foreigners invested them in Canadian assets, including making direct loans to the federal government and provincial governments. Thus, Canada's current account deficit was exactly offset by a capital account surplus, which is an excess of investment inflows over investment outflows. In fact, the current account deficit must always equal the capital account surplus, because of the following accounting convention. If foreigners earn excess Canadian dollars, there are two things they can do with them. They can invest them in Canadian assets such as corporate stock, government bonds, Toronto real estate, etc. Alternatively, they can simply hold the Canadian dollars in bank vaults or under mattresses or whatever. Both of these uses of Canadian dollars are counted as capital inflows to Canada. If a foreigner simply holds Canadian $100 bills under a mattress, that is viewed as an investment in a Canadian asset (i.e., in $100 bills). Thus, currency is itself viewed as an investment asset and holding currency counts as making an investment in Canada. In fact, very little of the accumulated earnings by foreigners from Canadian sources are held as currency, but this accounting convention ensures that the capital account surplus always exactly offsets the current account deficit.

A substantial part of the investment inflow (or capital account surplus) represents foreigners loaning money to (i.e., investing in) Canadian governments by purchasing interest-bearing government bonds. Therefore, the current account deficit and government budget deficits are related, and are sometimes referred to as twin deficits. From the mid-1970s to the mid-1990s Canadian governments were borrowing heavily from foreign sources (as well as from domestic residents).

Therefore, it is not surprising that the striking decline in Canadian government budget deficits at the end of the 1990s was accompanied by a sharp decline in the current account deficit. The "twin deficits" do not have to mirror each other, but there are forces that push in such a direction.

17.6 Macroeconomic Stabilization and Market Failure

In keeping with traditional discussions of public policy, this book has distinguished among four types of normative rationale for policy: efficiency (or market failure), fairness, macroeconomic stabilization, and other objectives. As some critics have pointed out, however, it is not obvious that stabilization policy should be regarded as an independent motivation for policy. According to this view, macroeconomic policy is properly viewed as part of the efficiency or market failure rationale for policy. After all, if workers and equipment that could be productively employed are standing idle, this is a clear example of economic inefficiency. Pareto improvements could be made by putting those resources to work.

In short, macroeconomic stabilization is not an end in itself. It is useful to the extent that it reduces or corrects market failure. The attractiveness of this idea is best appreciated by considering what we would recommend for policy if stabilizing some economic variable actually reduced economic efficiency. Suppose, for example, that we observe that unemployment is higher in January than in May. Suppose further that the main reason for this is that many industries, such as construction, are less productive in January than in May, because of weather conditions. We could, however, at some cost, stabilize employment between the two months by undertaking large amounts of employment generating deficit spending every January and restraining economic activity every May.

Such a policy would likely reduce real annual incomes, implying that it is (Pareto) inefficient. Would we advocate this efficiency-reducing policy? Obviously not. Macroeconomic policy is useful only to the extent that it serves either the efficiency rationale for intervention or, possibly, the fairness rationale for intervention. It is not really an end in itself. Macroeconomic failures are really microeconomic market failures writ large.

Why, then, do we distinguish between macro stabilization and efficiency rationales for intervention? In part, this reflects the history of economic thought and of actual policy, which have tended to separate micro-based policies, which focus on individual markets, from macro-based policies, which focus on aggregate business activity. Also, although stabilizing economic activity does not necessarily always improve economic efficiency, it usually does. It seems reasonable therefore, as a practical matter, to isolate stabilization as a specific subsidiary objective.

Conceptually, however, macro and micro policy principles cannot be logically different. To be logically complete, macro policy analysis must be based on the behaviour and efficiency properties of individual markets, just as micro policy analysis is. The Keynesian approach to deficit spending and stabilization, as described by Bernheim (1989), is based on the idea of significant failures in labour markets and in financial markets, and possibly simple failures on the part of individuals to make correct optimizing decisions. Under such conditions, active monetary and fiscal policy can have significant positive effects, if skilfully applied.

Bernheim (1989) also describes what he calls the neoclassical approach to macroeconomic policy. Under this approach, individuals are assumed to be rational calculating agents operating principally in a world of well-functioning competitive markets. In such a world, government deficit spending is primarily a transfer between generations. If the government decides to pay for current consumption by borrowing rather than by using taxes, the current generation is better off and consumes more than it otherwise would. It also saves less, leaving a lower capital stock and higher debts to future generations. This may be a reason for the pro-deficit bias described in Section 17.5.1.

17.7 Long-Run Economic Growth

Public policy tends to focus on short-run macrostabilization, perhaps to an excessive extent. Long-run economic growth is more important; after all, it has completely transformed the quality of life in Canada and many other countries from what it was when our grandparents were young. Cross-country comparisons of economic growth have been particularly striking in the 1960-98 period. While virtually all countries go through business cycles, in which the pace of economic activity rises and falls, some countries have performed consistently better than others, to an extent that has never been observed in previous eras. Figure 17.1 illustrates economic growth over the 1960-98 period for a handful of representative countries.

The fastest growing economies over this period have all been in Eastern Asia. A group of countries consisting of Japan, Singapore, Taiwan, Hong Kong, South Korea, and, more recently, Thailand, Malaysia, China itself, and now Indonesia have experienced faster per capita income growth rates than have previously been experienced by any

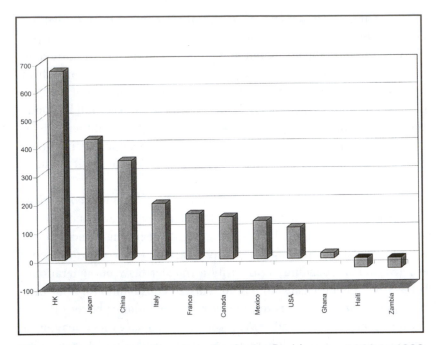

Figure 17.1 Percentage Growth in Per Capita Real Income, 1960 to 1998
Source: *World Bank.*

group of countries. From this group, Figure 17.1 shows Hong Kong (denoted HK), Japan, and China. Singapore (not shown in the graph) has actually had the world's most rapidly rising living standards over the 1960-98 period, since per capita real income has increased at least eight-fold in that time. Changes of this magnitude are so dramatic that quantitative comparisons lose some of their meaning. It is accurate to say, however, that the quality of life has been totally transformed in the space of 38 years. A young adult in Singapore today would find the living experience of his or her parents at a similar age so much poorer in material terms as to be difficult to comprehend.

On the other hand, there is a large group of countries, including much of sub-Saharan Africa and parts of Latin America and the Caribbean, where real incomes have stagnated or actually fallen between 1960 and 1998. As examples the graph shows Ghana, where real incomes rose marginally between 1960 and 1998, and Haiti (in the Caribbean), and Zambia, where real incomes fell about one-third. In 1960, Zambia was a slightly wealthier country (in per capita income) than South Korea. In 1998, real incomes in Zambia were less than one-sixth of those in South

Korea. Interestingly, this is exactly the opposite comparative pattern to that predicted by many development experts of the early 1960s, who based their reasoning largely on comparative resource endowments, and on excessively optimistic forecasts of what would happen to the African countries as they moved from colonial European control to independence.

As for Europe and North America, most countries have turned in strong performances by historical standards. Canadian real income per capita more than doubled between 1960 and 1998 (i.e., growth exceeded 100%, as indicated in Figure 17.1. Such growth rates are, however, somewhat anemic even with the late 1990s recession in Eastern Asia. Within European countries, the poorer ones have grown the fastest, so that Spain and Italy, in particular, have substantially closed the gap between them and the other European countries and North America. Thus, as far as East Asia, Europe, North America, and a few other countries are concerned, the period 1960-98 was a period of convergence, with all these countries experiencing rising real incomes, but with the poorer ones growing fastest. Interestingly, however, no country has actually passed the U.S. in real income as measured by purchasing power. Figure 17.2 shows the corresponding level of per capita real income for the countries shown in Figure 17.1.

Despite convergence in real incomes among the middle income and wealthier countries, aggregate world income has actually grown less equal, because of the very poor performance of the worst-off countries. It is a major challenge to explain why this pattern of growth has come about, and considerable current research is addressed to the area. Rather obviously, it is important for policymakers in any one country, such as Canada, to understand the causes of growth, and it is particularly important for development of the low income countries. The puzzle is far from being completely unravelled, but the following general statements can be made.

First, the basic type of economic system seems to be very important. Put bluntly, central planning, state socialism, and communism have not performed well, whereas market-based economies have performed well. There were centrally planned economies that produced quite good standards of living, such as the former East Germany, but compared to West Germany, East German performance was very poor. Similarly, centrally planned North Korea did better than most of Africa, but far worse than South Korea. In East Asia the comparison between market economies, such as Japan and Singapore, and centrally planned

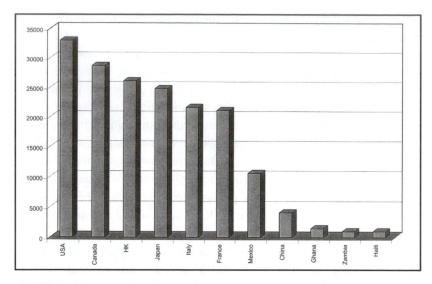

FIGURE 17.2 1998 Per Capital Real Income in 1998 C$
Source: *World Bank.*

or state socialist economies, such as Vietnam and Cambodia, is over-whelming. Even in Africa, the very worst performers were the communist regimes, such as Ethiopia, while some countries, notably market-oriented Botswana, turned in fairly good performances.

Second, basic economic theory suggests that investment rates should be very important. Countries that invest more should grow faster. It turns out to be true that investment rates are clearly correlated with income growth rates, but the amount of variation in income growth that can be explained in this way is surprisingly small. Using five-year periods, Brander and Dowrick (1994, p.15) found that only about 10% of the variation in income growth can be explained by variations in investment. Furthermore, high investment is far from sufficient for increases in per capita income. Zambia, for example, had among the world's highest investment rates between 1960 and 1992 and still experienced declines in per capita real income. However, the rapidly growing economics of East Asia have had high investment rates and high saving rates.

It is difficult to explain the dramatic decline of Zambia. As suggested in Brander and Dowrick (1994), high rates of population growth were a negative factor, but this was true throughout Africa and most African countries did better than Zambia (although still poorly). A second factor was the generally poor performance on world markets of its major export good (copper), and a third factor was unusually poor public policy as carried out by a well-meaning authoritarian socialist dictatorship. Also, as in other parts of Africa, periodic droughts in the face of rapid population growth created serious problems.

As suggested by this comment about Zambia, demography is an important factor in explaining real income changes. It has been well recognized that higher-income countries tend to have lower birth rates. (Furthermore, on a within-country basis, higher-income individuals tend to have fewer children.) It is widely accepted that rising incomes cause fertility to decline. What is less widely accepted is whether fertility declines might cause income growth. Brander and Dowrick (1994) found evidence consistent with the hypothesis that fertility declines cause real income improvement. In particular, the countries of East Asia that experienced dramatic income gains also experienced dramatic declines in birth rates that started before the acceleration of income gains. It is worth noting, however, that birth rates fell to low levels in most non-African communist countries over the 1960-90 period, and these countries still turned in poor performance. Demography and economic policy are both important.

It is apparent that the very rapid growth that has occurred in East Asia, parts of Europe, and elsewhere is largely the result of technology transfer. Firms in these countries have rapidly adopted technologies developed in the United States and elsewhere and have, as a result, greatly improved worker productivity and real incomes. The question, of course, is why has technology transfer occurred in some places but not others. Economists argue that successful technology transfer is related to human capital or workforce skills, but we still have to ask why the relevant human capital is available in some areas but not in others. One natural idea is that human capital might be closely related to years of schooling, but it turns out that variation in years of schooling does not explain much of the variation in apparent technology transfer. Education is no doubt important, but quality of education, which is very hard to measure, appears to be more important than mere years of schooling.

This is a book about government policy toward business. A natural question to ask is how such policies affect growth. They are important, although we would not get unanimous agreement on the growth consequences of many policies. Evidence suggests that having an open economy with few trade barriers and high capital mobility contributes to strong economic performance, as is consistent with the ideas discussed in Chapter 9.

High levels of regulation can be a problem. In a revealing experiment, described in de Soto (1989), a group of researchers tried to obtain permission to open a small clothing factory in Peru. Registering the factory took 289 days, and required, over this period, the efforts of several skilled people. Bribes were solicited on 10 occasions, but paid only twice, when the process would otherwise have been stopped. The total cost, not including the value of time spent by the researchers, was the equivalent of roughly three years' wages at Peru's minimum wage. Clearly, just getting the permission to start the factory, let alone equipping it with machinery and workers, would be beyond the means of most potential entrepreneurs.

The problem arises from several sources, the most important of which is simply overregulation. There is a strong political demand for regulation in Peru, as in many countries, and little respect for market forces. Incidentally, at no time during the 289 days did any of the regulatory authorities realize that they were dealing with a completely fictitious simulation. This suggests that the regulatory structure in Peru was incapable of accomplishing any substantive objective, but acts mainly as a source income for government workers and an impediment to private sector activity.

Provision of government infrastructure in the form of roads, communications facilities, ports, education, and so on seems to be important, but high levels of redistributive government activity seem to be a problem. Olson (1982) has advanced the thesis that mature societies decline largely because they allow redistributive transfer-seeking institutions to replace wealth-creating activity. He is particularly concerned about the highly litigious legal system in the United States, which is being increasingly copied in Canada.

The conduct of macroeconomic policy itself seems to be of some importance. Certainly, the uncontrolled deficit spending and resulting hyperinflations that have occurred in much of Latin America would seem to go a long way toward explaining their poor performance. Successful performance seems to be related to fiscally conservative deficit and demand management policy, which should serve as warning for Canada and other wealthy countries that are currently living beyond their means. It is worth recalling that Argentina was one of the world's richest countries as late as the 1940s, at which time its per capita income was not far from that of Canada. Venezuela had the world's fifth-highest per capita income as late as 1960. Both countries suffered from populist governments that sought to buy political popularity with government spending and now have living standards far lower than Canada's.

The role of research and development is subject to some debate, and is difficult to estimate, partly because research and development itself is so difficult to measure. It is clear that at a world level, economic growth depends upon technological progress. It is far from clear, however, that it is in one country's interest to subsidize research and development by public policy. The result of much research is freely available, and even proprietary research can be readily licensed. The rapidly growing economies of East Asia have, for the most part, purchased or borrowed technology rather than producing it themselves. The same is true of Canada.

One final point about economic growth should be made. While world economic growth over the 1960-98 period has been high by historical standards, it has been slowing down during the period. Furthermore, if we properly accounted for depreciation of natural resources, the slowdown in real income growth would be even more apparent. We do not have a good explanation for this slowdown in growth.

One possibility, following from the environmental issues raised in Chapters 10 and 11, might be expressed as follows. In 1960, world population was only about half of its 1998 level. In 1960, many important resources were in abundant supply. In most of the world, there was much unfarmed land, many undammed rivers, many unfished areas of ocean, etc. During the 1960-98 period, however, we may have begun to run up against resource limits. As resource limits are reached, extending the use of those fixed resources over an expanding population will have a dampening effect on economic growth.

17.8 Bibliographic Notes

The theory and practice of macroeconomic policy is too large a topic to reference adequately here. The origin of the economic theory of macroeconomic policy is associated with Keynes (1936). Modern textbooks on money and banking and macroeconomics are the best general sources for basic knowledge in the area. The development of the "policy neutrality" school is associated with Milton Friedman, who won the Nobel Prize for Economics in 1976. See Friedman (1968) for a statement of his position. The best-known recent proponent of the policy neutrality view is Lucas (1981). (Robert Lucas was awarded the 1995 Nobel Prize in Economics for his work in this area.) An insightful overview of modern macroeconmic theory by perhaps the most distinguished "Keynesian" macroeconomist is Tobin (1993). (Tobin won the Nobel Prize in 1981.) A valuable attempt to synthesize the main themes in modern macroeconomics is provided by Mankiw (1990). An accessible overview of modern growth theory can be found in Romer (1994).

References

Akerloff, George. 1970. "The Market for Lemons: Quantitative Uncertainty and the Market Mechanism." *Quarterly Journal of Economics* 84: pp. 488-500.

Alchian, Armen A., and Harold Demsetz. 1972. "Production, Information Costs, and Economic Organization." *American Economic Review* 62: pp. 777-795.

Anderson, F.J. 1991. *Natural Resources in Canada.* 2nd ed. Scarborough: Nelson.

Arrow, K.J. 1951, rev. ed. 1963. *Social Choice and Individual Values.* New York: John Wiley & Sons, Inc.

Arrow, K.J. 1974. *The Limits of Organization.* New York: Norton.

Arthur, John, and William H. Shaw. 1978. *Justice and Economic Distribution.* Englewood Cliffs, NJ: Prentice-Hall.

Atkinson, Michael M. 1993. *Governing Canada: Institutions and Public Policy.* Toronto: Harcourt Brace Jovanovich.

Averch, H., and L. Johnson. 1962. "Behaviour of the Firm under Regulatory Restraint." *American Economic Review* 52: pp. 1058-1059.

Axelrod, Robert. 1984. *The Evolution of Co-operation.* New York: Basic Books.

Bain, Joseph S. 1956. *Barriers to New Competition.* Cambridge, Mass. Harvard University Press.

Baetz, Mark C. 1993. *Readings and Canadian Cases in Business, Government, and Society.* Scarborough: Nelson.

Bakvis, H. 1989. "Regional Politics and Policy in the Mulroney Cabinet, 1984-88." *Canadian Public Policy* 15: pp. 121-134.

Bator, Francis M. 1957. "The Simple Analytics of Welfare Maximization." *American Economic Review* 47: pp. 22-59.

Bator, Francis M. 1958. "An Anatomy of Market Failure." *Quarterly Journal of Economics* 72: pp. 351-379.

Baumol, William, John Panzar, and Robert Willig. 1988. *Contestable Markets and the Theory of Industry Structure.* New York: Harcourt Brace Jovanovich.

Beck, R.L., and D. Hussey. 1989. "Politics, Property Rights, and Cottage Development." *Canadian Public Policy* 15: pp. 25-33.

Bernheim, B. Douglas. 1989. "A Neoclassical Perspective on Budget Deficits." *Journal of Economic Perspectives* 3: pp. 55-72.

Bernstein, Jeffrey. 1986. "The Effect of Direct and Indirect Tax Incentives on Canadian Industrial R&D Expenditures." *Canadian Public Policy* 12: pp. 438-448.

Bird, Richard. 1986. *Federal Finance in Comparative Perspective.* Toronto: Canadian Tax Foundation.

Black, D. 1958. *The Theory of Committees and Elections.* Cambridge: Cambridge University Press.

Blais, A. 1986. *Canadian Industrial Policy.* Royal Commission Research Studies. Vol. 44. Toronto: University of Toronto Press.

Blakeney, Allan, and Sandford Borins. 1992. *Political Management in Canada.* Whitby, ON: McGraw-Hill Ryerson.

Blinder, A. 1987. "Keynes, Lucas, and Scientific Progress." *American Economic Review Papers and Proceedings* 77: pp. 130-136.

Boadway, Robin, and David Wildasin. 1984. *Public Sector Economics.* 2nd ed. Boston: Little Brown.

Boardman, Anthony, Ruth Freedman, and Catherine Eckel. 1986. "The Price of Government Ownership A Study of the Domtar Takeover." *Journal of Public Economics* 31: pp. 269-285.

Boardman, Anthony E., et al. 1996. *Cost-Benefit Analysis: Concepts and Practice.* Englewood Cliffs, NJ: Prentice-Hall.

Borins, Sanford F., with L. Brown. 1986. *Investments in Failure: Five Government Enterprises that Cost the Canadian Taxpayer Billions.* Toronto: Methuen.

Brander, James A. 1986. "Rationales for Strategic Trade and Industrial Policy." In *Strategic Trade Policy and the New International Economics,* ed. Paul R. Krugman. Cambridge, MA: MIT Press.

Brander, James A. 1991. "Election Polls, Free Trade, and the Stock Market." *Canadian Journal of Economics* 24: pp. 827-843.

Brander, James A. 1995. "Strategic Trade Policy." *Handbook of International Economics,* vol. 3, pp. 1395-1454. New York: North-Holland.

Brander, James A., and Anming Zhang. 1993. "Dynamic Oligopoly Behaviour in the Airline Industry." *International Journal of Industrial Organization* 11: pp. 407-435.

Brander, James A., and Barbara J. Spencer. 1985. "Export Subsidies and International Market Share Rivalry." *Journal of International Economics* 18: pp. 83-100.

Brander, James A., and Steve Dowrick. 1994. "The Role of Fertility and Population in Economic Growth: Empirical Results from Aggregate Cross-National Data." *Journal of Population Economics* 7: pp. 1-25.

Brown, Alan. 1986. *Modern Political Philosophy: Theories of the Just Society.* Toronto: Penguin Group.

Brown, Lester R., et al. 1995. *State of the World 1995: A Worldwatch Institute Report on Progress toward a Sustainable Society.* New York: W.W. Norton & Company.

Brown, Stephen J., and David S. Sibley. 1986. *The Theory of Public Utility Pricing.* Cambridge: Cambridge University Press.

Brown, Wilson B. 1992. *Markets, Organizations, and Information.* Toronto: Butterworths.

Buchanan, James, and Gordon Tullock. 1962. *The Calculus of Consent.* Ann Arbor: University of Michigan Press.

Buchanan, J.M. 1967. *Public Finance in a Democratic Process.* Chapel Hill: University of North Carolina Press.

Cadsby, C., M. Frank, and V. Maksimovic. 1990. "Pooling, Separating, and Semi-Separating Equilibria in Financial Markets: Some Experimental Evidence." *Review of Financial Studies* 3: pp. 315-342.

Cadsby, Charles Bram, and Kenneth Woodside. 1993. "The Effect of the North American Free Trade Agreement on the Canada-United States Trade Relationship." *Canadian Public Policy* 19, 4: pp. 450-462.

Cameron, Duncan. 1986. *The Free Trade Papers.* Toronto: James Lorimer & Company, Publishers.

Canada. Department of the Environment. 1990. *Canada's Green Plan.* Ottawa: Supply and Services Canada.

Canada. 1995. *1995 Report of the Auditor General of Canada.* Ottawa: Office of Auditor General.

Canada Post Corporation. various years. *Annual Report Canada Post Corporation.* Ottawa: Canada Post Corporation.

Cape Breton Development Corporation. various years. *Annual Report Cape Breton Development Corporation.* Sydney, NS: The Corporation.

Carlton, Dennis W., and Jeffrey M. Perloff. 1994. *Modern Industrial Organization.* 2nd ed. New York: HarperCollins College.

Carmichael, Calum. 1987. "The Control of Export Credit Subsidies and it Welfare Consequences." *Journal of International Economics* 23: pp. 1-20.

Carr, J., F. Mathewson, and J. McManus. 1972. *Cents and Nonsense: the Economics of Canadian Policy Issues.* Toronto: Holt, Rinehart, and Winston.

Caves, Richard E. 1983. *Multinational Enterprise and Economic Analysis.* Cambridge: Cambridge University Press.

Chandler, Alfred. 1977. *The Visible Hand.* Cambridge, MA: Harvard University Press.

Chiras, Daniel E. 1994. *Environmental Science: Action for a Sustainable Future.* 4th ed. Redwood City, CA: Benjamin-Cummings.

Clark, Colin W. 1990. *Mathematical Bioeconomics: the Optimal Management of Renewable Resources.* 2nd ed. Toronto: John Wiley & Sons.

Coase, R.H. 1937. "The Nature of the Firm." *Economical:* Vol. 4. pp. 386-405.

Coase, R.H. 1960. "The Problem of Social Cost." *Journal of Law and Economics* 3: pp. 1-44.

Cockburn, Iain, and Z. Griliches. 1988. "Industry Effects and Appropriability Measures in the Stock Market's Valuation of R&D and Patents." *American Economic Review Papers and Proceedings* 78: pp. 419-423.

Consumer and Corporate Affairs Canada. 1985. *Competition Law Amendments: A Guide.* Ottawa: Minister of Supply and Services Canada.

———. 1986. *Competition Law Amendments: A Schematic Presentation of Bill C-91 and the Present Act.* Ottawa: Minister of Supply and Services Canada.

Copeland, Brian. 1989. "Tariffs and Quotas: Retaliation and Protection with Two Instruments of Protection." *Journal of International Economics* 26: pp. 179-188.

Courchene, T.J. 1980. "Towards a Protected Society: The Politicization of Economic Life." *Canadian Journal of Economics* 13: pp. 556-577.

———. 1994. *Social Canada in the Millennium: Reform Imperatives and Restructuring Principles.* Toronto: C.D. Howe Institute.

Cournot, Augustin. 1838. *Recherches sur les principes mathématiques de la théorie des richesses.* Paris: Hachette.

Couttie, Norm. 1985. *The Hoffman-LaRoche Case: Prerequisites for Predatory Pricing.* MBA graduating essay, University of British Columbia, April 1985.

Crookell, Harold. 1991. *Managing Business Relationships with Government.* Scarborough, ON: Prentice-Hall.

Cuddington, John T., and Ronald I. McKinnon. 1979. "Free Trade Versus Protectionism: A Perspective." In *Tariffs, Quotas and Trade: The Politics of Protectionism.* San Francisco: The Institute for Contemporary Studies.

Cyert, R., and J. March. 1963. *A Behavioural Theory of the Firm.* Englewood Cliffs, NJ: Prentice-Hall.

Dale, Richard. 1984. *The Regulation of International Banking.* Englewood Cliffs, NJ: Prentice-Hall.

Danaldson, Thomas, and Patricia H. Werhane. 1993. *Ethical Issues in Business: A Philosophical Approach.* 4th ed. Englewood Cliffs, NJ: Prentice-Hall.

Daub, Mervin. 1987. *Canadian Economic Forecasting in a World Where All's Unsure.* Kingston, ON: McGill-Queen's University Press.

Dauphinee, Mary M., and Ceta Ramkhalawansingh. 1991. "The Ethics of Managing a Diverse Workforce in Government." *Canadian Public Administration* 34: pp. 50-56.

de Condorcet, M. 1785. *Essai sur l'Application de L'Analyse à la Probabilité des Decisions Rendues à la Pluraliste des Voix.* Paris.

de Soto, Hernando. 1989. *The Other Path*. New York: Harper and Row.

Dixit, A. 1980. "The Role of Investment in Entry Deterrence." *Economic Journal* 90: pp. 95-106.

Doern, G. Bruce. 1990. *Getting it Green: Case Studies in Canadian Environmental Regulation*. Policy Study 12. Toronto: C.D. Howe Institute.

Doern, G. Bruce, and R.W. Phidd. 1992. *Canadian Public Policy: Ideas, Structure, Process*. 2nd ed. Scarborough: Nelson.

Dorfman, Robert, and Nancy S. Dorfman. 1993. *Economics of the Environment*. 2nd ed. New York: W.W. Norton & Company, Inc.

Downs, Anthony. 1957. *An Economic Theory of Democracy*. New York: Harper and Row.

D'Souza, Dinesh. 1991. *Illiberal Education: The Politics of Race and Sex on Campus*. New York: The Free Press.

Eastman, H.C., and S. Stykolt. 1967. *The Tariff and Competition in Canada*. Toronto: Macmillan.

Eaton, B.C., and R.G. Lipsey. 1981. "Capital, Commitment, and Entry Equilibrium." *Bell Journal of Economics* 12: pp. 593-604.

Eckbo, Espen. 1986. "Mergers and the Market for Corporate Control: the Canadian Evidence." *Canadian Journal of Economics* 19 (May): pp. 236-260.

Economic Council of Canada. 1981. *Reforming Regulation*. Ottawa: Minister of Supply and Services Canada.

———. 1986. *Minding the Public's Business*. Ottawa: Minister of Supply and Services Canada.

———. 1987. *A Framework for Financial Regulation*. Ottawa: Minister of Supply and Services Canada.

———. 1991. *New Faces in the Crowd: Economic and Social Impacts of Immigration*. Ottawa: Minister of Supply and Services Canada.

Elections Canada. 1992. *Referendum 92: Official Voting Results: Synopsis*. Ottawa: Chief Electoral Officer of Canada.

Estey, Willard I. (commissioner). 1986. *Report of the Inquiry into the Collapse of the CCB and Northland Bank*. Ottawa: Minister of Supply and Services Canada.

Ethier, Wilfred J. 1988. *Modern International Economics*. 2nd ed. New York: W.W. Norton & Company.

Evans, Robert G. 1984. *Strained Mercy: the Economics of Canadian Health Care*. Toronto: Butterworths.

Feldman, Fred. 1978. *Introductory Ethics*. Englewood Cliffs, NJ: Prentice-Hall.

Fleck, James D., and Joseph R. D'Cruz. 1985. *Canada Can Compete: Strategic Management of the Canadian Industrial Portfolio*. Halifax: Institute for Research on Public Policy.

Fleischmann, George. 1993. "Lobby Governments." *Business Quarterly* 58: pp. 23-28.

Frey, B.S., et al. 1984. "Consensus and Dissension Among Economists: An Empirical Enquiry." *American Economic Review* 74: pp. 986-994.

Friedman, Milton. 1962. *Capitalism and Freedom.* Chicago: University of Chicago Press.

———. 1968. "The Role of Monetary Policy." *American Economic Review* 58: pp. 1-18.

———. 1970. "The Social Responsibility of Business Is to Increase Its Profits." *New York Times Magazine,* September 13, p. 32.

———. 1983. *Oligopoly Theory.* New York: Cambridge University Press.

Gallant, Roy A. 1990. *The Peopling of Planet Earth: Human Population Growth Through the Ages.* New York: Macmillan.

Gaston, Noel, and Daniel Trefler. 1994. "An Assessment of the Labor Market Consequences of the Canada-U.S. Free Trade Agreement." Unpublished paper.

Ghemawat, P. 1991. *Commitment: The Dynamics of Strategy.* New York: The Free Press.

Gibbons, K.M., and D. Rowat, ed. 1976. *Political Corruption in Canada.* Toronto: McClelland and Stewart.

Gillen, David W., Tae Hoon Oum, and Michael W. Tretheway. 1985. *Airline Cost and Performance: Implications for Public and Industry Policies.* Vancouver: Centre for Transportation Studies.

Gleason, Richard. 1987. "The Common Agricultural Policy and the European Economic Community." Term paper, University of British Columbia.

Globerman, Steven. 1979. "Foreign Direct Investment and 'Spillover' Efficiency in Canadian Manufacturing Industries." *Canadian Journal of Economics* 12: pp. 42-50.

Globerman, Steven. 1979. *U.S. Ownership of Firms in Canada: Issues and Policy Approaches.* Montreal: C.D. Howe Institute.

Globerman, Steven, W.T. Stanbury, and Thomas A. Wilson. 1995. *The Future of Telecommunications Policy in Canada.* Vancouver: Bureau of Applied Research, Faculty of Commerce and Business Administration, University of British Columbia.

Gorecki, P.K., and W.T. Stanbury. 1984. *The Objectives of Canadian Competition Policy, 1888-1983.* Halifax: Institute for Research on Public Policy.

Green, Christopher. 1990. *Canadian Industrial Organization and Policy.* 3rd ed. Toronto: McGraw-Hill Ryerson.

Greenwald, B.C., and J.E. Stiglitz. 1986. "Externalities in Economies with Imperfect Information and Incomplete Markets." *Quarterly Journal of Economics* 51: pp. 229-264.

Grossman, Gene, and Ken Rogoff, ed. 1995. *Handbook of International Economics*. Vol. 3. New York: North-Holland.

Grubel, H. 1981. *International Economics*. 2nd ed. Homewood, IL: Irwin.

Grubel, H., and R. Schwindt. 1977. *The Real Cost of the B.C. Milk Board: A Case Study in Canadian Agricultural Policy*. Vancouver: Fraser Institute.

Hahn, Robert W. 1989. "Economic Prescriptions for Environmental Problems: How the Pateint Followed the Doctor's Orders." *Journal of Economic Prespectives* 3: 95-114.

Hardin, G. 1968. "The Tragedy of the Common." *Science* 162: pp. 1243-1248.

Harris, Richard G. 1984. "Applied General Equilibrium Analysis of Small Open Economies with Scale Economies and Imperfect Competition." *American Economic Review* 74: pp. 1016-1032.

Harris, Richard G. 1985a. *Trade, Industrial Policy and International Competition. Royal Commission Research Studies*. Vol. 13. Toronto: University of Toronto Press.

Harris, Richard G. 1985b. "Why Voluntary Export Restraints Are Voluntary." *Canadian Journal of Economics* 18: pp. 799-809.

Hartwick, John, and Nancy Olewiler. 1986. *The Economics of Natural Resource Use*. New York: Harper and Row.

Harvey, Charles M. 1992. "The reasonableness of non-constant discounting." *Journal of Public Economics* 53 (1994): pp. 31-51.

Hayek, F.A. 1960. *The Constitution of Liberty*. London: Routledge and Kegan Paul.

Hazledine, Tim. 1981. *The Costs of Protecting Jobs in 100 Canadian Manufacturing Industries*. Technical Study 16, Canada Employment and Immigration Commission. Ottawa: Minister of Supply and Services Canada.

Hazledine, Tim, and I. Wigington. 1987. "Canadian Auto Policy." *Canadian Public Policy* 13: pp. 490-501.

Head, Keith. 1994. "Infant Industry Protection in the Steel Rail Industry." *Journal of International Economics* 37: pp. 141-166.

Head, Keith, and John Ries. 1995. "Market-Access Effects of Trade Liberalization: Evidence from the Canada-U.S. Free Trade Agreement." Preliminary draft of a paper to be presented at the NBER conference.

Helpman, Elhanan, and Paul R. Krugman. 1985. *Market Structure and Foreign Trade: Increasing Returns, Imperfect Competition and the International Economy*. Cambridge, MA: MIT Press.

———. 1989. *Trade Policy and Market Structure*. Cambridge, MA: MIT Press.

Henderson, Rebecca and Iain Cockburn, 1995 (forthcoming). "Scale, Scope and Spillovers: Determinants of Productivity in the Pharmaceutical Industry" *Rand Journal of Economics*.

Herrnstein, Richard J., and Charles A. Murray. 1994. *The Bell Curve: Intelligence and Class Structure in American Life*. New York: Free Press.

Hotelling, H. 1929. "Stability in Competition." *Economic Journal* 39: pp. 41-57.

Hufbauer, Gary Clyde, and Jeffrey J. Schott. 1992. *North American Free Trade: Issues and Recommendations*. Washington: Institution for International Economics.

———. 1993. *NAFTA: An Assessment*. Washington: Institution for International Economics.

Hughes, E.N. 1991. *Report of the Honourable E. N. Hughes, Q.C. on the Sales of Fantasy Garden World Inc.* Victoria, BC: Crown Publications.

Hunter, Lawson A., and John F. Blakney. 1990. "Provisions of Competition Act Ruled Unconstitutional." *Canadian Competition Policy Record* 11, 2 (June): pp. 1-2.

Hyatt, Douglas E., and William J. Milne. 1991. "Can Public Policy Affect Fertility." *Canadian Public Policy* 17: pp. 77-85.

Industry Canada. 1986-1995. *Annual Report, Director of Investigation and Research Competition Act*. Ottawa: Minister of Supply and Service Canada.

Jackson, John H. 1989. *The World Trading System: Law and Policy of International Economic Relations*. Cambridge, MA: MIT Press.

Jackson, R.J., and M. Atkinson. 1980. *The Canadian Legislative System*. 2nd ed. Toronto: Macmillan.

Jensen, Michael C., and William H. Meckling. 1976. "Theory of the Firm: Managerial Behaviour, Agency Costs and Ownership Structure." *Journal of Financial Economics* 3: pp. 305-360.

Jones, J.C.H., Leonard Laudidio, and Michael Percy. 1973. "Market Structure and Profitability in Canadian Manufacturing Industry." *Canadian Journal of Economics* 6 (August): pp. 356-368.

Jones, R.W., and P. Kenen. 1984. *Handbook of International Economics*. Vol. 1. Amsterdam: North-Holland.

Kahn, A.E. 1970. *The Economics of Regulation*. Vol. 1. New York: John Wiley and Sons.

Kesselman, Jonathan. 1980. "Pitfalls of Selectivity in Income Security Programmes." *Canadian Taxation* 2: pp. 154-163.

Keynes, John Maynard. 1936. *The General Theory of Employment, Interest and Money*. London: Macmillan.

Khaneman, D., J. Knetsch, and R. Thaler. 1986. "Fairness as a Constraint on Profit Seeking." *American Economic Review* 76: pp. 728-741.

Khemani, R.S. 1988. "The Dimensions of Corporate Concentration in Canada." In *Mergers, Corporate Concentration and Power in Canada*, ed. R.S. Khemani, D. Shapiro, and W.T. Stanbury, pp. 17-38. Halifax: Institute for Research on Public Policy.

————. 1990. "Merger Policy and Small Open Economies: the Case of Canada." In *Perspectives in Industrial Organization*, ed. B. Dankbaar, J. Groenewegen, and H. Schenk. Boston: Kluwer.

Khemani, R.S., D. Shapiro, and W.T. Stanbury, ed. 1988. *Mergers, Corporate Concentration and Power in Canada*. Halifax: Institute for Research on Public Policy.

Kierans, Tom, and W.T. Stanbury, ed. 1985. *Papers on Privatization*. Montreal: The Institute for Research on Public Policy.

Kimball, Roger. 1990. *Tenured Radicals*. New York: Harper and Row.

Kreps, D., and R. Wilson. 1982. "Reputation and Imperfect Information." *Journal of Economic Theory* 27: pp. 253-279.

Krugman, Paul R. 1986. *Strategic Trade Policy and the New International Economics*. Cambridge, MA: MIT Press.

————. 1987. "Is Free Trade Passe?" *Journal of Economic Perspectives* 1: pp. 131-144.

Krugman, Paul R., and M. Obsfeldt. 1994. *International Economics*. 3rd ed. New York: Harper Collins.

Langford, John W. 1986. *Fear and Ferment: Public Sector Management Today*. Available as Canadian Public Administration, vol. 29, no. 4.

Leibenstein, H. 1966. "Allocative Efficiency vs. X-Efficiency." *American Economic Review* 56: pp. 392-415.

Lermer, George, ed. 1984. *Probing Leviathan: An Investigation of Government in the Economy*. Vancouver: Fraser Institute.

Lermer, George, and W.T. Stanbury. 1985. "The Cost of Redistributing Income by Means of Direct Regulation." *Canadian Journal of Economics 28*, 1: pp. 190-207.

Lind, R.C. 1982. *Discounting for Time and Energy Policy*. Washington, DC: Resources for Future.

Lipsey, R.G., and K. Lancaster. 1957. "The General Theory of the Second-Best." *Review of Economic Studies*. Vol. 24, pp. 11-32.

Lipsey R., D. Purvis, and P. Steiner. 1991. *Economics*. 5th ed. Toronto: McGraw-Hill.

Little, I.M.D. 1957. *A Critique of Welfare Economics*. 2nd ed. Oxford: Clarendon Press.

Litvak, I.A., and C.J. Maule. 1981. *The Canadian Multinationals*. Toronto: Butterworths.

Locke, J. 1939. "An Essay Concerning the True Original Extent and End of Civil Government." Reprinted in *The English Philosophers*. New York: Random House.

Lucas R.E. 1981. *Studies in Business Cycle Theory*. Cambridge, MA: MIT Press.

Lynn, Jonathan, and Anthony Jay. 1984. *The Complete Yes Minister*. London: BBC Books.

MacDonald, Donald S., Chairman. 1985. *Royal Commision of the Economic Union and Development Prospects for Canada*. Ottawa: Ministry of Supply and Services.

Magee, Stephen. 1991. "A Taxing Matter: The Negative Effect of Lawyers on Economic Activity." *International Economic Insights* 2 (January/February): pp. 34-35.

Magee, Stephen, William A. Brock, and Leslie Young. 1989. *Black Hole Tariffs and Endogenous Policy Theory*. New York: Cambridge University Press.

Malvern, Paul. 1985. *Persuaders: Lobbying, Influence Peddling and Political Corruption in Canada*. Toronto: Methuen.

Mankiw, Gregory N. 1990. "A Quick Referesher Course in Macroeconomics", *Journal of Economic Literature*. 28, pp. 1645-1660.

Marfels, C. 1988. "Aggregate Concentration in International Perspective." In *Mergers, Corporate Concentration and Power in Canada*, ed. R.S. Khemani, D. Shapiro, and W.T. Stanbury, pp. 53-88. Halifax: Institute for Research on Public Policy.

Mathewson, F., and R. Winter. 1985. *Competition Policy and Vertical Exchange. Royal Commission Research Studies*. Vol. 7. Toronto: University of Toronto Press.

Mathios, Alan D., and Robert P. Rogers. 1989. "The Impact of Alternative Forms of State Regulation of AT&T on Direct-Dial, Long-Distance Service Telephone Rates." *Rand Journal of Economics* Vol 20: pp. 437-453.

McCallum, John. 1995. "National Borders Matter: Canada-U.S. Regional Trade Patterns." *American Economic Review* 85: pp. 615-623.

McCready, Douglas J. 1984. *The Canadian Public Sector*. Toronto: John Wiley and Sons.

McDougall, John. 1991. "The Canada-US Free Trade Agreement and Canada's Energy Trade." *Canadian Public Policy* 17: pp. 1-13.

McFetridge, Donald G. 1974. "The Emergence of a Canadian Merger Policy: the ERCO Case." *Anti-trust Bulletin*. Vol 19: pp. 1-11.

————. 1985. *Canadian Industrial Policy in Action*. Royal Commission Research Studies. Vol. 4. Toronto: University of Toronto Press.

McRae, James J., and William Coffey. 1990. *Service Industries in Regional Economic Development*. Halifax: Institute for Research on Public Policy.

Meng, R.A., and D.A. Smith. 1990. "The Valuation of Risk of Death in Public Sector Decision-Making." *Canadian Public Policy* 16: pp. 137-144.

Milgrom, P., and J. Roberts. 1992. *Economics, Organization, and Management*. Englewood Cliffs, NJ: Prentice-Hall.

Milgrom, Paul, and John Roberts. 1992. *Economics, Organization and Management*. Englewood Cliffs, NJ: Prentice-Hall.

Mintz, Jack M., and Douglas D. Purvis. 1990. "Risk and Economic Policy." *Canadian Public Policy* 16: pp. 298-307.

Mintzberg, H., and J. Quinn. 1991. *The Strategy Process*. 2nd ed. Englewood Cliffs, NJ: Prentice-Hall.

Mitchell, Robert C., and Richard Carson. 1986. "Property Rights, Protest, and the Siting of Hazardous Waste Facilities." *American Economic Review*, Papers and Proceedings 76 (May): pp. 285-290.

Mueller, Dennis C. 1988. *Public Choice*. 2nd ed. London: Cambridge University Press.

Muller, R. Andrew. 1982. "The Eastman Stykholt Hypothesis Reconsidered." *Canadian Journal of Economics* 15: pp. 757-765.

Mumey, G., and J. Ostermann. 1990. "Alberta Heritage Fund: Measuring Value and Achievement." *Canadian Public Policy* 16: pp. 29-50.

Murray, V.V. 1985. *Theories of Business Government Relations*. Toronto: Trans-Canada Press.

Musgrave, R.A. 1959. *The Theory of Public Finance*. New York: McGraw-Hill.

Muzondo, T.R., and B. Pazderka. 1980. "Occupational Licensing and Professional Incomes in Canada." *Canadian Journal of Economics* 13: pp. 659-667.

Nelson, Richard R., and Sidney G. Winter. 1982. *An Evolutionary Theory of Economic Change*. Cambridge, MA: Harvard University Press.

Nemetz, Peter. 1986. "Federal Environmental Regulation in Canada." *Natural Resources Journal* 26: pp. 551-608.

Niskanen, W.A. 1971. *Bureaucracy and Representative Government*. Chicago: Aldine-Atherton.

Nozick, Robert. 1974. *Anarchy, State and Utopia*. New York: Basic Books.

Okun, Arthur M. 1975. *Equality and Efficiency: The Big Tradeoff*. Washington: The Brookings Institution.

Olson, Mancur. 1982. *The Rise and Decline of Nations: Economic Growth, Stagflation, and Social Rigidities*. New Haven, CT: Yale University Press.

Osbaldeston, G.F. 1989. *Keeping Deputy Ministers Accountable*. Toronto: McGraw-Hill.

Palda, Filip. 1994. *Provincial Trade Wars: Why the Blockade Must End*. Vancouver: The Fraser Institute.

Paltiel, K.Z. 1982. "The Changing Environment and Role of Special Interest Groups." *Canadian Public Administration* 25, 2 (Summer): pp. 198-210.

Panzar, J., and R. Willig. 1977. "Free Entry and the Sustainability of Natural Monopoly." *Bell Journal of Economics* 8: pp. 1-22.

Pauly, M.V. 1974. "Overinsurance and Public Provision of Insurance: The Roles of Moral Hazard and Adverse Selection." *Quarterly Journal of Economics* 88: pp. 44-54.

Pearce, D.W., G.D. Atkinson, and W.R. Dubourg. 1994. "The Economics of Sustainable Development." *Annual Review Energy Environment 1994* 19: pp. 457-74.

Pearce, D.W., and R. Kerry Turner. 1990. *Economics of Natural Resources and the Environment.* Baltimore: The John Hopkins University Press.

Petro-Canada. various years. *Annual Report Petro-Canada.* Ottawa: Minister of Supply and Service Canada.

Pindyck, Robert S., and Daniel L. Rubinfeld. 1995. *Microeconomics.* 3rd ed. Englewood Cliffs, NJ: Prentice-Hall.

Plourde, Andre. 1991. "The NEP Meets the FTA." *Canadian Public Policy* 17: pp. 14-24.

Poff, Deborah C., and Wilfrid J. Waluchow. 1991. *Business Ethics in Canada.* 2nd ed. Scarborough, ON: Prentice-Hall.

Porter, M.E. 1980. *Competitive Strategy: Techniques for Analyzing Industries and Competitors.* New York: Macmillan.

Porter, R.H. 1983. "A Study of Cartel Stability: the Joint Executive Committee, 1880-1886." *Bell Journal of Economics* 14: pp. 301-314.

Posner R.A. 1974. "Theories of Economic Regulation." *Bell Journal of Economics* 5: pp. 335-358.

Prichard, J. Robert S., ed. 1983. *Crown Corporations in Canada.* Toronto: Butterworths.

Pross, P., ed. 1992. *Group Politics and Public Policy.* 2nd ed. Toronto: Oxford University Press, Canada.

Rachels, James. 1993. *The Elements of Moral Philosophy.* 2nd ed. New York: McGraw-Hill.

Ramsey, F.P. 1927. "A Contribution to the Theory of Taxation." *Economic Journal* 89: pp. 66-83.

Ravenscraft, David J., and F.M. Scherer. 1987. *Mergers, Sell-Offs, and Economic Efficiency.* Washington, DC: Brookings.

Rawls, John. 1971. *A Theory of Justice.* Cambridge, MA: Harvard University Press.

Rea, K.J., and Nelson Wiseman, ed. 1985. *Government and Enterprise in Canada.* Toronto: Methuen.

Reschenthaler, G.B., and W.T. Stanbury. 1977a. "A Clarification of Canadian Merger Policy." *Anti-trust Bulletin* 22: pp. 673-685.

———. 1977b. "Benign Monopoly? Canadian Merger Policy and the K.C. Irving Case." *Canadian Business Law Journal* 2: pp. 135-168.

Restrictive Trade Practices Commission. 1986. *Competition in the Canadian Petroleum Industry.* Ottawa: Ministry of Supply and Services.

Rhoads, Steven E. 1985. *The Economist's View of the World Government, Markets, and Public Policy.* Cambridge: Cambridge University Press.

Ricardo, David. 1817; 1971. *The Principles of Political Economy and Taxation.* Baltimore: Penguin.

Ries, John C. 1993. "Windfall Profit and Vertical Relationships: Who Gained in the Japanese Auto Industry from VERs." *Journal of Industrial Economics* 41: pp. 259-277.

Ritchie, Gordon. 1994. "Free Trade: Year Five." *Canadian Competition Record* 15, 1: pp. 67-82.

Romer, Paul. 1994. 'The Origins of Endogenous Growth", *Journal of Economic Perspectives* 8, pp. 3-22.

Ross, Thomas. 1984. "Uncovering Regulator's Social Welfare Weights." *Rand Journal of Economics* 15: pp. 152-155.

————. 1991. "Proposals for a New Canadian Competition Law on Conspiracy." *Antitrust Bulletin* 36: 851-882.

————. 1993. "Sunk Costs as a Barrier to Entry in Merger Cases." *University of British Columbia Law Review* 27: pp. 75-92.

————, ed. 1996. Special Issue on Canadian Competition Policy. *Review of Industrial Organization.*

Rothschild, M., and J. Stiglitz. 1976. "Equilibrium in Competitive Insurance Markets: An Essay on the Economics of Imperfect Information." *Quarterly Journal of Economics* 90: pp. 629-650.

Rugman, Alan M., and John McIlveen. 1985. *Mega Firms Strategies for Canada's Multinationals.* Toronto: Methuen.

Samuelson, P.A. 1954. "The Pure Theory of Public Expenditure." *Review of Economic Statistics* 36 (November): pp. 386-389.

Schelling, Thomas. 1981. "Economic Reasoning and the Ethics of Policy." *Public Interest* 63 (Spring): p. 40.

Scherer, F.M. 1980. *Industrial Market Structure and Economic Performance.* 2nd ed. Boston: Houghton Mifflin.

Schmalensee, R., and R. Willig, ed. 1989. *Handbook of Industrial Organization.* Amsterdam: Elsevier.

Schultz, R.J., and A. Alexandroff. 1985. *Economic Regulation and the Federal System.* Royal Commission Research Studies. Vol. 42. Toronto: University of Toronto Press.

Schultze, Charles. 1977. *The Private Use of Public Interest.* Washington, DC: Brookings Institution.

Shearer, Ronald A., John F. Chant, and David E. Bond. 1984. *The Economics of the Canadian Financial System: Theory, Policy and Institutions.* 2nd ed. Scarborough, ON: Prentice-Hall.

Shepherd, William G. 1985. *Public Policies Toward Business.* 7th ed. Homewood, IL: Irwin.

Simeon, Richard, ed. 1986. *Division of Powers and Public Policy.* Royal Commission Research Studies. Vol. 63. Toronto: University of Toronto Press.

Simon, Herbert. 1979. "Rational Decision Making in Business Organizations." *American Economic Review* 69: pp. 493-513.

Simpson, Jeffrey. 1988. *Spoils of Power: The Politics of Patronage.* Toronto: Collins.

Sinclair, William F. 1991. "Controlling Effluent Discharges from Canadian Pulp and Paper Manufacturers." *Canadian Public Policy* 17: pp. 86-105.

Smith, Adam. 1776. *An Inquiry into the Nature and Causes of the Wealth of Nations.* Dublin: Printed for Messrs Whitestone, Chamberlaine etc.

Snyderman, Mark, and Stanley Rothman. 1988. *The IQ Controversy: The Media and Public Policy.* New Brunswick, NJ: Transaction Books.

Spence, M. 1973. "Job Market Signalling." *Quarterly Journal of Economics* 87: pp. 355-374.

Spencer, Barbara. 1980. "Outside Information and the Monopoly Power of a Public Bureau." *Southern Economic Journal* 47: pp. 228-233.

Stanbury, W.T., ed. 1980. *Government Regulation: Growth, Scope, Process.* Montreal: The Institute for Research on Public Policy.

————. 1986. "The New Competition Act and Competition Tribunal Act: Not with a Bang, but a Whimper." *The Canadian Business Law Journal* 12 (October): pp. 2-42.

————. 1991. *Money in Politics: Financing Federal Parties and Candidates in Canada.* A study for the Royal Commission on Electoral Reform and Party Financing.

————. 1993. *Business-Government Relations in Canada: Influencing Public Policy* 2nd ed. Scarborough: Nelson.

————. 1994. "The Extent of Privatization in Canada: 1979-1994." University of British Columbia, Vancouver.

Stanbury, W.T., and G. Reschenthaler. 1977. "Oligopoly and Conscious Parallelism: Theory, Policy and Canadian Cases." *Osgoode Hall Law Journal,* Vol. 15, pp. 617-700.

Stigler, G.J. 1971. "The Theory of Economic Regulation." *The Bell Journal of Economics and Management Science* 2 (Spring): pp. 3-21.

Stiglitz, J.E., and R.W. Boadway. 1994. *Economics and the Canadian Economy.* New York: Norton.

Summers, R., and A. Heston. 1991. "The Penn World Table (Mark 5): An Expanded Set of International Comparisons, 1950-1988." *Quarterly Journal of Economics* 105 (May): pp. 327-368.

Taylor, D. Wayne. 1991. *Business and Government Relations.* Toronto: Gage.

Tirole, Jean. 1988. *The Theory of Industrial Organization.* Cambridge, MA: MIT Press.

Tobin, James. 1993. "Price Flexibility and Output Stability: An Old Keynesian View", *Journal of Economic Perspectives* 7, pp. 45-65.

Trebilcock, M.J. 1986. *The Political Economy of Bailouts.* 2 vols. Toronto: University of Toronto Press.

Tullock, G. 1967. "The Welfare Costs of Tariffs, Monopolies, and Theft." *Western Economic Journal,* Vol. 5, pp. 224-232.

———. 1976. "The Transitional Gains Trap." *Bell Journal of Economics* 6: pp. 671-678.

Tupper, Allan, and G. Bruce Doern. 1981. *Public Corporations and Public Policy in Canada.* Montreal: The Institute for Research on Public Policy.

Turnovsky, S. 1977. *Macroeconomic Analysis and Stabilization Policy.* Cambridge: Cambridge University Press.

Usher, Dan. 1982. *The Private Cost of Public Funds: Variations on Themes by Browning, Atkinson and Stern.* Discussion paper, Queen's University.

Velasquez, Manuel G. 1992. *Business Ethics.* 3rd ed. Englewood Cliffs, NJ: Prentice-Hall.

VIA Rail Canada. various years. *Annual Report VIA Rail Canada.* Montreal: VIA Rail Canada Corporation.

Vining, Aidan, and Robert Botterell. 1983. "An Overview of the Origins, Growth, Size and Function of Provincial Crown Corporations." In *Crown Corporations in Canada,* ed. J. Robert S. Prichard, Toronto: Butterworths.

Viscusi, W. Kip, John M. Vernon, and Joseph E. Harrington. 1992. *Economics of Regulation and Antitrust.* Toronto: D.C. Heath and Company.

Vitousek, Peter M., Paul R. Ehrlich, and Anne H. Erlich. 1986. "Human Appropriation of the Products of Photosythesis." *BioScience* 36, pp. 368-373.

Walker, Michael. 1988. *Privatization: Tactics and Techniques.* Vancouver: The Fraser Institute.

Waters, W.G., T. Heaver, and T. Verrier, ed. 1980. *Oil Pollution from Tanker Operations: Costs, Causes, Controls.* Vancouver: Centre for Transportation Studies, University of British Columbia.

Watson, William G. 1983. *A Primer on the Economics of Industrial Policy.* Toronto: Ontario Economic Council.

Weimer, D., and Aidan Vining. 1992, 2nd ed. *Policy Analysis: Concepts and Practice.* New York: Prentice-Hall.

West, D. 1981. "Testing for Market Preemption Using Sequential Location Data." *Bell Journal of Economics* 12: pp. 129-143.

Whalley, J. 1985. *Canada and the Multilateral Trading System.* Royal Commission Research Studies. Vol. 10. Toronto: University of Toronto Press.

Whalley, J., C. Hamilton, and R. Hill. 1985. *Canadian Trade Policies and the World Economy.* Royal Commission Research Studies. Vol. 9. Toronto: University of Toronto Press.

Williamson, O.E. 1968. "Economies as an Anti-Trust Defence: The Welfare Tradeoffs." *American Economic Review* 58 (March): pp. 18-36.

–––. 1971. "The Vertical Integration of Production: Market Failure Considerations." *American Economic Review* 61 (May): pp. 112-123.

World Resources Institute. 1994. *World Resources: A Guide to the Global Environment.* New York: Oxford University Press.

Zerbe, Richard O., and Dwight D. Dively. 1994. *Benefit-Cost Analysis in Theory and Practice.* New York: Harper Collins.

Index